W9-BLI-249

EX LIBRIS

Deirdre Morse

TABLET ON THE BA

Incidents of Travel in
CENTRAL AMERICA CHIAPAS AND YUCATAN

By JOHN L. STEPHENS

WITH ILLUSTRATIONS BY
FREDERICK CATHERWOOD

IN TWO VOLUMES

Volume II

DOVER PUBLICATIONS, INC.

NEW YORK

Copyright © 1969 by Dover Publications, Inc.
All rights reserved under Pan American and
International Copyright Conventions.

Published in Canada by General Publishing Company, Ltd.,
30 Lesmill Road, Don Mills, Toronto, Ontario.
Published in the United Kingdom by Constable and Company,
Ltd., 10 Orange Street, London WC 2.

This Dover edition, first published in 1969, is an
unabridged republication of the work originally published in 1841 by Harper & Brothers, New York, to
which has been added certain material (as specified
in the Publisher's Note) from the edition published
by Arthur Hall, Virtue & Co., London, in 1854.

Standard Book Number: 486-22405-8
Library of Congress Catalog Card Number: 74-95745

Manufactured in the United States of America
Dover Publications, Inc.
180 Varick Street
New York, N.Y. 10014

CONTENTS

OF

THE SECOND VOLUME.

CHAPTER I.

CHAPTER II.

CHAPTER III.

CHAPTER IV.

CHAPTER V.

CHAPTER VI.

CHAPTER VII.

CHAPTER VIII.

CHAPTER IX.

CHAPTER X.

CHAPTER XI.

CHAPTER XII.

CHAPTER XIII.

CHAPTER XIV.

CHAPTER XV.

CHAPTER XVI.

CONTENTS.   5

CHAPTER XXII.

Embarcation.—An inundated Plain.—Rio Chico.—The Usumasinta.—Rio Palisada.—Yucatan.—More Revolutions.—Vespers.—Embarcation for the Laguna.—Shooting Alligators.—Tremendous Storm.—Boca Chico.—Lake of Terminos.—A Calm, succeeded by a Tempest.—Arrival at the Laguna . . Page 374

CHAPTER XXIII.

Laguna.—Journey to Merida.—Sisal.—A new Mode of Conveyance.—Village of Hunucama.—Arrival at Merida.—Aspect of the City.—Fête of Corpus Domini.—The Cathedral.—The Procession.—Beauty and Simplicity of the Indian Women.—Palace of the Bishop.—The Theatre.—Journey to Uxmal.—Hacienda of Vayalquex.—Value of Water.—Condition of the Indians in Yucatan.—A peculiar kind of Coach.—Hacienda of Mucuyche.—A beautiful Grotto 391

CHAPTER XXIV.

Journey resumed.—Arrival at Uxmal.—Hacienda of Uxmal. — Major-domos.—Adventures of a young Spaniard.—Visit to the Ruins of Uxmal.—First Sight of the Ruins.—Character of the Indians.—Details of Hacienda Life.—A delicate Case.—Illness of Mr. Catherwood.—Breaking up 410

CHAPTER XXV.

Ruins of Uxmal.—A lofty Building.—Magnificent View from its Doorway.—Peculiar sculptured Ornaments.—Another Building, called by the Indians the House of the Dwarf.—An Indian Legend.—The House of the Nuns.—The House of Turtles.—The House of Pigeons.—The Guard-house.—Absence of Water.—The House of the Governor.—Terraces.—*Wooden* Lintels.—Details of the House of the Governor.—Doorways.—Corridors.—A Beam of Wood, inscribed with Hieroglyphics.—Sculptured Stones, &c. 420

CHAPTER XXVI.

Exploration finished.—Who built these ruined Cities?—Opinion of Dupaix.—These Ruins bear no Resemblance to the Architecture of Greece and Rome.—Nothing like them in Europe.—Do not Resemble the known Works of Japan and China.—Neither those of Hindu.—No Excavations found.—The Pyramids of Egypt, in their original State, do not resemble what are called the Pyramids of America.—The Temples of Egypt not like those of America.—Sculpture not the same as that of Egypt.—Probable Antiquity of these Ruins.—Accounts of the Spanish Historians.—These Cities probably built by the Races inhabiting the Country at the time of the Spanish Conquest.—These Races not yet extinct 436

CHAPTER XXVII.

Journey to Merida.—Village of Moona.—A Pond of Water, a Curiosity.—Aboula.—Indian Runners.—Merida.—Departure.—Hunucama.—Siege of Campeachy.—Embarcation for Havana.—Incidents of the Passage.—Fourth of July at Sea.—Shark-fishing.—Getting lost at Sea.—Relieved by the Helen Maria.—Passage to New-York.—Arrival.—Conclusion 458

ILLUSTRATIONS

IN

VOLUME TWO

6A

INCIDENTS OF TRAVEL

OF

CENTRAL AMERICA, CHIAPAS, AND YUCATAN.

CHAPTER I.

MARCH 1. Anxious as I was to hurry on, I resolved nevertheless to give one day to the Volcano of Masaya. For this purpose I sent a courier ahead to procure me a guide up the volcano, and did not get off till eleven o'clock. At a short distance from the city we met a little negro on horseback, dressed in the black suit that nature made him, with two large plantain leaves sewed together for a hat, and plantain leaves for a saddle. At the distance of two leagues we came in sight of the volcano, and at four o'clock, after a hot ride, entered the town, one of the oldest and largest in Nicaragua, and though completely inland, containing, with its suburbs, a population of twenty thousand. We rode to the house of Don Sabino Satroon, who lay, with his mouth open, snoring in a hammock; but his wife, a pretty young half-blood, received me cordially, and with a proper regard for the infirmities of an old husband and for me, did not wake him up. All at once

7

he shut his mouth and opened his eyes, and gave me a cordial welcome.   Don Sabino was a Colombian, who had been banished for ten years, as he said, for services rendered his country ; and having found his way to Masaya, had married the pretty young half-breed, and set up as a doctor.   Inside the door, behind a little stock of sugar, rice, sausages, and chocolate, was a formidable array of jars and bottles, exhibiting as many colours and as puzzling labels as an apothecary's shop at home.

I had time to take a short walk around the town, and turning down the road, at the distance of half a mile came to the brink of a precipice, more than a hundred feet high, at the foot of which, and a short distance beyond, was the Lake of Masaya.   The descent was almost perpendicular, in one place by a rough ladder, and then by steps cut in the rock.   I was obliged to stop while fifteen or twenty women, most of them young girls, passed.   Their water-jars were made of the shell of a large gourd, round, with fanciful figures scratched on them, and painted or glazed, supported on the back by a strap across the forehead, and secured by fine network.   Below they were chattering gayly, but by the time they reached the place where I stood they were silent, their movements very slow, their breathing hard, and faces covered with profuse perspiration.   This was a great part of the daily labour of the women of the place, and in this way they procured enough for domestic use ; but every horse, mule, or cow was obliged to go by a circuitous road of more than a league for water. Why a large town has grown up and been continued so far from this element of life, I do not know.   The Spaniards found it a large Indian village, and as they immediately made the owners of the soil their drawers of water, they did not feel the burden ; nor do their descendants now.

In the mean time my guide arrived, who, to my great satisfaction, was no less a personage than the alcalde himself. The arrangements were soon made, and I was to join him the next morning at his house in Nindiri. I gave my mules and Nicolas a day's rest, and started on Don Sabino's horse, with a boy to act as guide and to carry a pair of alforgas with provisions. In half an hour I reached Nindiri, having met more people than on my whole road from San José to Nicaragua. The alcalde was ready, and in company with an assistant, who carried a pair of alforgas with provisions and a calabash of water, all mounted, we set out. At the distance of half a league we left the main road, and turned off on a small path in the woods on the left. We emerged from this into an open field covered with lava, extending to the base of the volcano in front and on each side as far as I could see, black, several feet deep, and in some places lying in high ridges. A faint track was beaten by cattle over this plain of lava. In front were two volcanoes, from both of which streams of lava had run down the sides into the plain. That directly in front my guide said was the Volcano of Masaya. In that on the right, and farthest from us, the crater was broken, and the great chasm inside was visible. This he said was called Ventero, a name I never heard before, and that it was inaccessible. Riding toward that in front, and crossing the field of lava, we reached the foot of the volcano. Here the grass was high, but the ground was rough and uneven, being covered with decomposed lava. We ascended on horseback until it became too steep for the horses to carry us, and then dismounted, tied them to a bush, and continued on foot. I was already uneasy as to my guides' knowledge of localities, and soon found that they were unwilling or unable to endure much fa-

tigue. Before we were half way up they disencumbered themselves of the water-jar and provisions, and yet
they lagged behind. The alcalde was a man about
forty, who rode his own horse, and being a man of consequence in the town, I could not order him to go fast-
er; his associate was some ten years older, and physi-
cally incapable; and seeing that they did not know any
particular path, I left them and went on alone.

At eleven o'clock, or three hours from the village of
Nindiri, I reached the high point at which we were
aiming; and from this point I expected to look down
into the crater of the volcano; but there was no crater,
and the whole surface was covered with gigantic masses of lava, and overgrown with bushes and scrub trees.
I waited till my guides came up, who told me that this
was the Volcano of Masaya, and that there was nothing
more to see. The alcalde insisted that two years before
he had ascended with the cura, since deceased, and a
party of villagers, and they all stopped at this place. I
was disappointed and dissatisfied. Directly opposite
rose a high peak, which I thought, from its position,
must command a view of the crater of the other volcano. I attempted to reach it by passing round the circumference of the mountain, but was obstructed by an
immense chasm, and returning, struck directly across.
I had no idea what I was attempting. The whole was
covered with lava lying in ridges and irregular masses,
the surface varying at every step, and overgrown with
trees and bushes. After an hour of the hardest work I
ever had in my life, I reached the point at which I aimed, and, to my astonishment, instead of seeing the crater of the distant volcano, I was on the brink of another.

Among the recorded wonders of the discoveries in
America, this mountain was one; and the Spaniards,

who in those days never stopped half way in any matter that touched the imagination, called it El Infierno
de Masaya, or the Hell of Masaya.   The historian, in
speaking of Nicaragua, says, " There are burning mountains in this province, the chief of which is Masaya,
where the natives at certain times offered up maids,
throwing them into it, thinking by their lives to appease
the fire, that it might not destroy the country, and they
went to it very chearful;" and in another place he
says, " Three leagues from the city of Masaya is a small
hill, flat and round, called Masaya, being a burning
Mountain, the Mouth of it being half a League in Compass, and the Depth within it two hundred and fifty
Fathoms.   There are no Trees nor Grass, but Birds
build without any Disturbance from the Fire.   There
is another Mouth like that of a Well about a Bowshot
over, the distance from which to the Fire is about a
hundred and fifty Fathoms, always boiling up, and that
mass of Fire often rises and gives a great Light, so
that it can be seen at a considerable Distance.   It
moves from one Side to the other, and sometimes roars
so loud that it is dreadful, yet never casts up anything but Smoak and Flame.   The Liquor never ceas-
ing at the Bottom, nor its Boiling, imagining the same
to be Gold, *F. Blase de Yniesta*, of the Order of *St.
Dominick*, and two other *Spaniards*, were let down into
the first Mouth in two Baskets, with a Bucket made of
one Piece of Iron, and a long Chain to draw up some of
that fiery Matter, and know whether it was Metal.
The Chain ran a hundred and fifty Fathoms, and as
soon as it came to the Fire, the Bucket melted, with
some Links of the Chain, in a very short Time, and
therefore they could not know what was below.   They
lay there that Night without any Want of Fire or Can-

dles, and came out again in their Baskets sufficiently frighted."

Either the monk, disappointed in his search for gold, had fibbed, or nature had made one of its most extraordinary changes. The crater was about a mile and a half in circumference, five or six hundred feet deep, with sides slightly sloping, and so regular in its proportions that it seemed an artificial excavation. The bottom was level, both sides and bottom covered with grass, and it seemed an immense conical green basin. There were none of the fearful marks of a volcanic eruption; nothing to terrify, or suggest an idea of el infierno ; but, on the contrary, it was a scene of singular and quiet beauty. I descended to the side of the crater, and walked along the edge, looking down into the area. Toward the other end was a growth of arbolitos or little trees, and in one place no grass grew, and the ground was black and loamy, like mud drying up. This was perhaps the mouth of the mysterious well that sent up the flame, which gave its light a " considerable distance," into which the Indian maidens were thrown, and which melted the monk's iron bucket. Like him, I felt curious to " know what was below;" but the sides of the crater were perpendicular. Entirely alone, and with an hour's very hard work between me and my guides, I hesitated about making any attempt to descend, but I disliked to return without. In one place, and near the black earth, the side was broken, and there were some bushes and scrub trees. I planted my gun against a stone, tied my handkerchief around it as a signal of my whereabout, and very soon was below the level of the ground. Letting myself down by the aid of roots, bushes, and projecting stones, I descended to a scrub tree which grew out of the side about half way from the bottom, and below this it was a naked and perpendicular wall. It was impossible to go any farther. I was even obliged to keep on the upper side of the tree, and here I was more anxious than ever to reach the bottom; but it was of no use. Hanging midway, impressed with the solitude and the extraordinary features of a scene upon which so few human eyes have ever rested, and the power of the great Architect who has scattered his wonderful works over the whole face of the earth, I could not but reflect, what a waste of the bounties of Providence in this favoured but miserable land! At home this volcano would be a fortune; with a good hotel on top, a railing round to keep children from falling in, a zigzag staircase down the sides, and a glass of iced lemonade at the bottom. Cataracts are good property with people who know how to turn them to account. Niagara and Trenton Falls pay well, and the owners of volcanoes in Central America might make money out of them by furnishing facilities to travellers. This one could probably be bought for ten dollars, and I would have given twice that sum for a rope and a man to hold it. Meanwhile, though anxious to be at the bottom, I was casting my eyes wistfully to the top. The turning of an ankle, breaking of a branch, rolling of a stone, or a failure of strength, might put me where I should have been as hard to find as the government of Central America. I commenced climbing up, slowly and with care, and in due time hauled myself out in safety.

On my right was a full view of the broken crater of the Volcano of Nindiri. The side toward me was hurled down, and showed the whole interior of the crater. This the alcalde had declared inaccessible; and partly from sheer spite against him, I worked my way

to it with extreme labour and difficulty. At length, after
five hours of most severe toil among the rugged heaps
of lava, I descended to the place where we had left our
provisions. Here I seized the calabash of water, and
stood for several minutes with my face turned up to the
skies, and then I began upon the alcalde and the eatables. Both he and his companion expressed their utter
astonishment at what I described, and persisted in saying
that they did not know of the existence of such a place.

I dwell upon this matter for the benefit of any future
traveller who may go out competent and prepared to
explore the interesting volcanic regions of Central
America. Throughout my journey my labours were
much increased by the ignorance and indifference of
the people concerning the objects of interest in their immediate neighbourhood. A few intelligent and educated men know of their existence as part of the history
of the country, but I never met one who had visited the
Volcano of Masaya; and in the village at its foot the
traveller will not obtain even the scanty information afforded in these pages. The alcalde was born near this
volcano; from boyhood had hunted stray cattle on its
side, and told me that he knew every foot of the ground;
yet he stopped me short of the only object of interest,
ignorant, as he said, of its existence. Now either the
alcalde lied, and was too lazy to encounter the toil which
I had undergone, or he was imposing upon me. In either case he deserves a flogging, and I beg the next
traveller, as a particular favour to me, to give him one.

I was too indignant with the alcalde to have anything
farther to do with him; and bent upon making another
attempt, on my return to the village I rode to the house
of the cura, to obtain his assistance in procuring men
and making other needful preparations. On the steps

of the back piazza I saw a young negro man, in a black
gown and cap, sitting by the side of a good-looking,
well-dressed white woman, and, if I mistake not, discoursing to her of other things than those connected with
his priestly duties. His black reverence was by no
means happy to see me. I asked him if I could make
an inn of his house, which, though it sounds somewhat
free, is the set phrase for a traveller to use ; and, without
rising from his seat, he said his house was small and in-
commodious, and that the alcalde had a good one. He
was the first black priest I had seen, and the only one
in the country who failed in hospitality. I must confess
that I felt a strong impulse to lay the butt of a pistol over
his head ; and spurring my horse so that he sprang almost upon him, I wheeled short and galloped out of the
yard. With the alcalde and cura both against me, I had
no chance in the village. It was nearly dark, and I returned to Masaya. My vexation was lost in a sense of
overpowering fatigue. It would be impossible to repeat
the severe labour of the day without an interval of rest,
and there was so much difficulty in making arrangements, that I determined to mount my macho and
push on.

The next morning I resumed my journey. My mules
had not been watered. To send them to the lake and
back would give them a journey of two leagues ; and
to save them I bought water, which was measured out
in a gourd holding about a quart. At about a league's
distance we came in sight of the Lake of Managua, and
before us the whole country was a bed of lava from the
base of the volcano to the lake. I met a travelling party, the principal of which I recognised as a stranger.
We had passed, when I turned round and accosted him
in English ; and after looking at me for a minute, to

my great surprise he called me by name. He was an
American named Higgins, whom I had seen last at my
own office in New-York. He was coming from Realejo, and was on his way to San Juan, with the intention
of embarking for the United States. We sent our luggage on and dismounted ; and besides the pleasure of
the meeting, I am under great obligation to him, for I
was riding at the time on an alvardo, or common saddle of the country, very painful for one not used to it.
My own saddle hurt my macho ; and as his journey
was nearly at an end, he gave me his in exchange, which
I rode on afterward till I left it on the shores of Yucatan. He gave me, too, a line in pencil to a lady in
Leon, and I charged him with messages to my friends
at home. When he rode off I almost envied him ; he
was leaving behind him tumults and convulsions, and
was going to a quiet home, but I had still a long and
difficult journey before me.

In about three hours, after a desperately hot ride, we
reached Managua, beautifully situated on the banks of
the lake. Entering through a collection of thatched
huts, we passed a large aristocratic house, with a courtyard occupying a whole square, the mansion of an ex-
patriated family, decaying and going to ruin.

Late in the afternoon I walked down to the lake.
It was not so grand as the Lake of Nicaragua, but it
was a noble sheet of water, and in full sight was the
Volcano of Momontanbo. The shore presented the
same animated spectacle of women filling their water-
jars, men bathing, horses and mules drinking, and in
one place was a range of fishermen's huts ; on the edge
of the water stakes were set up in a triangular form,
and women with small hand-nets were catching fish,
which they threw into hollow places dug, or rather

scraped, in the sand. The fish were called sardinitos, and at the door of the huts the men were building fires to cook them. The beauty of this scene was enhanced by the reflection that it underwent no change. Here was perpetual summer; no winter ever came to drive the inhabitants shivering to their fires; but still it may be questioned whether, with the same scenery and climate, wants few and easily supplied, luxuriating in the open air, and by the side of this lovely lake, even the descendants of the Anglo-Saxon race would not lose their energy and industry.

This lake empties into the Lake of Nicaragua by means of the River Tipitapa, and another communication between the two seas has been spoken of by means of a canal from it to the Pacific at the port of Realejo. The ground is perfectly level, and the port is perhaps the best in Spanish America; but the distance is sixty miles, and there are other difficulties which it seems to me are insuperable. The River Tipitapa has been represented as navigable the whole length for the largest ships; but no survey was ever made until Mr. Bailey's, according to which it is thirty miles in length. Beginning at the Lake of Nicaragua, for twenty-four miles the water is from one to three fathoms in depth. Above this there are rapids, and at the distance of four and a half miles a fall of thirteen feet. The whole rise within the six miles is twenty-eight feet eight inches. The Lake of Managua, from observation and information without survey, is about fifteen leagues long and thirty-five in circumference, and averages ten fathoms of water. There is not a single stream on the contemplated line of canal from this lake to the Pacific, and it would be necessary for this lake to furnish the whole supply of water for communication with both oceans.

At three o'clock the next morning we started. In all the tierras calientes it is the custom to travel at night, or, rather, very early in the morning. At eight o'clock we entered the village of Mateares, where we procured some eggs and breakfasted. From this village our road lay directly along the lake, but a few paces from the shore, and shaded by noble trees. Unfortunately, we were obliged to turn off to avoid a large rock which had rolled down several months before, and probably blocks up the road still; this brought us round by the Questa del Relox, so called from a venerable sundial which stands on one side of the road, of a dark gray stone, with an inscription in Castilian, but the characters so worn and indistinct that I could not make them out. It has no history except that it was erected by the conquerors, and it stands as an indication of the works with which the Spaniards began the settlement of the country.

At half past eleven we left the lake for the last time, and entered an open plain. We rode an hour longer, and reached Nagarotis, a miserable village, its houses built partly of mud, with yards in front, trodden bare by mules, and baked white by the sun. I entered one of the houses for shelter, and found in it a young negro priest on his way to Carthagena, with orders from the Church at Leon. The house was occupied by an old man alone. It had a bedstead with a mat over it, upon which I lay down, glad to rest a while, and to escape the scorching heat. Opposite the bed was a rude frame about six feet high, on the top of which was a sort of babyhouse, with the figure of the Virgin sitting on a chair, and dressed in cheap finery.

At three we started again. The sun had lost some of its force, the road was wooded, and I observed more

than the usual number of crosses. The people of Nicaragua are said to be the worst in the republic. The
inhabitants of the other states always caution a stranger against them, and they are proportionally devout.
Everywhere, in the cities and country, on the tops of
mountains, and by the side of rivers, these memorials
stared me in the face. I noticed one in a cleared place
by the roadside, painted black, with a black board suspended to it, containing an inscription in faded white
letters; it had been erected to the memory of a padre
who had been murdered and buried at its foot. I stopped to copy the inscription, and while so engaged saw
a travelling party approaching, and knowing the jealousy of the people, shut my notebook and rode on.
The party consisted of two men, with their servants,
and a woman. The younger man accosted me, and
said that he had seen me at Grenada, and regretted
that he had not known of my proposed journey. From
the style of his dress and equipments I supposed him
to be a gentleman, and was sure of it from the circumstance of his carrying a gamecock under his arm. As
we rode on the conversation turned upon these interesting birds, and I learned that my new acquaintance was
going to Leon to fight a match, of which he offered to
give me notice. The bird which he carried had won
three matches in Grenada; its fame had reached Leon,
and drawn forth a challenge from that place. It was
rolled up as carefully as a fractured leg, with nothing
but the head and tail visible; and suspended by a string,
was as easily carried as a basket. The young man
sighed over the miseries of the country, the distress and
ruin caused by the wars, and represented the pit at
Grenada as being in a deplorable condition; but in
Leon he said it was very flourishing, on account of its

being the headquarters of the military. The building, too, did honour to the city; it was only open on Sundays; but he knew the proprietor, and could at any time make an arrangement for a match. He made many inquiries about the state of the science in my country; told me that he had imported two cocks from England, which were game enough, but not sufficiently heavy for theirs; and gave me, besides, much valuable information on this subject, of which I neglected to make any memorandum.

Before dark we reached Pueblo Nuevo, and all went to the same posada. His companion was not so much of a sportsman, though he knew the qualities of a good bird, and showed a familiarity in handling them. It was the first time I had fallen in with travellers for the night. I have avoided details in all places where I was partaking of private hospitality, but this was like a hotel at home, in the main point that all were expected to pay. We had for supper poached eggs and beans, without plate, knife, fork, or spoon. My companions used their tortillas to take up an egg, and also, by turning up the edges, to scoop out frigoles from the dish; withal, they were courteous and gentlemanly. We had a species of chocolate, made of pounded cocoa and sweetened, and served in hickories, which, having bottoms like the butts of large eggs, could not stand on the table. My companions twisted their pocket-handkerchiefs, and winding them on the table in circular folds, set the hickories inside the hollow, and one of them did the same with my handkerchief for me. After supper the younger of the two dressed the birds in their robes de nuit, a cotton cloth wound tight around the body, compressing the wings, and then, with a string fastened to the back of the cloth, so that the body was balanced,

hooked each of them to the hammock. While he was
preparing them the woman was showing horn combs,
beads, earrings, and rosaries, and entrapped the daughter of the host into the purchase of a comb. The house
had an unusual influx of company. The young man,
the female merchant, and I do not know how many of
the family, slept in a back room. The elder traveller
offered me the hammock, but I preferred the long chest,
made from the trunk of a tree, which in every house in
Nicaragua served as a sort of cupboard.

CHAPTER II.

Beautiful Plain.—Leon.—Stroll through the Town.—Baneful Effects of Party
Spirit.—Scenes of Horror.—Unpleasant Intelligence.—Journey continued.—
A fastidious Beggar.—Chinandaga.—Gulf of Couchagua.—Visit to Realejo.—
Cotton Factory.—Harbour of Realejo.—El Viejo.—Port of Nagoscolo.—Im-
portance of a Passport.—Embarking Mules.—A Bungo.—Volcano of Cosagui-
na.—Eruption of 1835.—La Union.

AT two o'clock we were awakened by the crowing of
the cocks, and at three the cargo-mules were loaded
and we set off. The road was level and wooded, but
desperately dusty. For two hours after daylight we
had shade, when we came upon an open plain, bounded
on the Pacific side by a low ridge, and on the right by
a high range of mountains, forming part of the great
chain of the Cordilleras. Before us, at a great distance,
rising above the level of the plain, we saw the spires of
the Cathedral of Leon. This magnificent plain, in richness of soil not surpassed by any land in the world, lay
as desolate as when the Spaniards first traversed it.
The dry season was near its close ; for four months there
had been no rain, and the dust hung around us in thick
clouds, hot and fine as the sands of Egypt. At nine
o'clock we reached Leon, and I parted from my companions, but not without a courteous invitation from the
younger to take up my rest at the house of his brother.
The suburbs were more miserable than anything I had
yet seen. Passing up a long street, across which a sentinel was patrolling, I saw in front of the quartel a
group of vagabond soldiers, a match for Carrera's, who
cried out insolently, " Quittez el sombrero," " Take off
your hat." I had to traverse the whole extent of the

city before I reached the house to which I had been recommended. I dismounted, and entered it with confidence of a warm reception; but the lady, with considerable expedition, told me that her husband was not at home. I gave her a note with which I had been furnished, addressed to herself; but she said she could not read English, and handed it back. I translated it word for word, being a request that she would give me lodgings. Her brow actually knit with vexation; and she said she had but one spare room, and that was reserved for the English vice-consul from Realejo. I answered that the vice-consul did not intend leaving Realejo for the present. She asked me how long I intended to stay; and when I replied only that night, she said that if such was the case I might remain. The reader will perhaps wonder at my want of spirit; but the fact is, I was loth to consider any incivility personal. My only alternative was to seek out the young man whose invitation I had declined, and whose name I did not know, or to ask admission from door to door.

It is said that women are governed by appearances, and mine was not very seductive. My dress was the same with which I had left Grenada, soiled by the ascent of the Volcano of Masaya, and now covered with dust. Making the most of my moderate wardrobe, on my reappearance I was more favourably received. At least I had a capital breakfast; and as it was very hot, and I wanted to rest, I remained in doors and played with the children. At dinner I had the seat of honour at the head of the table, and had made such progress, that, if I had desired it, I would have ventured to broach the subject of remaining another day; and I owe it to the lady to say, that, having assented to my remaining, she treated me with great civility and attention, and particularly used great exertions in procuring me a guide to enable me to set out the next day.

After dinner Nicolas came to my room, and with uplifted hands cried out against the people of Leon, Gente indecente, sin verguenza (literally), indecent people, without shame. He had been hooted in the streets, and had heard such stories of the state of the country before us that he wanted to return home. I was extremely loth to make another change, and particularly for any of the assassin-looking scoundrels whom I had seen on my entry ; but I did not like the responsibility of taking him against his will, and told him that if he would procure me two honest men he might leave me. I had advanced him more than was due, but I had a security against his deserting me in his apprehension of being taken for a soldier.

This over, I walked out to take a view of the town. It had an appearance of old and aristocratic respectability, which no other city in Central America possessed. The houses were large, and many of the fronts were full of stucco ornaments ; the plaza was spacious, and the squares of the churches and the churches themselves magnificent. It was the seat of a bishopric, and distinguished for the costliness of its churches and convents, its seats of learning, and its men of science, down to the time of its revolution against Spain ; but in walking through its streets I saw palaces in which nobles had lived dismantled and roofless, and occupied by half-starved wretches, pictures of misery and want ; and on one side an immense field of ruins, covering half the city.

Almost immediately on the establishment of inde-

pendence, and the drawing of the great party-lines between the Centralists and Federalists, the State of Nicaragua became the theatre of a furious struggle.   In an
unfortunate hour the people elected a Central governor
and Liberal vice-governor.   A divided administration
led to drawing of blood and the most sanguinary con-
flict known in civil wars.   Inch by inch the ground
was disputed, till the whole physical force and deadly
animosity of the state were concentrated in the capital.
The contending parties fought up to the very heart of
the city; the streets were barricaded, and for three
months not a person could pass the line without being
shot at.   Scenes of horror surpassing human belief are
fresh in the memory of the inhabitants.   The Liberals
prevailed; the Central chief was killed, his forces massacred, and in the phrensy of the moment, the part of
the city occupied by the Centralists was burned and
razed to the ground; besides the blood of murdered
citizens, the tears and curses of widows and orphans,
the victors had the rich enjoyment of a desolated country and a ruined capital.   The same ruthless spirit still
characterized the inhabitants of Leon.   The heroes of
Taguzegalpa, without a single prisoner as a monument
of mercy, had been received with ringing of bells and
firing of cannon, and other demonstrations of joy, and
they were still in the city, flushed with their brutal victory, and anxious to be led on to more such triumphs.

I must confess that I felt a degree of uneasiness in
walking the streets of Leon that I never felt in any city
in the East.   My change of dress did not make my
presence more acceptable, and the eagle on my hat attracted particular attention.   At every corner was a
group of scoundrels, who stared at me as if disposed to
pick a quarrel.   With some my official character made

me an object of suspicion ; for in their disgraceful fights they thought that the eyes of the whole world were upon them, and that England, France, and the United States were secretly contending for the possession of their interesting country.   I intended to pay a visit to the chief of the state ; but, afraid of being insulted or getting into some difficulty that might detain me, I returned to the house.

By means of the servants Nicolas had found two men who were willing to accompany me, but I did not like their looks, or even to let them know when I intended to set out.   I had hardly disposed of them before my guide came to advise me not to set out the next day, as five hundred soldiers, who had been making preparations for several days, were to march the next morning against San Salvador.   This was most unpleasant intelligence.   I did not wish to travel with them, or to fall in with them on the road ; and calculating that their march would be slower than mine, told the guide to ascertain their time for starting, and we would set out two hours before them.   Nicolas went out with him to take the mules to water ; but they returned in great haste, with intelligence that piquets were scouring the city for men and mules, and had entered the yard of a padre near by and taken three of his animals.   The lady of the house ordered all the doors to be locked and the keys brought to her, and an hour before dark we were all shut in, and my poor mules went without water.

At about eight o'clock we heard the tramp of cavalry in the streets, and gathering inside the doorway, saw about six hundred men taking up their line of march. There was no music, no shouting, no waving of handkerchiefs, to cheer them as defenders of their country or as adventurers in the road to glory ; but in the dark, and barefooted, their tread seemed stealthy; people looked at them with fear; and it seemed rather the sally of a band of conspirators than a march by the soldiers of a republic.

My muleteer did not return till daylight the next morning. Fortunately for us, he had learned that the troops were destined on another, but even a more inglorious expedition. Expenses had been incurred in sending troops into Honduras, of which Grenada refused to pay its portion, on the ground that, by the constitution, it was not liable except for expenses incurred in defending the borders of its own state. This was admitted; but the expense had been incurred; Leon had fought the battle, and had the same materials with which she gained it to enforce the contribution. In order that Grenada might be taken unawares, it was given out that the troops were destined for San Salvador, and they were actually marched out on the San Salvador road; but at midnight made a circuit, and took the route for Grenada. War between different states was bad enough, but here the flame which had before laid the capital in ruins was lighted again within its own borders. What the result of this expedition was I never heard; but probably, taken unawares and without arms, Grenada was compelled by bayonets to pay what, by the constitution, she was not bound to pay.

Outside of Leon, and once more on the back of my macho, I breathed more freely. Nicolas was induced to continue by hearing that there was a vessel at Realejo for Costa Rica, and I hoped to find one for Zonzonate. The great plain of Leon was even more beautiful than before; too beautiful for the thankless people to whom the bounty of Providence had given it. On the left was the same low ridge separating it from the Pacific

Ocean, and on the right the great range of Cordilleras, terminated by the volcano of the Viejo.

I had passed through the village of Chichuapa when I heard a cry of " caballero" behind me, and turning, saw divers people waving their hands, and a woman running, almost out of breath, with a pocket-handkerchief which I had left at the house where I breakfasted. I was going on, when a respectable-looking gentleman stopped me, with many apologies for the liberty, and asked for a medio, sixpence. I gave him one, which he examined and handed back, saying, " No corre," " it does not pass." It was always, in paying money, a matter of course to have two or three pieces returned, and this I sometimes resisted ; but as in this land everything was al reverso, it seemed regular for beggars to be choosers, and I gave him another.

My stopping-place was at the house of Mr. Bridges, an Englishman from one of the West India Islands, who had been resident in the country many years, and was married to a lady of Leon, but, on account of the convulsions of the country, lived on his hacienda. The soil was rich for cotton and sugar, and Mr. B. said that here fifty men could manufacture sugar cheaper than two hundred in the islands ; but the difficulty was, no reliance could be placed upon Indian labour. Here again, thanks to the kindness of Mr. B. and his lady, and the magnificent wildness of hacienda life, I could have passed several days with much satisfaction ; but I stopped only for dinner, after which Mr. B. accompanied me to Chinandaga.

As usual, my first business was to make arrangements for continuing my journey. My whole road was along the coast of the Pacific, but beyond this the Gulf of Couchagua made a large indentation in the land, which it was customary to cross in a bungo, sending the mules around the head of the gulf. I was advised that the latter was hazardous, as the Honduras troops were marching upon San Salvador, and would seize them. I might save them by going myself; but it was a journey of six days, through a country so desolate that it was necessary to carry food for the mules; and as I had still a long road beyond, I felt it necessary to economize my strength. I was loth to run the risk of losing my mules, and sent a courier to El Viejo, where the owners of the bungoes lived, to hire the largest, determined to run the risk of taking them with me. The next morning the courier returned, having procured a bungo, to be ready the next evening, and with a message from the owner that the embarcation must be at my risk.

Obliged to wait the day, after breakfast I started for Realejo. On the way I met Mr. Foster, the English vice-consul, coming to see me. He turned back, and took me first to the machino or cotton factory, of which I had heard much on the road. It was the only one in the country, and owed its existence to the enterprise of a countryman, having been erected by Mr. Higgins, who, disappointed in his expectations, or disgusted with the country from other causes, sold it to Don Francisco and Mr. Foster. They were sanguine in their expectations of profit; for they supposed that, by furnishing a market, the people would be induced to work and raise cotton enough for exportation to Europe. The resources of this distracted country are incalculable. Peace and industry would open fountains which would overflow with wealth; and I have no doubt the influence of this single factory will be felt in quieting and enriching the whole district within its reach.

I accompanied Mr. Foster to Realejo, which was only half an hour's ride. The harbour, Huarros says, is capable of containing a thousand ships ; but, being two or three leagues distant, I was unable to visit it. The town, consisting of two or three streets, with low straggling houses, enclosed by a thick forest, was founded by a few of the companions of Alvarado, who stopped there on their expedition to Peru; but, being so near the sea, and exposed to the incursions of the bucaniers, the inhabitants moved inland, and founded Leon.

At dark we returned to the factory, and Don Francisco and I reached Chinandaga, where I was greeted with intelligence that the proprietor of the boat had sent word that he supposed I had a permission to embark from the chief of the state, as, by a late order, no person could embark without. He was most provokingly out in his supposition. I had entered the state by a frontier of wilderness, and had not once been asked for a passport. The reader may remember how I was prevented visiting the chief of the state ; and, besides, when at Leon, I did not know whether I should continue by land or cross the gulf, and supposed that at the port of embarcation I could procure all that was necessary. I was excessively disturbed ; but Don Francisco sent for the commandant of the town, who said that the order had not yet been sent to the port, but was in his hands, and he would retain it.

Early the next morning I sent on an ox wagon with the luggage and a stock of corn and grass for the mules during the voyage, and, after a pleasant ride of a league, reached the Viejo, one of the most respectable-looking towns in Nicaragua. The house of the owner of the bungo was one of the largest in the place, and furnished with two mahogany sofas made by a Yankee cabinet-maker in Lima, two looking-glasses with gilt frames, a French clock, gilt chairs with cane bottoms, and two Boston rocking-chairs, which had made the passage round Cape Horn. Don Francisco went over to the commandant. He, unluckily, had received his orders direct from the government, and dared not let me pass. I went over myself with Mr. Foster. The order was positive, and I was in agony. Here I made a push with my official character, and after an hour's torment, by the warm help of Mr. Foster, and upon his undertaking to save the commandant harmless, and to send an express immediately to Leon for a passport from the chief of the state, it was agreed that in the mean time I might go on.

I did not wait long, but, taking leave of Mr. Foster and Don Francisco, set out for the port. It was seven leagues, through an unbroken forest. On the way I overtook my bungo men, nearly naked, moving in single file, with the pilot at their head, and each carrying on his back an open network containing tortillas and provisions for the voyage. At half past two we reached the port of Nagoscolo. There was a single hut, at which a woman was washing corn, with a naked child near her on the ground, its face, arms, and body one running sore, a picture of squalid poverty. In front was a large muddy plain, through the centre of which ran a straight cut called a canal, with an embankment on one side dry, the mud baked hard and bleached by the sun. In this ditch lay several bungoes high and dry, adding to the ugliness of the picture. I had a feeling of great satisfaction that I was not obliged to remain there long; but the miserable woman, with a tone of voice that seemed to rejoice in the chance of making others as miserable as herself, desisted from washing

her maize, and screeched in my ears that a guarda had
been sent direct from the capital, with orders to let no
one embark without a passport.   The guarda had gone
down the river in a canoe, in search of a bungo which
had attempted to go away without a passport ; and I
walked down the bank of the canal in hope to catch him
alone when he returned.   The sun was scorching hot,
and as I passed the bungoes the boatmen asked me if I
had a passport.   At the end of the canal, under the shade
of a large tree, were two women ; and they had been in
that place three days, waiting for one of their party who
had gone to Leon to procure a passport.

It was more than an hour before the guarda appeared.   He was taken by the eagle on my hat, and while
I told him my story, said " Si, señor," to everything ;
but when I talked of embarking, said, " Señor, you
have no passport."   I will not inflict upon the reader
the details of all my vexations and anxiety that afternoon.   I was most eager to hurry on.   To send a courier to Leon would keep me in suspense insufferable.
Some difficulty might happen, and the only way for
peace of mind was to return myself.   I had already
made a longer journey than is ever made in the country without an interval of rest.   The road before me
led through the seat of war, and four days' detention
might throw me into the midst of it.   (In fact, the
result proved that one day would have done so.)   I
walked with the guarda to the hut, and in greater
anxiety than I had felt since my departure from home,
showed him my papers—a larger bundle, perhaps, than
he had ever seen before, and with bigger seals, particularly my original passport from my own government—
jumbling together his government and my government,
the amicable relations existing between them, and try-

ing to give him an overwhelming idea of my importance; but he knew no more what it meant than if I
had repeated to him in English the fifth problem in Eu-
clid. The poor man was almost in as great perplexity
as I was. Several times he assented and retracted; and
at length, upon my giving him a letter promising him
the protection of Mr. Foster and the commandant at
Viejo, he agreed to let the bungo go.

It was about an hour before dark when we went down
to embark the mules. My bungo was at the extreme
end of the canal, and the tide had risen so that she was
afloat. We began with the gray, by casting a noose
around her legs, drawing them together, and throwing
her down. The men then attempted to lift her up bodily over the side of the bungo; but failing in this, took
off the rudder, and leaning it against the side, hauled the
mule up it, then tilted the rudder, and dropped her into
the boat. In the mean time the macho stood under a
tree, looking on very suspiciously, and with fearful forebodings. The noose was put round his legs, with a rope
before and behind to pull on, and struggling desperately, he was thrown down, but hardly touched the
ground before, with a desperate effort, he broke the
ropes and rose upon his feet. A second attempt was
more successful; but the two abreast made a close fit,
and I was obliged to leave behind the luggage mule.
I paid the guarda to take her to Mr. Foster, but whether
she reached him or not I have never heard.

We were assisted by the boatmen of another bungo,
and I ordered supper and agua ardiente for the whole.
This was furnished at the hut by the guarda, and when
it was over, the men, all in good spirits, commenced
taking the luggage on board. At this time some who
were detained were grumbling, and a new man entered

the hut, as he said direct from the Pueblo, who croaked in my ears the odious order, and the guard again made objections.   I was excessively vexed by this last interruption ; and fairly bullying the new comer out of the hut, told the guard that the thing was settled and I would not be trifled with, took up my gun, and told the men to follow me.   I saw beforehand that they were elevated by their good cheer, and that I could rely upon them.   The guard, and all those compelled to wait, followed ; but we got on board, and my crew were so tipsy that they defied all opposition.   One push cleared the bungo from the canal, and as she was passing out a stranger unexpectedly stepped on board, and in the dark slipped down under the awning with the mules. I was surprised and a little indignant that he had not asked leave, and it occurred to me that he was a partisan who might compromise me ; but to return might lead to new difficulty, and, besides, he was probably some poor fellow escaping for his life, and it was better that I should know nothing about it.   In the midst of my doubts a man on the bank cried out that fifty soldiers had arrived from Leon.   It was pitchy dark ; we could see nothing, and my men answered with a shout of defiance.

In the mean time we were descending rapidly, whirling around and hitting against the branches of trees ; the mules were thrown down, the awning carried away, and in the midst of darkness and confusion we struck with a violent crash against another bungo, which knocked us all into a heap, and I thought would send us to the bottom.   The men rose with roars of laughter.   It was a bad beginning.   Still I was overjoyed at being clear of the port, and there was a wild excitement in the scene itself.   At length the men sat down to the oars, and pulled for a few minutes as if they would tear the old bungo out of the water, shouting all the time like spirits of darkness let loose. The pilot sat quietly at the helm, without speaking, and dark as it was, at times I saw a smile steal over his face at wild sallies of the boatmen. Again they began rowing furiously as before, and suddenly one of the sweeps broke and the oarsman fell backward. The bungo was run up among the trees, and the men climbed ashore by the branches. The blows of machetes, mingled with shouts and laughter, rang through the woods ; they were the noisiest party I met in Central America. In the dark they cut down a dozen saplings before they found what they wanted, and in about an hour returned, and the shattered awning was refitted. By this time they were more sobered ; and taking their sweeps, we moved silently down the dark river until one o'clock, when we came to anchor.

The bungo was about forty feet long, dug out of the trunk of a Guanacaste tree, about five feet wide and nearly as deep, with the bottom round, and a toldo or awning, round like the top of a market-wagon, made of matting and bulls' hides, covered ten feet of the stern. Beyond were six seats across the sides of the bungo for the oarsmen. The whole front was necessary for the men, and in reality I had only the part occupied by the awning, where, with the mules as tenants in common, there were too many of us. They stood abreast, with their halters tied to the first bench. The bottom was rounding, and gave them an unsteady foothold ; and when the boat heaved they had a scramble to preserve their centre of gravity. The space between their heels and the end of the log or stern of the bungo was my sleeping-room. Nicolas was afraid to pass between the mules to get a place among the men, and he could not climb over the awning. I had their heads tethered close up to the bench, and putting him outside to catch the first kick, drew up against the stern of the bungo and went to sleep.

At half past seven we weighed anchor, or hauled up a large stone, and started with oars. My boatmen were peculiar in their way of wearing pantaloons. First they pulled them off, folded them about a foot wide and two feet long, and then suspended them over the belts of their machetes like little aprons. At nine o'clock we reached the mouth of the river. Here we hoisted sail, and while the wind was fair did very well. The sun was scorching, and under the awning the heat was insufferable. Following the coast, at eleven o'clock we were opposite the Volcano of Cosaguina, a long, dark mountain range, with another ridge running below it, and then an extensive plain covered with lava to the sea. The wind headed us, and in order to weather the point of headland from which we could lay our course, the boatmen got into the water to tow the bungo. I followed them, and with a broad-brimmed straw hat to protect me from the sun, I found the water was delightful. During this time one of the men brought sand from the shore to break the roundness of the bottom of the boat, and give the mules a foothold. Unable to weather the point, at half past one we came to anchor, and very soon every man on board was asleep.

I woke with the pilot's legs resting on my shoulder. It was rather an undignified position, but no one saw it. Before me was the Volcano of Cosaguina, with its field of lava and its desolate shore, and not a living being was in sight except my sleeping boatmen. Five years before, on the shores of the Mediterranean, and at the foot of Mount Etna, I read in a newspaper an account of the eruption of this volcano. Little did I then ever

expect to see it ; the most awful in the history of volcanic eruptions, the noise of which startled the people
of Guatimala four hundred miles off; and at Kingston,
Jamaica, *eight hundred miles* distant, was supposed to
be signal guns of distress from some vessel at sea.   The
face of nature was changed ; the cone of the volcano
was gone ; a mountain and field of lava ran down to
the sea ; a forest old as creation had entirely disappeared, and two islands were formed in the sea; shoals
were discovered, in one of which a large tree was fixed
upside down ; one river was completely choked up, and
another formed, running in an opposite direction ; seven
men in the employ of my bungo-proprietor ran down to
the water, pushed off in a bungo, and were never heard
of more ; wild beasts, howling, left their caves in the
mountains, and ounces, leopards, and snakes fled for
shelter to the abodes of men.

This eruption took place on the 20th of January,
1835.   Mr. Savage was on that day on the side of the
Volcano of San Miguel, distant one hundred and twenty
miles, looking for cattle.   At eight o'clock he saw a
dense cloud rising in the south in a pyramidal form,
and heard a noise which sounded like the roaring of the
sea.   Very soon the thick clouds were lighted up by
vivid flashes, rose-coloured and forked, shooting and
disappearing, which he supposed to be some electrical
phenomenon.   These appearances increased so fast that
his men became frightened, and said it was a ruina,
and that the end of the world was nigh.   Very soon he
himself was satisfied that it was the eruption of a volcano ; and as Cosaguina was at that time a quiet
mountain, not suspected to contain subterraneous fires,
he supposed it to proceed from the Volcano of Tigris.
He returned to the town of San Miguel, and in riding

three blocks felt three severe shocks of earthquake. The inhabitants were distracted with terror. Birds flew wildly through the streets, and, blinded by the dust, fell dead on the ground. At four o'clock it was so dark that, as Mr. S. says, he held up his hand before his eyes, and could not see it. Nobody moved without a candle, which gave a dim and misty light, extending only a few feet. At this time the church was full, and could not contain half who wished to enter The figure of the Virgin was brought out into the plaza and borne through the streets, followed by the inhabitants, with candles and torches, in penitential procession, crying upon the Lord to pardon their sins. Bells tolled, and during the procession there was another earthquake, so violent and long that it threw to the ground many people walking in the procession. The darkness continued till eleven o'clock the next day when the sun was partially visible, but dim and hazy, and without any brightness. The dust on the ground was four inches thick; the branches of trees broke with its weight, and people were so disfigured by it that they could not be recognised.

At this time Mr. S. set out for his hacienda at Zonzonate. He slept at the first village, and at two or three o'clock in the morning was roused by a report like the breaking of most terrific thunder or the firing of thousands of cannon. This was the report which startled the people of Guatimala, when the commandant sallied out, supposing that the quartel was attacked, and which was heard at Kingston in Jamaica. It was accompanied by an earthquake so violent that it almost threw Mr. S. out of his hammock.*

---

* This may at first appear no great feat for an earthquake, but no stronger proof can be cited of the violence with which the shock affects the region in which it occurs.

Toward evening my men all woke ; the wind was fair, but they took things quietly, and after supper hoisted sail. About twelve o'clock, by an amicable arrangement, I stretched myself on the pilot's bench under the tiller, and when I woke we had passed the Volcano of Tigris, and were in an archipelago of islands more beautiful than the islands of Greece. The wind died away, and the boatmen, after playing for a little while with the oars, again let fall the big stone and went to sleep. Outside the awning the heat of the sun was withering, under it the closeness was suffocating, and my poor mules had had no water since their embarcation. In the confusion of getting away I had forgotten it till the moment of departure, and then there was no vessel in which to carry it. After giving them a short nap I roused the men, and with the promise of a reward induced them to take to their oars. Fortunately, before they got tired we had a breeze, and at about four o'clock in the afternoon the big stone was dropped in the harbour of La Union, in front of the town. One ship was lying at anchor, a whaler from Chili, which had put in in distress and been condemned.

The commandant was Don Manuel Romero, one of Morazan's veterans, who was anxious to retire altogether from public life, but remained in office because, in his present straits, he could be useful to his benefactor and friend. He had heard of me, and his attentions reminded me of, what I sometimes forgot, but which others very rarely did, my official character ; he invited me to his house while I remained in La Union, but gave me intelligence which made me more anxious than ever to hurry on. General Morazan had left the port but a few days before, having accompanied his family thither on their way to Chili. On his return to San Salvador

he intended to march directly against Guatimala.   By
forced marches I might overtake him, and go up under
the escort of his army, trusting to chance to avoid being
on the spot in case of a battle, or from my acquaintance
with Carrera get passed across the lines.   Fortunately,
the captain of the condemned ship wished to go to San
Salvador, and agreed to accompany me the next day.

There were two strangers in the place, Captain
R. of Honduras, and Don Pedro, a mulatto, both of
whom were particularly civil to me.   In the evening
my proposed travelling companion and I called upon
them, and very soon a game of cards was proposed.
The doors were closed, wine placed on the table, and
monte begun with doubloons.   Captain R. and Don
Pedro tried hard to make me join them; and when I
rose to leave, Captain R., as if he thought there could
be but one reason for my resisting, took me aside, and
said that if I wanted money he was my friend, while
Don Pedro declared that he was not rich, but that he
had a big heart; that he was happy of my acquaintance; he had had the honour to know a consul once
before at Panama, and I might count upon him for anything I wanted.   Gambling is one of the great vices of
the country, and that into which strangers are most apt
to fall.   The captain had fallen in with a set at San
Miguel, and these two had come down to the port expressly to fleece him.   During the night he detected
them cheating; and telling them that he had learned in
Chili to use a knife as well as they could, laid his cane
over the shoulders of him who had had the honour to
know a consul once before, and broke up the party.
There is an oldfashioned feeling of respect for a man
who wears a sword, but that feeling wears off in Central
America.

CHAPTER III.

Journey to San Salvador.—A new Companion.—San Alejo.—San Miguel.—War Alarms. — Another Countryman. — State of San Salvador. — River Lempa. — San Vicente.—Volcano of San Vicente.—Thermal Springs.—Cojutepeque.— Arrival at San Salvador. — Prejudice against Foreigners. — Contributions. — Pressgangs.—Vice-president Vigil.—Taking of San Miguel and San Vicente. —Rumours of a March upon San Salvador.—Departure from San Salvador.

AT five o'clock the next afternoon we set out for San Salvador. Don Manuel Romero furnished me with letters of introduction to all the Gefes Politicos, and the captain's name was inserted in my passport.

I must introduce the reader to my new friend. Captain Antonio V. F., a little over thirty, when six months out on a whaling voyage, with a leaky ship and a mutinous crew, steered across the Pacific for the Continent of America, and reached the port of La Union with seven or eight feet water in the hold and half his crew in irons. He knew nothing of Central America until necessity threw him upon its shore. While waiting the slow process of a regular condemnation and order for the sale of his ship, General Morazan, with an escort of officers, came to the port to embark his wife and family for Chili. Captain F. had become acquainted with them, and through them with their side of the politics of the country; and in the evening, while we were riding along the ridge of a high mountain, he told me that he had been offered a lieutenant-colonel's commission, and was then on his way to join Morazan in his march against Guatimala. His ship was advertised for sale, he had written an account of his misadventures to his owners and his wife, was tired of remaining at the port, and a campaign with Morazan was the only thing that offered. He liked General Morazan, and he liked the country, and thought his wife would ; if Morazan succeeded there would be vacant offices and estates without owners, and some of them worth having. He went from whaling to campaigning as coolly as a Yankee would from cutting down trees to editing a newspaper. It was no affair of mine, but I suggested that there was no honour to be gained ; that he would get his full share of hard knocks, bullets, and sword-cuts ; that if Morazan succeeded he would have a desperate struggle for his share of the spoils, and if Morazan failed he would certainly be shot. All this was matter he had thought on, and before committing himself he intended to make his observations at San Salvador.

At ten o'clock we reached the village of San Alejo, and stopped at a very comfortable house, where all were in a state of excitement from the report of an invasion from Honduras.

Early the next morning we started with a new guide, and a little beyond the village he pointed out a place where his uncle was murdered and robbed about a year before. Four of the robbers were caught, and sent by the alcalde, under a guard of the relations of the murdered man, to San Miguel, with directions to the guard to shoot them if refractory. The guard found them refractory at the very place where the murder had been committed, and shot them on the spot. At eight o'clock we came in sight of the Volcano of San Miguel, and at two entered the city. Riding up the street, we passed a large church with its front fallen, and saw paintings on the walls, and an altar forty feet high, with columns, and images sculptured and gilded, exposed to the open air. All along the road we had heard of war, and we found the city in a state of great excitement. The troops of Honduras were marching upon it, and then only twelve leagues distant. There were no soldiers to defend it; all had been drawn off for Morazan's expedition. Many of the citizens had already fled; in fact, the town was half depopulated, and the rest were preparing to save themselves by concealment or flight. We stopped at the house of John, or Don Juan, Denning, an American from Connecticut, who had sold an armed brig to the Federal Government, and commanded her himself during the blockade of Omoa, but had married in the country, and for several years lived retired on his hacienda. His house was deserted and stripped, the furniture and valuables were hidden, and his mother-in-law, an old lady, remained in the empty tenement. Nobody thought of resistance; and the captain bought a silver-mounted sword from one of the most respectable citizens, who was converting his useless trappings into money, and who, with a little trunk in his hand containing la plata, pointed to a fine horse in the courtyard, and without a blush on his face said that was his security.

The captain had great difficulty in procuring mules; he had two enormous trunks, containing, among other things, Peruvian chains and other gold trinkets to a large amount; in fact, all he was worth. In the evening we walked to the plaza; groups of men, wrapped in their ponchas, were discussing in low tones the movements of the enemy, how far they had marched that day, how long they would require for rest, and the moment when it would be necessary to fly. We returned to the house, placed two naked wooden-bottomed bedsteads in one, and having ascertained by calculation that we were not likely to be disturbed during the night, forgot the troubles of the flying inhabitants, and slept soundly.

On account of the difficulty of procuring mules, we did not set out till ten o'clock. The climate is the hottest in Central America, and insalubrious under exposure to the sun; but we would not wait. Every moment there were new rumours of the approach of the Honduras army, and it was all important for us to keep in advance of them. I shall hasten over our hurried journey through the State of San Salvador, the richest in Central America, extending a hundred and eighty miles along the shores of the Pacific, producing tobacco, the best indigo and richest balsam in the world. We had mountains and rivers, valleys and immense ravines, and the three great volcanoes of San Miguel, San Vicente, and San Salvador, one or the other of which was almost constantly in sight. The whole surface is volcanic; for miles the road lay over beds of decomposed lava, inducing the belief that here the whole shore of the Pacific is an immense arch over subterraneous fires. From the time of the independence this state stood foremost in the maintenance of liberal principles, and throughout it exhibits an appearance of improvement, a freedom from bigotry and fanaticism, and a development of physical and moral energy not found in any other. The San Salvadoreans are the only men who speak of sustaining the integrity of the Republic as a point of national honour.

In the afternoon of the second day we came in sight of the Lempa, now a gigantic river rolling on to the Pacific. Three months before I had seen it a little stream among the mountains of Esquipulas. Here we were overtaken by Don Carlos Rivas, a leading Liberal from Honduras, flying for life before partisan sol-

diers of his own state. We descended to the bank of
the river, and followed it through a wild forest, which
had been swept by a tornado, the trees still lying as
they fell. At the crossing-place the valley of the river
was half a mile wide ; but being the dry season, on this
side there was a broad beach of sand and stones. We
rode to the water's edge, and shouted for the boatman
on the opposite side. Other parties arrived, all fugitives, among them the wife and family of Don Carlos,
and we formed a crowd upon the shore. At length the
boat came, took on board sixteen mules, saddles, and
luggage, and as many men, women, and children as
could stow themselves away, leaving a multitude behind.
We crossed in the dark, and on the opposite side found
every hut and shed filled with fugitives ; families in
dark masses were under the trees, and men and wom-
en crawled out to congratulate friends who had put
the Lempa between them and the enemy. We slept
upon our luggage on the bank of the river, and before
daylight were again in the saddle.

That night we slept at San Vicente, and the next
morning the captain, in company with an invalid officer of Morazan's, who had been prevented by sickness from accompanying the general in his march
against Guatimala, rode on with the luggage, while I,
with Colonel Hoyas, made a circuit to visit El Infierno of
the Volcano of San Vicente. Crossing a beautiful plain
running to the base of the volcano, we left our animals
at a hut, and walked some distance to a stream in a deep
ravine, which we followed upward to its source, coming from the very base of the volcano. The water was
warm, and had a taste of vitriol, and the banks were
incrusted with white vitriol and flour of sulphur. At
a distance of one or two hundred yards it formed a ba-

sin, where the water was hotter than the highest grade
of my Reaumur's thermometer. In several places we
heard subterranean noises, and toward the end of the
ravine, on the slope of one side, was an orifice about
thirty feet in diameter, from which, with a terrific noise,
boiling water was spouted into the air. This is called
El Infiernillo, or the " little infernal regions." The inhabitants say that the noise is increased by the slightest agitation of the air, even by the human voice. Approaching to within range of the falling water, we shouted several times, and as we listened and gazed into
the fearful cavity, I imagined that the noise was louder
and more angry, and that the boiling water spouted
higher at our call. Colonel Hoyas conducted me to a
path, from which I saw my road, like a white line, over
a high verdant mountain. He told me that many of
the inhabitants of San Miguel had fled to San Vicente,
and at that place the Honduras arms would be repel-
led ; we parted, little expecting to see each other again
so soon, and under such unpleasant circumstances for
him.

I overtook the captain at a village where he had
breakfast prepared, and in the afternoon we arrived at
Cojutepeque, until within two days the temporary capital, beautifully situated at the foot of a small extinct
volcano, its green and verdant sides broken only by a
winding path, and on the top a fortress, which Morazan
had built as his last rallying-place, to die under the flag
of the Republic.

The next day at one o'clock we reached San Salvador. Entering by a fine gate, and through suburbs
teeming with fruit and flower trees, the meanness of the
houses was hardly noticed. Advancing, we saw heaps
of rubbish, and large houses with their fronts cracked

and falling, marks of the earthquakes which had broken it up as the seat of government, and almost depopulated the city. This series of earthquakes commenced on the third of the preceding October (the same day on which I sailed for that country), and for twenty days the earth was tremulous, sometimes suffering fifteen or twenty shocks in twenty-four hours, and one so severe that, as Mr. Chatfield told me, a bottle standing in his sleeping-room was thrown down. Most of the inhabitants abandoned the city, and those who remained slept under matting in the courtyards of their houses. Every house was more or less injured ; some were rendered untenantable, and many were thrown down. Two days before, the vice-president and officers of the Federal and State Governments, impelled by the crisis of the times, had returned to their shattered capital. It was about one o'clock, intensely hot, and there was no shade ; the streets were solitary, the doors and windows of the houses closed, the shops around the plaza shut, the little matted tents of the market-women deserted, and the inhabitants, forgetting earthquakes, and that a hostile army was marching upon them, were taking their noonday siesta. In a corner of the plaza was a barricado, constructed with trunks of trees, rude as an Indian fortress, and fortified with cannon, intended as the scene of the last effort for the preservation of the city. A few soldiers were asleep under the corridor of the quartel, and a sentinel was pacing before the door. Inquiring our way of him, we turned the corner of the plaza, and stopped at the house of Don Pedro Negrete, at that time acting as vice-consul both of England and France, and the only representative at the capital of any foreign power.

It was one of the features of this unhappy revolution,

that the Liberal party, before the friends and supporters of foreigners, manifested a violent feeling against
them, particularly the English, ostensibly on account
of their occupation of the miserable little Island of Roatan, in the Bay of Honduras.   The press, i. e., a little
weekly published at San Salvador, teemed with inflam-
matory articles against los Ingleses, their usurpation
and ambition, and their unjust design of adding to
their extended dominions the republic of Central
America.   It was a desperate effort to sustain a party menaced with destruction by rousing the national
prejudice against strangers.   A development of this
spirit was seen in the treaty of alliance between San
Salvador and Quezaltenango, the only two states that
sustained the Federal Government, by which, in Au-
gust preceding, it was agreed that their delegates to the
national convention should be instructed to treat, in
preference to all other things, upon measures to be taken for the recovery of the Island of Roatan ; and that
no production of English soil or industry, even though
it came under the flag of another nation, and no effect
of any other nation, though a friendly one, if it came
in an English vessel, should be admitted into the
territory until England restored to Central America
the possession of that island.   I do not mean to say
that they were wrong in putting forth their claims to
this island—the English flag was planted upon it in a
very summary way—nor that they were wrong in recommending the only means in their power to redress
what they considered an injury ; for, as England had
not declared war with China, it would have been rash
for the states of San Salvador and Los Altos to involve
themselves in hostilities with that overgrown power ;
but no formal complaint was ever made, and no nego-

tiation proposed; and on the publication of this treaty, which Mr. Chatfield, the British consul general, considered disrespectful and injurious to his government,
he addressed a note to the vice-president, requesting a
categorical answer to the question " if the Federal
Government did exist or not" (precisely what I was
anxious to know); to which he received no answer.
Afterward Mr. Chatfield visited Nicaragua, and the
government of that state sent him a communication, requesting his mediation in settling the difficulties between the states of San Salvador and Honduras, then
at war, and through him the guarantee of the Queen of
England to compel the fulfilment of any treaty made
between them.   Mr. Chatfield, in his answer, referred
to his letter to the vice-president, and spoke of the government as the " so-called Federal Government."
The correspondence was published, and increased the
exasperation against Mr. Chatfield and foreigners generally; they were denounced as instigators and supporters of the revolution; their rights and privileges as
residents discussed, and finally the injustice of their en-
joying the protection of the government! without contributing to the expenses of supporting it.   The result
was, that on the levying of a new forced loan, foreigners were included in the liability, and a peremptory order was issued, requiring them, in case of refusal to pay,
to leave the country in eight days.   The foreigners
were violently exasperated.   There were not more
than a dozen in the state, and most of them being engaged in business which it would be ruinous to leave,
were compelled to pay.   Two or three who wanted to
leave before walked off, and called themselves mar-
tyrs, threatened the vengeance of their government,
and talked of the arrival of a British ship-of-war.   Mr.

Kilgour, a British subject, refused to pay. The authorities had orders to give him his passport to leave the state. Don Pedro Negrete, as vice-consul of France, Encargado de la Ingelterra, presented a remonstrance. The vice-president's answer (in part but too true), as it contains the grounds of the law, and shows the state of feeling existing at the time, I give in his own words:

" Strangers in these barbarous countries, as they call them, ought not to expect to have the advantage of being protected in their property without aiding the government in it. We are poor, and if, in any of the convulsions which are so frequent in new countries that have hardly begun their political career, strangers suffer losses, they at once have recourse to their governments, that the nations in which they come to speculate, not without knowledge of the risks, pay them double or treble of what they have lost. This is unjust in every point of view, when they do not care with a slight loan to aid the government in its most urgent necessities. What ought the government to do ? to tell them, ' Away with you, I cannot secure your property ; or, lend me a certain sum in order to enable me to secure it.' On the other hand, if it happens that a strong party or faction, as it is called, prevails, and falls upon your property the same as upon the property of the sons of the country and the public rents, and you complain to your nation, she comes and blockades our ports, and makes the poor nation pay a thousand per cent."

Mr. Mercer, a French merchant, was absent at the time of enforcing the contributions. Don Pedro was his agent under a power of attorney, and had charge of his goods, and refused to pay. The government insisted ; Don Pedro was determined. The government sent soldiers to his house. Don Pedro said he would hoist the French flag; the chief of the state said he would tear it down.   Don Pedro was imprisoned in his own house, his family excluded from him, and his food handed in by a soldier, until a friend paid the money. Don Pedro contended that the majesty of France was violated in his person; the government said that the proceedings were against him as the agent of Mercer, and not as French consul; but any way, consul or agent, Don Pedro's body bore the brunt, and as this took place but two days before our arrival, Don Pedro was still in bed from the indisposition brought upon him by vexation and anxiety.   We received the above, with many details, from Don Pedro's son, as an apology for his father's absence, and an explanation of the ravings we heard in the adjoining room.

In the evening I called upon the vice-president. Great changes had taken place since I saw him at Zonzonate.   The troops of the Federal Government had been routed in Honduras; Carrera had conquered Quezaltenango, garrisoned it with his own soldiers, destroyed its existence as a separate state, and annexed it to Guatimala.   San Salvador stood alone in support of the Federal Government.   But Señor Vigil had risen with the emergency.   The chief of the state, a bold-looking mulatto, and other officers of the government, were with him.   They knew that the Honduras troops were marching upon the city, had reason to fear they would be joined by those of Nicaragua, but they were not dismayed; on the contrary, all showed a resolution and energy I had not seen before.   General Morazan, they said, was on his march against Guatimala.   Tired as they were of war, the people of San Salvador, Señor Vigil said, had risen with new enthusiasm.   Volunteers were flocking in from all quarters; and with a determination that was imposing, though called out by civil war, he added that they were resolved to sustain the Federation, or die under the ruins of San Salvador. It was the first time my feelings had been at all roused. In all the convulsions of the time I had seen no flash of heroism, no high love of country. Self-preservation and self-aggrandizement were the ruling passions. It was a bloody scramble for power and place; and sometimes, as I rode through the beautiful country, and saw what Providence had done for them, and how unthankful they were, I thought it would be a good riddance if they would play out the game of the Kilkenny cats. It was a higher tone than I was accustomed to, when the chief men of a single state, with an invading army at their door, and their own soldiers away, expressed the stern resolution to sustain the Federation, or die under the ruins of the capital. But they did not despair of the Republic; the Honduras troops would be repulsed at San Vicente, and General Morazan would take Guatimala. The whole subject of the revolution was discussed, and the conversation was deeply interesting to me, for I regarded it as touching matters of life and death. I could not compromise them by anything I might say, for they are all in exile, under sentence of death if they return. They did not speak in the ferocious and sanguinary spirit I afterward heard imputed to them at Guatimala, but they spoke with great bitterness of gentlemen whom I considered personal friends, who, they said, had been before spared by their lenity; and they added, in tones that could not be misunderstood, that they would not make such a mistake again.

In the midst of this confusion, where was my government? I had travelled all over the country, led on

by a glimmering light shining and disappearing, and I
could not conceal from myself that the crisis of my fortune was at hand. All depended upon the success of
Morazan's expedition. If he failed, my occupation was
gone ; but in this darkest hour of the Republic I did not
despair. In ten years of war Morazan had never been
beaten ; Carrera would not dare fight him ; Guatimala
would fall ; the moral effect would be felt all over the
country ; Quezaltenango would shake off its chains ;
the strong minority in the other states would rise ; the
flag of the Republic would once more wave triumphant-
ly, and out of chaos the government I was in search
of would appear.

Nevertheless, I was not so sure of it as to wait quietly till it came to me at San Salvador. The result was
very uncertain, and if it should be a protracted war, I
might be cut off from Guatimala, without any opportunity of serving my country by diplomatic arts, and prevented from prosecuting other objects more interesting
than the uncertain pursuit in which I was then engaged.
The design which the captain had in coming up to San
Salvador had failed ; he could not join Morazan's expedition ; but he had nothing to do at the port, was anxious to see Guatimala, had a stock of jewelry and other
things which he might dispose of there, and was so sure
of Morazan's success that he determined to go on and
pay him a visit, and have the benefits of balls and other
rejoicings attendant upon his triumph.

In the excitement and alarm of the place, it was very
difficult to procure mules. As to procuring them direct
for Guatimala, it was impossible. No one would move
on that road until the result of Morazan's expedition
was known ; and even to get them for Zonzonate it was
necessary to wait a day. That day I intended to ab-

stract myself from the tumult of the city and ascend the Volcano of San Salvador; but the next morning a woman came to inform us that one of our men had been taken by a pressgang of soldiers, and was in the carcel. We followed her to the place, and, being invited in by the officer to pick out our man, found ourselves surrounded by a hundred of Vigil's volunteers, of every grade in appearance and character, from the frightened servant-boy torn from his master's door to the worst of desperadoes; some asleep on the ground, some smoking stumps of cigars, some sullen, and others perfectly reckless. Two of the supreme worst did me the honour to say they liked my looks, called me captain, and asked me to take them into my company. Our man was not ambitious, and could do better than be shot at for a shilling a day; but we could not take him out without an order from the chief of the state, and went immediately to the office of the government, where I was sorry to meet Señor Vigil, as the subject of my visit and the secrets of the prison were an unfortunate comment upon his boasts of the enthusiasm of the people in taking up arms. With his usual courtesy, however, he directed the proper order to be made out, and the names of all in my service to be sent to the captains of the different pressgangs, with orders not to touch them. All day men were caught and brought in, and petty officers were stationed along the street drilling them. In the afternoon intelligence was received that General Morazan's advanced guard had defeated a detachment of Carrera's troops, and that he was marching with an accession of forces upon Guatimala. A feu de joie was fired in the plaza, and all the church bells rang peals of victory.

In the evening I saw Señor Vigil again and alone He was confident of the result. The Honduras troops would be repulsed at San Vicente ; Morazan would take Guatimala. He urged me to wait ; he had his preparations all made, his horses ready, and, on the first notice of Morazan's entry, intended to go up to Guatimala and establish that city once more as the capital. But I was afraid of delay, and we parted to meet in Guatimala ; but we never met again. A few days afterward he was flying for his life, and is now in exile, under sentence of death if he returns ; the party that rules Guatimala is heaping opprobrium upon his name ; but in the recollection of my hurried tour I never forget him who had the unhappy distinction of being vicepresident of the Republic.

I did not receive my passport till late in the evening, and though I had given directions to the contrary, the captain's name was inserted. We had already had a difference of opinion in regard to our movements. He was not so bent as I was upon pushing on to Guatimala, and besides, I did not consider it right, in an official passport, to have the name of a partisan. Accordingly, early in the morning I went to the Government House to have it altered. The separate passports were just handed to me when I heard a clatter in the streets, and fifteen or twenty horsemen galloped into the courtyard, covered with sweat and dust, among whom I recognised Colonel Hoyas, with his noble horse, so broken that I did not know him. They had ridden all night. The Honduras troops had taken San Miguel and San Vicente, and were then marching upon San Salvador. If not repulsed at Cojutepeque, that day they would be upon the capital. For four days I had been running before these troops, and now, by a strange caprice, at the prospect of actual collision, I regretted that my arrangements were so far advanced,

and that I had no necessity for remaining. I had a
strong curiosity to see a city taken by assault, but, unfortunately, I had not the least possible excuse. I had
my passport in my hand and my mules were ready.
Nevertheless, before I reached Don Pedro's house I
determined to remain. The captain had his sword and
spurs on, and was only waiting for me. I told him the
news, and he uttered an exclamation of thankfulness
that we were all ready, and mounted immediately, I
added that I intended to remain. He refused; said
that he knew the sanguinary character of the people
better than I did, and did not wish to see an affair
without having a hand in it. I replied, and after a
short controversy, the result was as usual between two
obstinate men: I would not go and he would not stay.
I sent my luggage-mules and servants under his charge,
and he rode off, to stop for me at a hacienda on the
road, while I unsaddled my horse and gave him another mess of corn.

In the mean time the news had spread, and great excitement prevailed in the city. Here there was no
thought of flight; the spirit of resistance was general.
The impressed soldiers were brought out from the prisons and furnished with arms, and drums beat through
the streets for volunteers. On my return from the Government House I noticed a tailor on his board at work;
when I passed again his horse was at the door, his sob-
bing wife was putting pistols in his holsters, and he was
fastening on his spurs. Afterward I saw him mounted
before the quartel, receiving a lance with a red flag,
and then galloping off to take his place in the line. In
two hours, all that the impoverished city could do
was done. Vigil, the chief of the state, clerks, and
household servants, were preparing for the last strug-

gle. At twelve o'clock the city was as still as death. I lounged on the shady side of the plaza, and the quiet was fearful. At two o'clock intelligence was received that the troops of San Vicente had fallen back upon Cojutepeque, and that the Honduras troops had not yet come up. An order was immediately issued to make this the rallying-place, and to send thither the mustering of the city. About two hundred lancers set off from the plaza with a feeble shout, under a burning sun, and I returned to the house. The commotion subsided; my excitement died away, and I regretted that I had not set out with the captain, when, to my surprise, he rode into the courtyard. On the road he thought that he had left me in the lurch, and that, as a travelling companion, he ought to have remained with me. I had no such idea, but I was glad of his return, and mounted, and left my capital to its fate, even yet uncertain whether I had any government.

CHAPTER IV.

Contributions.—El Baranco de Guaramal.—Volcano of Izalco.—Depredations of Rascon.—Zonzonate.—News from Guatimala.—Journey continued.—Aguisalco.—Apeneca.—Mountain of Aguachapa.—Subterranean Fires.—Aguachapa.—Defeat of Morazan.—Confusion and Terror.

THE captain had given me a hint in a led horse which he kept for emergencies, and I had bought one of an officer of General Morazan, who sold him because he would not stand fire, and recommended him for a way he had of carrying his rider out of the reach of bullets. At the distance of two leagues we reached a hacienda where our men were waiting for us with the luggage. It was occupied by a miserable old man alone, with a large swelling under his throat, very common all through this country, the same as is seen among the mountains of Switzerland. While the men were reloading, we heard the tramp of horses, and fifteen or twenty lancers galloped up to the fence; and the leader, a dark, stern, but respectable-looking man about forty, in a deep voice, called to the old man to get ready and mount; the time had come, he said, when every man must fight for his country; if they had done so before, their own ships would be floating on the Atlantic and the Pacific, and they would not now be at the mercy of strangers and enemies. Altogether the speech was a good one, and would have done for a fourth of July oration or a ward meeting at home; but made from the back of a horse by a powerful man, well armed, and with twenty lancers at his heels, it was not pleasant in the ears of the "strangers" for whom it was intended. Really I respected the man's energy, but his expression and manner precluded all courtesies; and though he looked at us for an answer, we said nothing. The old man answered that he was too old to fight, and the officer told him then to help others to do so, and to contribute his horses or mules. This touched us again; and taking ours apart, we left exposed and alone an object more miserable as a beast than his owner was as a man. The old man said this was his all. The officer, looking as if he would like a pretext for seizing ours, told him to give her up; and the old man, slowly untying her, without a word led her to the fence, and handed the halter across to one of the lancers. They laughed as they received the old man's all, and pricking the mule with their lances, galloped off in search of more " contributions."

Unluckily, they continued on our road, and we feared that parties were scouring the whole country to Zonzonate. This brought to mind a matter that gave us much uneasiness. As the mail-routes were all broken up, and there was no travelling, I was made letter-carrier all the way from Nicaragua. I had suffered so much anxiety from not receiving any letters myself, that I was glad to serve any one that asked me; but I had been treated with great frankness by the " party" at San Salvador, and was resolved not to be the means of communicating anything to their enemies; and with this view, always asked whether the letters contained any political information, never taking them until assured that they did not. But many of them were to Mr. Chatfield and the other Ingleses in Guatimala. There was a most bitter feeling against Mr. Chatfield, and the rudeness of this really respectable-looking man gave us some idea of the exasperation against foreigners generally; and as they were identified in the revolution, the directions alone might expose us to danger with any band of infuriated partisans who might take it into their

heads to search us on the road. If I had had a safe opportunity, I should have sent them back to San Salvador.
I could not intrust them with the old man, and we de-
liberated whether it was not better to return, and wait
the crisis at the capital; but we thought it an object to
get near the coast, and perhaps within reach of a vessel,
and determined to continue. In about an hour we passed the same party dismounted, at some distance from the
road, before the door of a large hacienda, with some of
the men inside, and, fortunately, so far off that, though
we heard them hallooing at us, we could not understand
what they said. Soon after we descended a wild mount-
ain-pass, and entered El Baranco de Guaramal, a narrow opening, with high perpendicular sides, covered
with bushes, wild flowers, and moss, and roofed over
by branches of large trees, which crossed each other
from the opposite banks. A large stream forced its way
through the ravine, broken by trunks of trees and huge
stones. For half a league our road lay in the bed of
the stream, knee-deep for the mules. In one place, on
the right-hand side, a beautiful cascade precipitated itself from the top of the bank almost across the ravine.
A little before dark, in a grassy recess at the foot of the
bank, a pig-merchant had encamped for the night. His
pigs were harnessed with straps and tied to a tree, and
his wife was cooking supper; and when we told him of
the foraging party at the other end of the ravine, he
trembled for his pigs. Some time after dark we reached the hacienda of Guaramal. There was plenty of sacate in an adjoining field, but we could not get any
one to cut it. The major-domo was an old man, and
the workmen were afraid of snakes. Bating this,
however, we fared well, and had wooden bedsteads to
sleep on; and in one corner was a small space partitioned off for the major-domo and his wife.

Before daylight we were in the saddle, and rode till eleven, when we stopped at a small village to feed our mules and avoid the heat of the day. At three we started. Toward evening I heard once more the deep rumbling noise of the Volcano of Izalco, sounding like distant thunder. We passed along its base, and stopped at the same house at which I had put up on my visit to the volcano. The place was in a state of perfect anarchy and misrule. Since my departure, Rascon, rendered more daring by the abject policy of the government, had entered Zonzonate, robbed the customhouse again, laid contributions upon some of the citizens, thence marched to Izalco, and quartered his whole band upon the town. Unexpectedly, he was surprised at night by a party of Morazan's soldiers; he himself escaped in his shirt, but nineteen of his men were killed and his band broken up. Lately the soldiers were called off to join Morazan's expedition, and the dispersed band emerged from their hiding-places. Some were then living publicly in the town, perfectly lawless; had threatened to kill the alcalde if he attempted to disturb them, and kept the town in a state of terror. Among those who reappeared I was told there was a young American del Norte, whom I recognised, from the description, as Jemmy, whom I had put on board his ship at Acajutla. He and the other American had deserted, and attempted to cross over to the Atlantic on foot. On the way they fell in with Rascon's band and joined them. The other man was killed at the time of the rout, but Jemmy escaped. I was happy to hear that Jemmy, by his manners and good conduct, had made a favourable impression upon the ladies of Izalco. He remained only three days, and whither he had gone no one knew.

While listening to this account we heard a noise in
the street, and looking out of the window, saw a man on
the ground, and another striking at him with a white
club, which by the moonlight looked like the blade of
a broadsword or machete. A crowd gathered, mostly
of women, who endeavoured to keep him off; but he
struck among them with blows that would have killed
the man if they had hit him. He was one of the Rascon gang, a native of the town, and known from boyhood as a bad fellow. All called him by name, and,
more by entreaties than force, made him desist. As he
walked off with several of his companions, he said that
the man was a spy of Morazan, and the next time he
met him he would kill him. The poor fellow was
senseless; and as the women raised up his head, we
saw with horror hairs white as snow, and the face of a
man of seventy. He was all in rags, and they told us
that he was a beggar and crazy; that he had given no
provocation whatever; but the young scoundrel, in passing, happened to fix his eyes upon him, and calling
him a spy of Morazan, knocked him down with his club.
Very soon the crowd dispersed, and the women remained to take care of the old man. These were
times which required the natural charity of woman to
be aided by supernatural strength. Every woman
dreaded that her husband, son, or brother should cross
the street at night, for fear of quarrels and worse weapons than clubs; and we saw five women, one with a
candle, without a single man or boy to help them, support the old man across the street, and set him up with
his back against the side of the house. Afterward a
woman came to the door and called to the woman
in our house, that if the young man passed again he
would kill him; and they went out again with a can-

dle, carried him into the courtyard of a house, and locked the door. The reader will perhaps cry shame upon us, but we went out once and were urged to retire, and two men were standing at the window all the time. It was natural to wish to break the head of the young man, but it was natural also to avoid bringing upon ourselves a gang which, though broken, was strong enough to laugh at the authorities of the town, and to waylay us in the wild road we had to pass. There was one ominous circumstance in the affair: that in a town in the State of San Salvador, a man dared threaten publicly to kill another because he was a partisan of Morazan, showed a disaffection in that state which surprised me more than anything I had yet encountered. Our men were afraid to take the mules to water, and it was indispensable for them to drink. We were cautioned against going with them; and at length, upon our standing in the doorway ready to go to their assistance, they set off with loaded pistols. When I passed through Izalco before it was a tranquil place.

Early in the morning we started, arrived at Zonzonate before breakfast, and rode to the house of my friend Mr. De Nouvelle. It was exactly two months since I left it, and, with the exception of my voyage on the Pacific and sickness at Costa Rica, I had not had a day of repose.

I was now within four days of Guatimala, but the difficulty of going on was greater than ever. The captain could procure no mules. No intelligence had been received of Morazan's movements; intercourse was entirely broken off, business at a stand, and the people anxiously waiting for news from Guatimala.. Nobody would set out on that road. I was very much distressed. My engagement with Mr. Catherwood was for a specific time; the rainy season was coming on, and by the loss of a month I should be prevented visiting Palenque. I considered it actually safer to pass through while all was in this state of suspense, than after the floodgates of war were opened. Rascon's band had prevented my passing the road before, and other Rascons might spring up. The captain had not the same inducement to push ahead that I had. I had no idea of incurring any unnecessary risk, and on the road would have had no hesitation at any time in putting spurs to my horse; but, on deliberate consideration, my mind was so fully made up that I determined to procure a guide at any price, and set out alone.

In the midst of my perplexity, a tall, thin, gaunt-looking Spaniard, whose name was Don Saturnino Tinocha, came to see me. He was a merchant from Costa Rica, so far on his way to Guatimala, and, by the advice of his friends rather than his own judgment, had been already waiting a week at Zonzonate. He was exactly in the humour to suit me, very anxious to reach Guatimala; and his views and opinions were just the same as mine. The captain was indifferent, and, at all events, could not go unless he could procure mules. I told Don Saturnino that I would go at all events, and he undertook to provide for the captain. In the evening he returned, with intelligence that he had scoured the town and could not procure a single mule, but he offered to leave two of his own cargoes and take the captain's, or to sell him two of his mules. I offered to lend him my horse or macho, and the matter was arranged.

In the midst of the war-rumours, the next day, which was Sunday, was one of the most quiet I passed in Central America. It was at the hacienda of Dr. Drivin, about a league from Zonzonate. This was one of the finest haciendas in the country. The doctor had imported a large steam engine, which was not yet set up, and was preparing to manufacture sugar upon a larger scale than any other planter in the country. He was from the island of St. Kitts, and, before sitting down in this out-of-the-way place, had travelled extensively in Europe and all the West India Islands, and knew America from Halifax to Cape Horn; but surprised me by saying that he looked forward to a cottage in Morristown, New-Jersey, as the consummation of his wishes. I learned from him that Jemmy, after his disappearance from Izalco, had straggled to his hacienda in wretched condition and sick of campaigning, and was then at the port on board the Cosmopolita, bound for Peru.

On our return to Zonzonate we were again in the midst of tumult. Two of Captain D'Yriarte's passengers for Guayaquil, whom he had given up, arrived that evening direct from Guatimala, and reported that Carrera, with two thousand men, had left the city at the same time with them to march upon San Salvador. Carrera knew nothing of Morazan's approach; his troops were a disorderly and tumultuous mass; and three leagues from the city, when they halted, the horses were already tired. Here our informants slipped away, and three hours afterward met Morazan's army, in good order, marching single file, with Morazan himself at their head, he and all his cavalry dismounted and leading their horses, which were fresh and ready for immediate action. Morazan stopped them, and made them show their passports and letters, and they told him of the sally of Carrera's army, and its condition; and we all formed the conclusion that Morazan had attacked them the same day, defeated them, and was then in possession of Guatimala. Upon the whole, we considered the news favourable to us, as his first business would be to make the roads secure.

At three o'clock the next morning we were again in the saddle. A stream of fire was rolling down the Volcano of Izalco, bright, but paler by the moonlight. The road was good for two leagues, when we reached the Indian village of Aguisalco. Our mules were overloaded, and one of Don Saturnino's gave out entirely. We tried to procure others or Indian carriers, but no one would move from home. Don Saturnino loaded his saddle-mule, and walked; and if it had not been for his indefatigable perseverance, we should have been compelled to stop.

At one o'clock we reached Apeneca, and rode up to one of the best houses, where an old man and his wife undertook to give us breakfast. Our mules presented a piteous spectacle. Mine, which had carried my light luggage like a feather all the way from La Union, had gone on with admirable steadiness up hill and down dale, but when we stopped she trembled in every limb, and before the cargo was removed I expected to see her fall. Nicolas and the muleteer said she would certainly die, and the faithful brute seemed to look at me reproachfully for having suffered so heavy a load to be put upon her back. I tried to buy or hire another, but all were removed one or two days' journey out of the line of march of the soldiers.

It was agreed that I should go on to Aguachapa and endeavour to have other mules ready early the next morning; but in the mean time the captain conceived some suspicions of the old man and woman, and resolved not to remain that night in the village. Fortunately, my mule revived and began to eat. Don Sat-

urnino repeated his 'sta bueno, with which he had
cheered us through all the perplexities of the day, and
we determined to set out again. Neither of us had any
luggage he was willing to leave, for in all probability
he would never see it again. We loaded our saddle-
beasts and walked. Immediately on leaving the village
we commenced ascending the mountain of Aguachapa,
the longest and worst in the whole road, in the wet season requiring two days to cross it. A steep pitch at
the beginning made me tremble for the result. The ascent was about three miles, and on the very crest, imbowered among the trees, was a blacksmith's shop,
commanding a view of the whole country back to the
village, and on the other side, of the slope of the mountain to the plain of Aguachapa. The clink of the hammer and the sight of a smith's grimed face seemed a
profanation of the beauties of the scene. Here our difficulties were over ; the rest of our road was down hill.
The road lay along the ridge of the mountain. On our
right we looked down the perpendicular side to a plain
two thousand feet below us; and in front, on another
part of the same plain, were the lake and town of
Aguachapa. Instead of going direct to the town, we
turned round the foot of the mountain, and came into
a field smoking with hot springs. The ground was
incrusted with sulphur, and dried and baked by subterranean fires. In some places were large orifices,
from which steam rushed out violently and with noise,
and in others large pools or lakes, one of them a
hundred and fifty feet in circumference, of dark brown
water, boiling with monstrous bubbles three or four feet
high, which Homer might have made the head-waters
of Acheron. All around, for a great extent, the earth
was in a state of combustion, burning our boots and

frightening the horses, and we were obliged to be careful to keep the horses from falling through. At some
distance was a stream of sulphur-water, which we followed up to a broad basin, made a dam with stones
and bushes, and had a most refreshing warm bath.

It was nearly dark when we entered the town, the
frontier of the state and the outpost of danger. All
were on the tiptoe of expectation for news from Guatimala. Riding through the plaza, we saw a new corps
of about two hundred "patriot soldiers," uniformed and
equipped, at evening drill, which was a guarantee against
the turbulence we had seen in Izalco. Colonel Angoula, the commandant, was the same who had broken up
the band of Rascon. Every one we met was astonished at our purpose of going on to Guatimala, and it was
vexatious and discouraging to have ominous cautions
perpetually dinned into our ears. We rode to the house
of the widow Padilla, a friend of Don Saturnino, whom
we found in great affliction. Her eldest son, on a visit
to Guatimala on business, with a regular passport, had
been thrown into prison by Carrera, and had then been
a month in confinement; and she had just learned, what
had been concealed from her, that the other son, a young
man just twenty-one, had joined Morazan's expedition.
Our purpose of going to Guatimala opened the fountain
of her sorrows. She mourned for her sons, but the case
of the younger seemed to give her most distress. She
mourned that he had become a soldier; she had seen
so much of the horrors of war; and, as if speaking of a
truant boy, begged us to urge General Morazan to send
him home. She was still in black for their father, who
was a personal friend of General Morazan, and had,
besides, three daughters, all young women, the eldest
not more than twenty-three, married to Colonel Molina,

the second in command; all were celebrated in that country for their beauty; and though the circumstances of the night prevented my seeing much of them, I looked upon this as one of the most ladylike and interesting family groups I had seen in the country.

Our first inquiry was for mules. Colonel Molina, the son-in-law, after endeavouring to dissuade us from continuing, sent out to make inquiries, and the result was that there were none to hire, but there was a man who had two to sell, and who promised to bring them early in the morning. We had vexations enough without adding any between ourselves; but, unfortunately, the captain and Don Saturnino had an angry quarrel, growing out of the breaking down of the mules. I was appealed to by both, and in trying to keep the peace came near having both upon me. The dispute was so violent that none of the female part of the family appeared in the sala, and while it was pending Colonel Molina was called off by a message from the commandant. In half an hour he returned, and told us that two soldiers had just entered the town, who reported that Morazan had been defeated in his attack on Guatimala, and his whole army routed and cut to pieces; that he himself, with fifteen dragoons, was escaping by the way of the coast, and the whole of Carrera's army was in full pursuit. The soldiers were at first supposed to be deserters, but they were recognised by some of the town's people; and after a careful examination and calculation of the lapse of time since the last intelligence, the news was believed to be true. The consternation it created in our little household cannot be described. Morazan's defeat was the death-knell of sons and brothers. It was not a moment for strangers to offer idle consolation, and we withdrew.

Our own plans were unsettled ; the very dangers I feared had happened ; the soldiers, who had been kept together in masses, were disbanded to sweep every road in the country with the ferocity of partisan war. But for the night we could do nothing. Our men were already asleep, and, not without apprehensions, the captain and I retired to a room opening upon the courtyard. Don Saturnino wrapped himself in his poncha and lay down under the corridor.

None of us undressed, but the fatigue of the day had been so great that I soon fell into a profound sleep. At one o'clock we were roused by Colonel Molina shouting in the doorway " La gente vienne !" " The people are coming!" His sword glittered, his spurs rattled, and by the moonlight I saw men saddling horses in the courtyard. We sprang up in a moment, and he told us to save ourselves; "la gente" were coming, and within two hours' march of the town. My first question was, What had become of the soldiers ? They were already marching out ; everybody was preparing to fly ; he intended to escort the ladies to a hiding-place in the mountains, and then to overtake the soldiers. I must confess that my first thought was "devil take the hindmost," and I ordered Nicolas, who was fairly blubbering with fright, to saddle for a start. The captain, however, objected, insisting that to fly would be to identify ourselves with the fugitives; and if we were overtaken with them we should certainly be massacred. Don Saturnino proposed to set out on our journey, and go straight on to a hacienda two leagues beyond ; if we met them on the road we would appear as travellers ; in their hurry they would let us pass;

and, at all events, we would avoid the dangers of a
general sacking and plunder of the town.   I approved
of this suggestion ; the fact is, I was for anything that
put us on horseback; but the captain again opposed it
violently.   Unluckily, he had four large, heavy trunks
containing jewelry and other valuables, and no mules
to carry them.   I made a hurried but feeling comment
upon the comparative value of life and property; but
the captain said that all he was worth in the world was
in those trunks; he would not leave them; he would
not risk them on the road; he would defend them as
long as he had life; and, taking them up one by one
from the corridor, he piled them inside of our little
sleeping-room, shut the door, and swore that nobody
should get into them without passing over his dead
body.   Now I, for my own part, would have taken a
quiet stripping, and by no means approved this desperate purpose of the captain's.   The fact is, I was very
differently situated from him.   My property was chiefly
in horseflesh and muleflesh, at the moment the most desirable thing in which money could be invested; and with
two hours' start, I would have defied all the Cachurecos in Guatimala to catch me.   But the captain's determination put an end to all thoughts of testing the sound-
ness of my investment; and perhaps, at all events, it
was best to remain.

I entered the house, where the old lady and her
daughters were packing up their valuables, and passed
through to the street.   The church bells were tolling
with a frightful sound, and a horseman, with a red ban-
neret on the point of his lance, was riding through the
streets warning the inhabitants to fly.   Horses were
standing before the doors saddled and bridled, and all
along men were issuing from the doors with loads on

their backs, and women with packages and bundles in
their hands, and hurrying children before them.   The
moon was beaming with unrivalled splendour ; the
women did not scream, the children did not cry ; terror was in every face and movement, but too deep for
utterance.   I walked down to the church ; the cura
was at the altar, receiving hurried confessions and ad-
ministering the sacrament ; and as the wretched inhabitants left the altar they fled from the town.   I saw a
poor mother searching for a missing child ; but her
friends, in hoarse whispers, said, " La gente vienne !"
and hurried her away.   A long line of fugitives, with
loaded mules interspersed, was moving from the door
of the church, and disappearing beneath the brow of
the hill.   It was the first time I ever saw terror operating
upon masses, and I hope never to see it again.   I went
back to the house.   The family of Padilla had not left,
and the poor widow was still packing up.   We urged
Colonel Molina to hasten ; as commandant, he would
be the first victim.   He knew his danger, but in a tone
of voice that told the horrors of this partisan war, said
he could not leave behind him the young women.   In
a few moments all was ready ; the old lady gave us the
key of the house, we exchanged the Spanish farewell
with a mutual recommendation to God, and sadly and
silently they left the town.   Colonel Molina remained
a moment behind.   Again he urged us to fly, saying
that the enemy were robbers, murderers, and assassins,
who would pay no respect to person or character, and
disappointment at finding the town deserted would
make them outrageous with us.   He drove his spurs
into his horse, and we never saw him again.   On the
steps of the church were sick and infirm old men and
children, and the cura's house was thronged with the

same helpless beings. Except these, we were left in sole possession of the town.

It was not yet an hour since we had been roused from sleep. We had not been able to procure any definite information as to the character of the approaching force. The alarm was " la gente vienne ;" no one knew or thought of more, no one paid any attention to us, and we did not know whether the whole army of Carrera was approaching, or merely a roving detachment. If the former, my hope was that Carrera was with them, and that he had not forgotten my diplomatic coat; I felt rejoiced that the soldiers had marched out, and that the inhabitants had fled ; there could be no resistance, no bloodshed, nothing to excite a lawless soldiery. Again we walked down to the church; old women and little boys gathered around us, and wondered that we did not fly. We went to the door of the cura's house; the room was small, and full of old women. We tried to cheer them, but old age had lost its garrulity; they waited their fate in silence. We returned to the house, smoked, and waited in anxious expectation. The enemy did not come, the bell ceased its frightful tolling, and after a while we began to wish they would come, and let us have the thing over. We went out, and looked, and listened ; but there was neither sound nor motion. We became positively tired of waiting ; there were still two hours to daylight ; we lay down, and, strange to say, again fell asleep.

CHAPTER V.

IT was broad daylight when we woke, without any machete cuts, and still in undisturbed possession of the town. My first thought was for the mules; they had eaten up their sacate, and had but a poor chance for more, but I sent them immediately to the river for water. They had hardly gone when a little boy ran in from the church, and told us that la gente were in sight. We hurried back with him, and the miserable beings on the steps, with new terrors, supposing that we were friends of the invaders, begged us to save them. Followed by three or four trembling boys, we ascended to the steeple, and saw the Cachurecos at a distance, descending the brow of a hill in single file, their muskets glittering in the sunbeams. We saw that it was not the whole of Carrera's army, but apparently only a pioneer company; but they were too many for us, and the smallness of their numbers gave them the appearance of a lawless predatory band. They had still to cross a long plain and ascend the hill on which the town was built. The bellrope was in reach of my hand; I gave it one strong pull, and telling the boys to sound loud the alarm, hurried down. As we passed out of the church, we heard loud cries from the old women in the house of the cura; and the old men and children on the steps asked us whether they would be murdered.

The mules had not returned, and, afraid of their being intercepted in the street, I ran down a steep hill toward the river, and meeting them, hurried back to the house. While doing so I saw at the extreme end of the street a single soldier moving cautiously; and watching carefully every house, as if suspecting treachery, he advanced with a letter directed to Colonel Angoula. The captain told him that he must seek Angoula among the mountains. We inquired the name of his commanding officer, how many men he had, said that there was no one to oppose him, and forthwith surrendered the town. The man could hardly believe that it was deserted. General Figoroa did not know it; he had halted at a short distance, afraid to make the attack at night, and was then expecting immediate battle. He himself could not have been much better pleased at avoiding it than we were. The envoy returned, and in a short time we saw at the extreme end of the street the neck of a horse protruding from the cross-street on the left. A party of cavalry armed with lances followed, formed at the head of the street, looking about them carefully as if still suspecting an ambush. In a few moments General Figoroa, mounted on a fierce little horse, without uniform, but with dark wool saddle-cloth, pistols, and basket-hilted sword, making a warlike appearance, came up, leading the van. We took off our hats as he approached our door, and he returned the salute. About a hundred lancers followed him, two abreast, with red flags on the ends of their lances, and pistols in their holsters. In passing, one ferocious-looking fellow looked fiercely at us, and grasping his lance, cried " Viva Carrera." We did not answer it immediately, and he repeated it in a tone that brought forth the response louder and more satisfactory, from the

spite with which it was given ; the next man repeated
it, and the next ; and before we were aware of our position, every lancer that passed, in a tone of voice reg-
ulated by the gentleness or the ferocity of his disposition, and sometimes with a most threatening scowl, put
to us as a touchstone " Viva Carrera."

The infantry were worse than the lancers in appearance, being mostly Indians, ragged, half naked, with
old straw hats and barefooted, armed with muskets and
machetes, and many with oldfashioned Spanish blun-
derbusses.   They vied with each other in sharpness and
ferocity, and sometimes actually levelling their pieces,
cried at us " Viva Carrera."   We were taken completely unawares ; there was no escape, and I believe
they would have shot us down on the spot if we had refused to echo the cry.   I compromised with my dignity
by answering no louder than the urgency of the case required, but I never passed through a more trying ordeal.
Don Saturnino had had the prudence to keep out of
sight ; but the captain, who had intended to campaign
against these fellows, never flinched, and when the last
man passed added an extra " Viva Carrera."   I again
felt rejoiced that the soldiers had left the town and that
there had been no fight.   It would have been a fearful
thing to fall into the hands of such men, with their passions roused by resistance and bloodshed.   Reaching
the plaza, they gave a general shout of " Viva Carrera,"
and stacked their arms.   In a few minutes a party of
them came down to our house and asked for breakfast ;
and when we could not give them that, they begged a
medio or sixpence.   By degrees others came in, until
the room was full.   They were really no great gainers
by taking the town.   They had had no breakfast, and
the town was completely stripped of eatables.   We in-

quired the news from Guatimala, and bought from them
several copies of the "Parte Official" of the Supreme
Government, headed "Viva la Patria! Viva el General
Carrera! The enemy has been completely extermi-
nated in his attack upon this city, which he intended to
devastate. The tyrant Morazan flies terrified, leaving
the plaza and streets strewed with corpses sacrificed to
his criminal ambition. The principal officers associated
in his staff have perished, &c. *Eternal glory to the Invincible Chief* General Carrera, and the valiant troops
under his command." They told us that Carrera, with
three thousand men, was in full pursuit. In a little
while the demand for sixpences became so frequent,
that, afraid of being supposed to have mucha plata,
we walked to the plaza to present ourselves to General
Figoroa, and settle the terms of our surrender, or, at all
events, to "define our position." We found him at
the cabildo, quite at home, with a parcel of officers,
white men, Mestitzoes, and mulattoes, smoking, and in-
terrogating some old men from the church as to the
movements of Colonel Angoula and the soldiers, the
time of their setting out, and the direction they took.
He was a young man—all the men in that country were
young—about thirty-two or three, dressed in a snuff-col-
oured cloth roundabout jacket, and pantaloons of the
same colour; and off his warhorse, and away from his
assassin-like band, had very much the air of an honest
man.

It was one of the worst evils of this civil war that no
respect was paid to the passports of opposite parties.
The captain had only his San Salvador passport, which
was here worse than worthless. Don Saturnino had a
variety from partisan commandants, and upon this occasion made use of one from a colonel under Ferrera.

The captain introduced me by the title of Señor Ministro del Norte America, and I made myself acceptable by
saying that I had been to San Salvador in search of a
government, and had not been able to find any.   The
fact is, although I was not able to get into regular business, I was practising diplomacy on my own account
all the time ; and in order to define at once and clearly
our relative positions, I undertook to do the honours of
the town, and invited General Figoroa and all his officers to breakfast.   This was a bold stroke, but Talleyrand could not have touched a nicer chord.   They had
not eaten anything since noon the day before, and I believe they would have evacuated their empty conquest
for a good breakfast all round.   They accepted my
invitation with a promptness that put an end to my
small stock of provisions for the road.   General Figoroa confirmed the intelligence of Morazan's defeat and
flight, and Carrera's pursuit, and the "invincible chief"
would perhaps have been somewhat surprised at the
pleasure I promised myself in meeting him.

With a very few moments' interchange of opinion,
we made up our minds to get out of this frontier town
as soon as possible, and again to go forward.   I had
almost abandoned ulterior projects, and looked only to
personal safety.   To go back, we reasoned, would carry us into the very focus of war and danger.   The San
Salvador people were furious against strangers, and the
Honduras troops were invading them on one side, and
Carrera's hordes on the other.   To remain where we
were was certain exposure to attacks from both parties.
By going on we would meet Carrera's troops, and if we
passed them we left war behind us.   We had but one
risk, and that would be tested in a day.   Under this belief,
I told the general that we designed proceeding to Gua-

timala, and that it would add to our security to have his
passport. It was the general's first campaign. He was
then only a few days in service, having set off in a hurry to get possession of this town, and cut off Morazan's
retreat. He was flattered by the request, and said that
his passport would be indispensable. His aid and secretary had been clerk in an apothecary's shop in Guatimala, and therefore understood the respect due to a
ministro, and said that he would make it out himself.
I was all eagerness to get possession of this passport.
The captain, in courtesy, said we were in no hurry. I
dismissed courtesy, and said that we were in a hurry;
that we must set out immediately after breakfast. I
was afraid of postponements, delays, and accidents,
and in spite of impediments and inconveniences, I persisted till I got the secretary down at the table, who,
without any trouble, and by a mere flourish of the pen,
made me "ministro plenipotentiario." The captain's
name was inserted in the passport, General Figoroa
signed it, and I put it in my pocket, after which I
breathed more freely.

We returned to the house, and in a few minutes the
general, his secretary, and two mulatto officers came
over to breakfast. It was very considerate in them that
they did not bring more. Our guests cared more for
quantity than quality, and this was the particular in
which we were most deficient. We had plenty of chocolate, a stock of bread for the road, and some eggs that
were found in the house. We put on the table all that
we had, and gave the general the seat of honour at the
head. One of the officers preferred sitting away on a
bench, and eating his eggs with his fingers. It is unpleasant for a host to be obliged to mark the quantity
that his guests eat, but I must say I was agreeably dis-

appointed. If I had been breakfasting with them instead of vice versa, I could have astonished them as
much as their voracious ancestors did the Indians.
The breakfast was a neat fit; there was none over, and
I believe nothing short.

There was but one unpleasant circumstance attendant upon it, viz., General Figoroa requested us to wait
an hour, until he could prepare despatches to Carrera,
advising him of his occupation of Aguachapa. I was
extremely anxious to get away while the game was
good. Of General Figoroa and his secretary we thought
favourably; but we saw that he had no control over his
men, and as long as we were in the town we should be
subject to their visits, inquiries, and importunities, and
some difficulties might arise. At the same time, despatches to Carrera would be a great security on the
road. Don Saturnino undertook to set off with the
luggage, and we, glad of the opportunity of travelling
without any encumbrance, charged him to push on as
fast as he could, not to stop for us, and we would overtake him.

In about an hour we walked over to the plaza for the
despatches, but unluckily found ourselves in a new scene
of confusion. Figoroa was already in the saddle, the
lancers were mounting in haste, and all running to
arms. A scout had brought in word that Colonel Angoula, with the soldiers of the town, was hovering on
the skirt of the mountain, and our friends were hurrying
to attack them. In a moment the lancers were off on a
gallop, and the ragged infantry snatched up their guns
and ran after them, keeping up with the horses. The
letter to Carrera was partly written, and the aiddecamp
asked us to wait, telling us that the affair would soon be
over. He was left in command of about seventy or

eighty men, and we sat down with him under the corridor of the quartel. He was several years younger
than Figoroa, more intelligent, and seemed very amiable except on political matters, and there he was savage
against the Morazan party. He was gentlemanly in his
manners, but his coat was out at the elbows, and his
pantaloons were torn. He said he had a new frock-
coat, for which he had paid sixteen dollars, but which
did not fit him, and he wished to sell it. I afterward
spoke of him to one of Morazan's officers, whom I
would believe implicitly except in regard to political
opponents, who told me that this same secretary stole
a pair of pantaloons from him, and he had no doubt
the coat was stolen from somebody else.

There was no order or discipline among the men ;
the soldiers lay about the quartel, joined in the conversation, or strolled through the town, as they pleased.
The inhabitants had fortunately carried away everything portable ; two or three times a foraging party returned with a horse or mule, and once they were all
roused by an alarm that Angoula was returning upon
the town in another direction. Immediately all snatched up their arms, and at least one half, without a moment's warning, took to their heels. We had a fair
chance of having the town again upon our hands, but
the alarm proved groundless. We could not, however,
but feel uncomfortable at the facility with which our
friends abandoned us, and the risk we ran of being
identified with them. There were three brothers, the
only lancers who did not go out with Figoroa, white
men, young and athletic, the best dressed and best
armed in the company ; swaggering in their manner,
and disposed to cultivate an acquaintance with us ; they

told us that they purposed going to Guatimala; but I
shrank from them instinctively, eluded their questions
as to when we intended to set out, and I afterward
heard that they were natives of the town, and had been
compelled to leave it on account of their notorious
characters as assassins. One of them, as we thought,
in a mere spirit of bravado, provoked a quarrel with
the aiddecamp, strutted before the quartel, and in the
hearing of all said that they were under no man's orders ; they only joined General Figoroa to please themselves, and would do as they thought proper. In the
mean time, a few of the townsmen who had nothing to
lose, among them an alguazil, finding there was no
massacring, had returned or emerged from their hiding-places, and we procured a guide to be ready the
moment General Figoroa should return, went back to
the house, and to our surprise found the widow Padilla
there. She had been secreted somewhere in the neighbourhood, and had heard, by means of an old woman-
servant, of the general's breakfasting with us, and our
intimacy with him. We inquired for her daughters'
safety, but not where they were, for we had already
found that we could answer inquiries better when we
knew nothing.

We waited till four o'clock, and hearing nothing of
General Figoroa, made up our minds that we should
not get off till evening. We therefore strolled up to
the extreme end of the street, where Figoroa had entered, and where stood the ruins of an old church. We
sat on the foundation walls and looked through the long
and desolate street to the plaza, where were a few
stacks of muskets and some soldiers. All around were
mountains, and among them rose the beautiful and verdant Volcano of Chingo. While sitting there two

women ran past, and telling us that the soldiers were
returning in that direction, hid themselves among the
ruins. We turned down a road and were intercepted
on a little eminence, where we were obliged to stop and
look down upon them as they passed. We saw that
they were irritated by an unsuccessful day's work, and
that they had found agua ardiente, for many of them
were drunk. A drummer on horseback, and so tipsy
that he could hardly sit, stopped the line to glorify General Carrera. Very soon they commenced the old
touchstone, " Viva Carrera !" and one fellow, with the
strap of his knapsack across his naked shoulders, again
stopped the whole line, and turning round with a ferocious expression, said, " You are counting us, are you?"

We disappeared, and by another street got back to
the house. We waited a moment, and, determined to
get out of the town and sleep at the first hacienda on
the road, left the house to go again to General Figoroa for his despatches; but before reaching it we
saw new confusion in the plaza, a general remounting
and rushing to arms. As soon as General Figoroa
saw us, he spurred his horse down the street to meet
us, and told us, in great haste, that General Morazan
was approaching and almost upon the town. He had
that moment received the news, and was going out to
attack him. He had no time to sign the despatches,
and while he was speaking the lancers galloped past.
He shook hands, bade us good-by, hasta luego (until
presently), asked us to call upon Carrera in case we
did not see him again, and dashing down the line, put
himself at the head of the lancers. The foot-soldiers
followed in single file on a run, carrying their arms as
was most convenient. In the hurry and excitement we
forgot ourselves till we heard some flattering epithets,

and saw two fellows shaking their muskets at us with the
expression of fiends ; but, hurried on by those behind,
they cried out ferociously, "Estos picaros otro vez,"
" Those rascals again." The last of the line had hardly
disappeared before we heard a volley of musketry, and
in a moment fifty or sixty men left in the plaza snatched up their arms and ran down a street opening from
the plaza. Very soon a horse without a rider came
clattering down the street at full speed ; three others
followed, and in five minutes we saw thirty or forty
horsemen, with our friend Figoroa at their head, dash
across the street, all running for their lives; but in a
few moments they rallied and returned. We walked
toward the church, to ascend the steeple, when a sharp
volley of musketry rolled up the street on that side, and
before we got back into the house there was firing
along the whole length of the street. We knew that
a chance shot might kill a non-combatant, and secured the doors and windows ; but finally, as the firing
was sharp, and the balls went beyond us and struck
the houses on the opposite side, with an old servant-
woman (what had become of the widow I do not know),
we retired into a small room on the courtyard, with delightful walls, and a door three inches thick and bullet-
proof, shutting which, and in utter darkness, we listened
valiantly. Here we considered ourselves out of harm's
way, but we had serious apprehensions for the result.
The spirit on both sides was to kill ; giving quarter was
not thought of. Morazan's party was probably small,
but they would not be taken without a desperate fight;
and from the sharpness of the firing and the time occupied, there was probably a sanguinary affair. Our
quondam friends, roused by bloodshed, wounds, and
loss of companions, without any one to control them,

would be very likely to connect " those rascals" with the arrival of Morazan. I will not say that we wished they might all be killed, but we did wish that their bad blood might be let out, and that was almost the same thing. In fact, I did most earnestly hope never to see their faces again. I preferred being taken by any roving band in the country rather than by them, and never felt more relieved than when we heard the sound of a bugle. It was the Morazan blast of victory; and, though sounding fiercely the well-known notes of " degollar, degollar," " cutthroat, cutthroat," it was music to our ears. Very soon we heard the tramp of cavalry, and leaving our hiding-place, returned to the sala, and heard a cry of " Viva la Federacion!" This was a cheering sound. It was now dark. We opened the door an inch or two, but a lancer riding by struck it open with his lance, and asked for water. We gave him a large calabash, which another took from his hands. We threw open the door, and kept two large calabashes on the sill; and the soldiers, as they passed, took a hasty draught. Asking a question of each, we learned that it was General Morazan himself, with the survivers of his expedition against Guatimala. Our house was well known; many of the officers inquired for the family, and an aiddecamp gave notice to the servant-woman that Morazan himself intended stopping there. The soldiers marched into the plaza, stacked their arms, and shouted " Viva Morazan." In the morning the shout was " Viva Carrera!" None cried " Viva la Patria!"

There was no end to our troubles. In the morning we surrendered to one party, and in the evening were captured out of their hands by another; probably before daylight Carrera would be upon us. There was

only one comfort : the fellows who had broken our rest
the night before, and scared the inhabitants from their
homes, were now looking out for lodgings in the mountains themselves.   I felt sorry for Figoroa and his aid,
and, on abstract principles, for the killed.   As for the
rest, I cared but little what became of them.

In a few moments a party of officers came down to
our house.   For six days they had been in constant
flight through an enemy's country, changing their direction to avoid pursuit, and only stopping to rest their
horses.   Entering under the excitement of a successful
skirmish, they struck me as the finest set of men I had
seen in the country.   Figoroa had come upon them so
suddenly, that General Morazan, who rode at the head
of his men, had two bullets pass by his head before he
could draw his pistol, and he had a narrower escape
than in the whole of his bloody battle in Guatimala.
Colonel Cabanes, a small, quiet, gentlemanly man, the
commander of the troops massacred in Honduras,
struck the first blow, broke his sword over a lancer, and,
wresting the lance out of its owner's hands, ran it
through his body, but was wounded himself in the hand.
A tall, gay, rattling young man, who was wiping warm
blood from off his sword, and drying it on his pocket-
handkerchief, mourned that he had failed in cutting off
their retreat ; and a quiet middle-aged man, wiping his
forehead, drawled out, that if their horses had not been
so tired they would have killed every man.   Even
they talked only of killing ; taking prisoners was never thought of.   The verb matar, to kill, with its in-
flexions, was so continually ringing in my ears that it
made me nervous.   In a few minutes the widow Padilla, who, I am inclined to believe, was secreted somewhere in the neighbourhood, knowing of General Mora-

zan's approach, rushed in, crying wildly for her sons. All answered that the eldest was with them; all knew her, and one after another put his right arm respectfully over her shoulder and embraced her; but the young man who was wiping his sword drove it into its scabbard, and, catching her up in his arms, lifted her off the floor and whirled her about the room. The poor old lady, half laughing and half crying, told him he was as bad as ever, and continued asking for her sons. At this moment a man about forty, whom I had noticed before as the only one without arms, with a long beard, pale and haggard, entered from the courtyard. The old lady screamed, rushed toward him, and fell on his neck, and for some moments rested her head upon his shoulder. This was the one who had been imprisoned by Carrera. General Morazan had forced his way into the plaza, broken open the prisons, and liberated the inmates; and when he was driven out this son made his escape. But where was her younger and dearer son? The young man answered that he had escaped and was safe. The old lady looked at him with distrust, and, calling him by his Christian name, told him he was deceiving her; but he persisted and swore that he had escaped; he himself had given him a fresh horse; he was seen outside the barrier, was probably concealed somewhere, and would soon make his appearance. The other officers had no positive knowledge. One had seen him at such a time, and another at such a time during the battle; and all agreed that the young man ought to know best, for their posts were near each other; and he, young, ardent, and reckless, the dearest friend of her son, and loving her as a mother, told me afterward that she should have one night's comfort, and that she would know the truth soon enough; but the brother, narrowly escaped from death himself, and who looked as if smiles had been forever driven from his face, told me he had no doubt his mother's darling was killed.

During these scenes the captain and I were not unnoticed. The captain found among the officers several whom he had become acquainted with at the port, and he learned that others had made their last campaign. In the first excitement of meeting them, he determined to turn back and follow their broken fortunes; but, luckily for me, those trunks had gone on. He felt that he had a narrow escape. Among those who had accompanied General Morazan were the former secretary of state and war, and all the principal officers, civil and military, of the shattered general government. They had heard of my arrival in the country. I had been expected at San Salvador, was known to them all by reputation, and very soon personally; particularly I became acquainted with Colonel Zerabia, a young man about twenty-eight, handsome, brave, and accomplished in mind and manners, with an enthusiastic attachment for General Morazan, from whom, in referring to one affair in the attack on Guatimala, with tears almost starting from his eyes, he said, Providence seemed to turn the bullets away. I had often heard of this gentleman in Guatimala, and his case shows the unhappy rending of private and social ties produced by these civil wars. His father was banished by the Liberal party eight years before, and was then a general in the Carlist service in Spain. His mother and three sisters lived in Guatimala, and I had visited at their house perhaps oftener than at any other in that city. They lived near the plaza, and while Morazan had possession of it, the colonel had run home to see them; and in the midst of a distracted meeting, rendered more poignant by the circumstance of his being joined in an attack upon his native city, he was called away to go into action; his horse was shot under him, he was wounded, and escaped with the wreck of the army. His mother and sisters knew nothing of his fate. He said, what I was sure was but too true, that they would have dreadful apprehensions about him, and begged me, immediately on my arrival at Guatimala, to visit them and inform them of his safety.

In the mean time, General Morazan, apprehensive of a surprise from Carrera during the night, sent word that he should sleep in the plaza; and escorted by Colonel Zerabia, I went to pay my respects to him. From the time of his entry I felt perfectly secure, and never had a moment of apprehension from unruly soldiers. For the first time I saw something like discipline. A sentinel was pacing the street leading from the plaza, to prevent the soldiers straggling into the town; but the poor fellows seemed to have no disposition for straggling. The town was stripped of everything; even the poor horses had no food. Some were gathered at the window of the cabildo, each in his turn holding up his hat for a portion of hard corn bread; some were sitting around fires eating this miserable fare; but most were stretched on the ground, already asleep. It was the first night they had lain down except in an enemy's country.

General Morazan, with several officers; was standing in the corridor of the cabildo; a large fire was burning before the door, and a table stood against the wall, with a candle and chocolate-cups upon it. He was about forty-five years old, five feet ten inches high, thin, with a black mustache and week's beard, and wore a military frock-coat, buttoned up to the throat, and sword. His hat was off, and the expression of his face mild and intelligent. Though still young, for ten years he had been the first man in the country, and eight president of the Republic. He had risen and had sustained himself by military skill and personal bravery ; always led his forces himself ; had been in innumerable battles, and often wounded, but never beaten. A year before, the people of Guatimala, of both parties, had implored him to come to their relief, as the only man who could save them from Carrera and destruction. At that moment he added another to the countless instances of the fickleness of popular favour. After the expiration of his term he had been elected chief of the State of San Salvador, which office he had resigned, and then acted as commander-in-chief under the Federal Government. Denounced personally, and the Federation under which he served disavowed, he had marched against Guatimala with fourteen hundred men, and forced his way into the plaza ; forty of his oldest officers and his eldest son were shot down by his side ; and cutting his way through masses of human flesh, with about four hundred and fifty men then in the plaza, made his escape. I was presented to him by Colonel Zerabia. From the best information I could acquire, and from the enthusiasm with which I had heard him spoken of by his officers, and, in fact, by every one else in his own state, I had conceived almost a feeling of admiration for General Morazan, and my interest in him was increased by his misfortunes. I was really at a loss how to address him ; and while my mind was full of his ill-fated expedition, his first question was if his family had arrived in Costa Rica, or if I had heard anything of them. I did **not** tell him, what I then thought, that his calamities would follow all who were connected with him, and probably that his wife and daughters would not be permitted an asylum in that state ; but it spoke volumes that, at such a moment, with the wreck of his followers before him, and the memory of his murdered companions fresh in his mind, in the overthrow of all his hopes and fortunes, his heart turned to his domestic relations. He express- ed his sorrow for the condition in which I saw his un- happy country; regretted that my visit was at such a most unfortunate moment; spoke of Mr. De Witt, and the relations of that country with ours, and his regret that our treaty had not been renewed, and that it could not be done now ; but these things were not in my mind. Feeling that he must have more important business, I remained but a short time, and returned to the house.

The moon had risen, and I was now extremely anx- ious to set out, but our plans were entirely deranged. The guide whom we had engaged to conduct us to the Rio Paz was missing, and no other could be found; in fact, not a man could be induced, either by promises or threats, to leave the town that night from fear of falling in with the routed troops. Several of the officers took chocolate with us, and at the head of the table sat a priest with a sword by his side. I had breakfasted men who would have been happy to cut their throats, and they were now hiding among the mountains or riding for life. If Carrera came, my new friends would be scattered. They all withdrew early, to sleep under arms in the plaza, and we were left with the widow and her son. A distressing scene followed, of inquiries and forebodings by the widow for her younger son, which the elder could only get rid of by pleading excessive fatigue, and begging to be permitted to go to sleep. It was rather singular, but it had not occurred to us before to inquire about the dead and wounded in the skirmish. There were none of the latter; all who fell were lanced, and the dead were left on the ground. He was in the rear of the Morazan party; the fire was scattering; but on the line by which he entered the town he counted eighteen bodies.

CHAPTER VI.

In the morning, to our surprise, we found several shops open, and people in the street, who had been concealed somewhere in the neighbourhood, and returned as soon as they knew of Morazan's entry. The alcalde reappeared, and our guide was found, but he would not go with us, and told the alcalde that he might kill him on the spot; that he would rather die there than by the hands of the Cachurecos.

While I was taking chocolate, General Morazan called upon me. Our conversation was longer and more general. I did not ask him his plans or purposes, but neither he nor his officers exhibited despondency. Once reference was made to the occupation of Santa Anna by General Cascara, and with a spirit that reminded me of Claverhouse in "Old Mortality," he said, "we shall visit that gentleman soon." He spoke without malice or bitterness of the leaders of the Central party, and of Carrera as an ignorant and lawless Indian, from whom the party that was now using him would one day be glad to be protected. He referred, with a smile, to a charge current among the Cachurecos of an effort made by him to have Carrera assassinated, of which a great parade had been made, with details of time and place, and which was generally believed. He had supposed the whole story a fabrication; but accidentally, in retreating from Guatimala, he found himself in the very house where the attempt was said to have been made; and the man of the house told him that Carrera, having offered outrage to a member of his family, he himself had stabbed him, as was supposed mortally; and in order to account for his wounds, and turn away inquiries from the cause, it was fastened upon Morazan, and so flew all through the country. One of his officers accompanied the story with details of the outrage; and I felt very sure that, if Carrera ever fell into his hands, he would shoot him on the spot.

With the opinion that he entertained of Carrera and his soldiers, he of course considered it unsafe for us to go on to Guatimala. But I was exceedingly anxious to set out; and the flush of excitement over, as the captain's trunks had gone on, he was equally so. Carrera might arrive at any moment, in which case we might again change owners, or, at all events, be the witnesses of a sanguinary battle, for Morazan would defend the frontier town of his own state to the death.

I told General Morazan my wish and purpose, and the difficulty of procuring a guide. He said that an escort of soldiers would expose us to certain danger; even a single soldier, without his musket and cartridge-box (these being the only distinguishing marks of a soldier), might be recognised; but he would send for the alcalde, and procure us some trusty person from the town. I bade him farewell with an interest greater than I had felt for any man in the country. Little did we then know the calamities that were still in store for him; that very night most of his soldiers deserted, having been kept together only by the danger to which they were exposed while in an enemy's country. With the rest he marched to Zonzonate, seized a vessel at the port, manning her with his own men, and sent her to Libertad, the port of San Salvador. He then marched to the capital, where the people, who had for years idolized him in power, turned their backs upon him in misfortune, and received him with open insults in the streets. With many of his officers, who were too deeply compromised to remain, he embarked for Chili. Suffering from confinement on board a small vessel, he stopped in Costa Rica, and asked permission for some of them to land. He did not ask it for himself, for he knew it would be refused. Leaving some of them behind, he went on to join his family in Chili. Amid the fierceness of party spirit it was impossible for a stranger to form a true estimate of the character of a public man. The great outcry against General Morazan was hostility to the church and forced loans. For his hostility to the church there is the justification that it is at this day a pall upon the spirit of free institutions, degrading and debasing instead of elevating the Christian character ; and for forced loans constant wars may plead. His worst enemies admit that he was exemplary in his private relations, and, what they consider no small praise, that he was not sanguinary. He is now fallen and in exile, probably forever, under sentence of death if he returns ; all the truckling worshippers of a rising sun are blasting his name and memory ; but I verily believe, and I know I shall bring down upon me the indignation of the whole Central party by the assertion, I verily believe they have driven from their shores the best man in Central America.

The population of the town was devoted to General Morazan, and an old man brought to us his son, a young man about twenty-two, as a guide ; but when he learned

that we wanted him to go with us all the way to Rio
Paz, he left us, as he said, to procure a horse. We
waited nearly an hour, when the old man reappeared
with a little boy about ten years old, dressed in a straw
hat and shirt, and mounted on a bare-backed horse.
The young man had disappeared and could not be
found; in fact, he was afraid to go, and it was thought
this little boy would run less risk. I was never much
disturbed by general reports of robbers or assassins,
but there was palpable danger in meeting any of the
routed troops. Desperate by defeat, and assassin-like
in disposition; not very amiable to us before; and
now, from having seen us lounging about the town
at that inauspicious moment, likely to connect us with
the movements of Morazan, I believed that if we fell
in with them we should be murdered. But, on the
other hand, they had not let the grass grow under
their feet; had probably been flying all night, in apprehension of pursuit; shunning the main road, had perhaps crossed the Rio Paz, and, once in Guatimala,
had dispersed to their own villages; besides which, the
rout had been so total that they were probably escaping
three or four together, and would be as likely to run
from us as we from them. At all events, it was better
to go than wait till Carrera came upon the town.

With these calculations and really uncomfortable
feelings, we bade farewell to some of the officers who
were waiting to see us off, and at nine o'clock set out.
Descending from the table-land on which the town is
built, we entered an open plain, over which we could
see to a great distance, and which would furnish, if necessary, a good field for the evolutions of our cavalry.
We passed the Lake of Aguachapa, the beauty of which,
under other circumstances, would have attracted our

admiration; and as our little guide seemed at fault, we stopped at a hut to inquire the road. The people were afraid to answer any questions. Figoroa's soldiers and Morazan's had passed by, but they did not know it; they could not tell whether any fugitive soldiers had passed, and only knew the road to the Rio Paz. It was easy to see that they thought of nothing else; but they said they were poor people, and at work all the time, and did not know what was going on. In half an hour we met three Indians, with loads of pottery on their backs. The poor fellows pulled off their hats, and trembled when we inquired if there were any routed soldiers on before. It occurred to us that this inquiry would expose us to the suspicion of being officers of Morazan in pursuit, and that, if we met any one, we had better ask no questions. Beyond this there were many roads, all of which, the boy said, led to the Rio Paz; but he had never been there before, and did not know the right one. We followed one which took us into the woods, and soon commenced descending. The road was broken, stony, and very steep; we descended rapidly, and soon it was manifest no horses had passed on this road for a long time before. Trees lay across it so low that we dismounted, and were obliged to slip our high-peaked saddles to pass under them. It was evidently an old cattle-path, now disused even by cattle. We descended some distance farther, and I proposed to return. My only argument was that it was safer; we knew we were wrong, and might get down so low that our physical strength would not carry us back. The captain said that I had chosen this path; if we had followed his advice, we should have been safe, and that now it was impossible to return. We had an angry quarrel, and, fortunately, in consideration of my having

led into the difficulty, I gave way, and very soon we
were cheered by hearing below us the rushing of the
river.　After a most difficult descent we reached the
bank; but here there was no fording-place, and no path
on the opposite side.

The river itself was beautiful.　The side which we
had descended was a high and almost perpendicular
mountain, and on both sides trees spread their branches
over the water.　It was called the River of Peace, but
was now the dividing-line of deadly war, the boundary
between Guatimala and San Salvador.　The inhabitants of the opposite side were in an enemy's country,
and the routed troops, both of Morazan and Figoroa,
had fled to it for refuge.　Riding some distance up the
stream, we worked our way across, and on the opposite
side found a waccal or drinking-shell, which had probably been left there by some flying soldier.　We drank
from it as if it had been intended for our use, and left
it on the bank for the benefit of the next comer.

We were now in the State of Guatimala, on the
banks of a wild river, without any visible path, and our
situation was rather more precarious than before, for
here the routed soldiers would consider themselves safe,
and probably many, after a day and night of toil and
fighting, would lie down to rest.　We were fortunate
in regard to a path, for, riding a short distance through
the woods along the bank of the river, we struck one
which turned off to the left, and terminated in the camino
real leading from the regular fording-place.　Here we
dismissed our little guide, and set out on the main road.
The face of the country was entirely changed, broken
and stony, and we saw no one till we reached the hacienda of Palmita.　This too seemed desolate.　We
entered the yard, and did not see a single person till

we pushed open the door of the house. The proprietor was an old gentleman, opposed to Morazan, who sat in the sala with his wife's saddle and his own, and two bundles of bed and bedding packed up on the floor, ready for a start. He seemed to feel that it was too late, and with an air of submission answered our questions, and then asked us how many men we had with us. It was amusing that, while half frightened to death ourselves, we carried terror wherever we went. We relieved him by inquiring about Don Saturnino and our luggage, remounted, and rode on. In an hour we reached the hacienda del Cacao, where Don Saturnino was to sleep. Owing to the position of the ground, we came suddenly upon the front of the house, and saw under the piazza three Cachureco soldiers eating tortillas. They saw us at the same moment, snatched up their muskets, and ran; but suddenly one stopped and levelled at us a blunderbuss. The barrel looked as big as a church door, and seemed to cover both the captain and me. We were in awful danger of being shot by mistake, when one of them rushed back, knocked up the blunderbuss, and crying out " amigos, los Ingleses!" gave us a chance to reach them. This amiable and sensible young Cachureco vagabond was one of those who had paid us a visit to beg a breakfast and a medio. Probably there never was a sixpence put out at better interest. He had seen us intimate with Figoroa, and taught by his betters to believe that General Morazan was a cutthroat and murderer, and not conceiving that we could be safe with him, considered us sharers of the same danger, and inquired how we had escaped. As it turned out, we were extremely happy to meet with these ; another party might have received us very differently ; and they relieved us in an important point,

for they told us that most of the routed soldiers had
fled on the Santa Anna road. Don Saturnino had
passed the night at this hacienda, and set out very early
in the morning. The soldiers returned to finish their
meal, and giving their thanks in payment, set out again
with us. They had a good horse which they had stolen
on the road, and which they said paid them very well
for the expedition, and rode by turns bare-backed.
Passing El Cacao their appearance created a sensation,
for they brought the first intelligence of the rout of Figoroa. This was ominous news, for all had considered
Morazan completely crushed by his defeat at Guatimala.
In his retreat he had avoided the villages, and they did
not know that he had escaped with so strong a force.
We endeavoured to procure a guide, but not a man
could be induced to leave the village, and we rode on.
In a short time it began to rain; the road was very
stony, and we crossed a high, bleak volcanic mountain.
Late in the afternoon the captain conceived suspicions
of the soldiers, and we rode on very unceremoniously,
leaving them behind. About five o'clock we avoided
the road that led to a village, and taking el Camino de
los Partidos, which was very rough and stony, soon
came to a place where there were branches, and we
were at a loss which to take; but the course lay through
a broad valley bounded by two ranges of mountains.
We felt sure that our road did not cross either of these
ranges, and these were our only guides. A little before
dark we passed beyond the range of mountains, and on
our right saw a road leading into the woods, and presently heard the sound of a bell, and saw through the
trees a hacienda, to arrive at which we had to go on
some distance, and then turn back by a private road.
It was situated in a large clearing, with cucinera and

sheds, and a large sugar-mill. Twenty or thirty workmen, principally Indians, were assembled to give an
account of their day's work, and receive orders for the
next. Our appearance created a great sensation. The
proprietors of the hacienda, two brothers, stood in the
door while we were talking with the men, and we rode
up and asked permission to stop there for the night.
The elder assented, but with an embarrassment that
showed the state of alarm and suspicion existing in the
country. The gentlemen wore the common hacienda
dress, and the interior was miserably poor, but had a
hammock, and two rude frames with matting over them
for beds. There was a small room adjoining, in which
was the wife of one of them with a child. The proprietors were men of education and intelligence, thoroughly acquainted with the condition of the country, and we
told them what had happened at Aguachapa, and that
we were hurrying on to Guatimala. We had supper at
a small table placed between the hammock and one of
the beds, consisting of fried eggs, frigoles, and tortillas,
as usual without knife, fork, or spoon.

After supper our elder host was called out, but in a
few minutes returned, and, closing the door, told us that
there was a great excitement among the workmen on our
account. They did not believe our story of going to
Guatimala, for a woman had seen us come in from the
Guatimala road, and they believed that we were officers
of Morazan retreating from the attack on Guatimala,
and endeavouring to escape into San Salvador. Here
was a ground of suspicion we had not anticipated. The
gentleman was much agitated; he regretted that he was
obliged to violate the laws of hospitality, but said we
knew the distracted state of the country, and the phrensy of party spirit. He himself was against Morazan,

his men were violent Cachurecos, and at this moment capable of committing any outrage. He had incurred great peril by receiving us for a moment under his roof, and begged us, both for our own sake and his, to leave his house ; adding that, even if we were of those unfortunate men, our horses should be brought up and we should go away unharmed ; more he could not promise. Now if we had really been the fugitives he supposed us, we should no doubt have been very thankful for his kindness ; but to be turned out by mistake in a dark night, an unknown country, and without any guide, was almost as bad as coming at us with a blunderbuss. Fortunately, he was not a suspicious man ; if he had been another Don Gregorio we should have " walked Spanish ;" and, more fortunately still, my pertinacity had secured Figoroa's passport ; it was the only thing that could have cleared our character. I showed it to him, pointing to the extra flourish which the secretary had made of plenipotentiario, and I believe he was not more astonished at finding who had honoured him by taking possession of his house, than pleased that we were not Morazan's officers. Though an intelligent man, he had passed a retired life on his hacienda. He had heard of such a thing as " a ministro plenipotentiario," but had never seen one. My accoutrements and the eagle on my hat sustained the character, and he called in the major-domo and two leading men on the hacienda, read to them the passport, and explained to them the character of a ministro plenipotentiario, while I sat up on the bed with my coat off and hat on to show the eagle, and the captain suppressed all partialities for Morazan, and talked of my intimacy with Carrera. The people are so suspicious that, having once formed an idea, they do not willingly abandon it, and it was un-

certain whether all this would satisfy them; but our
host was warm in his efforts, the major-domo was flattered by being made the medium of communicating with
the men, and his influence was at stake in satisfying
them. It was one of Talleyrand's maxims never to do
to-day what you can put off till to-morrow. On this
occasion at least of my diplomatic career I felt the benefit of the old opposite rule. From the moment I saw
Figoroa I had an eye only to getting his passport, and
did not rest until I had it in my pocket. If we had waited
to receive this with his letters, we should now have been
in a bad position. If we escaped immediate violence,
we should have been taken to the village, shut up in the
cabildo, and exposed to all the dangers of an ignorant
populace, at that moment excited by learning the success of Morazan and the defeat of Figoroa. In setting
out, our idea was that, if taken by the Cachurecos, we
should be carried up to Guatimala; but we found that
there was no accountability to Guatimala; the people
were in a state to act entirely from impulses, and nothing
could induce any party of men to set out for Guatimala,
or under any circumstances to go farther than from
village to village. This difficulty over, the major-domo
promised us a guide before daylight for the next village.
At three o'clock we were wakened by the creaking of
the sugar-mill. We waited till daylight for a guide, but
as none came we bade farewell to our kind host, and
set out alone. The name of the hacienda is San José,
but in the hurry of my movements I never learned the
name of the proprietor. In the constant revolutions of
Central America, it may happen that he will one day
be flying for his life; in his hour of need, may he meet
a heart as noble as his own.

At a distance of five leagues we reached the rancho

of Hocotilla, where Don Saturnino and our men had slept. The road lay in a magnificent ravine, with a fine bottom land and noble mountain sides. We passed through the straggling settlements of Oratorio and Leon, mostly single huts, where several times we saw women snatch up their children and run into the woods at sight of us. Bury the war-knife, and this valley would be equal to the most beautiful in Switzerland. At twelve o'clock we came upon four posts with a thatched roof, occupied by a scouting-party of Cachureco soldiers. We should have been glad to avoid them, but they could not have judged so from the way in which we shouted "amigos!" We inquired for Carrera; expected to meet him on the road; Figoroa had told us he was coming; Figoroa had entered Aguachapa; and, taking special good care not to tell them that Figoroa had been driven out, we bade them good-by and hurried on.

At twelve o'clock we reached the Rio de los Esclavos, a wild and noble river, the bridge across which is the greatest structure in Central America, a memorial of the Spanish dominion. We crossed it and entered the village, a mere collection of huts, standing in a magnificent situation on the bank of the river, looking up to a range of giant mountains on the other side, covered to the top with noble pines. The miserable inhabitants were insensible to its beauties, but there were reasons to make them so. Every hostile expedition between Guatimala and San Salvador passed through their village. Twice within one week Morazan's party had done so; the inhabitants carried off what they could, and, locking their doors, fled to the mountains. The last time, Morazan's army was so straitened for provisions, and pressed by fear of pursuit, that huts were torn down for firewood, and bullocks slain and eaten half raw in the street, without bread or tortillas.

At two we set off again, and from the village entered a country covered with lava. At four we reached the hacienda of Coral de Piedra, situated on the crest of a stony country, looking like a castle, very large, with a church and village, where, although it rained, we did not stop, for the whole village seemed to be intoxicated. Opposite one house we were hailed by a Cachureco officer, so tipsy that he could hardly sit on his horse, who came at us and told us how many of Morazan's men he had killed. A little before dark, riding through a forest, in the apprehension that we were lost, we emerged suddenly from the woods, and saw towering before us the great volcanoes of Agua and Fuego, and at the same moment were hailed by the joyful shouts of Don Saturnino and our men. They had encamped in a small hut on the borders of a large plain, and the mules were turned out to pasture. Don Saturnino had been alarmed about us, but he had followed our parting injunction to go on, as, if any accident had happened, he could be of more service in Guatimala. They had not met Morazan's army, having been at a hacienda off the road when it passed, and hurrying on, had not heard of the rout of Figoroa.

The rancho contained a single small room, barely large enough for the man and woman who occupied it, but there was plenty of room out of doors. After a rough ride of more than fifty miles, with the most comfortable reflection of being but one day from Guatimala, I soon fell asleep.

The next morning one of the mules was missing, and we did not get off till eight o'clock. Toward evening we descended a long hill, and entered the plain of

Guatimala. It looked beautiful, and I never thought I should be so happy to see it again. I had finished a journey of twelve hundred miles, and the gold of Peru could not have tempted me to undertake it again. At the gate the first man I saw was my friend Don Manuel Pavon. I could but think, if Morazan had taken the city, where would he be now ? Carrera was not in the city ; he had set out in pursuit of Morazan, but on the road received intelligence which induced him to turn off for Quezaltenango. I learned with deep satisfaction that not one of my acquaintances was killed, and, as I afterward found, not one of them had been in the battle.

I gave Don Manuel the first intelligence of General Morazan. Not a word had been heard of him since he left the Antigua. Nobody had come up from that direction ; the people were still too frightened to travel, and the city had not recovered from its spasm of terror. As we advanced I met acquaintances who welcomed me back to Guatimala. I was considered as having run the gauntlet for life, and escape from dangers created a bond between us. I could hardly persuade myself that the people who received me so cordially, and whom I was really glad to meet again, were the same whose expulsion by Morazan I had considered probable. If he had succeeded, not one of them would have been there to welcome me. Repeatedly I was obliged to stop and tell over the affair of Aguachapa ; how many men Morazan had ; what officers ; whether I spoke to him ; how he looked, and what he said. I introduced the captain ; each had his circle of listeners ; and the captain, as a slight indemnification for his forced " Viva Carreras" on the road, feeling, on his arrival once more among civilized and well-dressed people, a comparative security for liberty of speech, said that if Morazan's horses had not been so tired, every man of Figoroa's would have been killed. Unhappily, I could not but see that our news would have been more acceptable if we could have reported Morazan completely prostrated, wounded, or even dead. As we advanced I could perceive that the sides of the houses were marked by musket-balls, and the fronts on the plaza were fearfully scarified. My house was near the plaza, and three musket-balls, picked out of the woodwork, were saved for my inspection, as a sample of the battle. In an hour after my arrival I had seen nearly all my old friends. Engrossed by my own troubles, I had not imagined the full extent of theirs. I cannot describe the satisfaction with which I found myself once more among them, and for a little while, at least, at rest. I still had anxieties ; I had no letters from home, and Mr. Catherwood had not arrived ; but I had no uneasiness about him, for he was not in the line of danger ; and when I lay down I had the comfortable sensation that there was nothing to drive me forward the next day. The captain took up his abode with me. It was an odd finale to his expedition against Guatimala ; but, after all, it was better than remaining at the port.

Great changes had taken place in Guatimala since I left, and it may not be amiss here to give a brief account of what had occurred in my absence. The reader will remember the treaty between Carrera and Guzman, the general of the State of Los Altos, by which the former surrendered to the latter four hundred old muskets. Since that time Guatimala had adopted Carrera (or had been adopted by him, I hardly know which), and, on the ground that the distrust formerly entertained of him no longer existed, demanded a res-

titution of the muskets to him.   The State of Los Altos
refused.   This state was at that time the focus of Liberal
principles, and Quezaltenango, the capital, was the
asylum of Liberals banished from Guatimala.   Appre-
hending, or pretending to apprehend, an invasion from
that state, and using the restitution of the four hundred
worthless muskets as a pretext, Carrera marched against
Quezaltenango with one thousand men.   The Indians,
believing that he came to destroy the whites, assisted
him.   Guzman's troops deserted him, and Carrera with
his own hands took him prisoner, sick and encumbered
with a greatcoat, in the act of dashing his horse down
a deep ravine to escape : he sent to Guatimala Guzman's military coat, with the names of Omoa, Truxillos,
and other places where Guzman had distinguished himself in the service of the republic, labelled on it, and a
letter to the government, stating that he had sent the coat
as a proof that he had taken Guzman.   A gentleman
told me that he saw this coat on its way, stuck on a pole,
and paraded by an insulting rabble around the plaza of
the Antigua.   After the battle Carrera marched to the
capital, deposed the chief of the state and other officers, garrisoned it with his own soldiers, and, not understanding the technical distinctions of state lines, destroyed its existence as a separate state, and annexed it
to Guatimala, or, rather, to his own command.

    In honour of his distinguished services, public notice
was given that on Monday the seventeenth he would
make his triumphal entry into Guatimala, and on that
day he did enter, under arches erected across the streets,
amid the firing of cannon, waving of flags, and music,
with General Guzman, personally known to all the principal inhabitants, who but a year before had hastened
at their piteous call to save them from the hands of this

same Carrera, placed sidewise on a mule, with his feet tied under him, his face so bruised, swollen, and disfigured by stones and blows of machetes that he could not be recognised, and the prisoners tied together with ropes ; and the chief of the state, secretary of state, and secretary of the Constituent Assembly rode by Carrera's side in this disgraceful triumph.

General Guzman was one of those who had been liberated from prison by General Morazan. He had escaped from the plaza with the remnant of his forces, but, unable to endure the fatigues of the journey, he was left behind, secreted on the road ; and General Morazan told me that, in consequence of the cruelty exercised upon him, and the horrible state of anxiety in which he was kept, reason had deserted its throne, and his once strong mind was gone.

From this time the city settled into a volcanic calm, quivering with apprehensions of an attack by General Morazan, a rising of the Indians and a war of castes, and startled by occasional rumours that Carrera intended to bring Guzman and the prisoners out into the plaza and shoot them. On the fourteenth of March intelligence was received from Figoroa that General Morazan had crossed the Rio Paz and was marching against Guatimala. This swallowed up all other apprehensions. Carrera was the only man who could protect the city. On the fifteenth he marched out with nine hundred men toward Arazola, leaving the plaza occupied by five hundred men. Great gloom hung over the city. The same day Morazan arrived at the Coral de Piedra, eleven leagues from Guatimala. On the sixteenth the soldiers commenced erecting parapets at the corners of the plaza ; many Indians came in from the villages to assist, and Carrera took up his position at the Aceytuna,

a league and a half from the city. On the seventeenth
Carrera rode into the city, and with the chief of the
state and others, went around to visit the fortifications
and rouse the people to arms. At noon he returned to
the Aceytuna, and at four o'clock intelligence was received that Morazan's army was descending the Questa
de Pinula, the last range before reaching the plain of
Guatimala. The bells tolled the alarm, and great consternation prevailed in the city. Morazan's army slept
that night on the plain.

Before daylight he marched upon the city and entered the gate of Buena Vista, leaving all his cavalry
and part of his infantry at the Plaza de Toros and on
the heights of Calvario, under Colonel Cabanes, to
watch the movements of Carrera, and with seven hundred men occupied the Plaza of Guadaloupe, depositing
his parque, equipage, a hundred women (more or less of
whom always accompany an expedition in that country),
and all his train, in the Hospital of San Juan de Dios.
Hence he sent Perez and Rivas, with four or five hundred men, to attack the plaza. These passed up a street
descending from the centre of the city, and, while covered by the brow of the hill, climbed over the yard-wall
of the Church of Escuela de Cristo, and passed through
the church into the street opposite the mint, in the rear
of one side of the plaza. Twenty-seven Indians were
engaged in making a redoubt at the door, and twenty-six
bodies were found on the ground, nine killed and seventeen wounded. When I saw it the ground was still red
with blood. Entering the mint, the invaders were received with a murderous fire along the corridor; but,
forcing their way through, they broke open the front
portal, and rushed into the plaza. The plaza was occupied by the five hundred men left by Carrera, and two

or three hundred Indians, who fell back, closed up near
the porch of the Cathedral, and in a few moments all
fled, leaving the plaza, with all their ammunition, in the
possession of the assailants.   Rivera Paz and Don Luis
Bartres, the chief and secretary of the state, were in the
plaza at the time, and but few other white citizens.   Carrera did not want white soldiers, and would not permit
white men to be officers.   Many young men had presented themselves in the plaza, and were told that
there were no arms.

In the mean time, Carrera, strengthened by masses of
Indians from the villages around, attacked the division
on the heights of Calvario.   Morazan, with the small
force left at San Juan de Dios, went to the assistance of
Cabanes.   The battle lasted an hour and a half, fierce
and bloody, and fought hand to hand.   Morazan lost
some of his best officers.   Sanches was killed by Sotero
Carrera, a brother of the general.   Carrera and Morazan met, and Carrera says that he cut Morazan's saddle nearly in two.   Morazan was routed, pursued so
closely that he could not take up his equipage, and hurried on to the plaza, having lost three hundred muskets, four hundred men killed, wounded, and prisoners,
and all his baggage.   At ten o'clock his whole force
was penned up in the plaza, surrounded by an immense
mass of Indian soldiers, and fired upon from all the corners.   Manning the parapets and stationing pickets on
the roofs of the houses, he kept up a galling fire in return.

Pent up in this fearful position, Morazan had time to
reflect.   But a year before he was received with ringing
of bells, firing of cannon, joyful acclamations, and dep-
utations of grateful citizens, as the only man who could
save them from Carrera and destruction.   Among the
few white citizens in the plaza at the time of the entry

of the soldiers was a young man, who was taken prisoner and brought before General Morazan. The latter knew him personally, and inquired for several of his old partisans by name, asking whether they were not coming to join him. The young man answered that they were not, and Morazan and his officers seemed disappointed. No doubt he had expected a rising of citizens in his favour, and again to be hailed as a deliverer from Carrera. In San Salvador I had heard that he had received urgent solicitations to come up; but, whatever had been contemplated, there was no manifestation of any such intention; on the contrary, the hoarse cry was ringing in his ears, " Muera el tyranno! Muera el General Morazan!" Popular feeling had undergone an entire revolution, or else it was kept down by the masses of Indians who came in from the villages around to defend the city against him.

In the mean time the fire slackened, and at twelve o'clock it died away entirely; but the plaza was strewed with dead, dense masses choked up the streets, and at the corners of the plaza the soldiers, with gross ribaldry and jests, insulted and jeered at Morazan and his men. The firing ceased only from want of ammunition, Carrera's stock having been left in Morazan's possession. Carrera, in his eagerness to renew the attack, sat down to make cartridges with his own hands.

The house of Mr. Hall, the British vice-consul, was on one of the sides of the plaza. Mr. Chatfield, the consul general, was at Escuintla, about twelve leagues distant, when intelligence was received of Morazan's invasion. He mounted his horse, rode up to the city, and hoisted the English flag on Mr. Hall's house, to Morazan's soldiers the most conspicuous object on the plaza. Carrera himself was hardly more obnoxious to

them than Mr. Chatfield. A picket of soldiers was stationed on the roof of the house, commanding the plaza
on the one side and the courtyard on the other. Orellana, the former minister of war, was on the roof, and
cut into the staff with his sword, but desisted on a remonstrance from the courtyard that it was the house of
the vice-consul. At sundown the immense mass of Indians who now crowded the city fell on their knees,
and set up the Salve or hymn to the Virgin. Orellana
and others of Morazan's officers had let themselves
down into the courtyard, and were at the moment taking chocolate in Mr. Hall's house. Mrs. Hall, a
Spanish lady of the city, asked Orellana why he did
not fall on his knees; and he answered, in jest, that he
was afraid his own soldiers on the roof would take him
for a Cachureco and shoot him; but it is said that to
Morazan the noise of this immense chorus of voices
was appalling, bringing home to him a consciousness
of the immense force assembled to crush him, and for
the first time he expressed his sense of the danger they
were in. The prayer was followed by a tremendous
burst of " Viva la Religion! Viva Carrera! y muera el
General Morazan!" and the firing commenced more
sharply than before. It was returned from the plaza,
and for several hours continued without intermission.
At two o'clock in the morning Morazan made a desperate effort to cut his way out of the plaza, but was driv-
en back behind the parapets. The plaza was strewed
with dead. Forty of his oldest officers and his eldest son
were killed; and at three o'clock he stationed three
hundred men at three corners of the plaza, directed
them to open a brisk fire, threw all the powder into the
fountain, and while attention was directed to these
points, sallied by the other and left them to their fate.

I state this on the authority of the Guatimala official account of the battle—of course I heard nothing of it at Aguachapa—and if true, it is a blot on Morazan's character as a soldier and as a man. He escaped from the city with five hundred men, and strewing the road with wounded and dead, at twelve o'clock arrived at the Antigua. Here he was urged to proclaim martial law, and make another attack on the city; but he answered no; blood enough had been shed. He entered the cabildo, and, it is said, wrote a letter to Carrera recommending the prisoners to mercy; and Baron Mahelin, the French consul general, related to me an anecdote, which does not, however, seem probable, that he laid his glove on the table, and requested the alcalde to give it to Carrera as a challenge, and explain its meaning. From that place he continued his retreat by the coast until I met him at Aguachapa.

In the mean time Carrera's soldiers poured into the plaza with a tremendous feu de joie, and kept up a terrible firing in the air till daylight. Then they commenced searching for fugitives, and a general massacre took place. Colonel Arias, lying on the ground with one of his eyes out, was bayoneted to death. Perez was shot. Marescal, concealed under the Cathedral, was dragged out and shot. Padilla, the son of the widow at Aguachapa, found on the ground, while begging a Centralist whom he knew to save him, was killed with bayonets. The unhappy fugitives were brought into the plaza two, three, five, and ten at a time. Carrera stood pointing with his finger to this man and that, and every one that he indicated was removed a few paces from him and shot. Major José Viera, and several of the soldiers on the roof of Mr. Hall's house, let themselves down into the courtyard, and Carrera sent for all who had taken refuge there. Viera was taking chocolate with the family, and gave Mrs. Hall a purse of doubloons and a pistol to take care of for him. They were delivered up, with a recommendation to mercy, particularly in behalf of Viera ; but a few moments after Mr. Skinner entered the house, and said that he saw Viera's body in the plaza. Mr. Hall could not believe it, and walked round the corner, but a few paces from his own door, and saw him lying on his back, dead. In this scene of massacre the Padre Zezena, a poor and humble priest, exposed his own life to save his fellow-beings. Throwing himself on his knees before Carrera, he implored him to spare the unhappy prisoners, exclaiming, they are Christians like ourselves ; and by his importunities and prayers induced Carrera to desist from murder, and send the wretched captives to prison.

Carrera and his Indians had the whole danger and the whole glory of defending the city. The citizens, who had most at stake, took no part in it. The members of the government most deeply compromised fled or remained shut up in their houses. It would be hard to analyze the feelings with which they straggled out to gaze upon the scene of horror in the streets and in the plaza, and saw on the ground the well-known faces and mangled bodies of the leaders of the Liberal party. There was one overpowering sense of escape from immense danger, and the feeling of the Central government burst out in its official bulletin : " Eternal glory to the invincible chief General Carrera, and the valiant troops under his command !"

In the morning, as at the moment of our arrival, this subject was uppermost in every one's mind; no one could talk of anything else, and each one had something new to communicate. In our first walk through the streets our attention was directed to the localities, and everywhere we saw marks of the battle.   Vaga- bond soldiers accosted us, begging medios, pointing their muskets at our heads to show how they shot the enemy, and boasting how many they had killed.   These fellows made me feel uncomfortable, and I was not singular ; but if there was a man who had a mixture of uncomfortable and comfortable feelings, it was my friend the captain.   He was for Morazan ; had left La Union to join his expedition, left San Salvador to pay him a visit at Guatimala and partake of the festivities of his triumph, and left Aguachapa because his trunks had gone on before.   Ever since his arrival in the country he had been accustomed to hear Carrera spoken of as a robber and assassin, and the noblesse of Guatimala rid- iculed, and all at once he found himself in a hornet's nest.   He now heard Morazan denounced as a tyrant, his officers as a set of cutthroats, banded together to as- sassinate personal enemies, rob churches, and kill priests ; they had met the fate they deserved, and the universal sentiment was, so perish the enemies of Gua- timala.   The captain had received a timely caution. His story that Morazan would have killed every man of Figoroa's if the horses had not been so tired, had circu- lated ; it was considered very partial, and special inqui- ries were made as to who that captain was.   He was compelled to listen and assent, or say nothing.   On the road he was an excessively loud talker, spoke the lan- guage perfectly, with his admirable arms and horse equip- ments always made a dashing entrée into a village, and was called " muy valiante," " very brave ;" but here he was a subdued man, attracting a great deal of attention, but without any of the éclat which had attended him on the road, and feeling that he was an object of suspicion and distrust. But he had one consolation that nothing could take away : he had not been in the battle, or, to use his own expression, he might now be lying on the ground with his face upward.

In the afternoon, unexpectedly, Mr. Catherwood arrived. He had passed a month at the Antigua, and had just returned from a second visit to Copan, and had also explored other ruins, of which mention will be made hereafter. In our joy at meeting we tumbled into each other's arms, and in the very first moment resolved not to separate again while in that distracted country.

CHAPTER VII.

Ruins of Quirigua.—Visit to them.—Los Amates.—Pyramidal Structure.—A
Colossal Head.—An Altar.—A Collection of Monuments.—Statues.—Character of the Ruins.—A lost City.—Purchasing a ruined City.

To recur for a moment to Mr. Catherwood, who,
during my absence, had not been idle. On reaching
Guatimala the first time from Copan, I made it my business to inquire particularly for ruins. I did not meet
a single person who had ever visited those of Copan, and
but few who took any interest whatever in the antiquities of the country; but, fortunately, a few days after
my arrival, Don Carlos Meiney, a Jamaica Englishman,
long resident in the country, proprietor of a large hacienda, and extensively engaged in mining operations,
made one of his regular business visits to the capital.
Besides a thorough acquaintance with all that concerned
his own immediate pursuits, this gentleman possessed
much general information respecting the country, and a
curiosity which circumstances had never permitted him
to gratify in regard to antiquities; and he told me of
the ruins of Quirigua, on the Motagua River, near
Encuentros, the place at which we slept the second
night after crossing the Mico Mountain. He had never
seen them, and I hardly believed it possible they could
exist, for at that place we had made special inquiries for
the ruins of Copan, and were not informed of any others. I became satisfied, however, that Don Carlos was
a man who did not speak at random. They were on
the estate of Señor Payes, a gentleman of Guatimala
lately deceased. He had heard of them from Señor

Payes, and had taken such interest in the subject as to inquire for and obtain the details of particular monuments. Three sons of Señor Payes had succeeded to his estate, and at my request Don Carlos called with me upon them. Neither of the sons had ever seen the ruins or even visited the estate. It was an immense tract of wild land, which had come into their father's hands many years before for a mere trifle. He had visited it once ; and they too had heard him speak of these ruins. Lately the spirit of speculation had reached that country ; and from its fertility and position on the bank of a navigable river contiguous to the ocean, the tract had been made the subject of a prospectus, to be sold on shares in England. The prospectus set forth the great natural advantages of the location, and the inducements held out to emigrants, in terms and phrases that might have issued from a laboratory in New-York before the crash. The Señores Payes were in the first stage of anticipated wealth, and talked in the familiar strains of city builders at home. They were roused by the prospect of any indirect addition to the value of their real estate ; told me that two of them were then making arrangements to visit the tract, and immediately proposed that I should accompany them. Mr. Catherwood, on his road from Copan, had fallen in with a person at Chiquimula who told him of such ruins, with the addition that Colonel Galindo was then at work among them. Being in the neighbourhood, he had some idea of going to visit them ; but, being much worn with his labours at Copan, and knowing that the story was untrue as regarded Colonel Galindo, whom he knew to be in a different section of the country, he was incredulous as to the whole. We had some doubt whether they would repay the labour ; but as there was no occasion for him to accompany me to San Salvador, it was agreed that during my absence he should, with the Señores Payes, go to Quirigua, which he accordingly did.

The reader must go back to Encuentros, the place at which we slept the second night of our arrival in the country. From this place they embarked in a canoe about twenty-five feet long and four broad, dug out of the trunk of a mahogany-tree, and descending two hours, disembarked at Los Amates, near El Poso, on the main road from Yzabal to Guatimala, the place at which we breakfasted the second morning of our arrival in the country, and where the Señores Payes were obliged to wait two or three days. The place was a miserable collection of huts, scant of provisions, and the people drank a muddy water at their doors rather than take the trouble of going to the river.

On a fine morning, after a heavy rain, they set off for the ruins. After a ride of about half an hour, over an execrable road, they again reached the Amates. The village was pleasantly situated on the bank of the river, and elevated about thirty feet. The river was here about two hundred feet wide, and fordable in every part except a few deep holes. Generally it did not exceed three feet in depth, and in many places was not so deep ; but below it was said to be navigable to the sea for boats not drawing more than three feet water. They embarked in two canoes dug out of cedar-trees, and proceeded down the river for a couple of miles, where they took on board a negro man named Juan Lima, and his two wives. This black scoundrel, as Mr. C. marks him down in his notebook, was to be their guide. They then proceeded two or three miles farther, and stopped at a rancho on the left side of the river, and passing through two cornfields, entered a forest of large cedar

MONUMENT AT QUIRIGUA

23 Feet high

F. Catherwood del.

F. Catherwood   J. Halpin

IDOL AT QUIRIGUA.

and mahogany trees.   The path was exceedingly soft
and wet, and covered with decayed leaves, and the
heat very great.   Continuing through the forest toward
the northeast, in three quarters of an hour they reached
the foot of a pyramidal structure like those at Copan,
with the steps in some places perfect.   They ascended
to the top, about twenty-five feet, and descending by
steps on the other side, at a short distance beyond came
to a colossal head two yards in diameter, almost buried
by an enormous tree, and covered with moss.   Near it
was a large altar, so covered with moss that it was impossible to make anything out of it.   The two are within an enclosure.

Retracing their steps across the pyramidal structure,
and proceeding to the north about three or four hundred yards, they reached a collection of monuments of
the same general character with those at Copan, but
twice or three times as high.

The first is about twenty feet high, five feet six inches on two sides, and two feet eight on the other two.
The front represents the figure of a man, well preserved ; the back that of a woman, much defaced.   The
sides are covered with hieroglyphics in good preservation, but in low relief, and of exactly the same style as
those at Copan.

Another, represented in the engraving, is twenty-
three feet out of the ground, with figures of men on the
front and back, and hieroglyphics in low relief on the
sides, and surrounded by a base projecting fifteen or sixteen feet from it.

At a short distance, standing in the same position as
regards the points of the compass, is an obelisk or carved stone, twenty-six feet out of the ground, and probably six or eight feet under, which is represented in the

engraving opposite. It is leaning twelve feet two inches out of the perpendicular, and seems ready to fall,
which is probably prevented only by a tree that has
grown up against it and the large stones around the
base.   The side toward the ground represents the figure of man, very perfect and finely sculptured. The
upper side seemed the same, but was so hidden by vegetation as to make it somewhat uncertain.   The other
two contain hieroglyphics in low relief.   In size and
sculpture this is the finest of the whole.

A statue ten feet high is lying on the ground, covered with moss and herbage, and another about the same
size lies with its face upward.

There are four others erect, about twelve feet high,
but not in a very good state of preservation, and several
altars so covered with herbage that it was difficult to
ascertain their exact form.   One of them is round, and
situated on a small elevation within a circle formed by
a wall of stones.   In the centre of the circle, reached
by descending very narrow steps, is a large round stone,
with the sides sculptured in hieroglyphics, covered with
vegetation, and supported on what seemed to be two
colossal heads.

These are all at the foot of a pyramidal wall, near
each other, and in the vicinity of a creek which empties
into the Motagua.   Besides these they counted thirteen fragments, and doubtless many others may yet be
discovered.

At some distance from them is another monument,
nine feet out of ground, and probably two or three under, with the figure of a woman on the front and back,
and the two sides richly ornamented, but without hieroglyphics.

The next day the negro promised to show Mr. C.
eleven square columns higher than any he had seen,

standing in a row at the foot of a mountain; but after
dragging him three hours through the mud, Mr. C.
found by the compass that he was constantly changing
his direction; and as the man was armed with pistols,
notoriously a bad fellow, and indignant at the owners
of the land for coming down to look after their squat-
ters, Mr. C. became suspicious of him, and insisted upon
returning. The Payes were engaged with their own affairs, and having no one to assist him, Mr. Catherwood
was unable to make any thorough exploration or any
complete drawings.

The general character of these ruins is the same as at
Copan. The monuments are much larger, but they are
sculptured in lower relief, less rich in design, and more
faded and worn, probably being of a much older date.

Of one thing there is no doubt: a large city once
stood there; its name is lost, its history unknown; and,
except for a notice taken from Mr. C.'s notes, and inserted by the Señores Payes in a Guatimala paper after
the visit, which found its way to this country and Europe, no account of its existence has ever before been
published. For centuries it has lain as completely buried as if covered with the lava of Vesuvius. Every
traveller from Yzabal to Guatimala has passed within
three hours of it; we ourselves had done the same; and
yet there it lay, like the rock-built city of Edom, unvisited, unsought, and utterly unknown.

The morning after Mr. C. returned I called upon
Señor Payes, the only one of the brothers then in
Guatimala, and opened a negotiation for the purchase
of these ruins. Besides their entire newness and immense interest as an unexplored field of antiquarian research, the monuments were but about a mile from the
river, the ground was level to the bank, and the river

from that place was navigable; the city might be trans-
ported bodily and set up in New-York. I expressly
stated (and my reason for doing so will be obvious)
that I was acting in this matter on my own account,
that it was entirely a personal affair; but Señor Payes would consider me as acting for my government,
and said, what I am sure he meant, that if his family
was as it had been once, they would be proud to present the whole to the United States; in that country
they were not appreciated, and he would be happy to
contribute to the cause of science in ours; but they
were impoverished by the convulsions of the country;
and, at all events, he could give me no answer till his
brothers returned, who were expected in two or three
days.   Unfortunately, as I believe for both of us, Señor
Payes consulted with the French consul general, who
put an exaggerated value upon the ruins, referring him
to the expenditure of several hundred thousand dollars
by the French government in transporting one of the
obelisks of Luxor from Thebes to Paris.   Probably, before the speculating scheme referred to, the owners
would have been glad to sell the whole tract, consisting
of more than fifty thousand acres, with everything on it,
known and unknown, for a few thousand dollars.   I
was anxious to visit them myself, and learn with more
certainty the possibility of their removal, but was afraid
of increasing the extravagance of his notions.   His
brothers did not arrive, and one of them unfortunately
died on the road.   I had not the government for pay-
master; it might be necessary to throw up the purchase
on account of the cost of removal; and I left an offer
with Mr. Savage, the result of which is still uncertain;
but I trust that when these pages reach the hands of the
reader, two of the largest monuments will be on their
way to this city.

CHAPTER VIII.

Reception at the Government House.—The Captain in Trouble.—A Change of Character.—Arrangements for Journey to Palenque.—Arrest of the Captain.— His Release.—Visit from a Countryman.—Dangers in Prospect.—Last Stroll through the Suburbs.—Hospital and Cemetery of San Juan de Dios.—Fearful State of the Country.—Last Interview with Carrera.—Departure from Guati- mala. — A Don Quixote. — Ciudad Vieja. — Plain of El Vieja. — Volcanoes, Plains, and Villages.—San Andres Isapa.—Dangerous Road.—A Molina.

THE next day I called upon the chief of the state. At this time there was no question of presenting creden- tials, and I was received by him and all gentlemen connected with him without any distrust or suspicion, and more as one identified with them in feelings and in- terests than as a foreign agent. I had seen more of their country than any one present, and spoke of its ex- traordinary beauty and fertility, its volcanoes and mount- ains, the great canal which might make it known to all the civilized world, and its immense resources, if they would let the sword rest and be at peace among them- selves. Some of the remarks in these pages will per- haps be considered harsh, and a poor return for the kindness shown to me. My predilections were in fa- vour of the Liberal party, as well because they sustain- ed the Federation as because they gave me a chance for a government; but I have a warm feeling toward many of the leading members of the Central party. If I speak harshly, it is of their public and political char- acter only; and if I have given offence, I regret it.

As I was leaving the Government House a gentleman followed me, and asked me who that captain was that had accompanied me, adding, what surprised me not a little, that the government had advices of his travelling

up with me from La Union, his intention to join Morazan's expedition, and his change of purpose in consequence of meeting Morazan defeated on the road; that
as yet he was not molested only because he was stay-
ing at my house. I was disturbed by this communication. I was open to the imputation of taking advantage of my official character to harbour a partisan. I
was the only friend the captain had, and of course determined to stand by him; but he was not only an object of suspicion, but actually known; for much less
cause men were imprisoned and shot; in case of any
outbreak, my house would not be a protection; it was
best to avoid any excitement, and to have an understanding at once. With this view I returned to the
chief of the state, and mentioned the circumstances under
which we had travelled together, with the addition that,
as to myself, I would have taken a much more questionable companion rather than travel alone; and as to the
captain, if he had happened to be thrown ashore on their
coast, he would very likely have taken a campaign on
their side; that he was not on his way to join the expedition when we met Morazan, and assured him most
earnestly that now he understood better the other side
of the question, and I would answer for his keeping
quiet. Don Rivera Paz, as I felt well assured, was desirous to allay rather than create excitement in the city,
received my communication in the best spirit possible,
and said the captain had better present himself to the
government. I returned to my house, and found the
captain alone, already by no means pleased with the
turn of his fortunes. My communication did not relieve
him, but he accompanied me to the Government House.
I could hardly persuade myself that he was the same
man whose dashing appearance on the road had often

made the women whisper "muy valiente," and whose
answer to all intimations of danger was, that a man can
only die once. To be sure, the soldiers in the corridor
seemed to intimate that they had found him out; the
gentlemen in the room surveyed him from head to foot,
as if taking notes for an advertisement of his person,
and their looks appeared to say they would know him
when they met him again. On horseback and with a
fair field, the captain would have defied the whole noblesse of Guatimala; but he was completely cowed,
spoke only when he was spoken to, and walked out
with less effrontery than I supposed possible.

And now I would fain let the reader sit down and
enjoy himself quietly in Guatimala, but I cannot. The
place did not admit of it. I could not conceal from
myself that the Federal Government was broken up;
there was not the least prospect of its ever being restored, nor, for a long time to come, of any other being
organized in its stead. Under these circumstances I
did not consider myself justified in remaining any longer
in the country. I was perfectly useless for all the purposes of my mission, and made a formal return to the
authorities of Washington, in effect, "after diligent
search, no government found."

I was once more my own master, at liberty to go
where I pleased, at my own expense, and immediately
we commenced making arrangements for our journey
to Palenque. We had no time to lose; it was a thousand miles distant, and the rainy season was approaching, during which part of the road was impassable.
There was no one in the city who had ever made the
journey. The archbishop, on his exit from Guatimala
eight years before, had fled by that road, and since his
time it had not been travelled by any resident of Gua-

timala ; but we learned enough to satisfy us that it would be less difficult to reach Palenque from New-York than from where we were. We had many preparations to make, and, from the impossibility of getting servants upon whom we could rely, were obliged to attend to all the details ourselves. The captain was uncertain what to do with himself, and talked of going with us. The next afternoon, as we were returning to the house, we noticed a line of soldiers at the corner of the street. As usual, we gave them the sidewalk, and in crossing I remarked to the captain that they eyed us sharply and spoke to each other. The line extended past my door and up to the corner of the next street. Supposing that they were searching for General Guzman or other officers of General Morazan who were thought to be secreted in the city, and that they would not spare my house, I determined to make no difficulty, and let them search. We went in, and the porter, with great agitation, told us that the soldiers were in pursuit of the captain. He had hardly finished when an officer entered to summon the captain before the corregidor. The captain turned as pale as death. I do not mean it as an imputation upon his courage ; any other man would have done the same. I was as much alarmed as he, and told him that if he said so I would fasten the doors ; but he answered it was of no use ; they would break them down ; and it was better for him to go with the officers. I followed him to the door, telling him not to make any confessions, not to commit himself, and that I would be with him in a few minutes. I saw at once that the affair was out of the hands of the chief of the state, and had got before an inferior tribunal. Mr. Catherwood and Mr. Savage entered in time to see the captain moving down the street with his escort. Mr. S., who had charge of my house during my absence, and had hoisted the American flag during the attack upon the city, had lived so long in that country, and had beheld so many scenes of horror, that he was not easily disturbed, and knew exactly what to do. He accompanied me to the cabildo, where we found the captain sitting bolt upright within the railing, and the corregidor and his clerk, with pen, ink, and paper, and ominous formality, examining him. His face brightened at sight of the only man in Guatimala who took the least interest in his fate. Fortunately, the corregidor was an acquaintance, who had been pleased with the interest I took in the sword of Alvarado, an interesting relic in his custody, and was one of the many whom I found in that country proud of showing attentions to a foreign agent. I claimed the captain as my travelling companion, said that we had a rough journey together, and I did not like to lose sight of him. He welcomed me back to Guatimala, and appreciated the peril I must have encountered in meeting on the road the tyrant Morazan. The captain took advantage of the opportunity to detach himself, without any compunctions, from such dangerous fellowship, and we conversed till it was too dark to write, when I suggested that, as it was dangerous to be out at night, I wished to take the captain home with me, and would be responsible for his forthcoming. He assented with great courtesy, and told the captain to return at nine o'clock the next morning. The captain was immensely relieved ; but he had already made up his mind that he had come to Guatimala on a trading expedition, and to make great use of his gold chains.

The next day the examination was resumed. The

captain certainly did not commit himself by any confessions; indeed, the revolution in his sentiments was
most extraordinary. The Guatimala air was fatal to
partialities for Morazan. The examination, by favour
of the corregidor, was satisfactory; but the captain was
advised to leave the city. In case of any excitement
he would be in danger. Carrera was expected from
Quezaltenango in a few days, and if he took it up,
which he was not unlikely to do, it might be a bad
business. The captain did not need any urging. A
council was held to determine which way he should go,
and the road to the port was the only one open. He
had a horse and one cargo-mule, and wanted another
for those trunks. I had seven in my yard, and told
him to take one. On a bright morning he pulled off
his frockcoat, put on his travelling dress, mounted, and
set off for Balize. I watched him as he rode down the
street till he was out of sight. Poor captain, where is
he now? The next time I saw him was at my own
house in New-York. He was taken sick at Balize, and
got on board a brig bound for Boston, was there at the
time of my arrival, and came on to see me; and the
last that I saw of him, afraid to return across the country to get the account sales of his ship, he was about to
embark for the Isthmus of Panama, cross over, and go
up the Pacific. I was knocked about myself in that
country, but I think the captain will not soon forget
his campaign with Morazan.

At this time I received a visit from a countryman,
whom I regretted not to have seen before. It was
Dr. Weems, of Maryland, who had resided several
years at the Antigua, and lately returned from a visit
to the United States, with an appointment as consul.
He came to consult me in regard to the result of

my search for a government, as he was on the track
with his own credentials.   The doctor advised me not
to undertake the journey to Palenque.   In my race
from Nicaragua I had cheered myself with the idea
that, on reaching Guatimala, all difficulty was over,
and that our journey to Palenque would be attended
only by the hardships of travelling in a country destitute of accommodations ; but, unfortunately, the horizon in that direction was lowering.   The whole mass
of the Indian population of Los Altos was in a state
of excitement, and there were whispers of a general
rising and massacre of the whites.   General Prem, to
whom I have before referred, and his wife, while travelling toward Mexico, had been attacked by a band of
assassins ; he himself was left on the ground for dead,
and his wife murdered, her fingers cut off, and the
rings torn from them.   Lieutenant Nichols, the aiddecamp of Colonel M'Donald, arrived from the Balize
with a report that Captain Caddy and Mr. Walker, who
had set out for Palenque by the Balize River, had been
speared by the Indians ; and there was a rumour of
some dreadful atrocity committed by Carrera in Quezaltenango, and that he was hurrying back from that
place infuriate, with the intention of bringing all the
prisoners out into the plaza and shooting them.   Every
friend in Guatimala, and Mr. Chatfield particularly,
urged us not to undertake the journey.   We felt that
it was a most inauspicious moment, and almost shrunk ;
I have no hesitation in saying that it was a matter of
most serious consideration whether we should not abandon it altogether and go home ; but we had set out with
the purpose of going to Palenque, and could not return
without seeing it.

Among the petty difficulties of fitting ourselves I may

mention that we wanted four iron chains for trunks, but could only get two, for every blacksmith in the place was making chains for the prisoners. In a week from the time of my arrival everything was ready for our departure. We provided ourselves with all the facilities and safeguards that could be procured. Besides passports, the government furnished us special letters of recommendation to all the corregidors ; a flattering notice appeared in the government paper, El Tiempo, mentioning my travels through the provinces and my intended route, and recommending me to hospitality; and, upon the strength of the letter of the Archbishop of Baltimore, the venerable provesor gave me a letter of recommendation to all the curas under his charge. But these were not enough; Carrera's name was worth more than them all, and we waited two days for his return from Quezaltenango. On the sixth of April, early in the morning, he entered the city. At about nine o'clock I called at his house, and was informed that he was in bed, had ridden all night, and would not rise till the afternoon. The rumour of the atrocity committed at that place was confirmed.

After dinner, in company with Mr. Savage, I made my last stroll in the suburbs of the city. I never felt, as at that moment, its exceeding beauty of position, and for the third time I visited the hospital and cemetery of San Juan de Dios. In front was the hospital, a noble structure, formerly a convent, supported principally by the active charity of Don Mariano Aycinena. In the centre of the courtyard was a fine fountain, and beyond it the cemetery, which was established at the time of the cholera. The entrance was by a broad passage with a high wall on each side, intended for the burial of " her-

etics." There was but one grave, and the stone bore
the inscription

Teodoro Ashadl,
de la Religione Reformada.
July 19 de 1837.

At the end of this passage was a deadhouse, in which
lay, on separate beds, the bodies of two men, both poor,
one entirely naked, with his legs drawn up, as though
no friend had been by to straighten them, and the other
wrapped in matting. On the right of the passage a door
opened into a square enclosure, in which were vaults
built above the ground, bearing the names of the weal-
thy inhabitants of the city. On the left a door opened
into an enclosure running in the rear of the deadhouse,
about seven hundred and fifty feet long, and three hundred wide. The walls were high and thick, and the
graves were square recesses lengthwise in the wall,
three tiers deep, each closed up with a flat stone, on
which the name of the occupant was inscribed. These,
too, were for the rich. The area was filled with the
graves of the common people, and in one place was a
square of new-made earth, under which lay the bodies
of about four hundred men killed in the attack upon the
city. The table of land commanded a view of the green
plain of Guatimala and the volcanoes of the Antigua.
Beautiful flowers were blooming over the graves, and a
voice seemed to say,

"Oh do not pluck these flowers,
They're sacred to the dead."

A bier approached with the body of a woman, which
was buried without any coffin. Near by was a line of
new-made graves waiting for tenants. They were dug
through skeletons, and sculls and bones lay in heaps beside them. I rolled three sculls together with my foot.

It was a gloomy leave-taking of Guatimala. The earth slipped under my feet and I fell backward, but saved myself by stepping across a new-made grave. I verily believe that if I had fallen into it, I should have been superstitious, and afraid to set out on my journey.

I have mentioned that there were rumours in the city of some horrible outrage committed by Carrera at Quezaltenango. He had set out from Guatimala in pursuit of Morazan. Near the Antigua he met one of his own soldiers from Quezaltenango, who reported that there had been a rising in that town, and the garrison were compelled to lay down their arms. Enraged at this intelligence, he abandoned his pursuit of Morazan, and, without even advising the government of his change of plan, marched to Quezaltenango, and among other minor outrages seized eighteen of the municipality, the first men of the state, and without the slightest form of trial shot them in the plaza; and, to heighten the gloom which this news cast over the city, a rumour preceded him that, immediately on his arrival, he intended to order out all the prisoners and shoot them also. At this time the repressed excitement in the city was fearful. An immense relief was experienced on the repulse of Morazan, but there had been no rejoicing ; and again the sword seemed suspended by a single hair.

And here I would remark, as at a place where it has no immediate connexion with what precedes or what follows, and, consequently, where no application of it can be made, that some matters of deep personal interest, which illustrate, more than volumes, the dreadful state of the country, I am obliged to withhold altogether, lest, perchance, these pages should find their way to Guatimala and compromise individuals. In my long journey I had had intercourse with men of all parties, and was spoken to freely, and sometimes confidentially. Heretofore, in all the wars and revolutions the whites had the controlling influence, but at this time the Indians were the dominant power. Roused from the sloth of ages, and with muskets in their hands, their gentleness was changed into ferocity; and even among the adherents of the Carrera party there was a fearful apprehension of a war of castes, and a strong desire, on the part of those who could get away, to leave the country. I was consulted by men having houses and large landed estates, but who could only command two or three thousand dollars in money, as to their ability to live on that sum in the United States; and individuals holding high offices under the Central party told me that they had their passports from Mexico, and were ready at any moment to fly. There seemed ground for the apprehension that the hour of retributive justice was nigh, and that a spirit was awakened among the Indians to make a bloody offering to the spirits of their fathers, and recover their inheritance. Carrera was the pivot on which this turned. He was talked of as El rey de los Indios, the King of the Indians. He had relieved them from all taxes, and, as they said, supported his army by levying contributions upon the whites. His power by a word to cause the massacre of every white inhabitant, no one doubted. Their security was, as I conceived, that, in the constant action of his short career, he had not had time to form any plans for extended dominion, and knew nothing of the immense country from Texas to Cape Horn, occupied by a race sympathizing in hostility to the whites. He was a fanatic, and, to a certain extent, under the dominion of the priests; and his own acuteness told him that he was more powerful with the Indians themselves while supported by the priests and the aristocracy than at the head of the Indians only ; but all knew that, in the moment of passion, he forgot entirely the little of plan or policy that ever governed him ; and when he return-ed from Quezaltenango, his hands red with blood, and preceded by the fearful rumour that he intended to bring out two or three hundred prisoners and shoot them, the citizens of Guatimala felt that they stood on the brink of a fearful gulf. A leading member of the government, whom I wished to call with me upon him and ask him for his passport, declined doing so, lest, as he said, Carrera should think the government was trying to lead him. Others paid him formal visits of ceremony and congratulation upon his return, and compared notes with each other as to the manner in which they were received. Carrera made no report, official or verbal, of what he had done ; and though all were full of it, no one of them dared ask him any ques-tions, or refer to it. They will perhaps pronounce me a calumniator, but even at the hazard of wounding their feelings, I cannot withhold what I believe to be a true picture of the state of the country as it was at that time.

Unable to induce any of the persons I wished to call with me upon Carrera; afraid, after such a long interval and such exciting scenes as he had been engaged in, that he might not recognise me, and feeling that it was all important not to fail in my application to him, I re-membered that in my first interview he had spoken warmly of a doctor who had extracted a ball from his side. This doctor I did not know, but I called upon him, and asked him to accompany me, to which, with great civility, he immediately assented.

It was under these circumstances that I made my last visit to Carrera. He had removed into a much larger house, and his guard was more regular and formal. When I entered he was standing behind a table on one side of the room, with his wife, and Rivera Paz, and one or two others, examining some large Costa Rica chains, and at the moment he had one in his hands which had formed part of the contents of those trunks of my friend the captain, and which had often adorned his neck. I think it would have given the captain a spasm if he had known that anything once around his neck was between Carrera's fingers. His wife was a pretty, delicate-looking Mestitzo, not more than twenty, and seemed to have a woman's fondness for chains and gold. Carrera himself looked at them with indifference. My idea at the time was, that these jewels were sent in by the government as a present to his wife, and through her to propitiate him, but perhaps I was wrong. The face of Rivera Paz seemed anxious. Carrera had passed through so many terrible scenes since I saw him, that I feared he had forgotten me; but he recognised me in a moment, and made room for me behind the table next to himself. His military coat lay on the table, and he wore the same roundabout jacket, his face had the same youthfulness, quickness, and intelligence, his voice and manners the same gentleness and seriousness, and he had again been wounded. I regretted to meet Rivera Paz there, for I thought it must be mortifying to him, as the head of the government, to see that his passport was not considered a protection without Carrera's endorsement; but I could not stand upon ceremony, and took advantage of Carrera's leaving the table to say to him that I was setting out on a dangerous road, and considered it indispensable to for-

tify myself with all the security I could get. When
Carrera returned I told him my purpose; that I had
waited only for his return; showed him the passport
of the government, and asked him to put his stamp
upon it. Carrera had no delicacy in the matter; and
taking the passport out of my hand, threw it on the table, saying he would make me out a new one, and
sign it himself. This was more than I expected; but
in a quiet way telling me to "be seated," he sent his
wife into another room for the secretary, and told him
to make out a passport for the "Consul of the North."
He had an indefinite idea that I was a great man in
my own country, but he had a very indefinite idea as
to where my country was. I was not particular about
my title so that it was big enough, but the North was
rather a broad range, and to prevent mistakes I gave
the secretary the other passport. He took it into another room, and Carrera sat down at the table beside
me. He had heard of my having met Morazan on his
retreat, and inquired about him, though less anxiously
than others, but he spoke more to the purpose; said
that he was making preparations, and in a week he intended to march upon San Salvador with three thousand men, adding that if he had had cannon he would
have driven Morazan from the plaza very soon. I asked
him whether it was true that he and Morazan met personally on the heights of Calvary, and he said that they
did; that it was toward the last of the battle, when the
latter was retreating. One of Morazan's dismounted
troopers tore off his holsters; Morazan fired a pistol at
him, and he struck at Morazan with his sword, and cut
his saddle. Morazan, he said, had very handsome pistols; and it struck me that he thought if he had killed Morazan he would have got the pistols. I could

not but think of the strange positions into which I
was thrown : shaking hands and sitting side by side
with men who were thirsting for each other's blood,
well received by all, hearing what they said of each
other, and in many cases their plans and purposes, as
unreservedly as if I was a travelling member of both
cabinets. In a few minutes the secretary called him,
and he went out and brought back the passport himself,
signed with his own hand, the ink still wet. It had
taken him longer than it would have done to cut off a
head, and he seemed more proud of it. Indeed, it was
the only occasion in which I saw in him the slightest
elevation of feeling. I made a comment upon the ex-
cellence of the handwriting, and with his good wishes
for my safe arrival in the North and speedy return to
Guatimala, I took my leave. Now I do not believe, if
he knew what I say of him, that he would give me a
very cordial welcome ; but I believe him honest, and if
he knew how, and could curb his passions, he would do
more good for Central America than any other man
in it.

I was now fortified with the best security we could
have for our journey. We passed the evening in writing letters and packing up things to be sent home
(among which was my diplomatic coat), and on the seventh of April we rose to set out. The first movement
was to take down our beds. Every man in that country has a small cot called a cartaret, made to double
with a hinge, which may be taken down and wrapped up, with pillows and bedclothes, in an oxhide,
to carry on a journey. Our great object was to travel lightly. Every additional mule and servant gave
additional trouble, but we could not do with less than a
cargo-mule apiece. Each of us had two petacas, trunks

made of oxhide lined with thin straw matting, having a top like that of a box, secured by a clumsy iron chain with large padlocks, containing, besides other things, a hammock, blanket, one pair of sheets, and pillow, which, with alforgas of provisions, made one load apiece. We carried one cartaret, in case of sickness. We had one spare cargo-mule; the gray mule with which I had ascended the Volcano of Cartago and my macho for Mr. Catherwood and myself, and a horse for relief, in all six animals; and two mozos, or men of all work, untried. While in the act of mounting, Don Saturnino Tinoca, my companion from Zonzonate, rode into the yard, to accompany us two days on our journey. We bade farewell to Mr. Savage, my first, last, and best friend, and in a few minutes, with a mingled feeling of regret and satisfaction, left for the last time the barrier of Guatimala.

Don Saturnino was most welcome to our party. His purpose was to visit two brothers of his wife, curas, whom he had never seen, and who lived at Santiago Atitan, two or three days' journey distant. His father was the last governor of Nicaragua under the royal rule, with a large estate, which was confiscated at the time of the revolution; he still had a large hacienda there, had brought up a stock of mules to sell at San Salvador, and intended to lay out the proceeds in goods in Guatimala. He was about forty, tall, and as thin as a man could be to have activity and vigour, wore a roundabout jacket and trousers of dark olive cloth, large pistols in his holsters, and a long sword with a leather scabbard, worn at the point, leaving about an inch of steel naked. He sat his mule as stiff as if he had swallowed his own sword, holding the reins in his right hand, with his left arm crooked from the elbow, standing out like a pump-handle, the hand dropping from the wrist, and shaking with the movement of the mule. He rode on a Mexican saddle plated with silver, and carried behind a pair of alforgas with bread and cheese, and atole, a composition of pounded parched corn, cocoa, and sugar, which, mixed with water, was almost his living. His mozo was as fat as he was lean, and wore a bell-crowned straw hat, cotton shirt, and drawers reaching down to his knees. Excepting that instead of Rosinante and the ass the master rode a mule and the servant went afoot, they were a genuine Don Quixote and Sancho Panza, the former of which appellations, very early in our acquaintance, we gave to Don Saturnino.

We set out for Quezaltenango, but intended to turn aside and visit ruins, and that day we went three leagues out of our road to say farewell to our friend Padre Alcantra at Ciudad Vieja.

At five o'clock in the afternoon we reached the convent, where I had the pleasure of meeting again Padre Alcantra, Señor Vidaury, and Don Pepé, the same party with whom I had passed the day with so much satisfaction before. Mr. Catherwood had in the mean time passed a month at the convent. Padre Alcantra had fled at the approach of the *tyrant* Morazan ; Don Pepé had had a shot at him as he was retreating from the Antigua, and the padre had a musket left at night by a flying soldier against the wall of the convent.

The morning opened with troubles. The gray mule was sick. Don Saturnino bled her on both sides of her neck, but the poor animal was not in a condition to be ridden. Shortly afterward Mr. Catherwood had one of the mozos by the throat, but Padre Alcantra patched up a peace. Don Saturnino said that the gray mule would be better for exercise, and for the last time we bade farewell to our kind host.

Don Pepé escorted us, and crossing the plain of El Vieja in the direction in which Alvarado entered it, we ascended a high hill, and, turning the summit, through a narrow opening looked down upon a beautiful plain, cultivated like a garden, which opened to the left as we advanced, and ran off to the Lake of Duenos, between the two great volcanoes of Fire and Water. Descending to the plain, we entered the village of San Antonio, occupied entirely by Indians. The cura's house stood on an open plaza, with a fine fountain in front, and the huts of the Indians were built with stalks of sugarcane. Early in the occupation of Guatimala, the lands around the capital were partitioned out among certain canonigos, and Indians were allotted to cultivate them. Each village was called by the canonigo's own name. A church was built, and a fine house for himself, and by judicious management the Indians became settled and the artisans for the capital. In the stillness and quiet of the village, it seemed as if the mountains and volcanoes around had shielded it from the devastation and alarm of war. Passing through it, on the other side of the plain we commenced ascending a mountain. About half way up, looking back over the village and plain, we saw a single white line over the mountain we had crossed to the Ciudad Vieja, and the range of the eye embraced the plain and lake at our feet, the great plain of Escuintla, the two volcanoes of Agua and Fuego, extending to the Pacific Ocean. The road was very steep, and our mules laboured. On the other side of the mountain the road lay for some distance between shrubs and small trees, emerging from which we saw an immense plain, broken by the track of the direct road from Guatimala, and afar off the spires of the town of Chimaltenango. At the foot of the mountain we reached the village of Paramos. We had been three hours and a half making six miles. Don Pepé summoned the alcalde, showed him Carrera's passport, and demanded a guide to the next village. The alcalde called his alguazils, and in a very few minutes a guide was ready. Don Pepé told us that he left us in Europa, and with many thanks we bade him farewell.

We were now entering upon a region of country which, at the time of the conquest, was the most populous, the most civilized, and best cultivated in Guatimala. The people who occupied it were the descendants of those found there by Alvarado, and perhaps four fifths were Indians of untainted blood. For three centuries they had submitted quietly to the dominion of the whites, but the rising of Carrera had waked them up to a recollection of their fathers, and it was rumoured that their eyes rolled strangely upon the white men as the enemies of their race. For the first time we saw fields of wheat and peach-trees. The country was poetically called Europa; and though the Volcano de Agua still reared in full sight its stupendous head, it resembled the finest part of England on a magnificent scale.

But it was not like travelling in England. The young man with whose throat Mr. Catherwood had been so familiar loitered behind with the sick mule and a gun. He had started from Ciudad Vieja with a drawn knife in his hand, the blade about a foot and a half long, and we made up our minds to get rid of him; but we feared that he had anticipated us, and had gone off with the mule and gun. We waited till he came up, relieved him from the gun, and made him go forward,

while we drove the mule.   At the distance of two
leagues we reached the Indian village of San Andres
Isapa.   Don Saturnino flourished Carrera's passport, introduced me as El Ministro de Nueva-York, demanded
a guide, and in a few minutes an alguazil was trotting
before us for the next village.   At this village, on the
same requisition, the alcalde ran out to look for an alguazil, but could not find one immediately, and ventured to beg Don Saturnino to wait a moment.   Don
Saturnino told him he must go himself; Carrera would
cut off his head if he did not; "the minister of New-
York" could not be kept waiting.   Don Saturnino, like
many others of my friends in that country, had no very
definite notions in regard to titles or places.   A man
happened to be passing, whom the alcalde pressed into
service, and he trotted on before with the halter of the
led horse.   Don Saturnino hurried him along; as we
approached the next village Carrera's soldiers were in
sight, returning on the direct road to Guatimala, fresh
from the slaughter at Quezaltenango.   Don Saturnino
told the guide that he must avoid the plaza and go on
to the next village.   The guide begged, and Don Saturnino rode up, drew his sword, and threatened to cut
his head off.   The poor fellow trotted on, with his eye
fixed on the uplifted sword; and when Don Saturnino
turned to me with an Uncle Toby expression of face,
he threw down the halter, leaped over a hedge fence,
and ran toward the town.   Don Saturnino, not discon-
certed, caught up the halter, and, spurring his mule,
pushed on.   The road lay on a magnificent table-land,
in some places having trees on each side for a great
distance.   Beyond this we had a heavy rain-storm,
and late in the afternoon reached the brink of an immense precipice, in which, at a great distance, we

saw the molina or wheat-mill, looking like a New-England factory. The descent was very steep and muddy, winding in places close along the precipitous side of the ravine. Great care was necessary with the mules; their tendency was to descend sidewise, which was very dangerous; but in the steepest places, by keeping their heads straight, they would slip in the mud several paces, bracing their feet and without falling.

At dark, wet and muddy, and in the midst of a heavy rain, we reached the molina. The major-domo was a Costa Rican, a countryman of Don Saturnino, and, fortunately, we had a room to ourselves, though it was damp and chilly. Here we learned that Tecpan Guatimala, one of the ruined cities we wished to visit, was but three leagues distant, and the major-domo offered to go with us in the morning.

CHAPTER IX.

In the morning the major-domo furnished us with fine horses, and we started early. Almost immediately we commenced ascending the other side of the ravine which we had descended the night before, and on the top entered on a continuation of the same beautiful and extensive table-land. On one side, for some distance, were high hedge fences, in which aloes were growing, and in one place were four in full bloom. In an hour we arrived at Patzum, a large Indian village. Here we turned off to the right from the high road to Mexico by a sort of by-path; but the country was beautiful, and in parts well cultivated. The morning was bracing, and the climate like our own in October. The immense table-land was elevated some five or six thousand feet, but none of these heights have ever been taken. We passed on the right two mounds, such as are seen all over our own country, and on the left an immense barranca. The table was level to the very edge, where the earth seemed to have broken off and sunk, and we looked down into a frightful abyss two or three thousand feet deep. Gigantic trees at the bottom of the immense cavity looked like shrubs. At some distance beyond we passed a second of these immense barrancas, and in an hour and a half reached the Indian village of Tec-

pan Guatimala. For some distance before reaching it
the road was shaded by trees and shrubs, among which
were aloes thirty feet high. The long street by which
we entered was paved with stones from the ruins of the
old city, and filled with drunken Indians ; and rushing
across it was one with his arms around a woman's neck.
At the head of this street was a fine plaza, with a large
cabildo, and twenty or thirty Indian alguazils under the
corridor, with wands of office in their hands, silent, in
full suits of blue cloth, the trousers open at the knees,
and cloak with a hood like the Arab burnouse. Adjoining this was the large courtyard of the church,
paved with stone, and the church itself was one of the
most magnificent in the country. It was the second
built after the conquest. The façade was two hundred
feet, very lofty, with turrets and spires gorgeously ornamented with stuccoed figures, and a high platform, on
which were Indians, the first we had seen in picturesque
costume ; and with the widely-extended view of the
country around, it was a scene of wild magnificence in
nature and in art. We stopped involuntarily ; and
while the Indians, in mute astonishment, gazed at us, we
were lost in surprise and admiration. As usual, Don
Saturnino was the pioneer, and we rode up to the house
of the padre, where we were shown into a small room,
with the window closed and a ray of light admitted
from the door, in which the padre was dozing in a
large chair. Before he had fairly opened his eyes, Don
Saturnino told him that we had come to visit the ruins
of the old city, and wanted a guide, and thrust into his
hands Carrera's passport and the letter of the provesor.
The padre was old, fat, rich, and infirm, had been thirty-
five years cura of Tecpan Guatimala, and was not used
to doing things in a hurry ; but our friend, knowing the

particular objects of our visit, with great earnestness and haste told the padre that the minister of New-York had heard in his country of a remarkable stone, and the provesor and Carrera were anxious for him to see it. The padre said that it was in the church, and lay on the top of the grand altar; the cup of the sacrament stood upon it; it was covered up, and very sacred; he had never seen it, and he was evidently unwilling to let us see it, but said he would endeavour to do so when we returned from the ruins.   He sent for a guide, and we went out to the courtyard of the church; and while Mr. Catherwood was attempting a sketch, I walked up the steps.   The interior was lofty, spacious, richly ornamented with stuccoed figures and paintings, dark and solemn, and in the distance was the grand altar, with long wax candles burning upon it, and Indians kneeling before it.   At the door a man stopped me, and said that I must not enter with sword and spurs, and even that I must take off my boots.   I would have done so, but saw that the Indians did not like a stranger going into *their* church.   They were evidently entirely unaccustomed to the sight of strangers, and Mr. Catherwood was so annoyed by their gathering round him that he gave up his drawing; and fearing it would be worse on our return, I told Don Saturnino that we must make an effort to see the stone now.   Don Saturnino had a great respect for the priests and the Church. He was not a fanatic, but he thought a powerful religious influence good for the Indians.   Nevertheless, he said we ought to see it; and we went back in a body to the padre, and Don Saturnino told him that we were anxious to see the stone now, to prevent delay on our return.   The good padre's heavy body was troubled. He asked for the provesor's letter again, read it over, went out on the corridor and consulted with a brother about as old and round as himself, and at length told us to wait in that room and he would bring it. As he went out he ordered all the Indians in the courtyard, about forty or fifty, to go to the cabildo and tell the alcalde to send the guide. In a few minutes he returned, and opening with some trepidation the folds of his large gown, produced the stone.

Fuentes, in speaking of the old city, says, " To the westward of the city there is a little mount that commands it, on which stands a small round building about six feet in height, in the middle of which there is a pedestal formed of a shining substance resembling glass, but the precise quality of which has not been ascertained. Seated around this building, the judges heard and decided the causes brought before them, and their sentences were executed upon the spot. Previous to executing them, however, it was necessary to have them confirmed by the oracle, for which purpose three of the judges left their seats and proceeded to a deep ravine, where there was a place of worship containing a black transparent stone, on the surface of which the Deity was supposed to indicate the fate of the criminal. If the decision was approved, the sentence was executed immediately; if nothing appeared on the stone, the accused was set at liberty. This oracle was also consulted in the affairs of war. The Bishop Francisco Marroquin having obtained intelligence of this slab, ordered it to be cut square, and consecrated it for the top of the grand altar in the Church of Tecpan Guatimala. It is a stone of singular beauty, about a yard and a half each way." The " Modern Traveller" refers to it as an " interesting specimen of ancient art;" and in 1825 concludes, " we may hope, before long, to receive some more distinct account of this oracular stone."

The world—meaning thereby the two classes into which an author once divided it, of subscribers and non-subscribers to his work—the world that reads these pages is indebted to Don Saturnino for some additional information. The stone was sewed up in a piece of cotton cloth drawn tight, which looked certainly as old as the thirty-five years it had been under the cura's charge, and probably was the same covering in which it was enveloped when first laid on the top of the altar. One or two stitches were cut in the middle, and this was perhaps all we should have seen; but Don Saturnino, with a hurried jargon of "strange, curious, sacred, incomprehensible, the provesor's letter, minister of New-York," &c., whipped out his penknife, and the good old padre, heavy with agitation and his own weight, sunk into his chair, still holding on with both hands. Don Saturnino ripped till he almost cut the good old man's fingers, slipped out the sacred tablet, and left the sack in the padre's hands. The padre sat a picture of self-abandonment, helplessness, distress, and self-reproach. We moved toward the light, and Don Saturnino, with a twinkle of his eyes and a ludicrous earnestness, consummated the padre's fear and horror by scratching the sacred stone with his knife. This oracular slab is a piece of common slate, fourteen inches by ten, and about as thick as those used by boys at school, without characters of any kind upon it. With a strong predilection for the marvellous, and scratching it most irreverently, we could make nothing more out of it. Don Saturnino handed it back to the padre, and told him that he had better sew it up and put it back; and probably it is now in its place on the top of the grand altar,

with the sacramental cup upon it, an object of veneration to the fanatic Indians.

But the agitation of the padre destroyed whatever
there was of comic in the scene. Recovering from the
shock, he told us not to go back through the town; that
there was a road direct to the old city; and concealing
the tablet under his gown, he walked out with a firm
step, and in a strong, unbroken voice, rapidly, in their
own unintelligible dialect, called to the Indians to bring
up our horses, and directed the guide to put us in the
road which led direct to the molina. He feared that the
Indians might discover our sacrilegious act; and as we
looked in their stupid faces, we were well satisfied to
get away before any such discovery was made, rejoicing
more than the padre that we could get back to the molina without returning through the town.

We had but to mount and ride. At the distance of
a mile and a half we reached the bank of an immense
ravine. We descended it, Don Saturnino leading the
way; and at the foot, on the other side, he stopped at
a narrow passage, barely wide enough for the mule to
pass. This was the entrance to the old city. It was
a winding passage cut in the side of the ravine, twenty
or thirty feet deep, and not wide enough for two horsemen to ride abreast; and this continued to the high table
of land on which stood the ancient city of Patinamit.

This city flourished with the once powerful kingdom
of the Kachiquel Indians. Its name, in their language,
means "*the* city." It was also called Tecpan Guatimala, which, according to Vasques, means "the Royal
House of Guatimala," and he infers that it was the capital of the Kachiquel kings; but Fuentes supposes that
Tecpan Guatimala was the arsenal of the kingdom, and
not the royal residence, which honour belonged to Gua-

timala, and that the former was so called from its situation on an eminence with respect to the latter, the word Tecpan meaning " above."

According to Fuentes, Patinamit was seated on an eminence, and surrounded by a deep defile or natural fosse, the perpendicular height of which, from the level of the city, was more than one hundred fathoms. The only entrance was by a narrow causeway terminated by two gates, constructed of the chay stone, one on the exterior and the other on the interior wall of the city. The plane of this eminence extends about three miles in length from north to south, and about two in breadth from east to west. The soil is covered with a stiff clay about three quarters of a yard deep. On one side of the area are the remains of a magnificent building, perfectly square, each side measuring one hundred paces, constructed of hewn stones extremely well put together; in front of the building is a large square, on one side of which stand the ruins of a sumptuous palace, and near to it are the foundations of several houses. A trench three yards deep runs from north to south through the city, having a breastwork of masonry rising about a yard high. On the eastern side of this trench stood the houses of the nobles, and on the opposite side the houses of the maseguales or commoners. The streets were, as may still be seen, straight and spacious, crossing each other at right angles.

When we rose upon the table, for some distance it bore no marks of ever having been a city. Very soon we came upon an Indian burning down trees and preparing a piece of ground for planting corn. Don Saturnino asked him to go with us and show us the ruins, but he refused. Soon after we reached a hut, outside of which a woman was washing. We asked her to ac-

company us, but she ran into the hut.   Beyond this we
reached a wall of stones, but broken and confused.   We
tied our horses in the shade of trees, and commenced exploring on foot.   The ground was covered with mounds
of ruins.   In one place we saw the foundations of two
houses, one of them about a hundred feet long by fifty
feet broad.   It was one hundred and forty years since
Fuentes published the account of his visit; during that
time the Indians had carried away on their backs stones
to build up the modern village of Tecpan Guatimala,
and the hand of ruin had been busily at work.   We inquired particularly for sculptured figures; our guide
knew of two, and after considerable search brought us
to them.   They were lying on the ground, about three
feet long, so worn that we could not make them out,
though on one the eyes and nose of an animal were
distinguishable.   The position commanded an almost
boundless view, and it is surrounded by an immense ravine, which warrants the description given of it by Fuentes.   In some places it was frightful to look down
into its depths.   On every side it was inaccessible, and
the only way of reaching it was by the narrow passage
through which we entered, its desolation and ruin adding another page to the burdened record of human con-
tentions, and proving that, as in the world whose history we know, so in this of whose history we are ignorant, man's hand has been against his fellow.   The solitary Indian hut is all that now occupies the site of the
ancient city; but on Good Friday of every year a solemn procession of the whole Indian population is made
to it from the village of Tecpan Guatimala, and, as our
guide told us, on that day bells are heard sounding under the earth.

Descending by the same narrow passage, we trav-

ersed the ravine and ascended on the other side. Our
guide put us into the road that avoided the town, and
we set off on a gallop.

Don Saturnino possessed the extremes of good temper, simplicity, uprightness, intelligence, and perseverance. Ever since I fell in with him he had been most
useful, but this day he surpassed himself; and he was
so well satisfied with us as to declare that if it were not
for his wife in Costa Rica, he would bear us company to
Palenque. He had an engagement in Guatimala on a
particular day; every day that he lost with us was so
much deducted from his visit to his relatives; and at
his earnest request we had consented to pass a day with
them, though a little out of our road. We reached the
molina in time to walk over the mill. On the side of the
hill above was a large building to receive grain, and below it an immense reservoir for water in the dry season,
but which did not answer the purpose intended. The
mill had seven sets of grindstones, and working night
and day, ground from seventy to ninety negases of wheat
in the twenty-four hours, each negas being six arobas of
twenty-five pounds. The Indians bring the wheat, and
each one takes a stone and does his own grinding, paying a rial, twelve and a half cents, per negas for the
use of the mill. Flour is worth about from three dollars and a half to four dollars the barrel.

Don Saturnino was one of the best men that ever lived,
but in undress there was a lankness about him that was
ludicrous. In the evening, as he sat on the bed with his
thin arms wound around his thin legs, and we reproved
him for his sacrilegious act in cutting open the cotton
cloth, his little eyes twinkled, and Mr. C. and I laughed
as we had not before laughed in Central America.

But in that country one extreme followed close upon

another. At midnight we were roused from sleep by
that movement which, once felt, can never be mistaken.
The building rocked, our men in the corridor cried out
"temblor," and Mr. C. and I at the same moment ex-
claimed "an earthquake!" Our cartarets stood transversely. By the undulating movement of the earth he
was rolled from side to side, and I from head to foot.
The sinking of my head induced an awful faintness of
heart. I sprang upon my feet and rushed to the door.
In a moment the earth was still. We sat on the sides
of the bed, compared movements and sensations, lay
down again, and slept till morning.

Early in the morning we resumed our journey. Unfortunately, the gray mule was no better. Perhaps she
would recover in a few days, but we had no time to wait.
My first mule, too, purchased as the price of seeing Don
Clementino's sister, which had been a most faithful animal, was drooping. Don Saturnino offered me his
own, a strong, hardy animal, in exchange for the latter,
and the former I left behind, to be sent back and turned
out on the pasture-grounds of Padre Alcantra. There
were few trials greater in that country than that of
being obliged to leave on the road these tried and faithful companions.

To Patzum our road was the same as the day before.
Before reaching it we had difficulty with the luggage,
and left at a hut on the road our only cartaret. Leaving Patzum on the left, our road lay on the high, level
table of land, and at ten o'clock we came to the brink
of a ravine three thousand feet deep, saw an immense
abyss at our feet, and opposite, the high, precipitous
wall of the ravine. Our road lay across it. At the
very commencement the descent was steep. As we advanced the path wound fearfully along the edge of the

precipice, and we met a caravan of mules at a narrow place, where there was no room to turn out, and we were obliged to go back, taking care to give them the outside.   All the way down we were meeting them ; perhaps more than five hundred passed us, loaded with wheat for the mills and cloths for Guatimala.   In meeting so many mules loaded with merchandise, we lost the vague and indefinite apprehensions with which we had set out on this road.   We were kept back by them more than half an hour, and with great labour reached the bottom of the ravine.   A stream ran through it ; for some distance our road lay in the stream, and we crossed it thirty or forty times.   The sides of the ravine were of an immense height.   In one place we rode along a perpendicular wall of limestone rock smoking with spontaneous combustion.

At twelve o'clock we commenced ascending the opposite side.   About half way up we met another caravan of mules, with heavy boxes on their sides, tumbling down the steep descent.   They came upon us so suddenly that our cargo-mules got entangled among them, turned around, and were hurried down the mountain.   Our men got them disengaged, and we drew up against the side.   As we ascended, toward the summit, far above us, were rude fortifications, commanding the road up which we were toiling. This was the frontier post of Los Altos, and the position taken by General Guzman to repel the invasion of Carrera.   It seemed certain death for any body of men to advance against it ; but Carrera sent a detachment of Indians, who clambered up the ravine at another place, and attacked it in the rear.   The fortifications were pulled down and burned, the boundary lines demolished, and Los Altos annexed to Guatimala.   Here

we met an Indian, who confirmed what the muleteers
had told us, that the road to Santiago Atitan, the place
of residence of Don Saturnino's relatives, was five
leagues, and exceedingly bad, and, in order to save
our luggage-mules, we resolved to leave them at the
village of Godines, about a mile farther on. The village consisted of but three or four 'huts, entirely desolate ; there was not a person in sight. We were afraid
to trust our mozos alone; they might be robbed, or
they might rob us themselves; besides, they had nothing to eat. We were about at the head of the Lake
of Atitan. It was impossible, with the cargo-mules, to
reach Santiago Atitan that day; it lay on the left border of the lake ; our road was on the right, and it
was agreed for Don Saturnino to go on alone, and for
us to continue on our direct road to Panachahel, a village on the right border opposite Atitan, and cross the
lake to pay our visit to him. We were advised that
there were canoes for this purpose, and bade farewell to Don Saturnino with the confident expectation
of seeing him again the next day at the house of his
relatives; but we never met again.

At two o'clock we came out upon the lofty table of
land bordering the Lake of Atitan. In general I have
forborne attempting to give any idea of the magnificent
scenery amid which we were travelling, but here forbearance would be a sin. From a height of three or
four thousand feet we looked down upon a surface shining like a sheet of molten silver, enclosed by rocks
and mountains of every form, some barren, and some
covered with verdure, rising from five hundred to five
thousand feet in height. Opposite, down on the borders
of the lake, and apparently inaccessible by land, was the
town of Santiago Atitan, to which our friend was wend-

ing his way, situated between two immense volcanoes eight or ten thousand feet high. Farther on was another volcano, and farther still another, more lofty than all, with its summit buried in clouds. There were no associations connected with this lake; until lately we did not know it even by name; but we both agreed that it was the most magnificent spectacle we ever saw. We stopped and watched the fleecy clouds of vapour rising from the bottom, moving up the mountains and the sides of the volcanoes. We descended at first by a steep pitch, and then gently for about three miles along the precipitous border of the lake, leaving on our right the camino real and the village of San Andres, and suddenly reached the brink of the table-land, two thousand feet high. At the foot was a rich plain running down to the water; and on the opposite side another immense perpendicular mountain side, rising to the same height with that on which we stood. In the middle of the plane, buried in foliage, with the spire of the church barely visible, was the town of Panachahel. Our first view of the lake was the most beautiful we had ever seen, but this surpassed it. All the requisites of the grand and beautiful were there; gigantic mountains, a valley of poetic softness, lake, and volcanoes, and from the height on which we stood a waterfall marked a silver line down its sides. A party of Indian men and women were moving in single file from the foot of the mountain toward the village, and looked like children. The descent was steep and perpendicular, and, reaching the plain, the view of the mountain-walls was sublime. As we advanced the plain formed a triangle with its base on the lake, the two mountain ranges converged to a point, and communicated by a narrow defile beyond with the village of San Andres.

Riding through a thick forest of fruit and flower trees, we entered the village, and at three o'clock rode up to the convent. The padre was a young man, cura of four or five villages, rich, formal, and polite ; but all over the world women are better than men ; his mother and sister received us cordially. They were in great distress on account of the outrage at Quezaltenango. Carrera's troops had passed through on their return to Guatimala, and they feared that the same bloody scenes were to be enacted all through the country. Part of his outrages were against the person of a cura, and this seemed to break the only chain that was supposed to keep him in subjection. Unfortunately, we learned that there was little or no communication with Santiago Atitan, and no canoe on this side of the lake. Our only chance of seeing Don Saturnino again was that he would learn this fact at Atitan, and if there was a canoe there, send it for us. After dinner, with a servant of the house as guide, we walked down to the lake. The path lay through a tropical garden. The climate was entirely different from the table-land above, and productions which would not grow there flourished here. Sapotes, hocotes, aguacates, manzones, pineapples, oranges, and lemons, the best fruits of Central America, grew in profusion, and aloes grew thirty to thirty-five feet high, and twelve or fourteen inches thick, cultivated in rows, to be used for thatching miserable Indian huts. We came down to the lake at some hot springs, so near the edge that the waves ran over the spring, the former being very hot, and the latter very cold.

According to Huarros, " the Lake of Atitan is one of the most remarkable in the kingdom. It is about twenty-four miles from east to west, and ten from north to

south, entirely surrounded by rocks and mountains.
There is no gradation of depth from its shores, and the
bottom has not been found with a line of three hundred
fathoms. It receives several rivers, and all the waters
that descend from the mountains, but there is no known
channel by which this great body is carried off. The
only fish caught in it are crabs, and a species of small
fish about the size of the little finger. These are in such
countless myriads that the inhabitants of the surrounding
ten villages carry on a considerable fishing for them."

At that hour of the day, as we understood to be the
case always at that season of the year, heavy clouds
were hanging over the mountains and volcanoes, and
the lake was violently agitated by a strong southwest
wind ; as our guide said, la laguna esta mucha brava.
Santiago Atitan was nearly opposite, at a distance of
seven or eight leagues, and in following the irregular
and mountainous border of the lake from the point where
Don Saturnino left us, we doubted whether he could
reach it that night. It was much farther off than we
supposed, and with the lake in such a state of agitation,
and subject, as our guide told us, at all times to violent gusts of wind, we had but little inclination to cross
it in a canoe. It would have been magnificent to see
there a tropical storm, to hear the thunder roll among
the mountains, and see the lightnings flash down into
the lake. We sat on the shore till the sun disappeared
behind the mountains at the head of the lake. Mingled
with our contemplations of it were thoughts of other and
far distant scenes, and at dark we returned to the convent.

CHAPTER X.

EARLY in the morning we again went down to the lake. Not a vapour was on the water, and the top of every volcano was clear of clouds. We looked over to Santiago Atitan, but there was no indication of a canoe coming for us. We whiled away the time in shooting wild ducks, but could get only two ashore, which we afterward found of excellent flavour. According to the account given by Huarros, the water of this lake is so cold that in a few minutes it benumbs and swells the limbs of all who bathe in it. But it looked so inviting that we determined to risk it, and were not benumbed, nor were our limbs swollen. The inhabitants, we were told, bathed in it constantly; and Mr. C. remained a long time in the water, supported by his life preserver, and without taking any exercise, and was not conscious of extreme coldness. In the utter ignorance that exists in regard to the geography and geology of that country, it may be that the account of its fathomless depth, and the absence of any visible outlet, is as unfounded as that of the coldness of its waters.

The Modern Traveller, in referring to the want of specific information with regard to its elevation, and other circumstances from which to frame a conjecture as to its origin, and the probable communication of its

waters with some other reservoir, states that the " fish
which it contains are the same as are found in the Lake
of Amatitan," and asks, " May there not be some connexion between these lakes, at least the fathomless one,
and the Volcan de Agua ?"   We were told that the mo-
hara, the fish for which the Lake of Amatitan is celebrated in that country, was not found in the Lake of
Atitan at all ; so that on this ground at least there is no
reason to suppose a connexion between the two lakes.
In regard to any connexion with the Volcan de Agua,
if the account of Torquemada be true, the deluge of water from that volcano was not caused by an eruption,
but by an accumulation of water in a cavity on the top,
and consequently the volcano has no subterraneous water power.   The elevation of this lake has never been
taken, and the whole of this region of country invites
the attention of the scientific traveller.

While we were dressing, Juan, one of our mozos,
found a canoe along the shore.   It was an oblong " dug-
out," awkward and rickety, and intended for only one
person ; but the lake was so smooth that a plank seemed sufficient.   We got in, and Juan pushed off and
paddled out.   As we moved away the mountainous borders of the lake rose grandly before us ; and I had just
called Mr. C.'s attention to a cascade opening upon us
from the great height of perhaps three or four thousand feet, when we were struck by a flaw, which
turned the canoe, and drove us out into the lake.
The canoe was overloaded, and Juan was an unskilful
paddler.   For several minutes he pulled, with every
sinew stretched, but could barely keep her head straight.
Mr. C. was in the stern, I on my knees in the bottom of the canoe.   The loss of a stroke, or a tottering movement in changing places, might swamp her ;

and if we let her go she would be driven out into the
lake, and cast ashore, if at all, twenty or thirty miles
distant, whence we should have to scramble back over
mountains ; and there was a worse danger than this,
for in the afternoon the wind always came from the
other side, and might drive us back again into the
middle of the lake.   We saw the people on the shore
looking at us, and growing smaller every moment, but
they could not help us.   In all our difficulties we had
none that came upon us so suddenly and unexpectedly,
or that seemed more threatening.   It was hardly ten
minutes since we were standing quietly on the beach,
and if the wind had continued five minutes longer I do
not know what would have become of us ; but, most
fortunately, it lulled.   Juan's strength revived ; with a
great effort he brought us under cover of the high headland beyond which the wind first struck us, and in a
few minutes we reached the shore.

We had had enough of the lake ; time was precious,
and we determined to set out after dinner and ride four
leagues to Solola.   We took another mozo, whom the
padre recommended as a bobon, or great fool.   The first
two were at swords' points, and with such a trio there
was not much danger of combination.   In loading the
mules they fell to quarrelling, Bobon taking his share.
Ever since we left, Don Saturnino had superintended
this operation, and without him everything went wrong.
One mule slipped part of its load in the courtyard, and
we made but a sorry party for the long journey we had
before us.   From the village our road lay toward
the lake, to the point of the opposite mountain, which
shut in the plain of Panachahel.   Here we began to ascend.   For a while the path commanded a view of the
village and plain ; but by degrees we diverged from it,

and after an hour's ascent came out upon the lake,
rode a short distance upon the brink, with another immense mountain range before us, and breaking over the
top the cataract which I had seen from the canoe.
Very soon we commenced ascending ; the path ran zigzag, commanding alternately a view of the plain and
of the lake.   The ascent was terrible for loaded mules,
being in some places steps cut in the stone like a regular staircase.   Every time we came upon the lake there
was a different view.   At four o'clock, looking back
over the high ranges of mountains we had crossed, we
saw the great volcanoes of Agua and Fuego.   Six
volcanoes were in sight at once, four of them above
ten thousand, and two nearly fifteen thousand feet high.
Looking down upon the lake we saw a canoe, so small
as to present a mere speck on the water, and, as we
supposed, it was sent for us by our friend Don Saturnino.   Four days afterward, after diverging and returning to the main road, I found a letter from him, directed to " El Ministro de Nueva-York," stating that he
found the road so terrible that night overtook him, and
he was obliged to stop three leagues short of Atitan.
On arriving at that place he learned that *the* canoe was
on his side of the lake, but the boatmen would not
cross till the afternoon wind sprang up.   The letter
was written after the return of the canoe, and sent
by courier two days' journey, begging us to return,
and offering as a bribe a noble mule, which, in our
bantering on the road, he affirmed was better than
my macho.   Twice the mule-track led us almost within the fall of cataracts, and the last time we came
upon the lake we looked down upon a plain even more
beautiful than that of Panachahel.   Directly under
us, at an immense distance below, but itself elevated

fifteen hundred or two thousand feet, was a village, with its church conspicuous, and it seemed as if we could throw a stone down upon its roof. From the moment this lake first opened upon us until we left it, our ride along it presented a greater combination of beauties than any locality I ever saw. The last ascent occupied an hour and three quarters. As old travellers, we would have avoided it if there had been any other road; but, once over, we would not have missed it for the world. Very soon we saw Solola. In the suburbs drunken Indians stood in a line, and took off their old petates (straw hats) with both hands. It was Sunday, and the bells of the church were ringing for vespers, rockets were firing, and a procession, headed by violins, was parading round the plaza the figure of a saint on horseback, dressed like a harlequin. Opposite the cabildo the alcalde, with a crowd of Mestitzoes, was fighting cocks.

The town stands on the lofty borders of the Lake of Amatitan, and a hundred yards from it the whole water was visible. I tied my horse to the whipping-post, and, thanks to Carrera's passport, the alcalde sent off for sacate, had a room swept out in the cabildo, and offered to send us supper from his own house. He was about ten days in office, having been appointed since Carrera's last invasion. Formerly this place was the residence of the youngest branch of the house of the Kachiquel Indians.

It was our purpose at this place to send our luggage on by the main road to Totonicapan, one day's journey beyond, while we struck off at an angle and visited the ruins of Santa Cruz del Quiché. The Indians of that place, even in the most quiet times, bore a very bad name, and we were afraid of hearing such an account of them as would make it impossible to go there. Carrera had left a garrison of soldiers in Solola, and we called upon the commandant, a gentlemanly man, suspected of disaffection to Carrera's government, and therefore particularly desirous to pay respect to his passport, who told me that there had been less excitement at that place than in some of the other villages, and promised to send the luggage on under safe escort to the corregidor of Totonicapan, and give us a letter to his commissionado in Santa Cruz del Quiché.

On our return we learned that a lady had sent for us. Her house was on the corner of the plaza. She was a chapetone from Old Spain, which country she had left with her husband thirty years before, on account of wars. At the time of Carrera's last invasion her son was alcalde mayor, and fled. If he had been taken he would have been shot. The wife of her son was with her. They had not heard from him, but he had fled toward Mexico, and they supposed him to be in the frontier town, and wished us to carry letters to him, and to inform him of their condition. Their house had been plundered, and they were in great distress. It was another of the instances we were constantly meeting of the effects of civil war. They insisted on our remaining at the house all night, which, besides that they were interesting, we were not loth to do on our own account. The place was several thousand feet higher than where we slept the night before, and the temperature cold and wintry by comparison. Hammocks, our only beds, were not used at all. There were not even supporters in the cabildo to hang them on. The next morning the mules were all drawn up by the cold, their coats were rough, and my poor horse was so chilled that he could hardly move. In coming in he had attracted attention, and the

alcalde wanted to buy him.   In the morning he told me
that, being used to a hot climate, the horse could not
bear the journey across the Cordilleras, which was confirmed by several disinterested persons to whom he appealed.   I almost suspected him of having done the horse
some injury, so as to make me leave him behind.   However, by moving him in the sun his limbs relaxed, and
we sent him off with the men and luggage, and the
promised escort, to Totonicapan, recommended to the
corregidor.

At a quarter before nine we bade farewell to the
ladies who had entertained us so kindly, and, charged
with letters and messages for their son and husband,
set out with Bobon for Santa Cruz del Quiché.   At a
short distance from the town we again rose upon a
ridge which commanded a view of the lake and town;
the last, and, as we thought, the loveliest of all.   At a
league's distance we turned off from the camino real into
a narrow bridle-path, and very soon entered a well-cul-
tivated plain, passed a forest clear of brush and underwood, like a forest at home, and followed the course of
a beautiful stream.   Again we came out upon a rich
plain, and in several places saw clusters of aloes in full
bloom.   The atmosphere was transparent, and, as in an
autumn day at home, the sun was cheering and invig-
orating.

At twelve o'clock we met some Indians, who told us
that Santa Thomas was three leagues distant, and five
minutes afterward we saw the town apparently not more
than a mile off; but we were arrested by another immense ravine.   The descent was by a winding zigzag
path, part of the way with high walls on either side, so
steep that we were obliged to dismount and walk all
the way, hurried on by our own impetus and the mules

crowding upon us from behind.   At the foot of the ravine was a beautiful stream, at which, choked with dust
and perspiration, we stopped to drink.   We mounted
to ford the stream, and almost immediately dismounted
again to ascend the opposite side of the ravine.   This
was even more difficult than the descent, and when we
reached the top it seemed good three leagues.   We
passed on the right another awful barranca, broken off
from the table of land, and riding close along its edge,
looked down into an abyss of two or three thousand
feet, and very soon reached Santa Thomas.   A crowd
of Indians was gathered in the plaza, well dressed in
brown cloth, and with long black hair, without hats.
The entire population was Indian.   There was not a
single white man in the place, nor one who could speak
Spanish, except an old Mestitzo, who was the secretary
of the alcalde.   We rode up to the cabildo, and tied
our mules before the prison door.   Groups of villanous
faces were fixed in the bars of the windows.   We called for the alcalde, presented Carrera's passport, and
demanded sacate, eggs, and frigoles for ourselves, and
a guide to Quiché.   While these were got, the alcalde,
and as many alguazils as could find a place, seated
themselves silently on a bench occupied by us.   In
front was a new whipping-post.   There was not a word
spoken; but a man was brought up before it, his feet
and wrists tied together, and he was drawn up by a
rope which passed through a groove at the top of the
post.   His back was naked, and an alguazil stood on
his left with a heavy cowhide whip.   Every stroke
made a blue streak, rising into a ridge, from which
the blood started and trickled down his back.   The
poor fellow screamed in agony.   After him a boy was
stretched up in the same way.   At the first lash, with

a dreadful scream, he jerked his feet out of the ropes, and seemed to fly up to the top of the post. He was brought back and secured, and whipped till the alcalde was satisfied. This was one of the reforms instituted by the Central government of Guatimala. The Liberal party had abolished this remnant of barbarity; but within the last month, at the wish of the Indians themselves, and in pursuance of the general plan to restore old usages and customs, new whipping-posts had been erected in all the villages. Not one of the brutal beings around seemed to have the least feeling for the victims. Among the amateurs were several criminals, whom we had noticed walking in chains about the plaza, and among them a man and woman in rags, bareheaded, with long hair streaming over their eyes, chained together by the hand and foot, with strong bars between them to keep them out of each other's reach. They were a husband and wife, who had shocked the moral sense of the community by not living together. The punishment seemed the very refinement of cruelty, but while it lasted it was an effectual way of preventing a repetition of the offence.

At half past three, with an alguazil running before us and Bobon trotting behind, we set out again, and crossed a gently-rolling plain, with a distant side-hill on the left, handsomely wooded, and reminding us of scenes at home, except that on the left was another immense barranca, with large trees, whose tops were two thousand feet below us. Leaving a village on the right, we passed a small lake, crossed a ravine, and rose to the plain of Quiché. At a distance on the left were the ruins of the old city, the once large and opulent capital of Utatlan, the court of the native kings of Quiché, and the most sumptuous discovered by the Spaniards in this section of America. It was a site worthy to be the abode of a race of a kings. We passed between two small lakes, rode into the village, passed on, as usual, to the convent, which stood beside the church, and stopped at the foot of a high flight of stone steps. An old Indian on the platform told us to walk in, and we spurred our mules up the steps, rode through the corridor into a large apartment, and sent the mules down another flight of steps into a yard en-closed by a high stone fence. The convent was the first erected in the country by the Dominican friars, and dated from the time of Alvarado. It was built en-tirely of stone, with massive walls, and corridors, pave-ments, and courtyard strong enough for a fortress; but most of the apartments were desolate or filled with rubbish; one was used for sacate, another for corn, and another fitted up as a roosting-place for fowls. The padre had gone to another village, his own apartments were locked, and we were shown into one adjoining, about thirty feet square, and nearly as high, with stone floor and walls, and without a single article in it except a shattered and weather-beaten soldier in one corner, returning from campaigns in Mexico. As we had brought with us nothing but our ponchas, and the nights in that region were very cold, we were unwilling to risk sleeping on the stone floor, and with the padre's Indian servant went to the alcalde, who, on the strength of Carrera's passport, gave us the audience-room of the cabildo, which had at one end a raised platform with a railing, a table, and two long benches with high backs. Adjoining was the prison, being merely an enclosure of four high stone walls, without any roof, and filled with more than the usual number of criminals, some of whom,

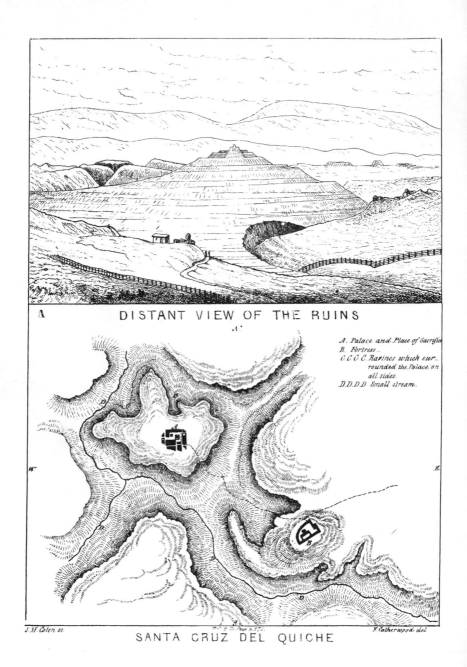

DISTANT VIEW OF THE RUINS

A. Palace and Place of Sacrifice
B. Fortress.
C.C.C.C. Ravines which sur-
rounded the Palace on
all sides.
D.D.D.D. Small stream.

J.H.Colen sc.

F. Catherwood del.

SANTA CRUZ DEL QUICHE

as we looked through the gratings, we saw lying on the ground, with only a few rags of covering, shivering in the cold. The alcalde provided us with supper, and promised to procure us a guide to the ruins.

Early in the morning, with a Mestitzo armed with a long basket-hilted sword, who advised us to carry our weapons, as the people were not to be trusted, we set out for the ruins. At a short distance we passed another immense barranca, down which, but a few nights before, an Indian, chased by alguazils, either fell or threw himself off into the abyss, fifteen hundred feet deep, and was dashed to pieces. At about a mile from the village we came to a range of elevations, extending to a great distance, and connected by a ditch, which had evidently formed the line of fortifications for the ruined city. They consisted of the remains of stone buildings, probably towers, the stones well cut and laid together, and the mass of rubbish around abounded in flint arrow-heads. Within this line was an elevation, which grew more imposing as we approached, square, with terraces, and having in the centre a tower, in all one hundred and twenty feet high. We ascended by steps to three ranges of terraces, and on the top entered an area enclosed by stone walls, and covered with hard cement, in many places still perfect. Thence we ascended by stone steps to the top of the tower, the whole of which was formerly covered with stucco, and stood as a fortress at the entrance of the great city of Utatlan, the capital of the kingdom of the Quiché Indians.

According to Fuentes, the chronicler of the kingdom of Guatimala, the kings of Quiché and Kachiquel were descended from the Toltecan Indians, who, when they came into this country, found it already inhab-

ited by people of different nations. According to
the manuscript of Don Juan Torres, the grandson of
the last king of the Quichés, which was in the possession of the lieutenant-general appointed by Pedro
de Alvarado, and which Fuentes says he obtained
by means of Father Francis Vasques, the historian
of the order of San Francis, the Toltecas themselves
descended from the house of Israel, who were released
by Moses from the tyranny of Pharaoh, and after crossing the Red Sea, fell into idolatry. To avoid the re-
proofs of Moses, or from fear of his inflicting upon them
some chastisement, they separated from him and his
brethren, and under the guidance of Tanub, their chief,
passed from one continent to the other, to a place which
they called the seven caverns, a part of the kingdom of
Mexico, where they founded the celebrated city of Tula.
From Tanub sprang the families of the kings of Tula
and Quiché, and the first monarch of the Toltecas. Nimaquiché, the fifth king of that line, and more beloved
than any of his predecessors, was directed by an oracle
to leave Tula, with his people, who had by this time
multiplied greatly, and conduct them from the kingdom
of Mexico to that of Guatimala. In performing this
journey they consumed many years, suffered extraordinary hardships, and wandered over an immense tract of
country, until they discovered the Lake of Atitan, and
resolved to settle near it in a country which they called
Quiché.

Nimaquiché was accompanied by his three brothers,
and it was agreed to divide the new country between
them. Nimaquiché died ; his son Axcopil became chief
of the Quichés, Kachiquels, and Zutugiles, and was at
the head of his nation when they settled in Quiché, and
the first monarch who reigned in Utatlan. Under him

the monarchy rose to a high degree of splendour. To relieve himself from some of the fatigues of administration, he appointed thirteen captains or governors, and at a very advanced age divided his empire into three kingdoms, viz., the Quiché, the Kachiquel, and the Zutugil, retaining the first for himself, and giving the second to his eldest son Jintemal, and the third to his youngest son Acxigual. This division was made on a day when three suns were visible at the same time, which extraordinary circumstance, says the manuscript, has induced some persons to believe that it was made on the day of our Saviour's birth. There were seventeen Toltecan kings who reigned in Utatlan, the capital of Quiché, whose names have come down to posterity, but they are so hard to write out that I will take it for granted the reader is familiar with them.

Their history, like that of man in other parts of the world, is one of war and bloodshed. Before the death of Axcopil his sons were at war, which, however, was settled by his mediation, and for two reigns peace existed. In the reign of Balam Acan, the next king of Quiché, while living on terms of great intimacy and friendship with his cousin Zutugilebpop, king of the Zutugiles, the latter abused his generosity and ran away with his daughter Ixconsocil; and at the same time Iloacab, his relative and favourite, ran away with Ecselixpua, the niece of the king. The rape of Helen did not produce more wars and bloodshed than the carrying off of these two young ladies with unpronounceable names. Balam Acan was naturally a mild man, but the abduction of his daughter was an affront not to be pardoned. With eighty thousand veterans, himself in the centre squadron, adorned with three diadems and other regal ornaments, carried in a rich chair of state,

splendidly ornamented with gold, emeralds, and other
precious stones, upon the shoulders of the nobles of his
court, he marched against Zutugilebpop, who met him
with sixty thousand men, commanded by Iloacab, his
chief general and accomplice. The most bloody battle ever fought in the country took place ; the field was
so deeply inundated with blood that not a blade of
grass could be seen. Victory long remained unde-
cided, and at length Iloacab was killed, and Balam
Acan remained master of the field. But the campaign
did not terminate here. Balam Acan, with thirty thousand veterans under his personal command and two
other bodies of thirty thousand each, again met Zutugilebpop with forty thousand of his own warriors and forty
thousand auxiliaries. The latter was defeated, and escaped at night. Balam Acan pursued and overtook
him ; but while his bearers were hastening with him to
the thickest of the fight, they lost their footing, and
precipitated him to the earth. At this moment Zutugilebpop was advancing with a chosen body of ten thousand lancers. Balam Acan was slain, and fourteen
thousand Indians were left dead on the field.

The war was prosecuted by the successor of Balam,
and Zutugilebpop sustained such severe reverses that
he fell into a despondency and died. The war was continued down to the time of Kicah Tanub, who, after a
sanguinary struggle, reduced the Zutugiles and Kachiquels to subjection to the kings of Quiché. At this time
the kingdom of the Quichés had attained its greatest
splendour, and this was contemporaneous with that
eventful era in American history, the reign of Montezuma
and the invasion of the Spaniards. The kings of Mexico and Quiché acknowledged the ties of relationship,
and in a manuscript of sixteen quarto leaves, preserved

by the Indians of San Andres Xecul, it is related that when Montezuma was made prisoner, he sent a private ambassador to Kicah Tanub, to inform him that some white men had arrived in his state, and made war upon him with such impetuosity that the whole strength of his people was unable to resist them; that he was himself a prisoner, surrounded by guards; and hearing it was the intention of his invaders to pass on to the kingdom of Quiché, he sent notice of the design, in order that Kicah Tanub might be prepared to oppose them. On receiving this intelligence, the King of Quiché sent for four young diviners, whom he ordered to tell him what would be the result of this invasion. They requested time to give their answers; and, taking their bows, discharged some arrows against a rock; but, seeing that no impression was made upon it, returned very sorrowfully, and told the king there was no way of avoiding the disaster; the white men would certainly conquer them. Kicah, dissatisfied, sent for the priests, desiring to have their opinions on this important subject; and they, from the ominous circumstance of a certain stone, brought by their forefathers from Egypt, having suddenly split into two, predicted the inevitable ruin of the kingdom. At this time he received intelligence of the arrival of the Spaniards on the borders of Soconusco to invade his territory; but, undismayed by the auguries of diviners or priests, he prepared for war. Messages were sent by him to the conquered kings and chiefs under his command, urging them to co-operate for the common defence; but, glad of an opportunity to rebel, Sinacam, the king of Guatimala, declared openly that he was a friend to the Teules or Gods, as the Spaniards were called by the Indians; and the King of the Zutugiles answered haughtily that he was able to defend his kingdom alone against a more numerous and less famished army than that which was approaching Quiché. Irritation, wounded pride, anxiety, and fatigue, brought on a sickness which carried Tanub off in a few days.

His son Tecum Umam succeeded to his honours and troubles. In a short time intelligence was received that the captain (Alvarado) and his Teules had marched to besiege Xelahuh (now Quezaltenango), next to the capital the largest city of Quiché. At that time it had within its walls eighty thousand men ; but such was the fame of the Spaniards that Tecum Umam determined to go to its assistance. He left the capital, at the threshold of which we stood, borne in his litter on the shoulders of the principal men of his kingdom, and preceded by the music of flutes, cornets, and drums, and seventy thousand men, commanded by his general Ahzob, his lieutenant Ahzumanche, the grand shield-bearer Ahpocob, other officers of dignity with still harder names, and numerous attendants bearing parasols and fans of feathers for the comfort of the royal person. An immense number of Indian carriers followed with baggage and provisions. At the populous city of Totonicapan the army was increased to ninety thousand fighting men. At Quezaltenango he was joined by ten more chiefs, well armed and supplied with provisions, displaying all the gorgeous insignia of their rank, and attended by twenty-four thousand soldiers. At the same place he was re-enforced by forty-six thousand more, adorned with plumes of different colours, and with arms of every description, the chiefs decorated with the skins of lions, tigers, and bears, as distinguishing marks of their bravery and warlike prowess. Tecum Umam marshalled under his banners on the plain of Tzaccapa two hundred and thirty thousand warriors, and fortified his camp with a wall of loose stones, enclosing within its circuit several mountains. In the camp were several military machines, formed of beams on rollers, to be moved from place to place. After a series of desperate and bloody battles, the Spaniards routed this immense army, and entered the city of Xelahuh. The fugitives rallied outside, and made a last effort to surround and crush the Spaniards. Tecum Umam commanded in person, singled out Alvarado, attacked him three times hand to hand, and wounded his horse; but the last time Alvarado pierced him with a lance, and killed him on the spot. The fury of the Indians increased to madness; in immense masses they rushed upon the Spaniards; and, seizing the tails of the horses, endeavoured by main force to bring horse and rider to the ground; but, at a critical moment, the Spaniards attacked in close column, broke the solid masses of the Quichés, routed the whole army, and slaying an immense number, became completely masters of the field. But few of the seventy thousand who marched out from the capital with Tecum Umam ever returned; and, hopeless of being able to resist any longer by force, they had recourse to treachery. At a council of war called at Utatlan by the king, Chinanivalut, son and successor of Tecum Umam, it was determined to send an embassy to Alvarado, with a valuable present of gold, suing for pardon, promising submission, and inviting the Spaniards to the capital. In a few days Alvarado, with his army, in high spirits at the prospect of a termination of this bloody war, encamped upon the plain.

This was the first appearance of strangers at Utatlan, the capital of the great Indian kingdom, the ruins of which were now under our eyes, once the most populous and opulent city, not only of Quiché, but of the whole kingdom of Guatimala. According to Fuentes, who visited it for the purpose of collecting information, and who gathered his facts partly from the remains and partly from manuscripts, it was surrounded by a deep ravine that formed a natural fossé, leaving only two very narrow roads as entrances, both of which were so well defended by the castle of Resguardo, as to render it impregnable. The centre of the city was occupied by the royal palace, which was surrounded by the houses of the nobility ; the extremities were inhabited by the plebeians; and some idea may be formed of its vast population from the fact, before mentioned, that the king drew from it no less than seventy-two thousand fighting men to oppose the Spaniards. It contained many very sumptuous edifices, the most superb of which was a seminary, where between five and six thousand children were educated at the charge of the royal treasury. The castle of the Atalaya was a remarkable structure, four stories high, and capable of furnishing quarters for a very strong garrison. The castle of Resguardo was five stories high, extending one hundred and eighty paces in front, and two hundred and thirty in depth. The grand alcazar, or palace of the kings of Quiché, surpassed every other edifice; and in the opinion of Torquemada, it could compete in opulence with that of Montezuma in Mexico, or that of the Incas in Cuzco. The front extended three hundred and seventy-six geometrical paces from east to west, and it was seven hundred and twenty-eight paces in depth. It was constructed of hewn stones of various colours. There were six principal divisions. The first contained lodgings for a numerous troop of lancers, archers, and other troops, constituting the royal body-guard. The second was assigned to the princes and relations of the king; the third to the monarch himself, containing distinct suites of apartments for the mornings, evenings, and nights. In one of the saloons stood the throne, under four canopies of feathers; and in this portion of the palace were the treasury, tribunals of the judges, armory, aviaries, and menageries. The fourth and fifth divisions were occupied by the queen and royal concubines, with gardens, baths, and places for breeding geese, which were kept to supply feathers for ornaments. The sixth and last division was the residence of the daughters and other females of the blood royal.

Such is the account as derived by the Spanish historians from manuscripts composed by some of the caciques who first acquired the art of writing; and it is related that from Tanub, who conducted them from the old to the new Continent, down to Tecum Umam, was a line of twenty monarchs.

Alvarado, on the invitation of the king, entered this city with his army; but, observing the strength of the place; that it was well walled, and surrounded by a deep ravine, having but two approaches to it, the one by an ascent of twenty-five steps, and the other by a causeway, and both extremely narrow; that the streets were but of trifling breadth, and the houses very lofty; that there were neither women nor children to be seen, and that the Indians seemed agitated, the soldiers began to suspect some deceit. Their apprehensions were soon confirmed by Indian allies of Quezaltenango, who discovered that the people intended that night to fire their capital, and while the flames were rising, to burst upon the Spaniards with large bodies of men concealed in the neighbourhood, and put every one to death. These tidings were found to be in accordance with the

movements of the Utatlans; and on examining the
houses, the Spaniards discovered that there were no
preparations of provisions to regale them, as had been
promised, but everywhere was a quantity of light dry
fuel and other combustibles.   Alvarado called his officers together, and laid before them their perilous situation, and the immediate necessity of withdrawing from
the place ; and pretending to the king and his caciques that their horses were better in the open fields,
the troops were collected, and without any appearance
of alarm, marched in good order to the plain.   The
king, with pretended courtesy, accompanied them, and
Alvarado, taking advantage of the opportunity, made
him prisoner, and after trial and proof of his treachery,
hung him on the spot.   But neither the death of Tecum nor the ignominious execution of his son could
quell the fierce spirit of the Quichés.   A new ebullition
of animosity and rage broke forth.   A general attack
was made upon the Spaniards ; but Spanish bravery and
discipline increased with danger ; and after a dreadful
havoc by the artillery and horses, the Indians abandoned a field covered with their dead, and Utatlan, the
capital, with the whole kingdom of Quiché, fell into
the hands of Alvarado and the Spaniards.

As we stood on the ruined fortress of Resguardo, the
great plain, consecrated by the last struggle of a brave
people, lay before us grand and beautiful, its blood-
stains all washed out, and smiling with fertility, but perfectly desolate.   Our guide leaning on his sword in the
area beneath was the only person in sight.   But very
soon Bobon introduced a stranger, who came stumbling
along under a red silk umbrella, talking to Bobon and
looking up at us.   We recognised him as the cura, and
descended to meet him.   He laughed to see us grope

our way down; by degrees his laugh became infectious, and when we met we all laughed together. All at once he stopped, looked very solemn, pulled off his neckcloth, and wiped the perspiration from his face, took out a paper of cigars, laughed, thrust them back, pulled out another, as he said, of Habaneras, and asked what was the news from Spain.

Our friend's dress was as unclerical as his manner, viz., a broad-brimmed black glazed hat, an old black coat reaching to his heels, glossy from long use, and pantaloons to match; a striped roundabout, a waistcoat, flannel shirt, and under it a cotton one, perhaps washed when he shaved last, some weeks before. He laughed at our coming to see the ruins, and said that he laughed prodigiously himself when he first saw them. He was from Old Spain; had seen the battle of Trafalgar, looking on from the heights on shore, and laughed whenever he thought of it; the French fleet was blown sky high, and the Spanish went with it; Lord Nelson was killed—all for glory—he could not help laughing. He had left Spain to get rid of wars and revolutions: here we all laughed; sailed with twenty Dominican friars; was fired upon and chased into Jamaica by a French cruiser: here we laughed again; got an English convoy to Omoa, where he arrived at the breaking out of a revolution; had been all his life in the midst of revolutions, and it was now better than ever. Here we all laughed incontinently. His own laugh was so rich and expressive that it was perfectly irresistible. In fact, we were not disposed to resist, and in half an hour we were as intimate as if acquainted for years. The world was our butt, and we laughed at it outrageously. Except the Church, there were few things which the cura did not laugh at; but politics was his fa-

vourite subject. He was in favour of Morazan, or Carrera, or el Demonio: " vamos adelante," " go ahead,"
was his motto; he laughed at them all. If we had parted
with him then, we should always have remembered him
as the laughing cura; but, on farther acquaintance, we
found in him such a vein of strong sense and knowledge, and, retired as he lived, he was so intimately acquainted with the country and all the public men, as a
mere looker on his views were so correct and his satire
so keen, yet without malice, that we improved his title
by calling him the laughing philosopher.

Having finished our observations at this place, stopping to laugh as some new greatness or folly of the
world, past, present, or to come, occurred to us, we
descended by a narrow path, crossed a ravine, and
entered upon the table of land on which stood the
palace and principal part of the city. Mr. Catherwood and I began examining and measuring the ruins,
and the padre followed us, talking and laughing all the
time; and when we were on some high place, out of
his reach, he seated Bobon at the foot, discoursing to
him of Alvarado, and Montezuma, and the daughter of
the King of Tecpan Guatimala, and books and manuscripts in the convent; to all which Bobon listened without comprehending a word or moving a muscle, looking
him directly in the face, and answering his long low
laugh with a respectful " Si, señor."

The plan in the division of the last engraving marked
A, represents the topography of the ground in the heart
of the city which was occupied by the palace and other
buildings of the royal house of Quiché. It is surrounded by an immense barranca or ravine, and the only entrance is through that part of the ravine by which we
reached it, and which is defended by the fortress before

referred to, marked B in the plate. The cura pointed out to us one part of the ravine which, he said, according to old manuscripts formerly existing in the convent, but now carried away, was artificial, and upon which forty thousand men had been employed at one time.

The whole area was once occupied by the palace, seminary, and other buildings of the royal house of Quiché, which now lie for the most part in confused and shapeless masses of ruins. The palace, as the cura told us, with its courts and corridors, once covering the whole diameter, is completely destroyed, and the materials have been carried away to build the present village. In part, however, the floor remains entire, with fragments of the partition walls, so that the plan of the apartments can be distinctly made out. This floor is of a hard cement, which, though year after year washed by the floods of the rainy season, is hard and durable as stone. The inner walls were covered with plaster of a finer description, and in corners where there had been less exposure were the remains of colours; no doubt the whole interior had been ornamented with paintings. It gave a strange sensation to walk the floor of that roofless palace, and think of that king who left it at the head of seventy thousand men to repel the invaders of his empire. Corn was now growing among the ruins. The ground was used by an Indian family which claimed to be descended from the royal house. In one place was a desolate hut, occupied by them at the time of planting and gathering the corn. Adjoining the palace was a large plaza or courtyard, also covered with hard cement, in the centre of which were the relics of a fountain.

The most important part remaining of these ruins is that which appears in the engraving, and which is called El Sacrificatorio, or the place of sacrifice. It is a quadrangular stone structure, sixty-six feet on each side at the base, and rising in a pyramidal form to the height, in its present condition, of thirty-three feet. On three sides there is a range of steps in the middle, each step seventeen inches high, and but eight inches on the upper surface, which makes the range so steep that in descending some caution is necessary. At the corners are four buttresses of cut stone, diminishing in size from the line of the square, and apparently intended to support the structure. On the side facing the west there are no steps, but the surface is smooth and covered with stucco, gray from long exposure. By breaking a little at the corners we saw that there were different layers of stucco, doubtless put on at different times, and all had been ornamented with painted figures. In one place we made out part of the body of a leopard, well drawn and coloured.

The top of the Sacrificatorio is broken and ruined, but there is no doubt that it once supported an altar for those sacrifices of human victims which struck even the Spaniards with horror. It was barely large enough for the altar and officiating priests, and the idol to whom the sacrifice was offered. The whole was in full view of the people at the foot.

The barbarous ministers carried up the victim entirely naked, pointed out the idol to which the sacrifice was made, that the people might pay their adorations, and then extended him upon the altar. This had a convex surface, and the body of the victim lay arched, with the trunk elevated and the head and feet depressed. Four priests held the legs and arms, and another kept his head firm with a wooden instrument made in the form of a coiled serpent, so that he was prevented

View of the Place of Sacrifice in Ruins
AT SANTA CRUZ DEL QUICHÈ

Section of the Place of Sacrifice

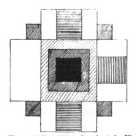

Place of Sacrifice shewing the Plan
of the Steps ascending to the top ,19 Steps
remain.On the West side there are no Steps.

Scale of Feet.

10   20   30   40   50

J.H.Cohen sc.   F.Catherwood del

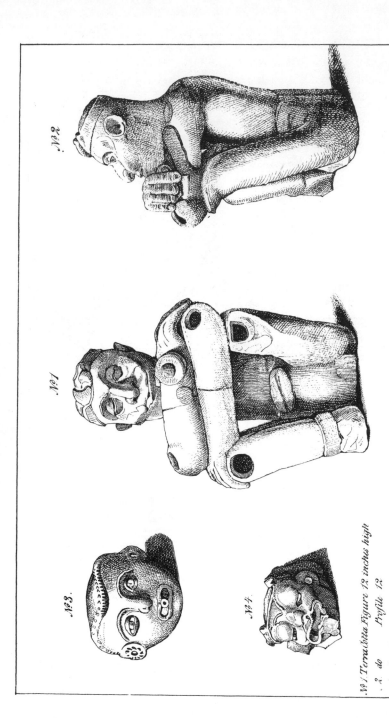

Nº2

Nº1

Nº3.

Nº4.

Nº 1 Terrachtta Figure 12 inches high
. 2   do   Profile 12
. 3   do   Head
. 4   do. Mask

F. Catherwood del.

J. H. Octen sc.

FICURES FOUND AT SANTA CRUZ DEL QUICHE

from making the least movement.   The head priest then
approached, and with a knife made of flint cut an aperture in the breast, and tore out the heart, which, yet pal-
pitating, he offered to the sun, and then threw it at the
feet of the idol.   If the idol was gigantic and hollow, it
was usual to introduce the heart of the victim into its
mouth with a golden spoon.   If the victim was a prisoner
of war, as soon as he was sacrificed they cut off the head
to preserve the scull, and threw the body down the steps,
when it was taken up by the officer or soldier to whom
the prisoner had belonged, and carried to his house to
be dressed and served up as an entertainment for his
friends.   If he was not a prisoner of war, but a slave
purchased for the sacrifice, the proprietor carried off the
body for the same purpose.   In recurring to the barbarous scenes of which the spot had been the theatre, it
seemed a righteous award that the bloody altar was
hurled down, and the race of its ministers destroyed.

It was fortunate for us, in the excited state of the
country, that it was not necessary to devote much time
to an examination of these ruins.   In 1834 a thorough
exploration had been made under a commission from
the government of Guatimala.   Don Miguel Rivera y
Maestre, a gentleman distinguished for his scientific and
antiquarian tastes, was the commissioner, and kindly
furnished me with a copy of his manuscript report to
the government, written out by himself.   This report is
full and elaborate, and I have no doubt is the result of
a thorough examination, but it does not refer to any
objects of interest except those I have mentioned.   He
procured, however, the image of which a front and side
view appear in the engraving opposite, and which,
without my venturing to express a wish for it, he kindly gave to me.   It is made of baked clay, very hard,

and the surface as smooth as if coated with enamel. It
is twelve inches high, and the interior is hollow, including the arms and legs.   In his report to the government, Don Miguel calls it Cabuahuil, or one of the dei-
ties of the ancient inhabitants of Quiché.   I do not
know upon what authority he has given it this name,
but to me it does not seem improbable that his supposition is true, and that to this earthen vessel human
victims have been offered in sacrifice.

The heads in the engraving were given me by the
cura.   They are of terra cotta; the lower one is hollow and the upper is solid, with a polished surface.
They are hard as stone, and in workmanship will compare with images in the same material by artists of the
present day.

In our investigation of antiquities we considered this
place important from the fact that its history is known
and its date fixed.   It was in its greatest splendour
when Alvarado conquered it.   It proves the character
of the buildings which the Indians of that day constructed, and in its ruins confirms the glowing accounts given
by Cortez and his companions of the splendour display-
ed in the edifices of Mexico.   The point to which we
directed our attention was to discover some resemblance
to the ruins of Copan and Quirigua; but we did not
find statues, or carved figures, or hieroglyphics, nor
could we learn that any had ever been found there.   If
there had been such evidences we should have considered these remains the works of the same race of people, but in the absence of such evidences we believed
that Copan and Quirigua were cities of another race
and of a much older date.

The padre told us that thirty years before, when he
first saw it, the palace was entire to the garden.   He was

then fresh from the palaces of Spain, and it seemed as if he was again among them. Shortly after his arrival a small gold image was found and sent to Zerabia, the president of Guatimala, who ordered a commission from the capital to search for hidden treasure. In this search the palace was destroyed; the Indians, roused by the destruction of their ancient capital, rose, and threatened to kill the workmen unless they left the country; and but for this, the cura said, every stone would have been razed to the ground. The Indians of Quiché have at all times a bad name; at Guatimala it was always spoken of as an unsafe place to visit; and the padre told us that they looked with distrust upon any stranger coming to the ruins. At that moment they were in a state of universal excitement; and coming close to us, he said that in the village they stood at swords' points with the Mestitzoes, ready to cut their throats, and with all his exertions he could barely keep down a general rising and massacre. Even this information he gave us with a laugh. We asked him if he had no fears for himself. He said no; that he was beloved by the Indians; he had passed the greater part of his life among them; and as yet the padres were safe: the Indians considered them almost as saints. Here he laughed. Carrera was on their side; but if he turned against them it would be time to fly. This was communicated and received with peals of laughter; and the more serious the subject, the louder was our cachinnation. And all the time the padre made continual reference to books and manuscripts, showing antiquarian studies and profound knowledge.

Under one of the buildings was an opening which the Indians called a cave, and by which they said one could reach Mexico in an hour. I crawled under, and

found a pointed-arch roof formed by stones lapping
over each other, but was prevented exploring it by
want of light, and the padre's crying to me that it was
the season of earthquakes; and he laughed more than
usual at the hurry with which I came out; but all at
once he stopped, and grasping his pantaloons, hopped
about, crying, "a snake, a snake." The guide and
Bobon hurried to his relief; and by a simple process,
but with great respect, one at work on each side, were
in a fair way of securing the intruder; but the padre
could not stand still, and with his agitation and restlessness tore loose from their hold, and brought to light a
large grasshopper. While Bobon and the guide, without a smile, restored him, and put each button in its
place, we finished with a laugh outrageous to the memory of the departed inhabitants, and to all sentiment
connected with the ruins of a great city.

As we returned to the village the padre pointed out
on the plain the direction of four roads, which led, and
which, according to him, are still open, to Mexico, Tecpan Guatimala, Los Altos, and Vera Paz.

CHAPTER XI.

Interior of a Convent.—Royal Bird of Quiché.—Indian Languages.—The Lord's Prayer in the Quiché Language.—Numerals in the same.—Church of Quiché. —Indian Superstitions.—Another lost City.—Tierra de Guerra.—The Aboriginals.—Their Conversion to Christianity.—They were never conquered.—A living City.—Indian Tradition respecting this City.—Probably has never been visited by the Whites.—Presents a noble Field for future Enterprise.—Departure.—San Pedro.—Virtue of a Passport.—A difficult Ascent.—Mountain Scenery.—Totonicapan.—An excellent Dinner.—A Country of Aloes.—" River of Blood."—Arrival at Quezaltenango.

It was late when we returned to the convent. The good padre regretted not being at home when we arrived, and said that he always locked his room to prevent the women throwing things into confusion. When we entered it was in what he called order, but this order was of a class that beggars description. The room contained a table, chairs, and two settees, but there was not a vacant place even on the table to sit down or to lay a hat upon. Every spot was encumbered with articles, of which four bottles, a cruet of mustard and another of oil, bones, cups, plates, sauce-boat, a large lump of sugar, a paper of salt, minerals and large stones, shells, pieces of pottery, sculls, bones, cheese, books, and manuscripts formed part. On a shelf over his bed were two stuffed quezales, the royal bird of Quiché, the most beautiful that flies, so proud of its tail that it builds its nest with two openings, to pass in and out without turning, and whose plumes were not permitted to be used except by the royal family.

Amid this confusion a corner was cleared on the table for dinner. The conversation continued in the same unbroken stream of knowledge, research, sagacity, and satire on his part. Political matters were spoken of in

whispers when any servants were in the rooms. A
laugh was the comment upon everything, and in the
evening we were deep in the mysteries of Indian history.

Besides the Mexican or Aztec language, spoken by
the Pipil Indians along the coast of the Pacific, there
are twenty-four dialects peculiar to Guatimala. Though
sometimes bearing such a strong resemblance in some
of their idioms that the Indians of one tribe can understand each other, in general the padres, after years of
residence, can only speak the language of the tribe
among which they live. This diversity of languages
had seemed to me an insuperable impediment in the
way of any thorough investigation and study of Indian
history and traditions; but the cura, profound in everything that related to the Indians, told us that the Quiché
was the parent tongue, and that, by one familiar with
it, the others are easily acquired. If this be true, a new
and most interesting field of research is opened. During my whole journey, even at Guatimala, I had not
been able to procure any grammar of an Indian language, nor any manuscripts. I made several vocabu-
laries, which I have not thought it worth while to publish; but the padre had a book prepared by some of the
early fathers for the church service, which he promised
to have copied for me and sent to a friend at Guatimala, and from which I copied the Lord's prayer in the
Quiché language. It is as follows:

Cacahan chicah lae coni Vtzah. Vcahaxtizaxie mayih
Bila Chipa ta pa Cani ahauremla Chibantah. Ahuamla
Uaxale Chiyala Chiqueeh hauta Vleus quehexi Caban
Chicah. Uacamic Chiyala. Chiqueeh hauta. Eihil
Caua. Zachala Camac quehexi Cacazachbep qui. Mac
Xemocum Chiqueeh: moho Estachcula maxa Copahic

Chupamtah Chibal mac xanare Cohcolta la ha Vonohel itgel quehe Chucoe.   Amen.

I will add the following numerals, as taken from the same book :

Hun, *one.*

Quieb, *two.*

Dxib, *three.*

Quieheb, *four.*

Hoob, *five.*

Uacacguil, *six.*

Veuib, *seven.*

Uahxalquib, *eight.*

Beleheb, *nine.*

Lahuh, *ten.*

Hulahuh, *eleven.*

Cablahuh, *twelve.*

Dxlahuh, *thirteen.*

Cahlahuh, *fourteen.*

Hoolahuh, *fifteen.*

Uaelahuh, *sixteen.*

Velahuh, *seventeen.*

Uapxaelahuh, *eighteen.*

Belehalahuh, *nineteen.*

Huuinac, *twenty.*

Huuina*chun*, *twenty-one.*

Huuinachlahuh, *thirty.*

Cauinae, *forty.*

Lahuh Raxcal, *fifty.*

Oxcal, *sixty.*

Lahuh Vhumuch, *seventy.*

Humuch, *eighty.*

Lahuh Rocal, *ninety.*

Ocal, *a hundred.*

Otuc Rox Ocob, *a thousand.*

Whether there is any analogy between this language and that of any of our own Indian tribes, I am not able to say.

For a man who has not reached that period when a few years tell upon his teeth and hair, I know of no place where, if the country becomes quiet, they might be passed with greater interest than at Santa Cruz del Quiché, in studying, by means of their language, the character and traditionary history of the Indians; for here they still exist, in many respects, an unchanged people, cherishing the usages and customs of their ancestors; and though the grandeur and magnificence of the churches, the pomp and show of religious ceremonies, affect their rude imaginations, the padre told us

that in their hearts they were full of superstitions, and
still idolaters; had their idols in the mountains and ravines, and in silence and secrecy practised the rites received from their fathers.   He was compelled to wink
at them; and there was one proof which he saw every
day.   The church of Quiché stands east and west.   On
entering it for vespers the Indians always bowed to the
west, in reverence to the setting sun.   He told us, too,
what requires confirmation, and what we were very curious to judge of for ourselves, that in a cave near a
neighbouring village were sculls much larger than the
natural size, and regarded with superstitious reverence
by the Indians.   He had seen them, and vouched for
their gigantic dimensions.   Once he placed a piece of
money in the mouth of the cave, and a year afterward
found the money still lying in the same place, while, he
said, if it had been left on his table, it would have disappeared with the first Indian who entered.

The padre's whole manner was now changed; his
keen satire and his laugh were gone.   There was interest enough about the Indians to occupy the mind
and excite the imagination of one who laughed at everything else in the world; and his enthusiasm, like
his laugh, was infectious.   Notwithstanding our haste
to reach Palenque, we felt a strong desire to track
them in the solitude of their mountains and deep ravines, and watch them in the observance of their idolatrous rites; but the padre did not give us any encouragement.   In fact, he opposed our remaining another
day, even to visit the cave of sculls.   He made no
apology for hurrying us away.   He lived in unbroken
solitude, in a monotonous routine of occupations, and
the visit of a stranger was to him an event most welcome; but there was danger in our remaining.   The

Indians were in an inflammable state; they were already inquiring what we came there for, and he could not answer for our safety. In a few months, perhaps, the excitement might pass away, and then we could return. He loved the subjects we took interest in, and would join us in all our expeditions, and aid us with all his influence.

And the padre's knowledge was not confined to his own immediate neighbourhood. His first curacy was at Coban, in the province of Vera Paz; and he told us that four leagues from that place was another ancient city, as large as Santa Cruz del Quiché, deserted and desolate, and almost as perfect as when evacuated by its inhabitants. He had wandered through its silent streets and over its gigantic buildings, and its palace was as entire as that of Quiché when he first saw it. This is within two hundred miles of Guatimala, and in a district of country not disturbed by war; yet, with all our inquiries, we had heard nothing of it. And now, the information really grieved us. Going to the place would add eight hundred miles to our journey. Our plans were fixed, our time already limited; and in that wild country and its unsettled state, we had superstitious apprehensions that it was ominous to return. My impression, however, of the existence of such a city is most strong. I do most earnestly hope that some future traveller will visit it. He will not hear of it even at Guatimala, and perhaps will be told that it does not exist. Nevertheless, let him seek for it; and if he do find it, experience sensations which seldom fall to the lot of man.

But the padre told us more; something that increased our excitement to the highest pitch. On the other side of the great traversing range of Cordilleras lies the

district of Vera Paz, once called Tierra de Guerra, or
land of war, from the warlike character of its aboriginal inhabitants.   Three times the Spaniards were driven
back in their attempts to conquer it.   Las Casas, vicar
of the convent of the Dominican order in the city of
Guatimala, mourning over the bloodshed caused by
what was called converting the Indians to Christianity,
wrote a treatise to prove that Divine Providence had
instituted the preaching of the Gospel as the only
means of conversion to the Christian faith; that war
could not with justice be made upon those who had
never committed any aggressions against Christians;
and that to harass and destroy the Indians was to prevent the accomplishing of this desired object.   This
doctrine he preached from the pulpit, and enforced in
private assemblies.   He was laughed at, ridiculed, and
sneeringly advised to put his theory in practice.   Undisturbed by this mockery, he accepted the proposal,
choosing as the field of his operations the unconquerable
district called Tierra de Guerra, and made an arrangement that no Spaniards should be permitted to reside in
that country for five years.   This agreed upon, the
Dominicans composed some hymns in the Quiché language, describing the creation of the world, the fall of
Adam, the redemption of mankind, and the principal
mysteries of the life, passion, and death of our Saviour.
These were learned by some Indians who traded with
the Quichés, and a principal cacique of the country,
afterward called Don Juan, having heard them sung,
asked those who had repeated them to explain in detail
the meaning of things so new to him.   The Indians
excused themselves, saying that they could only be explained by the fathers who had taught them.   The cacique sent one of his brothers with many presents, to

entreat that they would come and make him acquainted
with what was contained in the songs of the Indian
merchants. A single Dominican friar returned with the
ambassador, and the cacique, having been made to
comprehend the mysteries of the new faith, burned his
idols and preached Christianity to his own subjects.
Las Casas and another associate followed, and, like the
apostles of old, without scrip or staff, effected what
Spanish arms could not, bringing a portion of the Land
of War to the Christian faith. The rest of the Tierra
de Guerra never was conquered; and at this day the
northeastern section, bounded by the range of the Cordilleras and the State of Chiapas, is occupied by Candones or unbaptized Indians, who live as their fathers
did, acknowledging no submission to the Spaniards, and
the government of Central America does not pretend
to exercise any control over them. But the thing that
roused us was the assertion by the padre that, four days
on the road to Mexico, on the other side of the great
sierra, was a living city, large and populous, occupied
by Indians, precisely in the same state as before the
discovery of America. He had heard of it many years
before at the village of Chajul, and was told by the villagers that from the topmost ridge of the sierra this city
was distinctly visible. He was then young, and with
much labour climbed to the naked summit of the sierra,
from which, at a height of ten or twelve thousand feet, he
looked over an immense plain extending to Yucatan and
the Gulf of Mexico, and saw at a great distance a large
city spread over a great space, and with turrets white
and glittering in the sun. The traditionary account of
the Indians of Chajul is, that no white man has ever
reached this city; that the inhabitants speak the Maya
language, are aware that a race of strangers has con-

quered the whole country around, and murder any
white man who attempts to enter their territory.   They
have no coin or other circulating medium; no horses,
cattle, mules, or other domestic animals except fowls,
and the cocks they keep under ground to prevent their
crowing being heard.

There was a wild novelty—something that touched
the imagination—in every step of our journey in that
country; the old padre, in the deep stillness of the
dimly-lighted convent, with his long black coat like a
robe, and his flashing eye, called up an image of the
bold and resolute priests who accompanied the armies
of the conquerors; and as he drew a map on the table,
and pointed out the sierra to the top of which he had
climbed, and the position of the mysterious city, the interest awakened in us was the most thrilling I ever experienced.   One look at that city was worth ten years
of an every-day life.   If he is right, a place is left where
Indians and an Indian city exist as Cortez and Alvarado
found them; there are living men who can solve the
mystery that hangs over the ruined cities of America;
perhaps who can go to Copan and read the inscriptions
on its monuments.   No subject more exciting and attractive presents itself to my mind, and the deep impression of that night will never be effaced.

Can it be true ?   Being now in my sober senses, I do
verily believe there is much ground to suppose that what
the padre told us is authentic.   That the region referred
to does not acknowledge the government of Guatimala,
has never been explored, and that no white man ever
pretends to enter it, I am satisfied.   From other sources we heard that from that sierra a large *ruined* city
was visible, and we were told of another person who
had climbed to the top of the sierra, but, on account of

the dense cloud resting upon it, had been unable to see anything. At all events, the belief at the village of Chajul is general, and a curiosity is roused that burns to be satisfied. We had a craving desire to reach the mysterious city. No man, even if willing to peril his life, could undertake the enterprise with any hope of success, without hovering for one or two years on the borders of the country, studying the language and character of the adjoining Indians, and making acquaintance with some of the natives. Five hundred men could probably march directly to the city, and the invasion would be more justifiable than any ever made by the Spaniards; but the government is too much occupied with its own wars, and the knowledge could not be procured except at the price of blood. Two young men of good constitution, and who could afford to spare five years, might succeed. If the object of search prove a phantom, in the wild scenes of a new and unexplored country there are other objects of interest; but if real, besides the glorious excitement of such a novelty, they will have something to look back upon through life. As to the dangers, these are always magnified, and, in general, peril is discovered soon enough for escape. But in all probability, if any discovery is ever made it will be by the padres. As for ourselves, to attempt it alone, ignorant of the language, and with mozos who were a constant annoyance to us, was out of the question. The most we thought of was a climb to the top of the sierra, thence to look down upon the mysterious city; but we had difficulties enough in the road before us; it would add ten days to a journey already almost appalling in prospective; for days the sierra might be covered with clouds; in attempting too much we might lose all; Palenque was our great point, and we determined not to be diverted from the course we had marked out.

The next morning we had one painful moment with the cura, and that was the moment of parting. He was then calm and kind, his irresistible laugh and his enthusiasm all gone. We had one village to pass at which he told us the Indians were bad, for which reason he gave us a letter to the justitia; and in the kindness of his heart insisted on my accepting one of his beautiful quezales.

As this was Holy Week, we had great difficulty in procuring a guide. None of the Indians wished to leave the village, and the alcalde told an alguazil to take a man out of prison. After a parley with the inmates through the grating, one was selected, but kept in confinement till the moment of starting, when the alguazil opened the door and let him out, our roll of luggage was put on his back, and he set off. The battered soldier accompanied us a short distance, and Bobon went before, carrying on a stick the royal bird of Quiché. Crossing the plain and the ravine on which the city stood, we ascended a mountain in the rear, commanding a magnificent view of the plain of Quiché, and descending on the other side, at the distance of two leagues reached the village of San Pedro. A thatched church, with a cross before it, stood near the road, and the huts of the village were a little in the rear. The padre had told us that the Indians of this place were " muy malos," very bad; and as our guide, when he returned, had to be locked up in prison, to avoid the necessity of stopping we tried to induce him to continue; but he dropped his load at the foot of the cross, and ran back in such haste that he left behind his ragged chamar. The justitia was a Mestitzo, who sent for the alcalde, and presently that worthy trotted down with six alguazils, marching in single file, all with wands in their hands, and dressed in handsome cloth cloaks, the holyday costume for the Holy Week. We told them that we wanted a guide, and the whole six set off to look for one. In about ten minutes they returned single file, exactly on the same trot as before, and said they could not find any; the whole week was holyday, and no one wanted to leave home. I showed Carrera's passport, and told the justitia he must go himself, or send one of his alguazils, and they set off again in pursuit. After waiting a little while, I walked to the top of a hill near by, and saw them all seated below, apparently waiting for me to go. As soon as they saw me they ran back in a body to repeat that they could not find a guide. I offered them double price, but they were immovable; and feeling rather uncertain what turn things might take, I talked largely of Carrera's vengeance, not contenting myself with turning them out of office, but taking off their heads at once. After a few moments' consultation they all rose quietly; one doffed his dignity and dress, the rest rolled up the cargo, and throwing it on his bare back, placed the band across his forehead, and set him off on a run. We followed, the secretary begging me to write to Carrera that it was not through his fault I was kept waiting, and that he would have been my guide himself if I had not found another. At a short distance another alguazil, by a cross cut, intercepted and relieved the first, and they ran so fast that on the rough road we could not keep up with them.

The road was indeed rough and wild beyond all description; and very soon we reached another immense ravine, descended it, and commenced an ascent

on the opposite side, which occupied three hours.
Through openings in the woods we looked down precipices one or two thousand feet deep, while the
mountain side was still higher above us.   The whole
mountain was clothed with luxuriant vegetation, and
though wanting the rocky, savage grandeur of Alpine
scenery, at every turn the view was sublime.   As we
climbed up we met a few Indians who could speak no
language but their own, and reaching the top, saw a
wretched spectacle of the beings made in God's image.
A drunken Indian was lying on the ground, his face
cut with a machete, and weltering in his blood; and a
drunken woman was crying over him.   Our Indians
stopped and spoke to them, but we could not understand what they said.   At about three o'clock we emerged from the woods, and very soon saw Totonicapan,
at a great distance and far below us, on a magnificent
plain, with a high table of land behind it, a range of
mountains springing from the table, and rising above
them the Volcano of Quezaltenango.   The town was
spread over a large space, and the flat roofs of the
houses seemed one huge covering, broken only by the
steeple of the church.   We descended the mountain to
the banks of a beautiful stream, along which Indian
women were washing;   and following it, entered the
town, and rode up to the house of the corregidor, Don
José Azmitia.   Our luggage had arrived safely, and in
a few minutes our men presented themselves to receive
us.

Much might be said of Totonicapan as the head of a
department, and surrounded by mountains visible on all
sides from the plaza ; but I stop only to record an event.
All along, with the letters to corregidors, the passport
of Carrera, and the letter of the archbishop, our road

had been a sort of triumphal march; but at this place we dined, i. e., we had a dinner. The reader may remember that in Costa Rica I promised to offend but once more by referring to such a circumstance. That time has come, and I should consider myself an ingrate if I omitted to mention it. We were kept waiting perhaps two hours, and we had not eaten anything in more than twelve. We had clambered over terrible mountains; and at six o'clock, on invitation, with hands and faces washed, and in dress-coats, sat down with the corregidor. Courses came regularly and in right succession. Servants were well trained, and our host did the honours as if he was used to the same thing every day. But it was not so with us. Like Rittmaster Dugald Dalgetty, we ate very fast and very long, on his principle deeming it the duty of every commander of a fortress, on all occasions which offer, to secure as much munition and vivas as their magazines can possibly hold.

We were again on the line of Carrera's operations; the place was alive with apprehensions; white men were trembling for their lives; and I advised our host to leave the country and come to the United States.

The next morning we breakfasted with him, and at eleven o'clock, while a procession was forming in the plaza, we started for Quezaltenango, descended a ravine commanding at every point a beautiful view, ascended a mountain, from which we looked back upon the plain and town of Totonicapan, and on the top entered a magnificent plain, cultivated with cornfields and dotted with numerous flocks of sheep, the first we had seen in the country; on both sides of the road were hedges of gigantic aloes. In one place we counted upward of two hundred in full bloom. In the middle of the plain, at the distance of two and a half leagues, we

crossed, on a rude bridge of logs, a broad river, memorable for the killed and wounded thrown into it in Alvarado's battle with the Quiché Indians, and called the
" River of Blood." Two leagues beyond we came in
sight of Quezaltenango, standing at the foot of a great
range of mountains, surmounted by a rent volcano constantly emitting smoke, and before it a mountain ridge
of lava, which, if it had taken its course toward the city,
would have buried it like Herculaneum and Pompeii.

CHAPTER XII.

WE were again on classic soil. The reader perhaps
requires to be reminded that the city stands on the site of
the ancient Xelahuh, next to Utatlan the largest city in
Quiché, the word Xelahuh meaning " under the government of ten ;" that is, it was governed by ten principal
captains, each captain presiding over eight thousand
dwellings, in all eighty thousand, and containing, according to Fuentes, more than three hundred thousand
inhabitants ; that on the defeat of Tecum Umam by Alvarado, the inhabitants abandoned the city, and fled to
their ancient fortresses, Excansel the volcano, and Cek-
xak, another mountain adjoining ; that the Spaniards entered the deserted city, and, according to a manuscript
found in the village of San Andres Xecul, their videttes
captured the four celebrated caciques, whose names, the
reader doubtless remembers, were Calel Kalek, Ahpop-
gueham, Calelahan, and Calelaboy ; the Spanish records say that they fell on their knees before Pedro Alvarado, while a priest explained to them the nature of
the Christian faith, and they declared themselves ready
to embrace it. Two of them were retained as hostages,
and the others sent back to the fortresses, who returned
with such multitudes of Indians ready to be baptized,
that the priests, from sheer fatigue, could no longer lift
their arms to perform the ceremony.

As we approached, seven towering churches showed
that the religion so hastily adopted had not died away.
In a few minutes we entered the city. The streets
were handsomely paved, and the houses picturesque in
architecture; the cabildo had two stories and a corridor. The Cathedral, with its façade richly decorated,
was grand and imposing. The plaza was paved with
stone, having a fine fountain in the centre, and commanding a magnificent view of the volcano and mountains around. It was the day before Good Friday; the
streets and plaza were crowded with people in their
best attire, the Indians wearing large black cloaks,
with broad-brimmed felt sombreros, and the women a
white frock, covering the head except an oblong opening for the face; some wore a sort of turban of red
cord plaited with the hair. The bells were hushed,
and wooden clappers sounded in their stead. As we
rode through, armed to the teeth, the crowd made way
in silence. We passed the door of the church, and entered the great gate of the convent. The cura was
absent at the moment, but a respectable-looking servant-woman received us in a manner that assured us of
a welcome from her master. There was, however, an
air of excitement and trepidation in the whole household, and it was not long before the good woman unburdened herself of matters fearfully impressed upon
her mind.

After chocolate we went to the corregidor, to whom
we presented our letters from the government and Carrera's passport. He was one of Morazan's expulsados,
a fine, military-looking man, but, as he told us, not a
soldier by profession; he was in office by accident, and
exceedingly anxious to lay down his command; indeed, his brief service had been no sinecure. He in-

CITY OF QUEZALTENANGO.

troduced us to Don Juan Lavanigna, an Italian from Genoa, banished on account of a revolution headed by the present king, then heir apparent, and intended to put him on the throne, but out of which he basely drew himself, leaving his followers to their fate. How the signor found his way to this place I did not learn, but he had not found peace ; and, if I am not deceived, he was as anxious to get out of it as ever he was to leave Genoa.

On our return to the convent we found the cura, who gave us personally the welcome assured to us by his housekeeper. With him was a respectable-looking Indian, bearing the imposing title of Gobernador, being the Indian alcalde ; and it was rather singular that, in an hour after our arrival at Quezaltenango, we had become acquainted with the four surviving victims of Carrera's wrath, all of whom had narrowly escaped death at the time of the outrage, the rumour of which reached us at Guatimala. The place was still quivering under the shock of that event. We had heard many of the particulars on the road, and in Quezaltenango, except the parties concerned, no one could speak of anything else.

On the first entry of Morazan's soldiers into the plaza at Guatimala, in an unfortunate moment, a courier was sent to Quezaltenango to announce the capture of the city. The effect there was immediate and decided ; the people rose upon the garrison left by Carrera, and required them to lay down their arms. The corregidor, not wishing to fire upon the townsmen, and finding it would be impossible with his small force to repress the insurrection, by the advice of the cura and Don Juan Lavanigna, to prevent bloodshed and a general massacre, induced the soldiers to lay down their

arms and leave the town.   The same night the municipality, without his knowledge, nominated Don Juan
Lavanigna as commandant.   He refused to serve; but
the town was in a violent state of excitement, and they
urged him to accept for that night only, representing
that if he did not the fury of the populace would be directed against him.   The same night they made a pronunciamento in favour of Morazan, and addressed a letter of congratulation to him, which they despatched immediately by an Indian courier.   It will be remembered, however, that in the mean time Morazan had been
driven out of Guatimala, and that Carrera had pursued
him in his flight.   At the Antigua the latter met a disarmed sergeant, who informed him of the proceedings
at Quezaltenango, whereupon, abandoning his pursuit
of Morazan, he marched directly thither.   Early intelligence was received of his approach, and the corregidor,
the cura, and Don Juan Lavanigna were sent as a dep-
utation to receive him.   They met him at Totonicapan.
Carrera had heard on the road of their agency in inducing the soldiers to surrender their arms, and his first
greeting was a furious declaration that their heads should
lie at that place; laying aside his fanaticism and respect for the priests, he broke out against the cura in
particular, who, he said, was a relative of Morazan.
The cura said he was not a relative, but only a countryman (which in that region means a townsman), and
could not help the place of his birth; but Carrera forthwith ordered four soldiers to remove him a few paces
and shoot him on the spot.   The gobernador, the old
Indian referred to, threw himself on his knees and
begged the cura's life; but Carrera drew his sword
and struck the Indian twice across the shoulder, and the
wounds were still unhealed when we saw him; but he

desisted from his immediate purpose of shooting the cura, and delivered him over to the soldiers. Don Juan Lavanigna was saved by Carrera's secretary, who exhibited in El Tiempo, the government paper of Guatimala, an extract from a letter written by Don Juan to a friend in Guatimala, praising Carrera's deportment on his previous entry into Quezaltenango, and the discipline and good behaviour of his troops.

Early the next morning Carrera marched into Quezaltenango, with the cura and Don Juan as prisoners. The municipality waited upon him in the plaza ; but, unhappily, the Indian intrusted with the letter to Morazan had loitered in the town, and at this unfortunate moment presented it to Carrera. Before his secretary had finished reading it, Carrera, in a transport of fury, drew his sword to kill them on the spot with his own hand, wounded Molina, the alcalde-mayor, and two other members of the municipality, but checked himself and ordered the soldiers to seize them. He then rode to the corregidor, where he again broke out into fury, and drew his sword upon him. A woman in the room threw herself before the corregidor, and Carrera struck around her several times, but finally checked himself again, and ordered the corregidor to be shot unless he raised five thousand dollars by contributions upon the town. Don Juan and the cura he had locked up in a room with the threat to shoot them at five o'clock that afternoon unless they paid him one thousand dollars each, and the former two hundred, and the latter one hundred to his secretary. Don Juan was the principal merchant in the town, but even for him it was difficult to raise that sum. The poor cura told Carrera that he was not worth a cent in the world except his furniture and books. No one was allowed to visit him except the old housekeeper who first told us the story. Many of his friends had fled or hidden themselves away, and the old housekeeper ran from place to place with notes written by him, begging five dollars, ten dollars, anything she could get. One old lady sent him a hundred dollars. At four o'clock, with all his efforts, he had raised but seven hundred dollars; but, after undergoing all the mental agonies of death, when the cura had given up all hope, Don Juan, who had been two hours at liberty, made up the deficiency, and he was released.

The next morning Carrera sent to Don Juan to borrow his shaving apparatus, and Don Juan took them over himself. He had always been on good terms with Carrera, and the latter asked him if he had got over his fright, talking with him as familiarly as if nothing had happened. Shortly afterward he was seen at the window playing on a guitar; and in an hour thereafter, eighteen members of the municipality, without the slightest form of trial, not even a drum-head court-martial, were taken out into the plaza and shot. They were all the very first men in Quezaltenango; and Molina, the alcalde-mayor, in family, position, and character was second to no other in the republic. His wife was clinging to Carrera's knees, and begging for his life when he passed with a file of soldiers. She screamed " Robertito ;" he looked at her, but did not speak. She shrieked and fainted, and before she recovered her husband was dead. He was taken around the corner of the house, seated on a stone, and despatched at once. The others were seated in the same place, one at a time ; the stone and the wall of the house were still red with their blood. I was told that Carrera shed tears for the death of the first two, but for the rest he said he did not care. Heretofore, in all their revolutions, there had been some show of regard for the tribunals of justice, and the horror of the citizens at this lawless murder of their best men cannot be conceived. The facts were notorious to everybody in Quezaltenango. We heard them, with but little variation of detail, from more than a dozen different persons.

Having consummated this enormity, Carrera returned to Guatimala, and the place had not yet recovered from its consternation. It was considered a blow at the whites, and all feared the horrors of a war of castes. I have avoided speaking harshly of Carrera when I could. I consider myself under personal obligations to him, and without his protection I never could have travelled through the country; but it is difficult to suppress the feelings of indignation excited against the government, which, conscious of the enormity of his conduct and of his utter contempt for them, never dared call him to account, and now cajoles and courts him, sustaining itself in power by his favour alone.

To return to the cura: he was about forty-five, tall, stout, and remarkably fine-looking; he had several curacies under his charge, and next to a canonigo's, his position was the highest in the country; but it had its labours. He was at that time engrossed with the ceremonies of the Holy Week, and in the evening we accompanied him to the church. At the door the *coup d'œil* of the interior was most striking. The church was two hundred and fifty feet in length, spacious and lofty, richly decorated with pictures and sculptured ornaments, blazing with lights, and crowded with Indians. On each side of the door was a grating, behind which stood an Indian to receive offerings. The floor was strewed with pine-leaves. On the left was the figure of a dead Christ on a bier, upon which every woman who entered threw a handful of roses, and near it stood an Indian to receive money. Opposite, behind an iron grating, was the figure of Christ bearing the cross, the eyes bandaged, and large silver chains attached to the arms and other parts of the body, and fastened to the iron bars. Here, too, stood an Indian to receive con-tributions. The altar was beautiful in design and dec-orations, consisting of two rows of Ionic columns, one above another, gilded, surmounted by a golden glory, and lighted by candles ten feet high. Under the pulpit was a piano. After a stroll around the church, the cura led us to seats under the pulpit. He asked us to give them some of the airs of our country, and then himself sat down at the piano. On Mr. C.'s suggesting that the tune was from one of Rossini's operas, he said that this was hardly proper for the occasion, and chan-ged it.

At about ten o'clock the crowd in the church formed into a procession, and Mr. C. and I went out and took a position at the corner of a street to see it pass. It was headed by Indians, two abreast, each carrying in his hand a long lighted wax candle ; and then, borne aloft on the shoulders of four men, came the figure of Judith, with a bloody sword in one hand, and in the other the gory head of Holofernes. Next, also on the shoulders of four men, the archangel Gabriel, dressed in red silk, with large wings puffed out. The next were men in grotesque armour, made of black and silver paper, to resemble Moors, with shield and spear like ancient cav-aliers ; and then four little girls, dressed in white silk and gauze, and looking like little spiritualities, with men on each side bearing lighted candles. Then came a large figure of Christ bearing the cross, supported by four In-dians ; on each side were young Indian lads, carrying long poles horizontally, to keep the crowd from pressing upon it, and followed by a procession of townsmen. In turning the corner of the street at which we stood, a dark Mestitzo, with a scowl of fanaticism on his face, said to Mr. Catherwood, " Take off your spectacles and follow the cross." Next followed a procession of women with children in their arms, half of them asleep, fancifully dressed with silver caps and headdresses, and finally a large statue of the Virgin, in a sitting posture, magnificently attired, with Indian lads on each side, as before, supporting poles with candles. The whole was accompanied with the music of drums and violins ; and, as the long train of light passed down the street, we returned to the convent.

The night was very cold, and the next morning was like one in December at home. It was the morning of Good Friday ; and throughout Guatimala, in every village, preparations were making to celebrate, with the most solemn ceremonies of the Church, the resurrection of the Saviour. In Quezaltenango, at that early hour, the plaza was thronged with Indians from the country around ; but the whites, terrified and grieving at the murder of their best men, avoided, to a great extent, taking part in the celebration.

At nine o'clock the corregidor called for us, and we accompanied him to the opening ceremony. On one side of the nave of the church, near the grand altar, and opposite the pulpit, were high cushioned chairs for the corregidor and members of the municipality, and we had seats with them. The church was thronged with Indians, estimated at more than three thousand. Formerly, at this ceremony no women or children were admitted ; but now the floor of the church was filled with Indian women on their knees, with red cords

plaited in their hair, and perhaps one third of them had
children on their backs, their heads and arms only visible.   Except ourselves and the padre, there were no
white people in the church; and, with all eyes turned
upon us, and a lively recollection of the fate of those
who but a few days before had occupied our seats, we
felt that the post of honour was a private station.

At the steps of the grand altar stood a large cross,
apparently of solid silver, richly carved and ornamented, and over it a high arbour of pine and cypress
branches.   At the foot of the cross stood a figure of
Mary Magdalen weeping, with her hair in a profusion
of ringlets, her frock low in the neck, and altogether
rather immodest.   On the right was the figure of the
Virgin gorgeously dressed, and in the nave of the
church stood John the Baptist, placed there, as it
seemed, only because they had the figure on hand.
Very soon strains of wild Indian music rose from the
other end of the church, and a procession advanced,
headed by Indians with broad-brimmed felt hats, dark
cloaks, and lighted wax candles, preceding the body
of the Saviour on a bier borne by the cura and attendant padres, and followed by Indians with long wax candles.   The bier advanced to the foot of the cross; ladders were placed behind against it; the gobernador,
with his long black cloak and broad-brimmed felt hat,
mounted on the right, and leaned over, holding in his
hands a silver hammer and a long silver spike; another Indian dignitary mounted on the other side, while
the priests raised the figure up in front; the face was
ghastly, blood trickled down the cheeks, the arms and
legs were moveable, and in the side was a gaping
wound, with a stream of blood oozing from it.   The
back was affixed to the cross, the arms extended, spikes

driven through the hands and feet, the ladders taken away, and thus the figure of Christ was nailed to the cross.

This over, we left the church, and passed two or three hours in visiting. The white population was small, but equal in character to any in the republic ; and there was hardly a respectable family that was not afflicted by the outrage of Carrera. We knew nothing of the effect of this enormity until we entered domestic circles. The distress of women whose nearest connexions had been murdered or obliged to fly for their lives, and then wandering they knew not where, those only can realize who can appreciate woman's affection.

I was urged to visit the widow of Molina. Her husband was but thirty-five, and his death under any circumstances would have been lamented, even by political enemies. I felt a painful interest in one who had lived through such a scene, but at the door of her house I stopped. I felt that a visit from a stranger must be an intrusion upon her sorrows.

In the afternoon we were again seated with the municipality in the church, to behold the descent from the cross. The spacious building was thronged to suffocation, and the floor was covered by a dense mass of kneeling women, with turbaned headdresses, and crying children on their backs, their imaginations excited by gazing at the bleeding figure on the cross ; but among them all I did not see a single interesting face. A priest ascended the pulpit, thin and ghastly pale, who, in a voice that rang through every part of the building, preached emphatically a passion sermon. Few of the Indians understood even the language, and at times the cries of children made his words inaudible ; but the thrilling tones of his voice played upon every chord in their hearts; and mothers, regardless of their infants' cries, sat motionless, their countenances fixed in high and stern enthusiasm. It was the same church, and we could imagine them to be the same women who, in a phrensy and fury of fanaticism, had dragged the unhappy vice-president by the hair, and murdered him with their hands. Every moment the excitement grew stronger. The priest tore off his black cap, and leaning over the pulpit, stretched forward both his arms, and poured out a frantic apostrophe to the bleeding figure on the cross. A dreadful groan, almost curdling the blood, ran through the church. At this moment, at a signal from the cura, the Indians sprang upon the arbour of pine branches, tore it asunder, and with a noise like the crackling of a great conflagration, struggling and scuffling around the altar, broke into bits the consecrated branches to save as holy relics. Two Indians in broad-brimmed hats mounted the ladders on each side of the cross, and with embroidered cloth over their hands, and large silver pincers, drew out the spikes from the hands. The feelings of the women burst forth in tears, sobs, groans, and shrieks of lamentation, so loud and deep, that, coming upon us unexpectedly, our feelings were disturbed, and even with sane men the empire of reason tottered. Such screams of anguish I never heard called out by mortal suffering; and as the body, smeared with blood, was held aloft under the pulpit, while the priest leaned down and apostrophized it with frantic fervour, and the mass of women, wild with excitement, heaved to and fro like the surges of a troubled sea, the whole scene was so thrilling, so dreadfully mournful, that, without knowing why, tears started from our eyes. Four years before, at Jerusalem, on Mount Calvary itself, and in presence of the scoffing Mussul-

man, I had beheld the same representation of the descent from the cross; but the enthusiasm of Greek pil-
grims in the Church of the Holy Sepulchre was nothing
compared with this whirlwind of fanaticism and phrensy. By degrees the excitement died away; the cracking of the pine branches ceased, the whole arbour was
broken up and distributed, and very soon commenced
preparations for the grand procession.

We went out with the corregidor and officers of the
municipality, and took our place in the balcony of the
cabildo. The procession opened upon us in a manner
so extraordinary, that, screening myself from observation below, I endeavoured to make a note of it on the
spot. The leader was a man on horseback, called the
centurion, wearing a helmet and cuirass of pasteboard
covered with silver leaf, a black crape mask, black velvet shorts and white stockings, a red sash, and blue and
red ribands on his arms, a silver-hilted sword, and a
lance, with which, from time to time turning round, he
beckoned and waved the procession on. Then came a
led horse, having on its back an old Mexican saddle
richly plated with silver. Then two men wearing long
blue gowns, with round hoods covering their heads, and
having only holes for the eyes, leading two mules
abreast, covered with black cloth dresses enveloping
their whole bodies to their feet, the long trains of which
were supported by men attired like the other two.
Then followed the large silver cross of the crucifixion,
with a richly-ornamented silver pedestal, and ornaments
dangling from each arm of the cross that looked like
lanterns, supported by four men in long black dresses.
Next came a procession of Indians, two abreast, wearing
long black cloaks, with black felt hats, the brims six or
eight inches wide, all with lighted candles in their

hands, and then four Indians in the same costume, but
with crowns of thorns on their heads, dragging a long
low carriage or bier filled with pine-leaves, and having
a naked scull laid on the top at one end.

Next, and in striking contrast with this emblem of
mortality, advanced an angel in the attitude of an opera-
dancer, borne on the shoulders of six men, dressed in
flounced purple satin, with lace at the bottom, gauze
wings, and a cloud of gauze over her head, holding in
her right hand a pair of silver pincers, and in her left a
small wooden cross, and having a train of white muslin
ten yards long, supported by a pretty little girl fancifully dressed.   Then another procession of Indians with
lighted candles; then a group of devils in horrible mas-
querade.   Then another angel, still more like an opera-
dancer, dressed in azure blue satin, with rich lace wings,
and clouds, and fluttering ribands, holding in her right
hand a ladder, and in her left a silver hammer; her
train supported as before; and we could not help seeing that she wore black velvet smallclothes.   Then another angel, dressed in yellow, holding in her right hand
a small wooden cross, and in the other I could not tell
what.

The next in order was a beautiful little girl about ten
years old, armed cap-a-pie, with breastplate and helmet
of silver, also called the centurion, who moved along in
a slow and graceful dance, keeping time to the music,
turning round, stopping, resting on her sword, and waving on a party worthy of such a chief, being twelve
beautiful children fancifully dressed, intended to represent the twelve apostles; one of them carrying in his
arms a silver cock, to signify that he was the representative of St. Peter.   The next was the great object of
veneration, the figure of the Christ crucified, on a bier,

in a full length case of plate glass, strewed with roses inside and out, and protected by a mourning canopy of black cloth, supported by men in long black gowns, with hoods covering all but the eyes. This was followed by the cura and priests in their richest robes and bareheaded, the muffled drum, and soldiers with arms reversed; the Virgin Mary, in a long black mourning dress, closed the procession. It passed on to make the tour of the city; twice we intercepted it, and then went to the Church of El Calvario. It stands on an elevation at the extreme end of a long street, and the steps were already crowded with women dressed in white from the head to the feet, with barely an oval opening for the face. It was dark when the procession made its appearance at the foot of the street, but by the blaze of innumerable lighted candles every object was exhibited with more striking wildness, and fanaticism seemed written in letters of fire on the faces of the Indians. The centurion cleared a way up the steps; the procession, with a loud chant, entered the church, and we went away.

In the evening we made several visits, and late at night we were called to a conference by some friends of the cura, and on his behalf. His troubles were not yet over. On the day of our arrival he had received a peremptory order from the provesor to repair to Guatimala, with notice that "some proper person" would be appointed in his place. We knew that the terms of the order afflicted the cura, for they implied that he was not a proper person. All Quezaltenango, he said, could answer for his acts, and he could answer to God that his motives were only to prevent the effusion of blood. His house was all in confusion; he was packing up his books and furniture, and preparing to obey the provesor's order. But his friends considered that it was dangerous for him to go to Guatimala. At that place, they said, he would be under the eyes of Carrera, who, meeting him in an angry moment, might cut him down in the street. If he did not go, the provesor would send soldiers after him, such was the rigour of church discipline. They wished him to fly the country, to go with us into Mexico ; but he could not leave without a passport from Guatimala, and this would be refused. The reason of their unburdening themselves to us showed the helplessness of his condition. They supposed that I might have influence with the provesor, and begged me to write to Guatimala, and state the facts as they were known to all Quezaltenango. I had determined to take no part in the public or personal affairs of this unhappy revolution, but here I would not have hesitated to incur any trouble or risk to serve the cura could it have done him any good ; but I knew the sensitiveness of the men in power, and believed that the provesor and the government would resent my interference. I proposed, however, to write to a friend who I knew stood well with the provesor, and request him to call upon that dignitary and state the facts as from me ; and I suggested that he should send some friend to Guatimala expressly to see the provesor in person. Returned to a land of government and laws, I can hardly realize that so short a time since I was called in to counsel for the safety of a man of the cura's character and station. Relatively, the most respectable clergyman in our country does not stand higher than he did.

The next morning we were invited to breakfast with another friend and counsellor, and about as strange a one as myself, being the old lady who had sent the cura one hundred dollars, before mentioned. The plan was discussed and settled, and in the course of the day two friends undertook to visit Guatimala on the cura's behalf. We intended that day to ascend the Volcano of Quezaltenango, but were disappointed in our guide. In the morning we made purchases and provisions for continuing our journey, and as one of our mules' backs was badly galled, we requested the gobernador to procure us Indian carriers.

In the afternoon, in company with the corregidor, we rode to the warm springs of Almolonga. The road crosses a spur of the volcano, and descends precipitously into a deep valley, in which, about a league distant, stand the village and hot springs. There is a good bathing-house, at which we were not allowed to pay, being considered the guests of the city. Outside, in a beautiful natural reservoir, Indian men, women, and children were bathing together.

We returned by another road, passing up a valley of extraordinary beauty, and the theme of conversation was the happiness the country might enjoy but for wars and revolutions. Beautiful as it was, all wished to leave it, and seek a land where life was safe—*Mexico* or El Norte. Toward evening, descending the spur of the volcano, we met several hundred Indians returning from the ceremonies of the Holy Week, and exceeding in drunkenness all the specimens we had yet encountered. In one place a man and woman, the latter with a child on her back, were staggering so near the brink of a precipice, that the corregidor dismounted and took the child from them, and made them go before us into the town.

There was no place we had visited, except ruined cities, so unique and interesting, and which deserved to be so thoroughly explored, as Quezaltenango. A month, at least, might be satisfactorily and profitably employed in examining the many curious objects in the country around. For botanical researches it is the richest region in Central America. But we had no time even for rest.

I passed the evening in writing, packing things to be sent to Guatimala, among others my quezal, which, however, never arrived, and in writing letters, one of which was on account of the cura, and in which, intending, even if it fell into wrong hands, to be out of the country myself, I spoke in no measured terms of the atrocity committed by Carrera.

CHAPTER XIII.

EARLY in the morning our mules were saddled for
the journey.   The gobernador and another friend of the
cura came to receive parting instructions, and set off for
Guatimala.   The Indians engaged for us did not make
their appearance ; and, desirous to save the day, we
loaded the mules, and sent Juan and Bobon forward
with the luggage.   In a little while two women came
and told us that our Indians were in prison.   I accompanied them to two or three officials, and with much
difficulty and loss of time found the man having charge
of them, who said that, finding we had paid them part
of their hire in advance, and afraid they would buy
agua ardiente and be missing, he had shut them up the
night before to have them ready, and had left word to
that effect with one of the servants of the cura.   I went
with him to the prison, paid a shilling apiece for their
lodging, and took them over to the convent.   The poor
fellows had not eaten since they were shut up, and, as
usual, wanted to go home for tortillas for the journey.
We refused to let them go, but gave them money to
buy some in the plaza, and kept the woman and their
chamars as hostages for their return.   But we became
tired of waiting.   Mr. Catherwood picked up their chamars and threw them across his saddle as a guarantee
for their following, and we set off.

We had added to our equipments aguas de arma, being undressed goatskins embroidered with red leather,
which hung down from the saddlebow, to protect the
legs against rain, and were now fully accoutred in
Central American style.

It was cold and wintry. We ascended and crossed
a high plain, and at the distance of a league descended
to a village, where we learned that Juan and Bobon
had passed on some time before. Beyond this we ascended a high and rugged mountain, and on the top
reached a magnificent plain. We rode at a brisk pace,
and it was one o'clock before our jailbirds overtook us.
By this time we were surprised at not overtaking our
men with the luggage. We could not have passed
them, for there was but one road. Since leaving the
village we had not seen a single person, and at two
o'clock we met a man with a loaded mule coming from
Aguas Calientes, the end of our day's journey, who
had not met them. Mr. Catherwood became alarmed,
fearing that they had robbed us and run away. I was
always careless with luggage, but never lost any, and
was slow in coming to this belief. In half an hour we
met another man, who told us that he had not seen
them, and that there was no other road than the one by
which he came. Since our apprehensions began, we
had not been able to discover any tracks, but went on
to within two leagues of our halting-place, when we
stopped, and held one of the most anxious consultations
that occurred in our whole journey. We knew but little of the men. Juan cheated us every day in the little purchases for the road, and we had detected him in
the atrocity of keeping back part of the money we gave
him to buy corn and sacate, and starving the mules.
After a most unhappy deliberation, we concluded that

they had broken open the trunks, taken out the money, thrown the rest of the contents down some ravine, mounted the mules, and made off. Besides money, beds, and bedding, these trunks contained all Mr. Catherwood's drawings, and the precious notebooks to which the reader is indebted for these pages. The fruits of all our labour were gone. In all our difficulties and perplexities we never had a more trying moment. We were two leagues from Aguas Calientes. To go on, rouse the village, get fresh horses, and return in pursuit, was our first idea ; but this would widen the distance between us, and probably we should not be able to get horses.

With hearts so heavy that nothing but the feeble hope of catching them while dividing the money kept us from sinking, we turned back. It was four o'clock in the afternoon ; neither our mules nor we had eaten anything since early in the morning. Night would be upon us, and it was doubtful whether our mules would hold out. Our prisoners told us we had been very imprudent to let the men set out alone, and took it for granted that they had not let slip the opportunity of robbing us. As we rode back, both Mr. C. and I brooded over an apprehension which for some time neither mentioned to the other. It was the letter I had written on behalf of the cura. We should again be within reach of Carrera. If the letter by accident fell into his hands, he would be indignant at what he considered my ingratitude, and he could very easily take his revenge. Our plans, however, were made up at once. We determined, at all events, not to go back to Guatimala, nor, broken as we were in fortune and spirit, to give up Palenque, but, if possible, to borrow money for the road, even if we set out on foot; but, o GLORIA ETERNAL, as the official bulletin said of Carrera's victory, on reaching the top of a mountain we saw the men climbing up a deep ravine on the other side. We did not tell them our agony, but had not gone far before the Indians told all; and they were not surprised or hurt. How we passed them neither of us knew; but another such a spasm would have put a period to our journey of life; and from that time, however tedious, or whatever might be the inducements, we resolved to keep by our luggage. At dusk we reached the top of a high mountain, and by one of those long, steep, and difficult descents of which it is impossible to give the reader any idea, entered the village of Agua Calientes.

It was occupied entirely by Indians, who gathered round us in the plaza, and by the light of pine sticks looked at Carrera's passport. Not one of them could read it, but it was enough to pronounce the name, and the whole village was put in requisition to provide us with something to eat. The alcalde distributed the money we gave him, and one brought sixpence worth of eggs, another of beans, another of tortillas, another of lard, another of candles, and a dozen or more received sixpence apiece for sacate; not one of them would bring anything until he had the money in hand. A fire was kindled in the square, and in process of time we had supper. Our usual supper of fried eggs, beans, tortillas, and chocolate, any one of them enough to disturb digestion in a state of repose, with the excitement and vexation of our supposed loss, made me ill. The cabildo was a wretched shed, full of fleas, with a coat of dust an inch thick to soften the hard earthen floor. It was too cold to sleep out of doors, and there were no pins to hang hammocks on, for in this region hammocks were not used at all. We made inquiries with the view

of hiring for the night the bedsteads of the principal inhabitants, but there was not one in the village; all
slept on the bosom of mother earth, and we had part
of the family bed.   Fortunately, however, and most important for us, our mules fared well.

Early in the morning we resumed our journey.
There are warm springs in this neighbourhood, but we
did not go out of our way to visit them.   A short distance from the village we crossed a river and commenced ascending a mountain.   On the top we came upon
a narrow table of land, with a magnificent forest on
both sides far below us.   The wind swept over the lofty
height, so that with our ponchas, which were necessary
on account of the cold, it was difficult to keep the saddle.   The road was broken and stony, and the track
scarcely perceptible.   At about ten o'clock the whole
surface of the mountain was a bare ridge of limestone,
from which the sun was reflected with scorching heat,
and the whiteness was dazzling and painful to the eyes.
Below us, on each side, continued an immense forest
of gigantic pines.   The road was perfectly desolate;
we met no travellers.   In four hours we saw on our
left, at a great distance below, a single hacienda, with
a clearing around it, seemingly selected for a magnificent seclusion from the convulsions of a distracted
country.   The ridge was broken by gullies and deep
ravines; and we came to one across which, by way of
bridge, lay the trunks of two gigantic pines.   My macho
always pulled back when I attempted to lead him, and
I remained on his back, and was carried steadily over;
but at the other end we started at a noise behind us.
Our best cargo-mule had fallen, rolled over, and hung
on the brink of the precipice, with her feet kicking in
the air, kept from falling to the bottom only by being

entangled among bushes. In a moment we scrambled
down to her, got her head turned up the bank, and by
means of strong halters heaved her out; but she was
bruised and crippled, and barely able to stagger under
her load. Continuing along the ridge, swept by fierce
blasts of wind, we descended again to a river, rode some
distance along its bank, and passed a track up the side
of a mountain on the right, so steep that I had no idea
it could be our road, and passed it, but was called back.
It was the steepest ascent we had yet had in the country. It was cruel to push my brave macho, but I had
been tormented all day with a violent headache, and
could not walk; so I beat up, making the best tacks I
could, and stopping every time I put about. On the
top broke upon us one of those grand and magnificent
views which, when we had wiped off perspiration and
recovered breath, always indemnified us for our toil. It
was the highest ground on which we had yet stood.
Around us was a sea of mountains, and peeping above
them, but so little as to give full effect to our own great
height, were the conical tops of two new volcanoes.
The surface was of limestone rock, in immense strata,
with quartz, in one piece of which we discovered a
speck of gold. Here again, in this vast wilderness of
mountains, deep in the bowels of the earth, are those
repositories of the precious ores for which millions upon
millions all over the world are toiling, bargaining, craving, and cheating every day.

Continuing on this ridge, we came out upon a spur
commanding a view, far below us, of a cultivated valley, and the village of San Sebastiano. We descended to the valley, left the village on our right, crossed
the spur, and saw the end of our day's journey, the town
of Gueguetenango, situated on an extensive plain, with

a mild climate, luxuriant with tropical productions, surrounded by immense mountains, and before us the great
Sierra Madre, the natural bulwark of Central America,
the grandeur and magnificence of the view disturbed
only by the distressing reflection that we had to cross
it. My macho, brought up on the plains of Costa Rica,
had long seemed puzzled to know what mountains were
made for; if he could have spoken, he would have cried
out in anguish,

"Hills peep o'er hills, and Alps on Alps arise."

Our day's journey was but twenty-seven miles, but it
was harder for man and beast than any sixty since we
left Guatimala. We rode into the town, the chief place
of the last district of Central America and of the ancient kingdom of Quiché. It was well built, with a
large church or plaza, and again a crowd of Mestitzoes
were engaged in the favourite occupation of fighting
cocks. As we rode through the plaza the bell sounded
for the oracion or vesper prayers. The people fell on
their knees and we took off our hats. We stopped at
the house of Don Joaquim Monte, an old Spaniard of
high consideration, by whom we were hospitably received, and who, though a Centralist, on account of
some affair of his sons, had had his house at Chiantla
plundered by Carrera's soldiers. His daughters were
compelled to take refuge in the church, and forty or
fifty mules were driven from his hacienda. In a short
time we had a visit from the corregidor, who had seen
our proposed journey announced in the government
paper, and treated us with the consideration due to persons specially recommended by the government.

We reached Gueguetenango in a shattered condition.
Our cargo-mules had their backs so galled that it was

distressing to use them; and the saddle-horse was no
better off.   Bobon, in walking barefooted over the stony
road, had bruised the ball of one of his feet so that he
was disabled, and that night Juan's enormous supper
gave him an indigestion.   He was a tremendous feed-
er ; on the road nothing eatable was safe.   We owed
him a spite for pilfering our bread and bringing us
down to tortillas, and were not sorry to see him on
his back; but he rolled over the floor of the corridor,
crying out uproariously, so as to disturb the whole
household, " Voy morir !" " voy morir !" " I am going
to die !" " I am going to die !"   He was a hard subject to work upon, but we took him in hand strongly,
and unloaded him.

Besides our immediate difficulties, we heard of others in prospect.   In consequence of the throng of emigrants from Guatimala toward Mexico, no one was admitted into that territory without a passport from Ciudad Real, the capital of Chiapas, four or five days'
journey from the frontier.   The frontier was a long
line of river in the midst of a wilderness, and there
were two roads, a lower one but little travelled, on account of the difficulty of crossing the rivers, but at that
time passable.   As we intended, however, at all events,
to stop at this place for the purpose of visiting the ruins,
we postponed our decision till the next day.

The next morning Don Joaquim told us of the skeleton of a colossal animal, supposed to be a mastodon,
which had been found in the neighbourhood.   Some of
the bones had been collected, and were then in the
town, and having seen them, we took a guide and
walked to the place where they had been discovered,
on the borders of the Rio Chinaca, about half a mile
distant.   At this time the river was low, but the year

before, swelled by the immense floods of the rainy season, it had burst its bounds, carried away its left bank,
and laid bare one side of the skeleton. The bank was
perpendicular, about thirty feet high, and the animal had
been buried in an upright position. Besides the bones
in the town, some had been carried away by the flood,
others remained imbedded in the earth; but the impression of the whole animal, from twenty-five to thirty feet
long, was distinctly visible. We were told that about
eight leagues above, on the bank of the same river, the
skeleton of a much larger animal had been discovered.

In the afternoon we rode to the ruins, which in the
town were called *las cuevas*, the caves. They lie about
half a league distant, on a magnificent plain, bounded
in the distance by lofty mountains, among which is the
great Sierra Madre.

The site of the ancient city, as at Patinamit and
Santa Cruz del Quiché, was chosen for its security
against enemies. It was surrounded by a ravine, and
the general character of the ruins is the same as at Quiché, but the hand of destruction has fallen upon it more
heavily. The whole is a confused heap of grass-grown
fragments. The principal remains are two pyramidal
structures of this form:

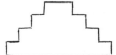

One of them measures at the base one hundred and two
feet; the steps are four feet high and seven feet deep,
making the whole height twenty-eight feet. They are
not of cut stone as at Copan, but of rough pieces cemented with lime, and the whole exterior was formerly
coated with stucco and painted. On the top is a small
square platform, and at the base lies a long slab of rough

stone, apparently hurled down from the top; perhaps the altar on which human victims were extended for sacrifice.

The owner of the ground, a Mestitzo, whose house was near by, and who accompanied us to the ruins, told us that he had bought the land from Indians, and that, for some time after his purchase, he was annoyed by their periodical visits to celebrate some of their ancient rites on the top of this structure. This annoyance continued until he whipped two or three of the principal men and drove them away.

At the foot of the structure was a vault, faced with cut stone, in which were found a collection of bones and a terra cotta vase, then in his possession. The vault was not long enough for the body of a man extended, and the bones must have been separated before they were placed there.

The owner believed that these structures contained interior apartments with hidden treasures; and there were several mounds, supposed to be sepulchres of the ancient inhabitants, which also, he had no doubt, contained treasure. The situation of the place was magnificent. We had never before enjoyed so good an opportunity of working, and agreed with him to come the next day and make excavations, promising to give him all the treasure, and taking for my share only the sculls, vases, and other curiosities.

The next morning, before we were up, the door was thrown open, and to our surprise we received a salutation in English. The costume of the stranger was of the country; his beard was long, and he looked as if already he had made a hard morning's ride. To my great surprise and pleasure I recognised Pawling, whom the reader will perhaps remember I had seen as

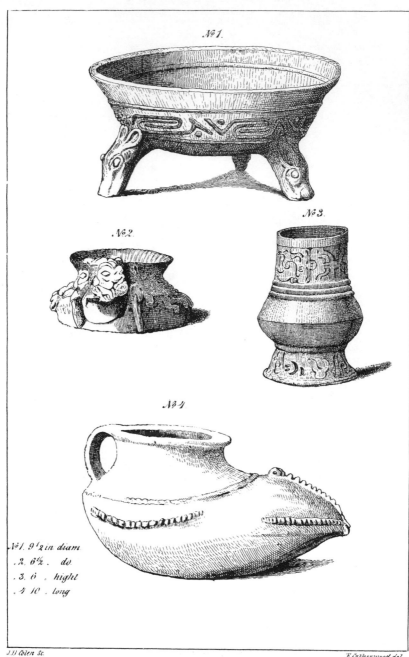

№ 1.

№ 2.

№ 3.

№ 4.

№1. 9½ in diam
.2. 6½ . do.
.3. 6 . hight
.4 10 . long

J.H. Colen Sc.   F. Catherwood del.

VASES FOUND AT GUEGUETENANGO

superintendent of a cochineal hacienda at Amatitan. He had heard of our setting out for Mexico, and, disgusted with his occupation and the country, had mounted his horse, and with all he was worth tied on behind his saddle, pushed on to overtake us. On the way he had bought a fine mule, and by hard riding, and changing from one animal to the other, had reached us in four days. He was in difficulty about a passport, and was anxious to have the benefit of mine in order to get out of the country, offering to attach himself to me in any capacity necessary for that purpose. Fortunately, my passport was broad enough to cover him, and I immediately constituted him the general manager of the expedition, the material of which was now reduced to Juan sick and but one cargo-mule sound.

At nine o'clock, attended by three men and a boy with machetes, being all we could procure at so short a notice, we were again among the ruins. We were not strong enough to pull down a pyramid, and lost the morning in endeavouring to make a breach in one of the sides, but did not accomplish anything.

In the afternoon we opened one of the mounds. The interior was a rough coat of stones and lime, and after an hour's digging we came to fragments of bones and the two lower vases in the plate opposite. The first of the two was entire when we discovered it, but, unfortunately, was broken in getting it out, though we obtained all the pieces. It is graceful in design, the surface is polished, and the workmanship very good. The last was already broken, and though more complicated, the surface is not polished. The tripod at the top of the engraving is a copy of the vase before referred to, found in the tomb, which I procured from the owner of the land. It is twelve inches in diameter, and the surface is polished. We discovered no treasure, but our day's work was most interesting, and we only regretted that we had not time to explore more thoroughly.

In the mean time Don Joaquim had made arrangements for us, and the next morning we resumed our journey. We left behind a mule, a horse, and Bobon, and were re-enforced by Pawling, well mounted, and armed with a pair of pistols, and a short double-barrelled gun slung to his saddle-bow, and Santiago, a Mexican fugitive soldier. Juan was an interesting invalid mounted on a mule, and the whole was under escort of a respectable old muleteer, who was setting out with empty mules to bring back a load of sugar.

At a short distance from the village we commenced ascending the Sierra Madre. The first range was stony, and on the top of it we came upon a cultivated plain, beyond which rose a second range, covered with a thick forest of oak. On the top of this range stood a cross. The spot was called Buena Vista, or Fine View, and commanded a magnificent expanse of mountains and plains, five lakes and two volcanoes, one of which, called Tajamulco, our guide said was a water volcano. Beyond this rose a third range. At some distance up was an Indian rancho, at which a fine little boy thrust his face through a bush fence, and said " adios" to every one that passed. Beyond was another boy, to whom we all in succession said " adios," but the surly little fellow would not answer one of us. On the summit of this range we were almost on a level with the tops of the volcanoes. As we ascended the temperature grew colder, and we were compelled to put on our ponchas. At half past two we reached the top of the Sierra Madre, the dividing line of the waters, being twelve miles from Gueguetenango, and in our devious course making the second time that we had crossed the sierra. The ridge of the mountain was a long level table about half a mile wide, with rugged sides rising on the right to a terrific peak. Riding about half an hour on this table, by the side of a stream of clear and cold water, which passed on, carrying its tribute to the *Pacific Ocean*, we reached a miserable rancho, in front of which the arriero proposed to encamp, as he said it would be impossible to reach the next village. At a distance it was a glorious idea, that of sleeping on the top of the Sierra Madre, and the scene was wild enough for the most romantic imagination; but, being poorly provided against cold, we would have gladly exchanged it for an Indian village.

The occupants of the hut were a man and woman, who lived there rent free. Like the eagle, they had fixed their habitation where they were not likely to be disturbed. While the men were unloading, Juan, as an invalid, asked permission to stretch his huge body before the fire, but the woman told him there was more room out of doors. I succeeded, however, in securing him a place inside. We had an hour to wander over the top of the sierra. It belonged to our friend Don Joaquim Monte, and was what would be called at home a pretty substantial piece of fast property. At every step there was some new opening, which presented a new view of the grand and magnificent in nature. In many places, between cliffs and under certain exposures, were fine pieces of ground, and about half a mile distant a potrero or pasture-ground for brood mares, which we visited to buy some corn for our mules. A vicious jack reigned lord of the sierra.

Adjoining the occupied hut was another about ten feet square, made of small upright poles, thatched with branches of cypress, and open on all sides to the wind.

We collected a quantity of wood, made a fire in the
centre, had supper, and passed a social evening.   The
muleteers had a large fire outside, and with their pack-
saddles and cargoes built a breastwork to shelter themselves against the wind.   Fancy called up a picture of
far-distant scenes : a small circle of friends, perhaps at
that moment thinking of us.   Perhaps, to tell the truth,
we wished to be with them ; and, above all, as we looked to our sleeping-places, thought of the comforts of
home.   Nevertheless, we soon fell asleep.   Toward
morning, however, we were reminded of our elevated
region.   The ground was covered with a hoar-frost,
and water was frozen a quarter of an inch thick.   Our
guide said that this happened regularly every night
in the year when the atmosphere was clear.   It was
the first ice we had seen in the country.   The men
were shivering around a large fire, and, as soon as they
could see, went out to look for the mules.   One of
them had strayed ; and while the men were looking for
her, we had breakfast, and did not get off till a quarter
before eight.   Our road traversed the ridge of the sierra, which for two leagues was a level table, a great part
composed of immense beds of red slate and blue limestone or chalk rock, lying in vertical strata.   At ten
o'clock we began to descend, the cold being still severe.
The descent surpassed in grandeur and magnificence
all that we had yet encountered.   It was by a broad
passage with perpendicular mountain-walls, rising in
rugged and terrific peaks, higher and higher as we descended, out of which gigantic cypress-trees were growing, their trunks and all their branches dead.   Before
us, between these immense walls, was a vista reaching
beyond the village of San Andres, twenty-four miles
distant.   A stream of water was dashing down over

rocks and stones, hurrying on to the Atlantic; we crossed it perhaps fifty times on bridges wild and rude as
the stream itself and the mountains between which it
rolled.   As we descended the temperature became
milder.   At twelve o'clock the immense ravine opened
into a rich valley a mile in width, and in half an hour
we reached the village of Todos Santos.   On the right,
far below us, was a magnificent table cultivated with
corn, and bounded by the side of the great sierra ; and
in the suburbs of the village were apple and peach trees
covered with blossoms and young fruit.   We had again
reached the tierras templadas, and in Europe or North
America the beauty of this miserable unknown village
would be a theme for poetry.

As we rode through it, at the head of the street we
were stopped by a drunken Indian, supported by two
men hardly able to stand themselves, who, we thought,
were taking him to prison; but, staggering before us,
they blocked up the passage, and shouted "Passeporte!"
Pawling, in anticipation, and to assume his new character, had tied his jacket around his waist by the sleeves,
and was dragging one of the mules by its halter.   Not
one of the three could read the passport, and they sent
for the secretary, a bare-headed Indian, habited in nothing but a ragged cotton shirt, who examined it very
carefully, and read aloud the name of Rafael Carrera,
which, I think, was all that he attempted to make out.
We were neither sentimental, nor philosophical, nor
moralizing travellers, but it gave us pangs to think that
such a magnificent country was in the possession of
such men.

Passing the church and convent, we ascended a ridge,
then descended an immense ravine, crossed another
magnificent valley, and at length reached the Indian

village of San Martin, which, with loveliness and grandeur all around us, might have been selected for its surpassing beauty of position.   We rode to the cabildo,
and then to the hut of the alcalde.   The people were
all Indians ; the secretary was a bare-legged boy, who
spelled out every word in the passport except our names;
but his reading sufficed to procure supper for us and
provender for the mules, and early in the morning we
pushed on again.

For some distance we rode on a lofty ridge, with a
precipitous ravine on each side, in one place so narrow
that, as our arriero told us, when the wind is high
there is danger of being blown off.   We continued descending, and at a quarter past twelve reached San
Andres Petapan, fifteen miles distant, blooming with
oranges, sapotes, and other fruit trees.   Passing through
the village, at a short distance beyond we were stopped
by a fire in the woods.   We turned back, and attempted to pass by another road, but were unable.   Before
we returned the fire had reached the place we left,
and increased so fast that we had apprehensions for
the luggage-mules, and hurried them back with the
men toward the village.   The flames came creeping
and crackling toward us, shooting up and whirled by
currents of wind, and occasionally, when fed with dry
and combustible materials, flashing and darting along
like a train of gunpowder.   We fell back, keeping as
near as we could to the line of fire, the road lying along
the side of a mountain ; while the fire came from the
ravine below, crossing the road, and moving upward.
The clouds of smoke and ashes, the rushing of currents
of wind and flames, the crackling of burning branches,
and trees wrapped in flames, and the rapid progress of
the destroying element, made such a wild and fearful

scene that we could not tear ourselves away. At
length we saw the flames rush up the side of the ravine, intercepting the path before us. We spurred our
horses, shot by, and in a moment the whole was a
sheet of flame. The fire was now spreading so rapidly that we became alarmed, and hurried back to the
church, which, on an elevation strongly defined against
the immense mountain in the background, stood before
us as a place of refuge. By this time the villagers
had become alarmed, and men and women were hurrying to the height to watch the progress of the flames.
The village was in danger of conflagration; it would
be impossible to urge the loaded mules up the hill we
had descended, and we resolved to deposite the luggage
in the church, and save the mules by driving them up
unburdened. It was another of those wild scenes to
which no effect can be given in words. We stopped
on the brow of the hill before the square of the church,
and while we were watching the fire, the black clouds
and sheets of flame rolled up the side of the mountain,
and spared the village. Relieved from apprehension,
we sat down under a tree in front of the church to the
calm enjoyment of the terrific spectacle and a cold fowl.
The cinders and ashes fell around, and the destructive
element rushed on, sparing the village before us, perhaps to lay some other in ruins.

We were obliged to wait two hours. From the foot
of the hill on which the village stood the ground was
hot and covered with a light coat of ashes; the brush
and underwood were burned away; in some places
were lying trees reduced to masses of live coal, and
others were standing with their trunks and branches
all on fire. In one place we passed a square of white
ashes, the remains of some miserable Indian hut. Our

faces and hands were scorched, and our whole bodies
heated when we emerged from the fiery forest.   For
a few moments the open air was delightful; but we
were hardly out of one trouble before we had another.
Swarms of enormous flies, perhaps driven out by the
fire, and hovering on the borders of the burned district, fell upon the mules.   Every bite drew blood, and
the tormentors clung to the suffering animals until brushed off by a stick.   For an hour we laboured hard, but
could not keep their heads and necks free.   The poor
beasts were almost frantic, and, in spite of all we could
do, their necks, the inside of their legs, mouths, ears,
nostrils, and every tender part of their skin, were trick-
ling with blood.   Hurrying on, in three hours we saw
the Church of San Antonio de Guista, and in a few minutes entered the village, beautifully situated on a table-
land projecting from the slope of a mountain, looking upon an immense opening, and commanding on all
sides a magnificent view.   At this time we were beyond
the reach of war, and free from all apprehensions.
With the addition of Pawling's pistols and double-barrelled gun, a faithful muleteer, Santiago, and Juan on
his legs again, we could have stormed an Indian village, and locked up a refractory alcalde in his own cabildo.   We took possession of San Antonio de Guista,
dividing ourselves between the cabildo and the convent,
sent for the alcalde (even on the borders of Central
America the name of Carrera was omnipotent), and
told him to stay there and wait upon us, or send an
alguazil.   The convent stood adjoining the church, on
an open table of land, commanding a view of a magnificent valley surrounded by immense mountains, and on
the left was a vista between two mountain ranges, wild,
rugged, and lofty, losing their tops in clouds.   Before

the door of the convent was a large cross on a high pedestal of stone, with the coating decayed, and covered with wild flowers. The convent was enclosed by a brush fence, without any opening until we made one. The padre was not at home, which was very fortunate for him, as there would not have been room enough for us all. In fact, everything seemed exactly intended for our party; there were three beds, just as many as we could conveniently occupy; and the style of them was new: they were made of long sticks about an inch thick, tied with bark strings at top and bottom, and resting on crotches about two feet high, driven into the dirt floor.

The alcalde and his major had roused the village. In a few moments, instead of the mortifying answer "no hay," there is none, the provision made for us was almost equal to the offers of the Turkish paradise. Twenty or thirty women were in the convent at one time, with baskets of corn, tortillas, dolces, plantains, hocotes, sapotes, and a variety of other fruits, each one's stock in trade being of the value of three cents; and among them was a species of tortillas, thin and baked hard, about twelve inches in diameter, one hundred and twenty for six cents, of which, as they were not expensive, we laid in a large supply.

At this place our muleteer was to leave us. We had but one cargo-mule fit for service, and applied to the alcalde for two carriers to go with us across the frontier to Comitan. He went out, as he said, to consult with the mozos, and told us that they asked six dollars apiece. We spoke to him of our friend Carrera, and on a second consultation the demand was reduced by two thirds. We were obliged to make provision for three days, and even to carry corn for the mules; and Juan and Santiago had a busy night, boiling fowls and eggs.

CHAPTER XIV.

Comfortable Lodgings.—Journey continued.—Stony Road.—Beautiful River.—
Suspension Bridge.—The Dolores.—Rio Lagertero.—Enthusiasm brought
down.—Another Bridge.—Entry into Mexico.—A Bath.—A Solitary Church.
—A Scene of Barrenness.—Zapolouta.—Comitan.—Another Countryman.—
More Perplexities. — Official Courtesy. — Trade of Comitan. — Smuggling. —
Scarcity of Soap.

THE next morning we found the convent was so comfortable, we were so abundantly served, the alcalde or
his major, staff in hand, being in constant attendance,
and the situation so beautiful, that we were in no hurry to go; but the alcalde told us that all was ready.
We did not see our carriers, and found that he and his
major were the mozos whom he had consulted. They
could not let slip two dollars apiece, and laying down
their staves and dignity, bared their backs, placed the
straps across their foreheads, took up the loads, and
trotted off.

We started at five minutes before eight. The weather was fine, but hazy. From the village we descended
a hill to an extensive stony plain, and at about a league's
distance reached the brink of a precipice, from which
we looked down into a rich oblong valley, two or three
thousand feet deep, shut in all around by a mountain
wall, and seeming an immense excavation. Toward
the other end of the valley was a village with a ruined
church, and the road led up a precipitous ascent to a
plain on the same level with that on which we stood,
undulating and boundless as the sea. Below us it
seemed as if we could drop a stone to the bottom. We
descended by one of the steepest and most stony paths
we had yet encountered in the country, crossing and

recrossing in a zigzag course along the side of the height, perhaps making the descent a mile and a half long. Very soon we reached the bank of a beautiful river, running lengthwise through the valley, bordered on each side by immense trees, throwing their branches clear across, and their roots washed by the stream; and while the plain beyond was dry and parched, they were green and luxuriant. Riding along it, we reached a suspension bridge of most primitive appearance and construction, called by the natives La Hammaca, which had existed there from time immemorial. It was made of oziers twisted into cords, about three feet apart, and stretched across the river with a hanging network of vines, the ends fastened to the trunks of two opposite trees. It hung about twenty-five feet above the river, which was here some eighty feet wide, and was supported in different places by vines tied to the branches. The access was by a rude ladder to a platform in the crotch of the tree. In the bottom of the hammaca were two or three poles to walk on. It waved with the wind, and was an unsteady and rather insecure means of transportation. From the centre the vista of the river both ways under the arches of the trees was beautiful, and in every direction the hammaca was a most picturesque-looking object. We continued on to the village, and after a short halt and a smoke with the alcalde, rode on to the extreme end of the valley, and by a steep and stony ascent, at twenty minutes past twelve reached the level ground above. Here we dismounted, slipped the bridles of our mules, and seated ourselves to wait for our Indians, looking down into the deep imbosomed valley, and back at the great range of Cordilleras, crowned by the Sierra Madre, seeming a barrier fit to separate worlds.

Free from all apprehensions, we were now in the full enjoyment of the wild country and wild mode of travelling. But our poor Indians, perhaps, did not enjoy it so much. The usual load was from three to four arrobas, seventy-five to one hundred pounds; ours were not more than fifty; but the sweat rolled in streams down their naked bodies, and every limb trembled. After a short rest they started again. The day was hot and sultry, the ground dry, parched, and stony. We had two sharp descents, and reached the River Dolores. On both sides were large trees, furnishing a beautiful shade, which, after our scorching ride, we found delightful. The river was about three hundred feet broad. In the rainy season it is impassable, but in the dry season not more than three or four feet deep, very clear, and the colour a grayish green, probably from the reflection of the trees. We had had no water since we left the suspension bridge, and both our mules and we were intemperate.

We remained here half an hour; and now apprehensions, which had been operating more or less all the time, made us feel very uncomfortable. We were approaching, and very near, the frontier of Mexico. This road was so little travelled, that, as we were advised, there was no regular guard; but piquets of soldiers were scouring the whole line of frontier to prevent smuggling, who might consider us contraband. Our passports were good for going out of Central America; but to go into Mexico, the passport of the Mexican authorities at Ciudad Real, four days' journey, was necessary. Turning back was not in our vocabulary; perhaps we should be obliged to wait in the wilderness till we could send for one.

In half an hour we reached the Rio Lagertero, the

boundary-line between Guatimala and Mexico, a scene
of wild and surpassing beauty, with banks shaded by
some of the noblest trees of the tropical forests, water
as clear as crystal, and fish a foot long playing in it as
gently as if there were no fish-hooks.   No soldiers were
visible; all was as desolate as if no human being had
ever crossed the boundary before.   We had a moment's consultation on which side to encamp, and determined to make a lodgment in Mexico.   I was riding
Pawling's horse, and spurred him into the water, to be
the first to touch the soil.   With one plunge his fore-
feet were off the bottom, and my legs under water.
For an instant I hesitated; but as the water rose to my
holsters my enthusiasm gave way, and I wheeled back
into Central America.   As we afterward found, the
water was ten or twelve feet deep.

We waited for the Indians, in some doubt whether it
would be possible to cross at all with the luggage.   At a
short distance above was a ledge of rocks, forming rapids, over which there had been a bridge with a wooden
arch and stone abutments, the latter of which were still
standing, the bridge having been carried away by the
rising of the waters seven years before.   It was the last
of the dry season; the rocks were in some places dry,
the body of the river running in channels on each side,
and a log was laid to them from the abutments of the
bridge.   We took off the saddles and bridles of the
mules, and cautiously, with the water breaking rapidly
up to the knees, carried everything across by hand; an
operation in which an hour was consumed.   One night's
rain on the mountains would have made it impassable.
The mules were then swum across, and we were all
landed safely in Mexico.

On the bank opposite the place where I attempted to

cross was a semicircular clearing, from which the only
opening was the path leading into the Mexican provinces.   We closed this up, and turned the mules loose,
hung our traps on the trees, and bivouacked in the centre.   The men built a fire, and while they were preparing supper we went down to the river to bathe.   The
rapids were breaking above us.   The wildness of the
scene, its seclusion and remoteness, the clearness of the
water, the sense of having accomplished an important
part of our journey, all revived our physical and moral
being.   Clean apparel consummated the glory of the
bath.   For several days our digestive organs had been
out of order, but when we sat down to supper they
could have undertaken the bridles of the mules ; and
my brave macho—it was a pleasure to hear him craunch
his corn.   We were out of Central America, safe from
the dangers of revolution, and stood on the wild borders
of Mexico, in good health, with good appetites, and
something to eat.   We had still a tremendous journey
before us, but it seemed nothing.   We strode the little
clearing as proudly as the conquerors of Mexico, and
in our extravagance resolved to have a fish for breakfast.   We had no hooks, and there was not even a pin
in our travelling equipage ; but we had needles and
thread.   Pawling, with the experience of seven years'
" roughing," had expedients, and put a needle in the
fire, which softened its temper, so that he bent it into a
hook.   A pole was on every tree, and we could see the
fish in the water ; all that we wanted was for them to
open their mouths and hook themselves to the needle ;
but this they would not do, and for this reason alone
we did not catch any.   We returned.   Our men cut
some poles, and resting them in the crotch of a tree, covered them with branches.   We spread our mats under,

and our roof and beds were ready.   The men piled logs
of wood on the fire, and our sleep was sound and glorious.

At daylight the next morning we were again in the
water.   Our bath was even better than that of the night
before, and when I mounted I felt able to ride through
Mexico and Texas to my own door at home.   Returned
once more to steamboats and railroads, how flat, tame,
and insipid all their comforts seem.

We started at half past seven.   At a very short distance three wild boars crossed our path, all within gun-
shot ; but our men carried the guns, and in an instant
it was too late.   Very soon we emerged from the woods
that bordered the river, and came out into an open
plain.   At half past eight we crossed a low stony hill
and came to the dry bed of a river.   The bottom was
flat and baked hard, and the sides smooth and regular
as those of a canal.   At the distance of half a league
water appeared, and at half past nine it became a considerable stream.   We again entered a forest, and riding by a narrow path, saw directly before us, closing
the passage, the side of a large church.   We came out,
and saw the whole gigantic building, without a single
habitation, or the vestige of one, in sight.   The path led
across the broken wall of the courtyard.   We dismounted in the deep shade of the front.   The façade
was rich and perfect.   It was sixty feet front and two
hundred and fifty feet deep, but roofless, with trees
growing out of the area above the walls.   Nothing could
exceed the quiet and desolation of the scene ; but there
was something strangely interesting in these roofless
churches, standing in places entirely unknown.   Santiago told us that this was called Conata, and the tradition is, that it was once so rich that the inhabitants car-

ried their water-jars by silken cords. Giving our mules
to Santiago, we entered the open door of the church.
The altar was thrown down, the roof lay in broken
masses on the ground, and the whole area was a forest
of trees. At the foot of the church, and connected with
it, was a convent. There was no roof, but the apartments were entire as when a good padre stood to welcome a traveller. In front of the church, on each side,
was a staircase leading up to a belfry in the centre of
the façade. We ascended to the top. The bells which
had called to matin and vesper prayers were gone ; the
crosspiece was broken from the cross. The stone of
the belfry was solid masses of petrified shells, worms,
leaves, and insects. On one side we looked down into
the roofless area, and on the other over a region of
waste. One man had written his name there :

Joaquim Ruderigos,
Conata, Mayo 1º, 1836.

We wrote our names under his and descended,
mounted, rode over a stony and desolate country,
crossed a river, and saw before us a range of hills, and
beyond a range of mountains. Then we came upon a
bleak stony table, and after riding four hours and a
half, saw the road leading across a barren mountain on
our right, and, afraid we had missed our way, halted
under a low spreading tree to wait for our men. We
turned the mules loose, and after waiting some time,
sent Santiago back to look for them. The wind
was sweeping over the plain, and while Mr. Catherwood was cutting wood, Pawling and I descended
to a ravine to look for water. The bed was entirely
dry, and one took his course up and the other down.
Pawling found a muddy hole in a rock, which, even
to thirsty men, was not tempting. We returned, and

found Mr. Catherwood warming himself by the blaze of
three or four young trees, which he had piled one upon
another. The wind was at this time sweeping furiously over the plain. Night was approaching; we had not
eaten anything since morning; our small stock of provisions was in unsafe hands, and we began to fear that
none would be forthcoming. Our mules were as badly
off. The pasture was so poor that they required a wide
range, and we let all go loose except my poor macho,
which, from certain roving propensities acquired before
he came into my possession, we were obliged to fasten
to a tree. It was some time after dark when Santiago
appeared with the alforgas of provisions on his back.
He had gone back six miles when he found the track
of Juan's foot, one of the squarest ever planted, and
followed it to a wretched hut in the woods, at which
we had expected to stop. We had lost nothing by not
stopping; all they could get to bring away was four
eggs. We supped, piled up our trunks to windward,
spread our mats, lay down, gazed for a few moments
at the stars, and fell asleep. During the night the wind
changed, and we were almost blown away.

The next morning, preparatory to entering once more
upon habitable regions, we made our toilet; i. e., we
hung a looking-glass on the branch of a tree, and shaved
the upper lip and a small part of the chin. At a quarter past seven we started, having eaten up our last fragment. Since we left Guista we had not seen a human
being; the country was still desolate and dreary; there
was not a breath of air; hills, mountains, and plains
were all barren and stony; but, as the sun peeped
above the horizon, its beams gladdened this scene of
barrenness. For two hours we ascended a barren
stony mountain. Even before this the desolate fron-

tier had seemed almost an impregnable barrier; but Alvarado had crossed it to penetrate an unknown country teeming with enemies, and twice a Mexican army has invaded Central America.

At half past ten we reached the top of the mountain, and on a line before us saw the Church of Zapolouta, the first village in Mexico. Here our apprehensions revived from want of a passport. Our great object was to reach Comitan, and there bide the brunt. Approaching the village, we avoided the road that led through the plaza, and leaving the luggage to get along as it could, hurried through the suburbs, startled some women and children, and before our entry was known at the cabildo we were beyond the village. We rode briskly for about a mile, and then stopped to breathe. An immense weight was removed from our minds, and we welcomed each other to Mexico. Coming in from the desolate frontier, it opened upon us like an old, long-settled, civilized, quiet, and well-governed country.

Four hours' ride over an arid and sandy plain brought us to Comitan. Santiago, being a deserter from the Mexican army, afraid of being caught, left us in the suburbs to return alone across the desert we had passed, and we rode into the plaza. In one of the largest houses fronting it lived an American. Part of the front was occupied as a shop, and behind the counter was a man whose face called up the memory of home. I asked him in English if his name was M'Kinney, and he answered " Si, señor." I put several other questions in English, which he answered in Spanish. The sounds were familiar to him, yet it was some time before he could fully comprehend that he was listening to his native tongue; but when he did, and understood that I was a countryman, it awakened feelings to which he had long been a stranger, and he received us as one in whom absence had only strengthened the links that bound him to his country.

Dr. James M'Kinney, whose unpretending name is in Comitan transformed to the imposing one of Don Santiago Maquene, was a native of Westmoreland county, Virginia, and went out to Tobasco to pass a winter for the benefit of his health and the practice of his profession. Circumstances induced him to make a journey into the interior, and he established himself at Ciudad Real. At the time of the cholera in Central America he went to Quezaltenango, where he was employed by the government, and lived two years on intimate terms with the unfortunate General Guzman, whom he described as one of the most gentlemanly, amiable, intelligent, and best men in the country. He afterward returned to Comitan, and married a lady of a once rich and powerful family, but stripped of a portion of its wealth by a revolution only two years before. In the division of what was left, the house on the plaza fell to his share ; and disliking the practice of his profession, he abandoned it, and took to selling goods. Like every other stranger in the country, by reason of constant wars and revolutions he had become nervous. He had none of this feeling when he first arrived, and at the time of the first revolution in Ciudad Real he stood in the plaza looking on, when two men were shot down by his side. Fortunately, he took them into a house to dress their wounds, and during this time the attacking party forced their way into the plaza, and cut down every man in it.

Up to this place we had travelled on the road to Mexico ; here Pawling was to leave us and go on to the capital ; Palenque lay on our right, toward the coast of the Atlantic. The road Dr. M'Kinney described as more

frightful than any we had yet travelled; and there were
other difficulties. War was again in our way; and,
while all the rest of Mexico was quiet, Tobasco and
Yucatan, the two points in our journey, were in a state
of revolution. This might have disturbed us greatly
but for another difficulty. It was necessary to present
ourselves at Ciudad Real, three days' journey directly
out of our road, to procure a passport, without which we
could not travel in any part of the Mexican republic.
And, serious as these things were, they merged in a
third; viz., the government of Mexico had issued a peremptory order to prevent all strangers visiting the ruins
of Palenque. Dr. M'Kinney told us of his own knowledge that three Belgians, sent out on a scientific expedition by the Belgian government, had gone to Ciudad
Real expressly to ask permission to visit them, and had
been refused. These communications damped somewhat the satisfaction of our arrival in Comitan.

By Dr. M'Kinney's advice we presented ourselves
immediately to the commandant, who had a small garrison of about thirty men, well uniformed and equipped,
and, compared with the soldiers of Central America, giving me a high opinion of the Mexican army. I showed
him my passport, and a copy of the government paper
of Guatimala, which fortunately stated that I intended
going to Campeachy to embark for the United States.
With great courtesy he immediately undertook to relieve
us from the necessity of presenting ourselves in person
at Ciudad Real, and offered to send a courier to the
governor for a passport. This was a great point, but
still there would be detention; and by his advice we
called upon the prefeto, who received us with the same
courtesy, regretted the necessity of embarrassing my
movements, showed us a copy of the order of the gov-

ernment, which was imperative, and made no exceptions in favour of Special Confidential Agents. He was really anxious, however, to serve us, said he was willing to incur some responsibility, and would consult with the commandant. We left him with a warm appreciation of the civility and good feeling of the Mexican officials, and satisfied that, whatever might be the result, they were disposed to pay great respect to their neighbours of the North. The next morning the prefeto sent back the passport, with a courteous message that they considered me in the same light as if I had come accredited to their own government, would be happy to render me every facility in their power, and that Mexico was open to me to travel which way I pleased. Thus one great difficulty was removed. I recommend all who wish to travel to get an appointment from Washington.

As to the revolutions, after having gone through the crash of a Central American, we were not to be put back by a Mexican. But the preventive order against visiting the ruins of Palenque was not so easily disposed of. If we made an application for permission, we felt sure of the good disposition of the local authorities ; but if they had no discretion, were bound by imperative orders, and obliged to refuse, it would be uncourteous and improper to make the attempt. At the same time, it was discouraging, in the teeth of Dr. M'Kinney's information, to undertake the journey without. To be obliged to retrace our steps, and make the long journey to the capital to ask permission, would be terrible ; but we learned that the ruins were removed some distance from any habitation ; we did not believe that, in the midst of a formidable revolution, the government had any spare soldiers to station there as a guard. From what we knew of other ruins, we had reason to believe that the place was entirely desolate ; we might be on the ground before any one knew we were in the neighbourhood, and then make terms either to remain or evacuate, as the case might require ; and it was worth the risk if we got one day's quiet possession. With this uncertain prospect we immediately commenced repairing and making preparations for our journey.

The comfort of finding ourselves at this distant place in the house of a countryman can hardly be appreciated. In dress, manner, appearance, habits, and feelings, the doctor was as natural as if we had met him at home. The only difference was his language, which he could not speak connectedly, but interlarded it with Spanish expressions. He moved among the people, but he was not of them ; and the only tie that bound him was a dark-eyed Spanish beauty, one of the few that I saw in that country for whom a man might forget kindred and home. He was anxious to leave the country, but was trammelled by a promise made his mother-in-law not to do so during her life. He lived, however, in such constant anxiety, that he hoped she would release him.

Comitan, the frontier town of Chiapas, contains a population of about ten thousand. It has a superb church, and well-filled convent of Dominican friars. The better classes, as in Central America, have dwelling-houses in the town, and derive their subsistence from the products of their haciendas, which they visit from time to time. It is a place of considerable trade, and has become so by the effect of bad laws ; for, in consequence of the heavy duties on regular importations at the Mexican ports of entry, most of the European goods consumed in this region are smuggled in from Balize and Guatimala. The proceeds of confiscations and the perquisites of officers are such an important item of revenue that the officers are vigilant, and the day before we arrived twenty or thirty mule-loads that had been seized were brought into Comitan; but the profits are so large that smuggling is a regular business, the risk of seizure being considered one of the expenses of carrying it on. The whole community, not excepting the revenue officers, are interested in it, and its effect upon public morals is deplorable. The markets, however, are but poorly supplied, as we found. We sent for a washerwoman, but there was no soap in the town. We wanted our mules shod, but there was only iron enough to shoe one. Buttons for pantaloons, in size, made up for other deficiencies. The want of soap was a deplorable circumstance. For several days we had indulged in the pleasing expectation of having our sheets washed. The reader may perhaps consider us particular, as it was only three weeks since we left Guatimala, but we had slept in wretched cabildoes, and on the ground, and they had become of a very doubtful colour. In time of trouble, however, commend me to the sympathy of a countryman. Don Santiago, alias Doctor M'Kinney, stood by us in our hour of need, provided us with soap, and our sheets were purified.

I have omitted a circumstance which from the time of our arrival in the country we had noticed as extraordinary. The horses and mules are never shod, except perhaps a few pleasure horses used for riding about the streets of Guatimala. On the road, however, we were advised, after we had set out, that it was proper to have ours shod; but there was no good blacksmith except at Quezaltenango, and as we were at that place during a fiesta he would not work. In crossing long ranges of stony mountains, not one of them suffered except Mr. Catherwood's riding mule, and her hoofs were worn down even with the flesh.

Pawling's difficulties were now over.   I procured for him a separate passport, and he had before him a clear road to Mexico; but his interest had been awakened; he was loth to leave us, and after a long consultation and deliberation resolved that he would go with us to Palenque.

CHAPTER XV.

On the first of May, with a bustle and confusion like those of May-day at home, we moved out of Don Santiago's house, mounted, and bade him farewell. Doubtless his daily routines have not since been broken by the visit of a countryman, and communication is so difficult that he never hears from home. He charged us with messages to his friend Doctor Coleman, United States consul at Tobasco, who was then dead; and the reader will perhaps feel for him when I mention that probably a copy of this work, which I intend to send him, will never reach his hands.

I must pass over the next stage of our journey, which was through a region less mountainous, but not less solitary than that we had already traversed. The first afternoon we stopped at the hacienda of Sotaná, belonging to a brother-in-law of Don Santiago, in a soft and lovely valley, with a chapel attached, and bell that at evening called the Indian workmen, women, and children to vesper prayers. The next day, at the abode of Padre Solis, a rich old cura, short and broad, living on a fine hacienda, we dined off solid silver dishes, drank out of silver cups, and washed in a silver basin. He had lived at Palenque, talked of Candones or unbaptized Indians, and wanted to buy my macho, prom-

ising to keep him till he died ; and the only thing that
relieves me from self-reproach in not securing him such
pasture-grounds is the recollection of the padre's weight.

At four o'clock on the third day we reached Ocosingo, likewise in a beautiful situation, surrounded by
mountains, with a large church ; and in the wall of the
yard we noticed two sculptured figures from the ruins
we proposed to visit, somewhat in the same style as those
at Copan.   In the centre of the square was a magnificent
Ceiba tree.   We rode up to the house of Don Manuel
Pasada, the prefet, which, with an old woman-servant,
we had entirely to ourselves, the family being at his
hacienda.   The house was a long enclosure, with a
shed in front, and furnished with bedsteads made of
reeds split into two, and supported on sticks resting in
the ground.

The alcalde was a Mestitzo, very civil, and glad to
see us, and spoke of the neighbouring ruins in the most
extravagant terms, but said they were so completely
buried in El Monte that it would require a party of men
for two or three days to cut a way to them ; and he laid
great stress upon a cave, the mouth of which was completely choked up with stones, and which communicated by a subterraneous passage with the old city of Palenque, about one hundred and fifty miles distant.   He
added that if we would wait a few days to make preparations, he and all the village would go with us, and
make a thorough exploration.   We told him that first
we wished to make preliminary observations, and he
promised us a guide for the next morning.

That night broke upon us the opening storm of the
rainy season.   Peals of crashing thunder reverberated
from the mountains, lightning illuminated with fearful
flashes the darkness of night, rain poured like a deluge

upon our thatched roof, and the worst mountains in the whole road were yet to be crossed. All our efforts to anticipate the rainy season had been fruitless.

In the morning dark clouds still obscured the sky, but they fell back and hid themselves before the beams of the rising sun. The grass and trees, parched by six months' drought, started into a deeper green, and the hills and mountains seemed glad. The alcalde, I believe vexed at our not being willing to make an immediate affair of exploring the ruins, had gone away for the day without sending us any guide, and leaving word that all the men were engaged in repairing the church. We endeavoured to entice one of them away, but unsuccessfully. Returning, we found that our piazza was the schoolhouse of the village. Half a dozen children were sitting on a bench, and the schoolmaster, half tipsy, was educating them, i. e., teaching them to repeat by rote the formal parts of the church service. We asked him to help us, but he advised us to wait a day or two ; in that country nothing could be done violenter. We were excessively vexed at the prospect of losing the day ; and at the moment when we thought we had nothing left but to submit, a little girl came to tell us that a woman, on whose hacienda the ruins were, was then about going to visit it, and offered to escort us. Her horse was already standing before the door, and before our mules were ready she rode over for us. We paid our respects, gave her a good cigar, and, lighting all around, set out. She was a pleasant Mestitzo, and had a son with her, a fine lad about fifteen. We started at half past nine, and, after a hot and sultry ride, at twenty minutes past eleven reached her rancho. It was a mere hut, made of poles and plastered with mud, but the situation was one of those that warmed us to

country life. Our kind guide sent with us her son and
an Indian with his machete, and in half an hour we
were at the ruins.

Soon after leaving the rancho, and at nearly a mile
distant, we saw, on a high elevation, through openings
in trees growing around it, one of the buildings of
Tonila, the Indian name in this region for stone houses. Approaching it, we passed on the plain in front
two stone figures lying on the ground, with the faces
upward; they were well carved, but the characters
were somewhat faded by long exposure to the elements,
although still distinct. Leaving them, we rode on to
the foot of a high structure, probably a fortress, rising in a pyramidal form, with five spacious terraces.
These terraces had all been faced with stone and stuccoed, but in many places they were broken and overgrown with grass and shrubs. Taking advantage of
one of the broken parts, we rode up the first pitch, and,
following the platform of the terrace, ascended by another breach to the second, and in the same way to the
third. There we tied our horses and climbed up on
foot. On the top was a pyramidal structure overgrown
with trees, supporting the building which we had seen
from the plain below. Among the trees were several
wild lemons, loaded with fruit, and of very fine flavour,
which, if not brought there by the Spaniards, must be
indigenous. The building is fifty feet front and thirty-
five feet deep; it is constructed of stone and lime, and
the whole front was once covered with stucco, of which
part of the cornice and mouldings still remain. The
entrance is by a doorway ten feet wide, which leads
into a sort of antechamber, on each side of which is a
small doorway leading into an apartment ten feet
square. The walls of these apartments were once cov-

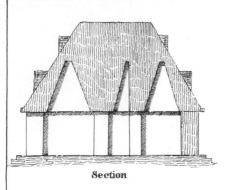

Section

Elevation of the Building with the
Pyramidal Structure on which it stands

Ornament to a large scale over Door marked A on the Plan.

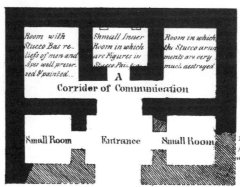

Room with
Stucco Bas re-
liefs of men and
Apes well preser-
ved & painted.

Small Inner
Room in which
are Figures in
Stucco Pain...

Room in which
the Stucco orna-
ments are very
much destroyed

A
Corridor of Communication

Small Room   Entrance   Small Room

The parts tinted Black are
perfect. Those tinted light
are in a ruined State.

PLAN OF ONE OF THE ANCIENT BUILDINGS AT OCOSINGO

Scale of Feet
10   5   0   10   20   30   40   50 Ft

J. H. Colen sc   F. Catherwood del

ered with stucco, which had fallen down; part of the
roof had given way, and the floor was covered with
ruins. In one of them was the same pitchy substance
we had noticed in the sepulchre at Copan. The roof
was formed of stones, lapping over in the usual style,
and forming as near an approach to the arch as was
made by the architects of the Old World.

In the back wall of the centre chamber was a doorway of the same size with that in front, which led to an
apartment without any partitions, but in the centre was
an oblong enclosure eighteen feet by eleven, which was
manifestly intended as the most important part of the
edifice. The door was choked up with ruins to within
a few feet of the top, but over it, and extending along
the whole front of the structure, was a large stucco ornament, which at first impressed us most forcibly by its
striking resemblance to the winged globe over the doors
of Egyptian temples. Part of this ornament had fallen
down, and, striking the heap of rubbish underneath,
had rolled beyond the door of entrance. We endeavoured to roll it back and restore it to its place, but it
proved too heavy for the strength of four men and a
boy. The part which remains is represented in the engraving, and differs in detail from the winged globe.
The wings are reversed; there is a fragment of a circular ornament which may have been intended for a
globe, but there are no remains of serpents entwining it.

There was another surprising feature in this door.
The lintel was *a beam of wood;* of what species we did
not know, but our guide said it was of the sapote-tree.
It was so hard that, on being struck, it rang like metal,
and perfectly sound, without a worm-hole or other
symptom of decay. The surface was smooth and
even, and from a very close examination we were of

the opinion that it must have been trimmed with an instrument of metal.

The opening under this doorway was what the alcalde had intended as the mouth of the cave that led to Palenque, and which, by-the-way, he had told us was so completely buried in El Monte that it would require two days digging and clearing to reach it. Our guide laughed at the ignorance prevailing in the village in regard to the difficulty of reaching it, but stoutly maintained the story that it led to Palenque. We could not prevail on him to enter it. A short cut to Palenque was exactly what we wanted. I took off my coat, and, lying down on my breast, began to crawl under. When I had advanced about half the length of my body, I heard a hideous hissing noise, and starting back, saw a pair of small eyes, which in the darkness shone like balls of fire. The precise portion of time that I employed in backing out is not worth mentioning. My companions had heard the noise, and the guide said it was " un tigre." I thought it was a wildcat; but, whatever it was, we determined to have a shot at it. We took it for granted that the animal would dash past us, and in a few moments our guns and pistols, swords and machetes, were ready ; taking our positions, Pawling, standing close against the wall, thrust under a long pole, and with a horrible noise out fluttered a huge turkey-buzzard, which flapped itself through the building and took refuge in another chamber.

This peril over, I renewed the attempt, and holding a candle before me, quickly discovered the whole extent of the cave that led to Palenque. It was a chamber corresponding with the dimensions given of the outer walls. The floor was encumbered with rubbish two or three feet deep, the walls were covered with stuccoed figures, among which that of a monkey was conspicuous, and against the back wall, among curious and interesting ornaments, were two figures of men in profile, with their faces toward each other, well drawn and as large as life, but the feet concealed by the rubbish on the floor. Mr. Catherwood crawled in to make a drawing of them, but, on account of the smoke from the candles, the closeness, and excessive heat, it was impossible to remain long enough. In general appearance and character they were the same as we afterward saw carved on stone at Palenque.

By means of a tree growing close against the wall of this building I climbed to the top, and saw another edifice very near and on the top of a still higher structure. We climbed up to this, and found it of the same general plan, but more dilapidated. Descending, we passed between two other buildings on pyramidal elevations, and came out upon an open table which had probably once been the site of the city. It was protected on all sides by the same high terraces, overlooking for a great distance the whole country round, and rendering it impossible for an enemy to approach from any quarter without being discovered. Across the table was a high and narrow causeway, which seemed partly natural and partly artificial, and at some distance on which was a mound, with the foundations of a building that had probably been a tower. Beyond this the causeway extended till it joined a range of mountains. From the few Spanish books within my reach I have not been able to learn anything whatever of the history of this place, whether it existed at the time of the conquest or not. I am inclined to think, however, that it did, and that mention is made of it in some Spanish authors. At all events, there was no place we had seen which gave us such an idea of the vastness of the works erected by the aboriginal inhabitants. Pressed as we were, we determined to remain and make a thorough exploration.

It was nearly dark when we returned to the village. Immediately we called upon the alcalde, but found on the very threshold detention and delay. He repeated the schoolmaster's warning that nothing could be done violenter. It would take two days to get together men and implements, and these last of the kind necessary could not be had at all. There was not a crowbar in the place ; but the alcalde said one could be made, and in the same breath that there was no iron; there was half a blacksmith, but no iron nearer than Tobasco, about eight or ten days' journey. While we were with him another terrible storm came on. We hurried back in the midst of it, and determined forthwith to push on to Palenque. I am strongly of opinion that there is at this place much to reward the future traveller. We were told that there were other ruins about ten leagues distant, along the same range of mountains; and it has additional interest in our eyes, from the circumstance that this would be the best point from which to attempt the discovery of the mysterious city seen from the top of the Cordilleras.

At Ocosingo we were on the line of travel of Captain Dupaix, whose great work on Mexican Antiquities, published in Paris in 1834–5, awakened the attention of the learned in Europe. His expedition to Palenque was made in 1807. He reached this place from the city of Mexico, under a commission from the government, attended by a draughtsman and secretary, and part of a regiment of dragoons. "Palenque," he says, "is eight days' march from Ocosingo. The journey is very fatiguing. The roads, if they can be so called, are only narrow and difficult paths, which wind across mountains and precipices, and which it is necessary to follow sometimes on mules, sometimes on foot, sometimes on the shoulders of Indians, and sometimes in hammocks. In some places it is necessary to pass on bridges, or, rather, trunks of trees badly secured, and over lands covered with wood, desert and dispeopled, and to sleep in the open air, excepting a very few villages and huts.

"We had with us thirty or forty vigorous Indians to carry our luggage and hammocks. After having experienced in this long and painful journey every kind of fatigue and discomfort, we arrived, thank God, at the village of Palenque."

This was now the journey before us; and, according to the stages we had arranged, to avoid sleeping out at night, it was to be made in five instead of eight days. The terrible rains of the two preceding nights had infected us with a sort of terror, and Pawling was completely shaken in his purpose of continuing with us. The people of the village told him that after the rains had fairly set in it would be impossible to return, and in the morning, though reluctantly, he determined abruptly to leave us and go back. We were very unwilling to part with him, but, under the circumstances, could not urge him to continue. Our luggage and little traps, which we had used in common, were separated; Mr. Catherwood bade him good-by and rode on; but while mounted, and in the act of shaking hands to pursue our opposite roads, I made him a proposition which induced him again to change his determination, at the risk of remaining on the other side of the mountains until the rainy season was over. In a few minutes we overtook Mr. Catherwood.

The fact is, we had some apprehensions from the

badness of the roads.   Our route lay through an Indian
country, in parts of which the Indians bore a notoriously
bad character.   We had no dragoons, our party of attendants was very small, and, in reality, we had not a
single man upon whom we could rely ; under which
state of things Pawling's pistols and double-barrelled
gun were a matter of some consequence.

We left Ocosingo at a quarter past eight.   So little
impression did any of our attendants make upon me,
that I have entirely forgotten every one of them.   Indeed, this was the case throughout the journey.   In
other countries a Greek muleteer, an Arab boatman, or
a Bedouin guide was a companion ; here the people
had no character, and nothing in which we took any
interest except their backs.   Each Indian carried, besides his burden, a net bag containing his provisions for
the road, viz., a few tortillas, and large balls of mashed
Indian corn wrapped in leaves.   A drinking cup, being
half a calabash, he carried sometimes on the crown of
his head.   At every stream he filled his cup with water,
into which he stirred some of his corn, making a sort
of cold porridge ; and this throughout the country is
the staff of life for the Indian on a journey.   In half an
hour we passed at some distance on our right large
mounds, formerly structures which formed part of the
old city.   At nine o'clock we crossed the Rio Grande
or Huacachahoul, followed some distance on the bank,
and passed three cascades spreading over the rocky
bed of the river, unique and peculiar in beauty, and
probably many more of the same character were breaking unnoticed and unknown in the wilderness through
which it rolled ; but, turning up a rugged mountain, we
lost sight of it.   The road was broken and mountainous.   We did not meet a single person, and at three

o'clock, moving in a north-northwest direction, we entered the village of Huacachahoul, standing in an open situation, surrounded by mountains, and peopled entirely by Indians, wilder and more savage than any we had yet seen. The men were without hats, but wore their long black hair reaching to their shoulders; and the old men and women, with harsh and haggard features and dark rolling eyes, had a most unbaptized appearance. They gave us no greetings, and their wild but steady glare made us feel a little nervous. A collection of naked boys and girls called Mr. Catherwood " Tata," mistaking him for a padre. We had some misgivings when we put the village behind us, and felt ourselves enclosed in the country of wild Indians. We stopped an hour near a stream, and at half past six arrived at Chillon, where, to our surprise and pleasure, we found a sub-prefect, a white man, and intelligent, who had travelled to San Salvador, and knew General Morazan. He was very anxious to know whether there was any revolution in Ciudad Real, as, with a pliancy becoming an office-holder, he wished to give in his adhesion to the new government.

The next morning, at a quarter before seven, we started with a new set of Indians. The road was good to Yahalon, which we reached at ten o'clock. Before entering it we met a young Indian girl with her father, of extraordinary beauty of face, in the costume of the country, but with a modest expression of countenance, which we all particularly remarked as evidence of her innocence and unconsciousness of anything wrong in her appearance. Every village we passed was most picturesque in position, and here the church was very effective; as in the preceding villages, it was undergoing repairs.

Here we were obliged to take another set of Indians, and perhaps we should have lost the day but for the padre, who called off some men working at the church. At a quarter past eleven we set off again ; at a quarter before one we stopped at the side of a stream to lunch. At this place a young Indian overtook us, with a very intelligent face, who seated himself beside me, and said, in remarkably good Spanish, that we must beware of the Indians. I gave him some tortillas. He broke off a small piece, and holding it in his fingers, looked at me, and with great emphasis said he had eaten enough; it was of no use to eat; he ate all he could get, and did not grow fat ; and, thrusting his livid face into mine, told me to see how thin he was. His face was calm, but one accidental expression betrayed him as a ma-niac ; and I now noticed in his face, and all over his body, white spots of leprosy, and started away from him. I endeavoured to persuade him to go back to the vil-lage, but he said it made no difference whether he went to the village or not ; he wanted a remedio for his thinness.

Soon after we came upon the banks of the River of Yahalon. It was excessively hot, the river as pure as water could be, and we stopped and had a delightful bath. After this we commenced ascending a steep mountain, and when high up saw the poor crazed young Indian standing in the same place on the bank of the river. At half past five, after a toilsome ascent, we reached the top of the mountain, and rode along the borders of a table of land several thousand feet high, looking down into an immense valley, and turning to the left, around the corner of the forest, entered the outskirts of Tumbala. The huts were distributed among high, rugged, and pictu-resque rocks, which had the appearance of having once formed the crater of a volcano. Drunken Indians were lying in the path, so that we had to turn out to avoid treading on them. Riding through a narrow passage between these high rocks, we came out upon a corner of the lofty perpendicular table several thousand feet high, on which stood the village of Tumbala. In front were the church and convent; the square was filled with wild-looking Indians preparing for a fiesta, and on the very corner of the immense table was a high conical peak, crowned with the ruins of a church. Altogether it was the wildest and most extraordinary place we had yet seen, and though not consecrated by associations, for unknown ages it had been the site of an Indian village.

It was one of the circumstances of our journey in this country that every hour and day produced something new. We never had any idea of the character of the place we were approaching until we entered it, and one surprise followed close upon another. On one corner of the table of land stood the cabildo. The justitia was the brother of our silver-dish friend Padre Solis, as poor and energetic as the padre was rich and inert. At the last village we had been told that it would be impossible to procure Indians for the next day on account of the fiesta, and had made up our minds to remain; but my letters from the Mexican authorities were so effective, that immediately the justitia held a parley with forty or fifty Indians, and, breaking off occasionally to cuff one of them, our journey was arranged through to Palenque in three days, and the money paid and distributed. Although the wildness of the Indians made us feel a little uncomfortable, we almost regretted this unexpected promptness; but the justitia told us we had come at a fortunate moment, for many of the Indians of San Pedro, who were notori-

ously a bad set, were then in the village, but he could
select those he knew, and would send an alguazil of
his own with us all the way.   As he did not give us
any encouragement to remain, and seemed anxious to
hurry us on, we made no objections, and in our anxiety
to reach the end of our journey, had a superstitious apprehension of the effect of any voluntary delay.

With the little of daylight that remained, he conducted us along the same path trodden by the Indians
centuries before, to the top of the cone rising at the corner of the table of land, from which we looked down on
one side into an immense ravine several thousand feet
in depth, and on the other, over the top of a great
mountain range, we saw the village of San Pedro, the
end of our next day's journey, and beyond, over the
range of the mountains of Palenque, the Lake of Terminos and the Gulf of Mexico.   It was one of the
grandest, wildest, and most sublime scenes I ever beheld.   On the top were ruins of a church and tower,
probably once used as a lookout, and near it were thirteen crosses erected over the bodies of Indians, who,
a century before, tied the hands and feet of the curate,
and threw him down the precipice, and were killed and
buried on the spot.   Every year new crosses are set up
over their bodies, to keep alive in the minds of the Indians the fate of murderers.   All around, on almost inaccessible mountain heights, and in the deepest ravines,
the Indians have their milpas or corn-patches, living almost as when the Spaniards broke in upon them, and
the justitia pointed with his finger to a region still occupied by the " unbaptized :" the same strange people
whose mysterious origin no man knows, and whose des-
tiny no man can foretell.   Among all the wild scenes
of our hurried tour, none is more strongly impressed

upon my mind than this; but with the untamed Indians around, Mr. Catherwood was too much excited and too nervous to attempt to make a sketch of it.

At dark we returned to the cabildo, which was decorated with evergreens for the fiesta, and at one end was a table, with a figure of the Virgin fantastically dressed, sitting under an arbour of pine-leaves.

In the evening we visited the padre, the delegate of Padre Solis, a gentlemanly young man from Ciudad Real, who was growing as round, and bade fair to grow as rich out of this village as Padre Solis himself. He and the justitia were the only white men in the place. We returned to the cabildo; the Indians came in to bid the justitia buenos noces, kissed the back of his hand, and we were left to ourselves.

Before daylight we were roused by an irruption of Indian carriers with lighted torches, who, while we were still in bed, began tying on the covers of our trunks to carry them off. At this place the mechanic arts were lower than in any other we had visited. There was not a rope of any kind in the village; the fastenings of the trunks and the straps to go around the forehead were all of bark strings; and here it was customary for those who intended to cross the mountains to take hammacas or sillas; the former being a cushioned chair, with a long pole at each end, to be borne by four Indians before and behind, the traveller sitting with his face to the side, and, as the justitia told us, only used by very heavy men and padres; and the latter an armchair, to be carried on the back of an Indian. We had a repugnance to this mode of conveyance, considering, though unwilling to run any risk, that where an Indian could climb with one of us on his back we could climb alone, and set out without either silla or hammaca.

Immediately from the village the road, which was a mere opening through the trees, commenced descending, and very soon we came to a road of palos or sticks, like a staircase, so steep that it was dangerous to ride down them. But for these sticks, in the rainy season the road would be utterly impassable. Descending constantly, at a little after twelve we reached a small stream, where the Indians washed their sweating bodies.

From the banks of this river we commenced ascending the steepest mountain I ever knew. Riding was out of the question; and encumbered with sword and spurs, and leading our mules, which sometimes held back, and sometimes sprang upon us, the toil was excessive. Every few minutes we were obliged to stop and lean against a tree or sit down. The Indians did not speak a word of any language but their own. We could hold no communication whatever with them, and could not understand how far it was to the top. At length we saw up a steep pitch before us a rude cross, which we hailed as being the top of the mountain. We climbed up to it, and, after resting a moment, mounted our mules, but, before riding a hundred yards, the descent began, and immediately we were obliged to dismount. The descent was steeper than the ascent. In a certain college in our country a chair was transmitted as an heirloom to the laziest man in the senior class. One held it by unanimous consent; but he was seen running down hill, was tried and found guilty, but avoided sentence by the frank avowal that a man pushed him, and he was too lazy to stop himself. So it was with us. It was harder work to resist than to give way. Our mules came tumbling after us; and after a most rapid, hot, and fatiguing descent, we reached a stream covered with leaves and insects. Here two of our Indians left us to return that night to Tumbala! Our labour was excessive; what must it have been to them! though probably accustomed to carry loads from their boyhood, they suffered less than we; and the freedom of their naked limbs relieved them from the heat and confinement which we suffered from clothes wet with perspiration. It was the hottest day we had experienced in the country. We had a farther violent descent through woods of almost impenetrable thickness, and at a quarter before four reached San Pedro. Looking back over the range we had just crossed, we saw Tumbala, and the towering point on which we stood the evening before, on a right line, only a few miles distant, but by the road twenty-seven.

If a bad name could kill a place, San Pedro was damned. From the hacienda of Padre Solis to Tumbala, every one we met cautioned us against the Indians of San Pedro. Fortunately, however, nearly the whole village had gone to the fête at Tumbala. There was no alcalde, no alguazils; a few Indians were lying about in a state of utter nudity, and when we looked into the huts the women ran away, probably alarmed at seeing men with pantaloons. The cabildo was occupied by a travelling party, with cargoes of sugar for Tobasco. The leaders of the party and owners of the cargoes were two Mestitzoes, having servants well armed, with whom we formed an acquaintance and tacit alliance. One of the best houses was empty; the proprietor, with his family and household furniture, except reed bedsteads fixed in the ground, had gone to the fiesta. We took possession, and piled our luggage inside.

Without giving us any notice, our men deserted us to return to Tumbala, and we were left alone. We could not speak the language, and could get nothing for the mules or for ourselves to eat ; but, through the leader of the sugar party, we learned that a new set of men would be forthcoming in the morning to take us on. With the heat and fatigue I had a violent headache. The mountain for the next day was worse, and, afraid of the effort, and of the danger of breaking down on the road, Mr. C. and Pawling endeavoured to procure a hammaca or silla, which was promised for the morning.

CHAPTER XVI.

EARLY the next morning the sugar party started, and at five minutes before seven we followed, with silla and men, altogether our party swelled to twenty Indians.

The country through which we were now travelling was as wild as before the Spanish conquest, and without a habitation until we reached Palenque. The road was through a forest so overgrown with brush and underwood as to be impenetrable, and the branches were trimmed barely high enough to admit a man's travelling under them on foot, so that on the backs of our mules we were constantly obliged to bend our bodies, and even to dismount. In some places, for a great distance around, the woods seemed killed by the heat, the foliage withered, the leaves dry and crisp, as if burned by the sun ; and a tornado had swept the country, of which no mention was made in the San Pedro papers.

We met three Indians carrying clubs in their hands, naked except a small piece of cotton cloth around the loins and passing between the legs, one of them, young, tall, and of admirable symmetry of form, looking the freeborn gentleman of the woods. Shortly afterward we passed a stream, where naked Indians were setting rude nets for fish, wild and primitive as in the first ages of savage life.

At twenty minutes past ten we commenced ascending

the mountain.   It was very hot, and I can give no idea of the toil of ascending these mountains.   Our mules could barely clamber up with their saddles only.   We disencumbered ourselves of sword, spurs, and all useless trappings; in fact, came down to shirt and pantaloons, and as near the condition of the Indians as we could.   Our procession would have been a spectacle in Broadway.   First were four Indians, each with a rough oxhide box, secured by an iron chain and large padlock, on his back; then Juan, with only a hat and pair of thin cotton drawers, driving two spare mules, and carrying a double-barrelled gun over his naked shoulders; then ourselves, each one driving before him or leading his own mule; then an Indian carrying the silla, with relief carriers, and several boys bearing small bags of provisions, the Indians of the silla being much surprised at our not using them according to contract and the price paid.   Though toiling excessively, we felt a sense of degradation at being carried on a man's shoulders. At that time I was in the worst condition of the three, and the night before had gone to bed at San Pedro without supper, which for any of us was sure evidence of being in a bad way.

We had brought the silla with us merely as a measure of precaution, with much expectation of being obliged to use it; but at a steep pitch, which made my head almost burst to think of climbing, I resorted to it for the first time.   It was a large, clumsy armchair, put together with wooden pins and bark strings.   The Indian who was to carry me, like all the others, was small, not more than five feet seven, very thin, but symmetrically formed.   A bark strap was tied to the arms of the chair, and, sitting down, he placed his back against the back of the chair, adjusted the length of the strings,

RIDING IN A SILLA.

F. Catherwood.

and smoothed the bark across his forehead with a little
cushion to relieve the pressure. An Indian on each
side lifted it up, and the carrier rose on his feet, stood
still a moment, threw me up once or twice to adjust me
on his shoulders, and set off with one man on each side.
It was a great relief, but I could feel every movement,
even to the heaving of his chest. The ascent was one
of the steepest on the whole road. In a few minutes he
stopped and sent forth a sound, usual with Indian carriers, between a whistle and a blow, always painful to
my ears, but which I never felt so disagreeably before.
My face was turned backward; I could not see where
he was going, but observed that the Indian on the left
fell back. Not to increase the labour of carrying me,
I sat as still as possible; but in a few minutes, looking
over my shoulder, saw that we were approaching the
edge of a precipice more than a thousand feet deep.
Here I became very anxious to dismount; but I could
not speak intelligibly, and the Indians could or would
not understand my signs. My carrier moved along
carefully, with his left foot first, feeling that the stone
on which he put it down was steady and secure before
he brought up the other, and by degrees, after a particularly careful movement, brought both feet up within
half a step of the edge of the precipice, stopped, and
gave a fearful whistle and blow. I rose and fell with
every breath, felt his body trembling under me, and his
knees seemed giving way. The precipice was awful,
and the slightest irregular movement on my part might
bring us both down together. I would have given him
a release in full for the rest of the journey to be off his
back; but he started again, and with the same care ascended several steps, so close to the edge that even on
the back of a mule it would have been very uncomfort-

able.   My fear lest he should break down or stumble was
excessive.   To my extreme relief, the path turned away ;
but I had hardly congratulated myself upon my escape
before he descended a few steps.   This was much worse
than ascending ; if he fell, nothing could keep me from
going over his head ; but I remained till he put me
down of his own accord.   The poor fellow was wet
with perspiration, and trembled in every limb.   Another stood ready to take me up, but I had had enough.
Pawling tried it, but only for a short time.   It was bad
enough to see an Indian toiling with a dead weight on
his back ; but to feel him trembling under one's own
body, hear his hard breathing, see the sweat rolling
down him, and feel the insecurity of the position, made
this a mode of travelling which nothing but constitu-
tional laziness and insensibility could endure.   Walking, or rather climbing, stopping very often to rest,
and riding when it was at all practicable, we reached
a thatched shed, where we wished to stop for the night,
but there was no water.

We could not understand how far it was to Nopa,
our intended stopping-place, which we supposed to be
on the top of the mountain.   To every question the Indians answered una legua.   Thinking it could not be
much higher, we continued.   For an hour more we had
a very steep ascent, and then commenced a terrible
descent.   At this time the sun had disappeared ; dark
clouds overhung the woods, and thunder rolled heavily
on the top of the mountain.   As we descended a heavy
wind swept through the forest ; the air was filled with
dry leaves ; branches were snapped and broken, trees
bent, and there was every appearance of a violent tornado.   To hurry down on foot was out of the question.
We were so tired that it was impossible ; and, afraid of

being caught on the mountain by a hurricane and deluge of rain, we spurred down as fast as we could go. It was a continued descent, without any relief, stony, and very steep. Very often the mules stopped, afraid to go on ; and in one place the two empty mules bolted into the thick woods rather than proceed. Fortunately for the reader, this is our last mountain, and I can end honestly with a climax : it was the worst mountain I ever encountered in that or any other country, and, under our apprehension of the storm, I will venture to say that no travellers ever descended in less time. At a quarter before five we reached the plain. The mountain was hidden by clouds, and the storm was now raging above us. We crossed a river, and continuing along it through a thick forest, reached the rancho of Nopa.

It was situated in a circular clearing about one hundred feet in diameter, near the river, with the forest around so thick with brush and underwood that the mules could not penetrate it, and with no opening but for the passage of the road through it. The rancho was merely a pitched roof covered with palm-leaves, and supported by four trunks of trees. All around were heaps of snail-shells, and the ground of the rancho was several inches deep with ashes, the remains of fires for cooking them. We had hardly congratulated ourselves upon our arrival at such a beautiful spot, before we suffered such an onslaught of moschetoes as we had not before experienced in the country. We made a fire, and, with appetites sharpened by a hard day's work, sat down on the grass to dispose of a San Pedro fowl; but we were obliged to get up, and while one hand was occupied with eatables, use the other to brush off the venomous insects. We soon saw that we had bad prospects for the night, lighted fires all around the rancho, and smoked inordinately. We were in no hurry to lie down, and sat till a late hour, consoling ourselves with the reflection that, but for the moschetoes, our satisfaction would be beyond all bounds. The dark border of the clearing was lighted up by fireflies of extraordinary size and brilliancy darting among the trees, not flashing and disappearing, but carrying a steady light; and, except that their course was serpentine, seeming like shooting stars. In different places there were two that remained stationary, emitting a pale but beautiful light, and seemed like rival belles holding levees. The fiery orbs darted from one to the other; and when one, more daring than the rest, approached too near, the coquette withdrew her light, and the flutterer went off. One, however, carried all before her, and at one time we counted seven hovering around her.

At length we prepared for sleep. Hammocks would leave us exposed on every side to the merciless attacks of the moschetoes, and we spread our mats on the ground. We did not undress. Pawling, with a great deal of trouble, rigged his sheets into a moscheto-net, but it was so hot that he could not breathe under them, and he roamed about or was in the river nearly all night. The Indians had occupied themselves in catching snails and cooking them for supper, and then lay down to sleep on the banks of the river; but at midnight, with sharp thunder and lightning, the rain broke in a deluge, and they all came under the shed, and there they lay perfectly naked, mechanically, and without seeming to disturb themselves, slapping their bodies with their hands. The incessant hum and bite of the insects kept us in a constant state of wakefulness and irritation. Our bodies we could protect, but with a covering over the face the heat was insufferable. Before daylight I walked to the river, which was broad and shallow, and stretched myself out on the gravelly bottom, where the water was barely deep enough to run over my body. It was the first comfortable moment I had had. My heated body became cooled, and I lay till daylight. When I rose to dress they came upon me with appetites whetted by a spirit of vengeance. Our day's work had been tremendously hard, but the night's was worse. The morning air, however, was refreshing, and as day dawned our tormentors disappeared. Mr. Catherwood had suffered least, but in his restlessness he had lost from his finger a precious emerald ring, which he had worn for many years, and prized for associations. We remained some time looking for it, and at length mounted and made our last start for Palenque. The road was level, but the woods were still as thick as on the mountain. At a quarter before eleven we reached a path which led to the ruins, or somewhere else. We had abandoned the intention of going directly to the ruins; for, besides that we were in a shattered condition, we could not communicate at all with our Indians, and probably they did not know where the ruins were. At length we came out upon an open plain, and looked back at the range we had crossed, running off to Peten and the country of unbaptized Indians.

As we advanced we came into a region of fine pasture grounds, and saw herds of cattle. The grass showed the effect of early rains, and the picturesque appearance of the country reminded me of many a scene at home; but there was a tree of singular beauty that was a stranger, having a high, naked trunk and spreading top, with leaves of vivid green, covered with yellow flowers. Continuing carelessly, and stopping from time to time to enjoy the smiling view around, and realize our escape from the dark mountains behind, we rose upon a slight table of land and saw the village before us, consisting of one grass-grown street, unbroken even by a mule-path, with a few straggling white houses on each side, on a slight elevation at the farther end a thatched church, with a rude cross and belfry before it. A boy could roll on the grass from the church door out of the village. In fact, it was the most dead-and-alive place I ever saw; but, coming from villages thronged with wild Indians, its air of repose was most grateful to us. In the suburbs were scattered Indian huts; and as we rode into the street, eight or ten white people, men and women, came out, more than we had seen since we left Comitan, and the houses had a comfortable and respectable appearance. In one of them lived the alcalde, a white man, about sixty, dressed in white cotton drawers, and shirt outside, respectable in his appearance, with a stoop in his shoulders, but the expression of his face was very doubtful. With what I intended as a most captivating manner, I offered him my passport; but we had disturbed him at his siesta; he had risen wrong side first; and, looking me steadily in the face, he asked me what he had to do with my passport. This I could not answer; and he went on to say that he had nothing to do with it, and did not want to have; we must go to the prefeto. Then he turned round two or three times in a circle, to show he did not care what we thought of him; and, as if conscious of what was passing in our minds, volunteered to add that complaints had been made against him before, but it was of no use; they couldn't remove him, and if they did he didn't care.

This greeting at the end of our severe journey was rather discouraging, but it was important for us not to

have any difficulty with this crusty official; and, endeavouring to hit a vulnerable point, told him that we wished
to stop a few days to rest, and should be obliged to
purchase many things. We asked him if there was
any bread in the village; he answered, "no hay,"
"there is none;" corn? "no hay;" coffee? "no hay;"
chocolate? "no hay." His satisfaction seemed to increase as he was still able to answer "no hay;" but
our unfortunate inquiries for bread roused his ire. In-
nocently, and without intending any offence, we betrayed our disappointment; and Juan, looking out for
himself, said that we could not eat tortillas. This he
recurred to, repeated several times to himself, and to
every new-comer said, with peculiar emphasis, they
can't eat tortillas. Following it up, he said there was
an oven in the place, but no flour, and the baker went
away seven years before; the people there could do
without bread. To change the subject, and determined
not to complain, I threw out the conciliatory remark,
that, at all events, we were glad to escape from the rain
on the mountains, which he answered by asking if we
expected anything better in Palenque, and he repeated
with great satisfaction an expression common in the
mouths of Palenquians: "tres meres de agua, tres meres
aguacero, y tres meres del norte," "three months rains,
three months heavy showers, and six months north
wind," which in that country brings cold and rain.

Finding it impossible to hit a weak point, while the
men were piling up the luggage I rode to the prefeto,
whose reception at that critical moment was most
cheering and reviving. With habitual courtesy he offered me a chair and a cigar, and as soon as he saw my
passport said he had been expecting me for some time.
This surprised me; and he added that Don Patricio had

told him I was coming, which surprised me still more, as I did not remember any friend of that name, but soon learned that this imposing cognomen meant my friend Mr. Patrick Walker, of Balize. This was the first notice of Mr. Walker and Captain Caddy I had received since Lieutenant Nicols brought to Guatimala the report that they had been speared by the Indians. They had reached Palenque by the Balize River and Lake of Peten, without any other difficulties than from the badness of the roads, had remained two weeks at the ruins, and left for the Laguna and Yucatan.   This was most gratifying intelligence, first, as it assured me of their safety, and second, as I gathered from it that there would be no impediment to our visiting the ruins. The apprehension of being met at the end of our toil-some journey with a peremptory exclusion had con-stantly disturbed us more or less, and sometimes weighed upon us like lead. We had determined to make no reference to the ruins until we had an oppor-tunity of ascertaining our ground, and up to that mo-ment I did not know but that all our labour was boot-less.   To heighten my satisfaction, the prefeto said that the place was perfectly quiet ; it was in a retired nook, which revolutions and political convulsions never reach-ed.   He had held his office twenty years, acknowledg-ing as many different governments.

I returned to make my report, and in regard to the old alcalde, in the language of a ward-meeting mani-festo, determined to ask for nothing but what was right, and to submit to nothing that was wrong.   In this spirit we made a bold stand for some corn.   The alcalde's " no hay" was but too true ; the corn-crop had failed, and there was an actual famine in the place.   The In-dians, with accustomed improvidence, had planted barely enough for the season, and this turning out bad, they were reduced to fruits, plantains, and roots instead of tortillas. Each white family had about enough for its own use, but none to spare. The shortness of the corn-crop made everything else scarce, as they were obliged to kill their fowls and pigs from want of anything to feed them with. The alcalde, who to his other offences added that of being rich, was the only man in the place who had any to spare, and he was holding on for a greater pressure. At Tumbala we had bought good corn at thirty ears for sixpence; here, with great difficulty, we prevailed upon the alcalde to spare us a little at eight ears for a shilling, and these were so musty and worm-eaten that the mules would hardly touch them. At first it surprised us that some enterprising capitalist did not import several dollars' worth from Tumbala; but on going deeper into the matter we found that the cost of transportation would not leave much profit, and, besides, the course of exchange was against Palenque. A few back-loads would overstock the market; for as each white family was provided till the next crop came in, the Indians were the only persons who wished to purchase, and they had no money to buy with. The brunt of the famine fell upon us, and particularly upon our poor mules. Fortunately, however, there was good pasture, and not far off. We slipped the bridles at the door and turned them loose in the streets; but after making the circuit they came back in a body, and poked their heads in at the door with an imploring look for corn.

Our prospects were not very brilliant; nevertheless, we had reached Palenque, and toward evening storms came on, with terrific thunder and lightning, which made us feel but too happy that our journey was over.

The house assigned to us by the alcalde was next his own, and belonged to himself. It had a cucinera adjoining, and two Indian women, who did not dare look at us without permission from the alcalde. It had an earthen floor, three beds made of reeds, and a thatched roof, very good, except that over two of the beds it leaked. Under the peaked roof and across the top of the mud walls there was a floor made of poles, serving as a granary for the alcalde's mouldy corn, inhabited by industrious mice, which scratched, nibbled, squeaked, and sprinkled dust upon us all night. Nevertheless, we had reached Palenque, and slept well.

The next day was Sunday, and we hailed it as a day of rest. Heretofore, in all my travels, I had endeavoured to keep it as such, but in this country I had found it impossible. The place was so tranquil, and seemed in such a state of repose, that as the old alcalde passed the door we ventured to wish him a good-morning; but again he had got up wrong; and, without answering our greeting, stopped to tell us that our mules were missing, and, as this did not disturb us sufficiently, he added that they were probably stolen; but when he had got us fairly roused and on the point of setting off to look for them, he said there was no danger; they had only gone for water, and would return of themselves.

The village of Palenque, as we learned from the prefeto, was once a place of considerable importance, all the goods imported for Guatimala passing through it; but Balize had diverted that trade and destroyed its commerce, and but a few years before more than half the population had been swept off by the cholera. Whole families had perished, and their houses were desolate and falling to ruins. The church stood at the head of the street, in the centre of a grassy square. On each side of the square were houses with the forest directly upon them ; and, being a little elevated in the plaza, we were on a line with the tops of the trees. The largest house on the square was deserted and in ruins. There were a dozen other houses occupied by white families, with whom, in the course of an hour's stroll, I became acquainted. It was but to stop before the door, and I received an invitation, "Pasen adelante," "Walk in, captain," for which title I was indebted to the eagle on my hat. . Each family had its hacienda in the neighbourhood, and in the course of an hour I knew all that was going on in Palenque ; i., e., I knew that nothing was going on.

At the upper end of the square, commanding this scene of quiet, was the house of an American named William Brown! It was a strange place for the abode of an American, and Mr. Brown was a regular "go-ahead" American. In the great lottery he had drawn a Palenquian wife, which in that quiet place probably saved him from dying of ennui. What first took him to the country I do not know ; but he had an exclusive privilege to navigate the Tobasco River by steam, and would have made a fortune, but his steamboat foundered on the second trip. He then took to cutting logwood on a new plan, and came very near making another fortune, but something went wrong. At the time of our visit he was engaged in canalling a short cut to the sea, to connect two rivers near his hacienda. To the astonishment of the Palenquians, he was always busy, when he might live quietly on his hacienda in the summer, and pass his winters in the village. Very much to our regret, he was not then in the village. It would have been interesting to meet a countryman of his stamp in that quiet corner of the world.

The prefeto was well versed in the history of Palenque. It is in the province of Tzendales, and for a century after the conquest of Chiapas it remained in possession of the Indians. Two centuries ago, Lorenzo Mugil, an emissary direct from Rome, set up among them the standard of the cross. The Indians still preserve his dress as a sacred relic, but they are jealous of showing it to strangers, and I could not obtain a sight of it. The bell of the church, too, was sent from the holy city. The Indians submitted to the dominion of the Spaniards until the year 1700, when the whole province revolted, and in Chillon, Tumbala, and Palenque they apostatized from Christianity, murdered the priests, profaned the churches, paid impious adoration to an Indian female, massacred the white men, and took the women for their wives. But, as soon as the intelligence reached Guatimala, a strong force was sent against them, the revolted towns were reduced and recovered to the Catholic faith, and tranquillity was restored. The right of the Indians, however, to the ownership of the soil was still recognised, and down to the time of the Mexican Independence they received rent for land in the villages and the milpas in the neighbourhood.

A short distance from Palenque the River Chacamal separates it from the country of the unbaptized Indians, who are here called Caribs. Fifty years ago the Padre Calderon, an uncle of the prefeto's wife, attended by his sacristan, an Indian, was bathing in the river, when the latter cried out in alarm that some Caribs were looking at them, and attempted to fly; but the padre took his cane and went toward them. The Caribs fell down before him, conducted him to their huts, and gave him an invitation to return, and make them a visit on a certain day. On the day appointed the padre went with his sacristan, and found a gathering of Caribs and a great feast prepared for him. He remained with them some time, and invited them in return to the village of Palenque on the day of the fête of St. Domingo. A large party of these wild Indians attended, bringing with them tiger's meat, monkey's meat, and cocoa as presents. They listened to mass, and beheld all the ceremonies of the Church; whereupon they invited the padre to come among them and teach them, and they erected a hut at the place where they had first met him, which he consecrated as a church; and he taught his sacristan to say mass to them every Sunday. As the prefeto said, if he had lived, many of them would probably have been Christianized; but, unfortunately, he died; the Caribs retired into the wilderness, and not one had appeared in the village since.

The ruins lie about eight miles from the village, perfectly desolate. The road was so bad, that, in order to accomplish anything, it was necessary to remain there, and we had to make provision for that purpose. There were three small shops in the village, the stock of all together not worth seventy-five dollars; but in one of them we found a pound and a half of coffee, which we immediately secured. Juan communicated the gratifying intelligence that a hog was to be killed the next morning, and that he had engaged a portion of the lard; also, that there was a cow with a calf running loose, and an arrangement might be made for keeping her up and milking her. This was promptly attended to, and all necessary arrangements were made for vis-

iting the ruins the next day. The Indians generally
knew the road, but there was only one man in the
place who was able to serve as a guide on the ground,
and he had on hand the business of killing and distributing the hog, by reason whereof he could not set out
with us, but promised to follow.

Toward evening the quiet of the village was disturbed by a crash, and on going out we found that a house
had fallen down. A cloud of dust rose from it, and the
ruins probably lie as they fell. The cholera had stripped it of tenants, and for several years it had been deserted.

CHAPTER XVII.

Preparations for visiting the Ruins. — A Turn-out. — Departure.—The Road.—
Rivers Micol and Otula.—Arrival at the Ruins.—The Palace.—A Feu-de-joie.
—Quarters in the Palace.—Inscriptions by former Visiters.—The Fate of
Beanham.—Discovery of the Ruins of Palenque.—Visit of Del Rio.—Expedition of Dupaix.—Drawings of the present Work.—First Dinner at the Ruins.—Mammoth Fireflies.—Sleeping Apartments.—Extent of the Ruins.—Ob-
stacles to Exploration.—Suffering from Moschetoes.

EARLY the next morning we prepared for our move to
the ruins. We had to make provision for housekeeping
on a large scale ; our culinary utensils were of rude
pottery, and our cups the hard shells of some round
vegetables, the whole cost, perhaps, amounting to one
dollar. We could not procure a water-jar in the place,
but the alcalde lent us one free of charge unless it
should be broken, and as it was cracked at the time he
probably considered it sold. By-the-way, we forced
ourselves upon the alcalde's affections by leaving our
money with him for safe-keeping. We did this with
great publicity, in order that it might be known in the
village that there was no "plata" at the ruins, but the
alcalde regarded it as a mark of special confidence.
Indeed, we could not have shown him a greater. He
was a suspicious old miser, kept his own money in a
trunk in an inner room, and never left the house without locking the street door and carrying the key with
him. He made us pay beforehand for everything we
wanted, and would not have trusted us half a dollar
on any account.

It was necessary to take with us from the village all
that could contribute to our comfort, and we tried hard
to get a woman ; but no one would trust herself alone

with us. This was a great privation; a woman was desirable, not, as the reader may suppose, for embellishment, but to make tortillas. These, to be tolerable, must be eaten the moment they are baked; but we were obliged to make an arrangement with the alcalde to send them out daily with the product of our cow.

Our turn-out was equal to anything we had had on the road. One Indian set off with a cowhide trunk on his back, supported by a bark string, as the groundwork of his load, while on each side hung by a bark string a fowl wrapped in plantain leaves, the head and tail only being visible. Another had on the top of his trunk a live turkey, with its legs tied and wings expanded, like a spread eagle. Another had on each side of his load strings of eggs, each egg being wrapped carefully in a husk of corn, and all fastened like onions on a bark string. Cooking utensils and water-jar were mounted on the backs of other Indians, and contained rice, beans, sugar, chocolate, &c.; strings of pork and bunches of plantains were pendent; and Juan carried in his arms our travelling tin coffee-canister filled with lard, which in that country was always in a liquid state.

At half past seven we left the village. For a short distance the road was open, but very soon we entered a forest, which continued unbroken to the ruins, and probably many miles beyond. The road was a mere Indian footpath, the branches of the trees, beaten down and heavy with the rain, hanging so low that we were obliged to stoop constantly, and very soon our hats and coats were perfectly wet. From the thickness of the foliage the morning sun could not dry up the deluge of the night before. The ground was very muddy, broken by streams swollen by the early rains, with gullies in which the mules floundered and stuck fast, in some places very difficult to cross.   Amid all the wreck of empires, nothing ever spoke so forcibly the world's mutations as this immense forest shrouding what was once a great city.   Once it had been a great highway, thronged with people who were stimulated by the same passions that give impulse to human action now ; and they are all gone, their habitations buried, and no traces of them left.

In two hours we reached the River Micol, and in half an hour more that of Otula, darkened by the shade of the woods, and breaking beautifully over a stony bed. Fording this, very soon we saw masses of stones, and then a round sculptured stone.   We spurred up a sharp ascent of fragments, so steep that the mules could barely climb it, to a terrace so covered, like the whole road, with trees, that it was impossible to make out the form. Continuing on this terrace, we stopped at the foot of a second, when our Indians cried out " el Palacio," " the palace," and through openings in the trees we saw the front of a large building richly ornamented with stuccoed figures on the pilasters, curious and elegant; trees growing close against it, and their branches entering the doors ; in style and effect unique, extraordinary, and mournfully beautiful.   We tied our mules to the trees, ascended a flight of stone steps forced apart and thrown down by trees, and entered the palace, ranged for a few moments along the corridor and into the courtyard, and after the first gaze of eager curiosity was over, went back to the entrance, and, standing in the doorway, fired a *feu-de-joie* of four rounds each, being the last charge of our firearms.   But for this way of giving vent to our satisfaction we should have made the roof of the old palace ring with a hurrah.   It was intended, too, for effect upon the Indians, who had probably never heard such a cannonade before, and almost, like their ancestors in the time of Cortez, regarded our weapons as instruments which spit lightning, and who, we knew, would make such a report in the village as would keep any of their respectable friends from paying us a visit at night.

We had reached the end of our long and toilsome journey, and the first glance indemnified us for our toil. For the first time we were in a building erected by the aboriginal inhabitants, standing before the Europeans knew of the existence of this continent, and we prepared to take up our abode under its roof. We selected the front corridor as our dwelling, turned turkey and fowls loose in the courtyard, which was so overgrown with trees that we could barely see across it; and as there was no pasture for the mules except the leaves of the trees, and we could not turn them loose into the woods, we brought them up the steps through the palace, and turned them into the courtyard also. At one end of the corridor Juan built a kitchen, which operation consisted in laying three stones anglewise, so as to have room for a fire between them. Our luggage was stowed away or hung on poles reaching across the corridor. Pawling mounted a stone about four feet long on stone legs for a table, and with the Indians cut a number of poles, which they fastened together with bark strings, and laid them on stones at the head and foot for beds. We cut down the branches that entered the palace, and some of the trees on the terrace, and from the floor of the palace overlooked the top of an immense forest stretching off to the Gulf of Mexico.

The Indians had superstitious fears about remaining at night among the ruins, and left us alone, the sole tenants of the palace of unknown kings. Little did they who built it think that in a few years their royal line would perish and their race be extinct, their city a ruin, and Mr. Catherwood, Pawling, and I and Juan its sole tenants.   Other strangers had been there, wondering like ourselves.   Their names were written on the walls, with comments and figures ; and even here were marks of those low, grovelling spirits which delight in profaning holy places.   Among the names, but not of the latter class, were those of acquaintances : Captain Caddy and Mr. Walker; and one was that of a countryman, Noah O. Platt, New-York.   He had gone out to Tobasco as supercargo of a vessel, ascended one of the rivers for logwood, and while his vessel was loading visited the ruins.   His account of them had given me a strong desire to visit them long before the opportunity of doing so presented itself.

High up on one side of the corridor was the name of William Beanham, and under it was a stanza written in lead-pencil.   By means of a tree with notches cut in it, I climbed up and read the lines.   The rhyme was faulty and the spelling bad, but they breathed a deep sense of the moral sublimity pervading these unknown ruins. The author seemed, too, an acquaintance.   I had heard his story in the village.   He was a young Irishman, sent by a merchant of Tobasco into the interior for purposes of small traffic ; had passed some time at Palenque and in the neighbourhood; and, with his thoughts and feelings turned strongly toward the Indians, after dwelling upon the subject for some time, resolved to penetrate into the country of the Caribs.   His friends endeavoured to dissuade him, and the prefect told him, " You have red hair, a florid complexion, and white skin, and they will either make a god of you and keep you among them, or else kill and eat you;" but he set off alone and on

foot, crossed the River Chacamal, and after an absence
of nearly a year returned safe, but naked and emacia-
ted, with his hair and nails long, having been eight days
with a single Carib on the banks of a wild river, searching for a crossing-place, and living upon roots and herbs.
He built a hut on the borders of the Chacamal River,
and lived there with a Carib servant, preparing for another and more protracted journey among them, until
at length some boatmen who came to trade with him
found him lying in his hammock dead, with his scull
split open. He had escaped the dangers of a journey
which no man in that country dared encounter, to die by
the hands of an assassin in a moment of fancied security. His arm was hanging outside, and a book lying on
the ground; probably he was struck while reading.
The murderers, one of whom was his servant, were
caught, and were then in prison in Tobasco. Unfortunately, the people of Palenque had taken but little interest in anything except the extraordinary fact of his
visit among the Caribs and his return safe. All his
papers and collection of curiosities were scattered and
destroyed, and with him died all the fruits of his labours ; but, were he still living, he would be the man,
of all others, to accomplish the discovery of that mysterious city which had so much affected our imaginations.

As the ruins of Palenque are the first which awakened
attention to the existence of ancient and unknown cities
in America, and as, on that account, they are perhaps
more interesting to the public, it may not be amiss to
state the circumstances of their first discovery.

The account is, that in the year 1750, a party of
Spaniards travelling in the interior of Mexico penetrated to the lands north of the district of Carmen, in
the province of Chiapas, when all at once they found

in the midst of a vast solitude ancient stone buildings, the remains of a city, still embracing from eighteen to twenty-four miles in extent, known to the Indians by the name of Casas de Piedras. From my knowledge of the country I am at a loss to conjecture why a party of Spaniards were travelling in that forest, or how they could have done so. I am inclined to believe rather that the existence of the ruins was discovered by the Indians, who had clearings in different parts of the forest for their corn-fields, or perhaps was known to them from time immemorial, and on their report the inhabitants were induced to visit them.

The existence of such a city was entirely unknown; there is no mention of it in any book, and no tradition that it had ever been. To this day it is not known by what name it was called, and the only appellation given to it is that of Palenque, after the village near which the ruins stand.

The news of the discovery passed from mouth to mouth, was repeated in some cities of the province, and reached the seat of government; but little attention was paid to it, and the members of the government, through ignorance, apathy, or the actual impossibility of occupying themselves with anything except public affairs, took no measures to explore the ruins, and it was not till 1786, thirty years subsequent to the discovery, that the King of Spain ordered an exploration; on the third of May, 1787, Captain Antonio del Rio arrived at the village, under a commission from the government of Guatimala, and on the fifth he proceeded to the site of the ruined city. In his official report he says, on making his first essay, owing to the thickness of the woods, and a fog so dense that it was impossible for the men to distinguish each other at five paces' distance, the principal building was completely concealed from their view.

He returned to the village, and after concerting measures with the deputy of the district, an order was issued to the inhabitants of Tumbala, requiring two hundred Indians with axes and billhooks. On the 17th seventy-nine arrived, furnished with twenty-eight axes, after which twenty more were obtained in the village ; and with these he again moved forward, and immediately commenced felling trees, which was followed by a general conflagration.

The report of Captain Del Rio, with the commentary of Doctor Paul Felix Cabrera of New Guatimala, deducing an Egyptian origin for the people, through either the supineness or the jealousy of the Spanish government was locked up in the archives of Guatimala until the time of the Revolution, when, by the operation of liberal principles, the original manuscripts came into the hands of an English gentleman long resident in that country, and an English translation was published at London in 1822. This was the first notice in Europe of the discovery of these ruins ; and, instead of electrifying the public mind, either from want of interest in the subject, distrust, or some other cause, so little notice was taken of it, that in 1831 the Literary Gazette, a paper of great circulation in London, announced it as a new discovery made by Colonel Galindo, whose unfortunate fate has been before referred to. If a like discovery had been made in Italy, Greece, Egypt, or Asia, within the reach of European travel, it would have created an interest not inferior to the discovery of Herculaneum, or Pompeii, or the ruins of Pæstum.

While the report and drawings of Del Rio slept in the archives of Guatimala, Charles the Fourth of

Spain ordered another expedition, at the head of which was placed Captain Dupaix, with a secretary and draughtsman, and a detachment of dragoons. His expeditions were made in 1805, 1806, and 1807, the last of which was to Palenque.

The manuscripts of Dupaix, and the designs of his draughtsman Castenada, were about to be sent to Madrid, which was then occupied by the French army, when the revolution broke out in Mexico; they then became an object of secondary importance, and remained during the wars of independence under the control of Castenada, who deposited them in the Cabinet of Natural History in Mexico. In 1828 M. Baradere disentombed them from the cartons of the museum, where, but for this accident, they might still have remained, and the knowledge of the existence of this city again been lost. The Mexican Congress had passed a law forbidding any stranger not formally authorized to make researches or to remove objects of art from the country; but, in spite of this interdict, M. Baradere obtained authority to make researches in the interior of the republic, with the agreement that after sending to Mexico all that he collected, half should be delivered to him, with permission to transport them to Europe. Afterward he obtained by exchange the original designs of Castenada, and an authentic copy of the itinerary and descriptions of Captain Dupaix was promised in three months. From divers circumstances, that copy did not reach M. Baradere till long after his return to France, and the work of Dupaix was not published until 1834, '5, twenty-eight years after his expedition, when it was brought out in Paris, in four volumes folio, at the price of eight hundred francs, with notes and commentaries by M. Alexandre Lenoir,

M. Warden, M. Charles Farcy, M. Baradere, and M. De St. Priest.

Lord Kingsborough's ponderous tomes, so far as regards Palenque, are a mere reprint of Dupaix, and the cost of his work is four hundred dollars per copy. Colonel Galindo's communications to the Geographical Society of Paris are published in the work of Dupaix, and since him Mr. Waldeck, with funds provided by an association in Mexico, had passed two years among the ruins. His drawings, as he states in a work on another place, were taken away by the Mexican government; but he had retained copies, and before we set out his work on Palenque was announced in Paris. It, however, has never appeared, and in the mean time Dupaix's is the text-book.

I have two objections to make to this work, not affecting Captain Dupaix, who, as his expedition took place thirty-four years since, is not likely to be affected, if he is even living, but his Paris editors. The first is the very depreciating tone in which mention is made of the work of his predecessor Del Rio, and, secondly, this paragraph in the introduction :

"It must be considered that a government only can execute such undertakings. A traveller relying upon his own resources cannot hope, whatever may be his intrepidity, to penetrate, and, above all, to live in those dangerous solitudes ; and, supposing that he succeeds, it is beyond the power of the most learned and skilful man to explore alone the ruins of a vast city, of which he must not only measure and draw the edifices still existing, but also determine the circumference and examine the remains, dig the soil and explore the subterraneous constructions. M. Baradere arrived within fifty leagues of Palenque, burning with the desire of going there ; but what could a single man do with domestics or other auxiliaries, without moral force or intelligence, against a people still half savage, against serpents and other hurtful animals, which, according to Dupaix, infest these ruins, and also against the vegetative force of a nature fertile and powerful, which in a few years re-covers all the monuments and obstructs all the avenues ?"

The effect of this is to crush all individual enterprise, and, moreover, it is untrue. All the accounts, founded upon this, represent a visit to these ruins as attended with immense difficulty and danger, to such an extent that we feared to encounter them; but there is no difficulty whatever in going from Europe or the United States to Palenque. Our greatest hardships, even in our long journey through the interior, were from the revolutionary state of the countries and want of time ; and as to a residence there, with time to construct a hut or to fit up an apartment in the palace, and to procure stores from the seaboard, " those dangerous solitudes" might be anything rather than unpleasant.

And to show what individuals can accomplish, I state that Mr. Catherwood's drawings include all the objects represented in the work of Dupaix, and others besides which do not appear in that work at all, and have never before been presented to the public ; among which are the frontispiece of this volume and the large tablets of hieroglyphics, the most curious and interesting pieces of sculpture at Palenque. I add, with the full knowledge that I will be contradicted by future travellers if I am wrong, that the whole of Mr. C.'s are more correct in proportions, outline, and filling up than his, and furnish more true material for speculation and study. I would not have said thus much but from a wish to give confidence to the reader who may be disposed to investigate and study these interesting remains. As to most of the places visited by us, he will find no materials whatever except those furnished in these pages. In regard to Palenque he will find a splendid work, the materials of which were procured under the sanction of a commission from government, and brought out with explanations and commentaries by the learned men of Paris, by the side of which my two octavoes shrink into insignificance; but I uphold the drawings against these costly folios, and against every other book that has ever been published on the subject of these ruins. My object has been, not to produce an illustrated work, but to present the drawings in such an inexpensive form as to place them within reach of the great mass of our reading community.

But to return to ourselves in the palace. While we were making our observations, Juan was engaged in a business that his soul loved. As with all the mozos of that country, it was his pride and ambition to servir a mano. He scorned the manly occupation of a muleteer, and aspired to that of a menial servant. He was anxious to be left at the village, and did not like the idea of stopping at the ruins, but was reconciled to it by being allowed to devote himself exclusively to cookery. At four o'clock we sat down to our first dinner. The tablecloth was two broad leaves, each about two feet long, plucked from a tree on the terrace before the door. Our saltcellar stood like a pyramid, being a case made of husks of corn put together lengthwise, and holding four or five pounds, in lumps from the size of a pea to that of a hen's egg. Juan was as happy as if he had prepared the dinner exclusively for his own eating; and all went merry as a marriage-bell, when the sky became overcast, and a sharp thunder-clap heralded the

afternoon's storm.   From the elevation of the terrace,
the floor of the palace commanded a view of the top of
the forest, and we could see the trees bent down by the
force of the wind; very soon a fierce blast swept through
the open doors, which was followed instantaneously
by heavy rain.   The table was cleared by the wind,
and, before we could make our escape, was drenched
by the rain.   We snatched away our plates, and finished our meal as we could.

The rain continued, with heavy thunder and lightning, all the afternoon.   In the absolute necessity of
taking up our abode among the ruins, we had hardly
thought of our exposure to the elements until it was
forced upon us.   At night we could not light a candle,
but the darkness of the palace was lighted up by fireflies of extraordinary size and brilliancy, shooting
through the corridors and stationary on the walls,
forming a beautiful and striking spectacle.   They were
of the description with those we saw at Nopa, known
by the name of shining beetles, and are mentioned by
the early Spaniards, among the wonders of a world
where all was new, " as showing the way to those who
travel at night."   The historian describes them as
" somewhat smaller than Sparrows, having two stars
close by their Eyes, and two more under their Wings,
which gave so great a Light that by it they could spin,
weave, write, and paint; and the Spaniards went by
night to hunt the Utios or little Rabbits of that country ;
and a-fishing, carrying these Animals tied to their great
Toes or Thumbs : and they called them Locuyos, being also of use to save them from the Gnats, which
are there very troublesome.   They took them in the
Night with Firebrands, because they made to the Light,
and came when called by their Name ; and they are so

unwieldy that when they fall they cannot rise again; and the Men stroaking their Faces and Hands with a sort of Moisture that is in those Stars, seemed to be afire as long as it lasted."

It always gave us high pleasure to realize the romantic and seemingly half-fabulous accounts of the chroniclers of the conquest. Very often we found their quaint descriptions so vivid and faithful as to infuse the spirit that breathed through their pages. We caught several of these beetles, not, however, by calling them by their names, but with a hat, as school-boys used to catch fireflies, or, less poetically, light-ning-bugs, at home. They are more than half an inch long, and have a sharp movable horn on the head ; when laid on the back they cannot turn over except by pressing this horn against a membrane upon the front. Behind the eyes are two round transparent substances full of luminous matter, about as large as the head of a pin, and underneath is a larger membrane containing the same luminous substance. Four of them together threw a brilliant light for several yards around, and by the light of a single one we read distinctly the finely-printed pages of an American newspaper. It was one of a packet, full of debates in Congress, which I had as yet barely glanced over, and it seemed stranger than any incident of my journey to be reading by the light of beetles, in the ruined palace of Palenque, the say-ings and doings of great men at home. In the midst of it Mr. Catherwood, in emptying the capacious pocket of a shooting-jacket, handed me a Broadway omnibus ticket :

" Good to the bearer for a ride,
" A. Brower."

These things brought up vivid recollections of home, and among the familiar images present were the good beds into which our friends were about that time turning. Ours were set up in the back corridor, fronting the court-yard. This corridor consisted of open doors and pilasters alternately. The wind and rain were sweeping through, and, unfortunately, our beds were not out of reach of the spray. They had been set up with some labour on four piles of stones each, and we could not then change their position. We had no spare articles to put up as screens; but, happily, two umbrellas, tied up with meas-uring rods and wrapped in a piece of matting, had sur-vived the wreck of the mountain-roads. These Mr. C. and I secured at the head of our beds. Pawling swung a hammock across the corridor so high that the sweep of the rain only touched the foot; and so passed our first night at Palenque. In the morning, umbrellas, bed-clothes, wearing apparel, and hammocks were wet through, and there was not a dry place to stand on. Already we considered ourselves booked for a rheuma-tism. We had looked to our residence at Palenque as the end of troubles, and for comfort and pleasure, but all we could do was to change the location of our beds to places which promised a better shelter for the next night.

A good breakfast would have done much to restore our equanimity; but, unhappily, we found that the tor-tillas which we had brought out the day before, proba-bly made of half-mouldy corn, by the excessive damp-ness were matted together, sour, and spoiled. We went through our beans, eggs, and chocolate without any substitute for bread, and, as often before in time of trouble, composed ourselves with a cigar. Blessed be the man who invented smoking, the soother and com-poser of a troubled spirit, allayer of angry passions, a comfort under the loss of breakfast, and to the roamer in desolate places, the solitary wayfarer through life, serving for "wife, children, and friends."

At about ten o'clock the Indians arrived with fresh tortillas and milk. Our guide, too, having finished cutting up and distributing the hog, was with them. He was the same who had been employed by Mr. Waldeck, and also by Mr. Walker and Captain Caddy, and was recommended by the prefect as the only man acquainted with the ruins. Under his escort we set out for a preliminary survey. Of ourselves, leaving the palace, in any direction, we should not have known which way to direct our steps.

In regard to the extent of these ruins. Even in this practical age the imagination of man delights in wonders. The Indians and the people of Palenque say that they cover a space of sixty miles; in a series of well-written articles in our own country they have been set down as ten times larger than New-York; and lately I have seen an article in some of the newspapers, referring to our expedition, which represents this city, *discovered* by us, as having been three times as large as London! It is not in my nature to discredit any marvellous story. I am slow to disbelieve, and would rather sustain all such inventions; but it has been my unhappy lot to find marvels fade away as I approached them: even the Dead Sea lost its mysterious charm; and besides, as a traveller and "writer of a book," I know that if I go wrong, those who come after me will not fail to set me right. Under these considerations, not from any wish of my own, and with many thanks to my friends of the press, I am obliged to say that the Indians and people of Palenque really know nothing of the ruins personally, and the other accounts do not rest upon any sufficient foundation. The whole country for miles around is cov-

ered by a dense forest of gigantic trees, with a growth
of brush and underwood unknown in the wooded des-
erts of our own country, and impenetrable in any direction except by cutting a way with a machete.   What
lies buried in that forest it is impossible to say of my
own knowledge ; without a guide, we might have gone
within a hundred feet of all the buildings without dis-
covering one of them.

Captain Del Rio, the first explorer, with men and
means at command, states in his report, that in the execution of his commission he cut down and burned all
the woods ; he does not say how far, but, judging from
the breaches and excavations made in the interior of the
buildings, probably for miles around.   Captain Dupaix,
acting under a royal commission, and with all the resources such a commission would give, did not discover
any more buildings than those mentioned by Del Rio,
and we saw only the same ; but, having the benefit of
them as guides, at least of Del Rio (for at that time we
had not seen Dupaix's work), we of course saw things
which escaped their observation, just as those who come
after us will see what escaped ours.   This place, however, was the principal object of our expedition, and it was
our wish and intention to make a thorough exploration.
Respect for my official character, the special tenour of
my passport, and letters from Mexican authorities, gave
me every facility.   The prefect assumed that I was sent
by my government expressly to explore the ruins ; and
every person in Palenque except our friend the alcalde,
and even he as much as the perversity of his disposition would permit, was disposed to assist us.   But there
were accidental difficulties which were insuperable.
First, it was the rainy season.   This, under any circumstances, would have made it difficult ; but as the rains

did not commence till three or four o'clock, and the
weather was clear always in the morning, it alone would
not have been sufficient to prevent our attempting it;
but there were other difficulties, which embarrassed us
from the beginning, and continued during our whole residence among the ruins. There was not an axe or spade
in the place, and, as usual, the only instrument was the
machete, which here was like a short and wide-bladed
sword; and the difficulty of procuring Indians to work
was greater than at any other place we had visited. It
was the season of planting corn, and the Indians, under
the immediate pressure of famine, were all busy with
their milpas. The price of an Indian's labour was
eighteen cents per day; but the alcalde, who had the
direction of this branch of the business, would not let
me advance to more than twenty-five cents, and the
most he would engage to send me was from four to six
a day. They would not sleep at the ruins, came late,
and went away early; sometimes only two or three appeared, and the same men rarely came twice, so that
during our stay we had all the Indians of the village in
rotation. This increased very much our labour, as it
made it necessary to stand over them constantly to direct their work; and just as one set began to understand
precisely what we wanted, we were obliged to teach the
same to others; and I may remark that their labour,
though nominally cheap, was dear in reference to the
work done.

At that time I expected to return to Palenque;
whether I shall do so now or not is uncertain; but I am
anxious that it should be understood that the accounts
which have been published of the immense labour and
expense of exploring these ruins, which, as I before remarked, made it almost seem presumptuous for me to

undertake it with my own resources, are exaggerated and untrue. Being on the ground at the commencement of the dry season, with eight or ten young " pioneers," having a spirit of enterprise equal to their bone and muscle, in less than six months the whole of these ruins could be laid bare. Any man who has ever "cleared" a hundred acres of land is competent to undertake it, and the time and money spent by one of our young men in a " winter in Paris" would determine beyond all peradventure whether the city ever did cover the immense extent which some have supposed.

But to return : Under the escort of our guide we had a fatiguing but most interesting day. What we saw does not need any exaggeration. It awakened admiration and astonishment. In the afternoon came on the regular storm. We had distributed our beds, however, along the corridors, under cover of the outer wall, and were better protected, but suffered terribly from moschetoes, the noise and stings of which drove away sleep. In the middle of the night I took up my mat to escape from these murderers of rest. The rain had ceased, and the moon, breaking through the heavy clouds, with a misty face lighted up the ruined corridor. I climbed over a mound of stones at one end, where the wall had fallen, and, stumbling along outside the palace, entered a lateral building near the foot of the tower, groped in the dark along a low damp passage, and spread my mat before a low doorway at the extreme end. Bats were flying and whizzing through the passage, noisy and sinister ; but the ugly creatures drove away moschetoes. The dampness of the passage was cooling and refreshing ; and, with some twinging apprehensions of the snakes and reptiles, lizards and scorpions, which infest the ruins, I fell asleep.

CHAPTER XVIII.

Precautions against the Attacks of Moschetoes.—Mode of Life at Palenque.—
Description of the Palace.— Piers.— Hieroglyphics.— Figures.— Doorways.—
Corridors.—Courtyards.—A wooden Relic.—Stone Steps.—Towers.—Tablets.
—Stucco Ornaments, &c., &c.—The Royal Chapel.—Explorations.—An Aque-
duct.—An Alarm.—Insects.—Effect of Insect Stings.—Return to the Village
of Palenque.

At daylight I returned, and found Mr. C. and Pawling sitting on the stones, half dressed, in rueful con-
clave.　They had passed the night worse than I, and
our condition and prospects were dismal.　Rains, hard
work, bad fare, seemed nothing ; but we could no more
exist without sleep than the " foolish fellow" of Æsop,
who, at the moment when he had learned to live without eating, died.　In all his travels through the country
Pawling had never encountered such hard work as since
he met us.

The next night the moschetoes were beyond all en-
durance ; the slightest part of the body, the tip end of a
finger, exposed, was bitten.　With the heads covered
the heat was suffocating, and in the morning our faces
were all in blotches.　Without some remedy we were
undone.　It is on occasions like this that the creative
power of genius displays itself.　Our beds, it will be
remembered, were made of sticks lying side by side,
and set on four piles of stones for legs.　Over these we
laid our pellons and armas de aguas, or leathern armour against rain, and over these our straw matting.
This prevented our enemies invading us from between
the sticks.　Our sheets were already sewed up into
sacks.　We ripped one side, cut sticks, and bent them

F. Catherwood

J. Halpin.

PALACE AT PALENQUE.

in three bows about two feet high over the frame of the beds. Over these the sheets were stretched, and, sewed down all around, with a small space open at the head, had much the appearance of biers. At night, after a hard day's work, we crawled in. Hosts were waiting for us inside. We secured the open places, when each, with the stump of a lighted candle, hunted and slew, and with a lordly feeling of defiance we lay down to sleep. We had but one pair of sheets apiece, and this was a new way of sleeping under them; but, besides the victory it afforded us over the moschetoes, it had another advantage; the heat was so great that we could not sleep with our clothes on; it was impossible to place the beds entirely out of the reach of the spray, and the covering, held up a foot or two above us and kept damp, cooled the heated atmosphere within.

In this way we lived: the Indians came out in the morning with provisions, and as the tortillas were made in the alcalde's own kitchen, not to disturb his household arrangements, they seldom arrived till after breakfast.

In the mean time work went on. As at Copan, it was my business to prepare the different objects for Mr. Catherwood to draw. Many of the stones had to be scrubbed and cleaned; and as it was our object to have the utmost possible accuracy in the drawings, in many places scaffolds were to be erected on which to set up the camera lucida. Pawling relieved me from a great part of this labour. That the reader may know the character of the objects we had to interest us, I proceed to give a description of the building in which we lived, called the palace.

A front view of this building is given in the engraving. It does not, however, purport to be given with the same accuracy as the other drawings, the front being in a more ruined condition. It stands on an artificial elevation of an oblong form, forty feet high, three hundred and ten feet in front and rear, and two hundred and sixty feet on each side. This elevation was formerly faced with stone, which has been thrown down by the growth of trees, and its form is hardly distinguishable.

The building stands with its face to the east, and measures two hundred and twenty-eight feet front by one hundred and eighty feet deep. Its height is not more than twenty-five feet, and all around it had a broad projecting cornice of stone. The front contained fourteen doorways, about nine feet wide each, and the intervening piers are between six and seven feet wide. On the left (in approaching the palace) eight of the piers have fallen down, as has also the corner on the right, and the terrace underneath is cumbered with the ruins. But six piers remain entire, and the rest of the front is open.

The engraving opposite represents the ground-plan of the whole. The black lines represent walls still standing; the faint lines indicate remains only, but, in general, so clearly marked that there was no difficulty in connecting them together.

The building was constructed of stone, with a mortar of lime and sand, and the whole front was covered with stucco and painted. The piers were ornamented with spirited figures in bas-relief, one of which is represented

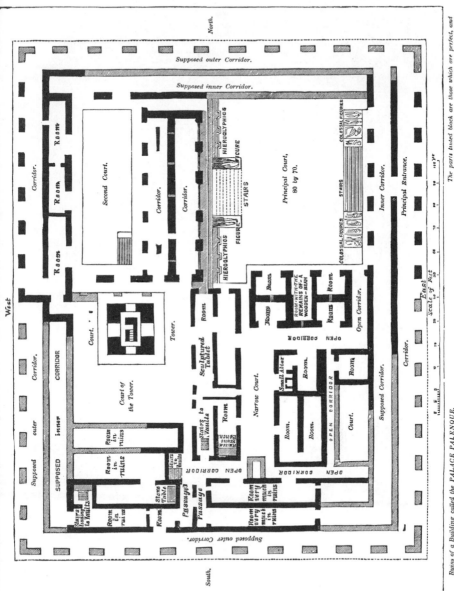

Ruins of a Building called the PALACE PALENQUE.

The parts tinted black are those which are perfect, and those tinted light are restored.

North.

South.

West.

East.

Scale of Feet

Supposed outer Corridor.

Supposed inner Corridor.

Supposed outer Corridor.

Supposed inner Corridor.

Principal Entrance.

Inner Corridor.

Supposed Corridor.

Corridor.

Corridor.

Corridor.

Corridor.

Corridor.

Corridor.

Supposed outer Corridor.

SUPPOSED inner CORRIDOR.

Court of the Tower.

Court.

Tower.

Second Court.

HIEROGLYPHICS

FIGURE

HIEROGLYPHICS

FIGURE

STAIRS

STAIRS

Principal Court, 80 by 70.

COLOSSAL FIGURES

COLOSSAL FIGURES

Room.

Room.

ROOM WITH THE REMAINS OF A WOODEN BEAM

Room.

Room.

OPEN CORRIDOR

Open Corridor.

Open Corridor.

Small Altar

Room.

Room.

Room.

Room.

Court.

Room.

OPEN CORRIDOR

OPEN CORRIDOR

Sculptured Tablet

Narrow Court.

Room.

Room.

Stairs to Vaults

MASSIVE STONE STEPS

Room very much in ruins

Passage

Passage

Stairs to Vaults

Slate Table

Stairs leading to Vaults

Room in ruins

Room in ruins

Room.

Room.

Room.

Room very much in ruins

Room in ruins

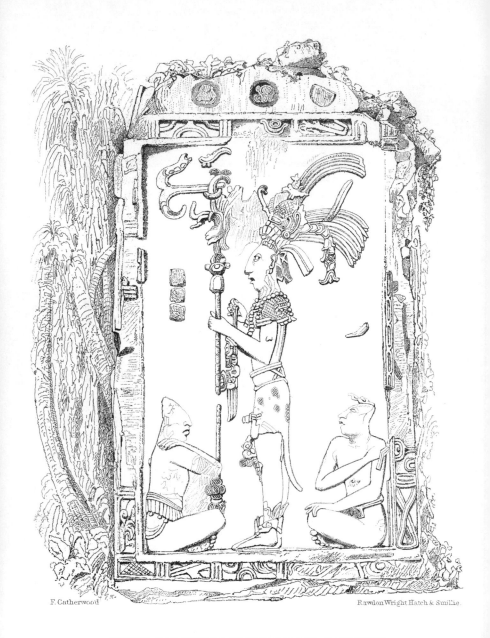

F. Catherwood

Rawdon Wright Hatch & Smillie.

STUCCO BAS RELIEF AT THE PALACE, PALENQUE.

in the engraving opposite. On the top are three hieroglyphics sunk in the stucco. It is enclosed by a richly-
ornamented border, about ten feet high and six wide, of
which only a part now remains. The principal personage stands in an upright position and in profile, exhibiting an extraordinary facial angle of about forty-five degrees. The upper part of the head seems to have been
compressed and lengthened, perhaps by the same process employed upon the heads of the Choctaw and Flat-
head Indians of our own country. The head represents
a different species from any now existing in that region
of country; and supposing the statues to be images of
living personages, or the creations of artists according
to their ideas of perfect figures, they indicate a race of
people now lost and unknown. The headdress is evidently a plume of feathers. Over the shoulders is a
short covering decorated with studs, and a breastplate;
part of the ornament of the girdle is broken; the tunic
is probably a leopard's skin; and the whole dress no
doubt exhibits the costume of this unknown people.
He holds in his hand a staff or sceptre, and opposite his
hands are the marks of three hieroglyphics, which have
decayed or been broken off. At his feet are two naked
figures seated cross-legged, and apparently suppliants.
A fertile imagination might find many explanations for
these strange figures, but no satisfactory interpretation
presents itself to my mind. The hieroglyphics doubtless tell its history. The stucco is of admirable consist-
ency, and hard as stone. It was painted, and in different places about it we discovered the remains of red,
blue, yellow, black, and white.

The piers which are still standing contained other figures of the same general character, but which, unfortunately, are more mutilated, and from the declivity of

the terrace it was difficult to set up the camera lucida
in such a position as to draw them.   The piers which
are fallen were no doubt enriched with the same ornaments.   Each one had some specific meaning, and the
whole probably presented some allegory or history ; and
when entire and painted, the effect in ascending the
terrace must have been imposing and beautiful.

The principal doorway is not distinguished by its
size or by any superior ornament, but is only indicated
by a range of broad stone steps leading up to it on the
terrace.   The doorways have no doors, nor are there
the remains of any.   Within, on each side, are three niches in the wall, about eight or ten inches square, with a
cylindrical stone about two inches in diameter fixed upright, by which perhaps a door was secured.   Along
the cornice outside, projecting about a foot beyond the
front, holes were drilled at intervals through the stone;
and our impression was, that an immense cotton cloth,
running the whole length of the building, perhaps painted in a style corresponding with the ornaments, was attached to this cornice, and raised and lowered like a
curtain, according to the exigencies of sun and rain.
Such a curtain is used now in front of the piazzas of
some haciendas in Yucatan.

The tops of the doorways were all broken.   They
had evidently been square, and over every one were
large niches in the wall on each side, in which the lintels had been laid.   These lintels had all fallen, and the
stones above formed broken natural arches.   Underneath were heaps of rubbish, but there were no remains
of lintels.   If they had been single slabs of stone, some
of them must have been visible and prominent ; and we
made up our minds that these lintels were of *wood*.
We had no authority for this.   It is not suggested ei-

FRONT CORRIDOR OF THE PALACE PALENQUE.

ther by Del Rio or Captain Dupaix, and perhaps we should not have ventured the conclusion but for the wooden lintel which we had seen over the doorway at Ocosingo ; and by what we saw afterward in Yucatan, we were confirmed, beyond all doubt, in our opinion. I do not conceive, however, that this gives any conclusive data in regard to the age of the buildings. The wood, if such as we saw in the other places, would be very lasting ; its decay must have been extremely slow, and centuries may have elapsed since it perished altogether.

The building has two parallel corridors running lengthwise on all four of its sides. In front these corridors are about nine feet wide, and extend the whole length of the building upward of two hundred feet. In the long wall that divides them there is but one door, which is opposite the principal door of entrance, and has a corresponding one on the other side, leading to a courtyard in the rear. The floors are of cement, as hard as the best seen in the remains of Roman baths and cisterns. The walls are about ten feet high, plastered, and on each side of the principal entrance ornamented with medallions, of which the borders only remain ; these perhaps contained the busts of the royal family. The separating-wall had apertures of about a foot, probably intended for purposes of ventilation. Some were of this form ⊹, and some of this ⊤, which have been called the Greek Cross and the Egyptian Tau, and made the subject of much learned speculation.

The ceiling of each corridor was in this form △. The builders were evidently ignorant of the principles of the arch, and the support was made by stones lapping over as they rose, as at Ocosingo, and among the

Cyclopean remains in Greece and Italy. Along the top was a layer of flat stone, and the sides, being plastered, presented a flat surface. The long, unbroken corridors in front of the palace were probably intended for lords and gentlemen in waiting; or perhaps, in that beautiful position, which, before the forest grew up, must have commanded an extended view of a cultivated and inhabited plain, the king himself sat in it to receive the reports of his officers and to administer justice. Under our dominion Juan occupied the front corridor as a kitchen, and the other was our sleeping apartment.

From the centre door of this corridor a range of stone steps thirty feet long leads to a rectangular courtyard, eighty feet long by seventy broad. On each side of the steps are grim and gigantic figures, carved on stone in basso-relievo, nine or ten feet high, and in a position slightly inclined backward from the end of the steps to the floor of the corridor. The engraving opposite represents this side of the courtyard, and the one next following shows the figures alone, on a larger scale. They are adorned with rich headdresses and necklaces, but their attitude is that of pain and trouble. The design and anatomical proportions of the figures are faulty, but there is a force of expression about them which shows the skill and conceptive power of the artist.   When we first took possession of the palace this courtyard was encumbered with trees, so that we could hardly see across it, and it was so filled up with rubbish that we were obliged to make excavations of several feet before these figures could be drawn.

On each side of the courtyard the palace was divided into apartments, probably for sleeping. On the right the piers have all fallen down. On the left they are still standing, and ornamented with stucco figures. In

F. Catherwood.

A. L. Dick.

EAST SIDE OF COURT YARD OF PALACE AT PALENQUE.

F. Catherwood.

A.L. Dick.

EAST SIDE OF COURTYARD OF PALACE AT PALENQUE.

COLOSSAL BAS RELIEFS IN STONE
on the East side of Principal Court of the Palace Palenque.

F. Catherwood del

the centre apartment, in one of the holes before referred to of the arch, are the remains of a wooden pole about a foot long, which once stretched across, but the rest had decayed. It was the only piece of wood we found at Palenque, and we did not discover this until some time after we had made up our minds in regard to the wooden lintels over the doors. It was much worm-eaten, and probably, in a few years, not a vestige of it will be left.

At the farther side of the courtyard was another flight of stone steps, corresponding with those in front, on each side of which are carved figures, and on the flat surface between are single cartouches of hieroglyphics. The plate opposite represents this side.

The whole courtyard was overgrown with trees, and it was encumbered with ruins several feet high, so that the exact architectural arrangements could not be seen. Having our beds in the corridor adjoining, when we woke in the morning, and when we had finished the work of the day, we had it under our eyes. Every time we descended the steps the grim and mysterious figures stared us in the face, and it became to us one of the most interesting parts of the ruins. We were exceedingly anxious to make excavations, clear out the mass of rubbish, and lay the whole platform bare ; but this was impossible. It is probably paved with stone or cement ; and from the profusion of ornament in other parts, there is reason to believe that many curious and interesting specimens may be brought to light. This agreeable work is left for the future traveller, who may go there better provided with men and materials, and with more knowledge of what he has to encounter ; and, in my opinion, if he finds nothing new, the mere spectacle of the courtyard entire will repay him for the labour and expense of clearing it.

The part of the building which forms the rear of the courtyard, communicating with it by the steps, consists of two corridors, the same as the front, paved, plastered, and ornamented with stucco. The floor of the corridor fronting the courtyard sounded hollow, and a breach had been made in it which seemed to lead into a subterraneous chamber; but in descending, by means of a tree with notches cut in it, and with a candle, we found merely a hollow in the earth, not bounded by any wall.

In the farther corridor the wall was in some places broken, and had several separate coats of plaster and paint. In one place we counted six layers, each of which had the remains of colours. In another place there seemed a line of written characters in black ink. We made an effort to get at them; but, in endeavouring to remove a thin upper stratum, they came off with it, and we desisted.

This corridor opened upon a second courtyard, eighty feet long and but thirty across. The floor of the corridor was ten feet above that of the courtyard, and on the wall underneath were square stones with hieroglyphics sculptured upon them. On the piers were stuccoed figures, but in a ruined condition.

On the other side of the courtyard were two ranges of corridors, which terminated the building in this direction. The first of them is divided into three apartments, with doors opening from the extremities upon the western corridor. All the piers are standing except that on the northwest corner. All are covered with stucco ornaments, and one with hieroglyphics. The rest contain figures in bas-relief, three of which, being those least ruined, are represented in the opposite plates.

BAS RELIEF IN STUCCO
on one of the Piers of the West Front of the Palace Palenque

F. Catherwood del

BAS RELIEF IN STUCCO

on West Side of Palace Palenque

F. Catherwood del

BAS RELIEF IN STUCCO
on West Side of Palace Palenque.

F. Catherwood del.

The first was enclosed by a border, very wide at the bottom, part of which is destroyed. The subject consists of two figures with facial angles similar to that in the plate before given, plumes of feathers and other decorations for headdresses, necklaces, girdles, and sandals ; each has hold of the same curious baton, part of which is destroyed, and opposite their hands are hieroglyphics, which probably give the history of these incomprehensible personages. The others are more ruined, and no attempt has been made to restore them. One is kneeling as if to receive an honour, and the other a blow.

So far the arrangements of the palace are simple and easily understood ; but on the left are several distinct and independent buildings, as will be seen by the plan, the particulars of which, however, I do not consider it necessary to describe. The principal of these is the tower, on the south side of the second court. This tower is conspicuous by its height and proportions, but on examination in detail it is found unsatisfactory and uninteresting. The base is thirty feet square, and it has three stories. Entering over a heap of rubbish at the base, we found within another tower, distinct from the outer one, and a stone staircase, so narrow that a large man could not ascend it. The staircase terminates against a dead stone ceiling, closing all farther passage, the last step being only six or eight inches from it. For what purpose a staircase was carried up to such a bootless termination we could not conjecture. The whole tower was a substantial stone structure, and in its arrangements and purposes about as incomprehensible as the sculptured tablets.

East of the tower is another building with two corridors, one richly decorated with pictures in stucco, and having in the centre the elliptical tablet represented in the engraving opposite. It is four feet long and three wide, of hard stone set in the wall, and the sculpture is in bas-relief. Around it are the remains of a rich stucco border. The principal figure sits cross-legged on a couch ornamented with two leopards' heads; the attitude is easy, the physiognomy the same as that of the other personages, and the expression calm and benevolent. The figure wears around its neck a necklace of pearls, to which is suspended a small medallion containing a face; perhaps intended as an image of the sun. Like every other subject of sculpture we had seen in the country, the personage had earrings, bracelets on the wrists, and a girdle round the loins. The headdress differs from most of the others at Palenque in that it wants the plumes of feathers. Near the head are three hieroglyphics.

The other figure, which seems that of a woman, is sitting cross-legged on the ground, richly dressed, and apparently in the act of making an offering. In this supposed offering is seen a plume of feathers, in which the headdress of the principal person is deficient. Over the head of the sitting personage are four hieroglyphics. This is the only piece of sculptured stone about the palace except those in the courtyard. Under it formerly stood a table, of which the impression against the wall is still visible, and which is given in the engraving in faint lines, after the model of other tables still existing in other places.

At the extremity of this corridor there is an aperture in the pavement, leading by a flight of steps to a platform; from this a door, with an ornament in stucco over it, opens by another flight of steps upon a narrow, dark passage, terminating in other corridors, which run

OVAL BAS RELIEF IN STONE

in the Wall of one of the Apartments of the Palace Palenque

F. Catherwood del

BAS RELIEF IN STUCCO

on the Side of a doorway at Palenque

F. Catherwood del.

transversely. These are called subterraneous apartments; but there are windows opening from them above the ground, and, in fact, they are merely a ground-floor below the pavement of the corridors. In most parts, however, they are so dark that it is necessary to visit them with candles. There are no bas-reliefs or stucco ornaments; and the only objects which our guide pointed out or which attracted our attention, were several stone tables, one crossing and blocking up the corridor, about eight feet long, four wide, and three high. One of these lower corridors had a door opening upon the back part of the terrace, and we generally passed through it with a candle to get to the other buildings. In two other places there were flights of steps leading to corridors above. Probably these were sleeping apartments.

In that part of the plan marked Room No. 1, the walls were more richly decorated with stucco ornaments than any other in the palace; but, unfortunately, they were much mutilated. On each side of the doorway was a stucco figure, one of which, being the most perfect, is given in the engraving opposite. Near it is an apartment in which is marked " small altar." It was richly ornamented, like those which will be hereafter referred to in other buildings; and from the appearance of the back wall we supposed there had been stone tablets. In our utter ignorance of the habits of the people who had formerly occupied this building, it was impossible to form any conjecture for what uses these different apartments were intended; but if we are right in calling it a palace, the name which the Indians give it, it seems probable that the part surrounding the courtyards was for public and state occasions, and that the rest was occupied as the place of residence of the royal family; this room with the small altar, we may suppose, was what would be called, in our own times, a royal chapel.

With these helps and the aid of the plan, the reader will be able to find his way through the ruined palace of Palenque; he will form some idea of the profusion of its ornaments, of their unique and striking character, and of their mournful effect, shrouded by trees; and perhaps with him, as with us, fancy will present it as it was before the hand of ruin had swept over it, perfect in its amplitude and rich decorations, and occupied by the strange people whose portraits and figures now adorn its walls.

The reader will not be surprised that, with such objects to engage our attention, we disregarded some of the discomforts of our princely residence. We expected at this place to live upon game, but were disappointed. A wild turkey we could shoot at any time from the door of the palace; but, after trying one, we did not venture to trifle with our teeth upon another; and besides these, there was nothing but parrots, monkeys, and lizards, all very good eating, but which we kept in reserve for a time of pressing necessity. The density of the forest and the heavy rains would, however, have made sporting impracticable.

Once only I attempted an exploration. From the door of the palace, almost on a line with the front, rose a high steep mountain, which we thought must command a view of the city in its whole extent, and perhaps itself contain ruins. I took the bearing, and, with a compass in my hand and an Indian before me with his machete, from the rear of the last-mentioned building cut a straight line up east-northeast to the top. The ascent was so steep that I was obliged to haul myself up by the branches. On the top was a high mound of stones, with a foundation-wall still remaining. Probably a tower or temple had stood there, but the woods were as thick as below, and no part of the ruined city, not even the palace, could be seen. Trees were growing out of the top, up one of which I climbed, but could not see the palace or any one of the buildings. Back toward the mountain was nothing but forest; in front, through an opening in the trees, we saw a great wooded plain extending to Tobasco and the Gulf of Mexico; and the Indian at the foot of the tree, peering through the branches, turned his face up to me with a beaming expression, and pointing to a little spot on the plain, which was to him the world, cried out, "esta el pueblo," "there is the village." This was the only occasion on which I attempted to explore, for it was the only time I had any mark to aim at.

I must except, however, the exploration of an aqueduct which Pawling and I attempted together. It is supplied by a stream which runs at the base of the terrace on which the palace stands. At the time of our arrival the whole stream passed through this aqueduct. It was now swollen, and ran over the top and alongside. At the mouth we had great difficulty in stemming the torrent. Within it was perfectly dark, and we could not move without candles. The sides were of smooth stones about four feet high, and the roof was made by stones lapping over like the corridors of the buildings. At a short distance from the entrance the passage turned to the left, and at a distance of one hundred and sixty feet it was completely blocked up by the ruins of the roof, which had fallen down. What was its direction beyond it was impossible to determine, but certainly it did not pass under the palace, as has been supposed.

Besides the claps of thunder and flashes of lightning, we had one alarm at night. It was from a noise that sounded like the cracking of a dry branch under a stealthy tread, which, as we all started up together, I thought was that of a wild beast, but which Mr. Catherwood, whose bed was nearer, imagined to be that of a man. We climbed up the mound of fallen stones at the end of this corridor, but beyond all was thick darkness. Pawling fired twice as an intimation that we were awake, and we arranged poles across the corridor as a trap, so that even an Indian could not enter from that quarter without being thrown down with some considerable noise and detriment to his person.

Besides moschetoes and garrapatas, or ticks, we suffered from another worse insect, called by the natives *niguas*, which, we are told, pestered the Spaniards on their first entry into the country, and which, says the historian, " ate their Way into the Flesh, under the Nails of the Toes, then laid their Nits there within, and multiplied in such manner that there was no ridding them but by Cauteries, so that some lost their Toes, and some their Feet, whereas they should at first have been picked out ; but being as yet unacquainted with the Evil, they knew not how to apply the Remedy."

This description is true even to the last clause. We had escaped them until our arrival at Palenque, and being unacquainted with the evil, did not know how to apply the remedy. I carried one in my foot for several days, conscious that something was wrong, but not knowing what, until the nits had been laid and multiplied. Pawling undertook to pick them out with a penknife, which left a large hole in the flesh; and, unluckily, from the bites of various insects my foot became so inflamed that I could not get on shoe or stock-

ing. I was obliged to lie by, and, sitting an entire day
with my foot in a horizontal position, uncovered, it was
assaulted by small black flies, the bites of which I did
not feel at the moment of infliction, but which left
marks like the punctures of a hundred pins. The irritation was so great, and the swelling increased so much,
that I became alarmed, and determined to return to the
village. It was no easy matter to get there. The foot
was too big to put in a stirrup, and, indeed, to keep it
but for a few moments in a hanging position made it
feel as if the blood would burst through the skin, and
the idea of striking it against a bush makes me shudder
even now. It was indispensable, however, to leave the
place. I sent in to the village for a mule, and on the
tenth day after my arrival at the ruins, hopped down
the terrace, mounted, and laid the unfortunate member
on a pillow over the pommel of the saddle. This gave
me, for that muddy road, a very uncertain seat. I had
a man before me to cut the branches, yet my hat was
knocked off three or four times, and twice I was obliged
to dismount; but in due season, to my great relief, we
cleared the woods. After the closeness and confinement of the forest, coming once more into an open
country quickened every pulse.

As I ascended to the table on which the village stood,
I observed an unusual degree of animation, and a crowd
of people in the grass-grown street, probably some fifteen or twenty, who seemed roused at the sight of me,
and presently three or four men on horseback rode toward me. I had borne many different characters in
that country, and this time I was mistaken for three
padres who were expected to arrive that morning from
Tumbala. If the mistake had continued I should have
had dinner enough for six at least; but, unluckily, it

was soon discovered, and I rode on to the door of our old house. Presently the alcalde appeared, with his keys in his hands and in full dress, i. e., his shirt was inside of his pantaloons; and I was happy to find that he was in a worse humour at the coming of the padres than at our arrival ; indeed, he seemed now rather to have a leaning toward me, as one who could sympathize in his vexation at the absurdity of making such a fuss about them. When he saw my foot, too, he really showed some commiseration, and endeavoured to make me as comfortable as possible. The swelling had increased very much. I was soon on my back, and, lying perfectly quiet, by the help of a medicine-chest, starvation, and absence of irritating causes, in two days and nights I reduced the inflammation very sensibly.

CHAPTER XIX.

THE third day I heard from the ruins a voice of wailing. Juan had upset the lard, and every drop was gone. The imploring letter I received roused all my sensibilities; and, forgetting everything in the emergency, I hurried to the alcalde's, and told him a hog must die. The alcalde made difficulties, and to this day I cannot account for his concealing from me a fact of which he must have been aware, to wit, that on that very night a porker had been killed. Very early the next morning I saw a boy passing with some strings of fresh pork, hailed him, and he guided me to a hut in the suburbs, but yesterday the dwelling of the unfortunate quadruped. I procured the portion of some honest Palenquian, and returned, happy in the consciousness of making others so. That day was memorable, too, for another piece of good fortune ; for a courier arrived from Ciudad Real with despatches for Tobasco, and a back-load of bread on private account. As soon as the intelligence reached me, I despatched a messenger to negotiate for the whole stock. Unfortunately, it was sweetened, made up into diamonds, circles, and other fanciful forms, about two inches long and an inch thick, to be eaten with chocolate, and that detestable lard was oozing out of the crust. Nevertheless, it was

bread ; and placing it carefully on a table, with a fresh
cheese, the product of our cow, I lay down at night
full of the joy that morning would diffuse over the ruins of Palenque ; but, alas! all human calculations are
vain.   In my first sleep I was roused by a severe clap
of thunder, and detected an enormous cat on the table.
While my boot was sailing toward her, with one bound
she reached the wall and disappeared under the eaves
of the roof.   I fell asleep again ; she returned, and the
consequences were fatal.

The padres were slow in movement, and after keeping
the village in a state of excitement for three days, this
morning they made a triumphal entry, escorted by citizens, and with a train of more than a hundred Indians,
carrying hammocks, chairs, and luggage.   The villages
of Tumbala and San Pedro had turned out two or three
hundred strong, and carried them on their backs and
shoulders to Nopa, where they were met by a deputa-
tion from Palenque, and transferred to the village.   It
is a glorious thing in that country to be a padre, and
next to being a padre one's self is the position of being a
padre's friend.   In the afternoon I visited them, but
after the fatigues of the journey they were all asleep,
and the Indians around the door were talking in low
tones so as not to disturb them.   Inside were enormous
piles of luggage, which showed the prudent care the
good ecclesiastics took of themselves.   The siesta over,
very soon they appeared, one after the other, in dresses,
or rather undresses, difficult to describe, but certainly
by no means clerical ; neither of them had coat or jacket.
Two of them were the curas of Tumbala and Ayalon,
whom we had seen on our journey.   The third was a
Franciscan friar from Ciudad Real, and they had come
expressly to visit the ruins.   All had suffered severely

from the journey. The cura of Ayalon was a deputy to Congress, and in Mexico many inquiries had been made of him about the ruins, on the supposition that they were in his neighbourhood, which erroneous supposition he mentioned with a feeling reference to the intervening mountains. The padre of Tumbala was a promising young man of twenty-eight, and weighed at that time about twelve stone, or two hundred and forty pounds: a heavy load to carry about with him over such roads as they had traversed; but the Dominican friar suffered most, and he sat sideways in a hammock, with his vest open, wiping the perspiration from his breast. They were all intelligent men, and, in fact, the circumstance of their making the journey for no other purpose than to visit the ruins was alone an indication of their superior character. The Congressman we had seen on our way through his village, and then were struck with his general knowledge, and particularly with his force of character. He had borne an active part in all the convulsions of the country from the time of the revolution against Spain, of which he had been an instigator, and ever since, to the scandal of the Church party, stood forth as a Liberal; he had played the soldier as well as priest, laying down his blood-stained sword after a battle to confess the wounded and dying; twice wounded, once chronicled among the killed, an exile in Guatimala, and with the gradual recovery of the Liberal party restored to his place and sent as a deputy to Congress, where very soon he was to take part in new convulsions. They were all startled by the stories of moschetoes, insects, and reptiles at the ruins, and particularly by what they had heard of the condition of my foot.

While we were taking chocolate the cura of Palenque

entered.   At the time of our first arrival he was absent
at another village under his charge, and I had not seen
him before.   He was more original in his appearance
than either of the others, being very tall, with long black
hair, an Indian face and complexion, and certainly four
fifths Indian blood.   Indeed, if I had seen him in Indian costume, and what that is the reader by this time
understands, I should have taken him for a " puro," or
Indian of unmixed descent.   His dress was as unclerical as his appearance, consisting of an old straw hat,
with the rim turned up before, behind, and at the sides,
so as to make four regular corners, with a broad blue
velvet riband for a hatband, both soiled by long exposure to wind and rain.   Beneath this were a check shirt,
an old blue silk neckcloth with yellow stripes, a striped
roundabout jacket, black waistcoat, and pantaloons
made of bedticking, not meeting the waistcoat by two
inches, the whole tall figure ending below in yellow
buckskin shoes.   But under this outré appearance existed a charming simplicity and courtesy of manner, and
when he spoke his face beamed with kindness.   The
reception given him showed the good feeling existing
among the padres; and after some general conversation, the chocolate cups were removed, and one of the
padres went to his chest, whence he produced a pack
of cards, which he placed upon the table.   He said that
he always carried them with him, and it was very pleasant to travel with companions, as, wherever they stopped,
they could have a game at night.   The cards had evidently done much service, and there was something
orderly and systematic in the preliminary arrangements,
that showed the effect of regular habits and a well-train-
ed household.   An old Indian servant laid on the table a handful of grains of corn and a new bundle of

paper cigars. The grains of corn were valued at a medio. I declined joining in the game, whereupon one of
the reverend fathers kept aloof to entertain me, and the
other three sat down to Monté, still taking part in the
conversation. Very soon they became abstracted, and
I left them playing as earnestly as if the souls of uncon-
verted Indians were at stake. I had often heard the
ill-natured remark of foreigners, that two padres cannot
meet in that country without playing cards, but it was
the first time I had seen its verification; perhaps (I feel
guilty in saying so) because, except on public occasions,
it was the first time I had ever seen two padres together. Before I left them the padres invited me to dine
with them the next day, and on returning to my own
quarters I found that Don Santiago, the gentleman who
gave them the dinner, and, next to the prefect, the principal inhabitant, had called upon me with a like invitation, which I need not say I accepted.

The next day was Sunday; the storm of the night
had rolled away, the air was soft and balmy, the grass
was green, and, not being obliged to travel, I felt what
the natives aver, that the mornings of the rainy season
were the finest in the year. It was a great day for the
little church at Palenque. The four padres were there,
all in their gowns and surplices, all assisted in the ceremonies, and the Indians from every hut in the village
went to mass. This over, all retired, and in a few minutes the village was as quiet as ever.

At twelve o'clock I went to the house of Don Santiago
to dine. The three stranger padres were there, and most
of the guests were assembled. Don Santiago, the richest
man in Palenque, and the most extensive merchant, received us in his tienda or store, which was merely a few
shelves with a counter before them in one corner, and his

whole stock of merchandise was worth perhaps twenty
or thirty dollars; but Don Santiago was entirely a different style of man from one in such small business in this
country or Europe; courteous in manners, and intelligent for that country; he was dressed in white pantaloons and red slippers, a clean shirt with an embroidered bosom, and suspenders, which probably cost more
than all the rest of his habiliments, and were not to be
hidden under coat and waistcoat. In this place, which
had before seemed to me so much out of the world, I
was brought more directly in contact with home than
at any other I visited. The chair on which I sat came
from New-York; also a small looking-glass, two pieces
of American "cottons," and the remnant of a box of
vermicelli, of the existence of which in the place I was
not before advised. The most intimate foreign relations
of the inhabitants were with New-York, through the
port of Tobasco. They knew a man related to a family
in the village who had actually been at New-York, and
a barrel of New-York flour, the bare mention of which
created a yearning, had once reached the place. In
fact, New-York was more familiar to them than any
other part of the world except the capital. Don Santiago had a copy of Zavala's tour in the United States,
which, except a few volumes of the lives of saints, was
his library, and which he knew almost by heart; and
they had kept up with our political history so well as to
know that General Washington was not president, but
General Jackson.

The padre of Tumbala, he of two hundred and forty
pounds' weight, was somewhat of an exquisite in dress
for that country, and had brought with him his violin.
He was curious to know the state of musical science in
my country, and whether the government supported

good opera companies; regretted that I could not play some national airs, and entertained himself and the company with several of their own.

In the mean time the padre of Palenque was still missing, but, after being sent for twice, made his appearance. The dinner was in fact his; but, on account of want of conveniences in the convent from his careless housekeeping, was given by his friend Don Santiago on his behalf, and the answer of the boy sent to call him was that he had forgotten all about it. He was absent and eccentric enough for a genius, though he made no pretensions to that character. Don Santiago told us that he once went to the padre's house, where he found inside a cow and a calf; the cura, in great perplexity, apologized, saying that he could not help himself, they would come in; and considered it a capital idea when Don Santiago suggested to him the plan of driving them out.

As soon as he appeared the other padres rallied him upon his forgetfulness, which they insisted was all feigned; they had won sixteen dollars of him the night before, and said that he was afraid to come. He answered in the same strain that he was a ruined man. They offered him his revenge, and forthwith the table was brought out, cards and grains of corn were spread upon it as before, and while the padre of Tumbala played the violin, the other three played Monté. Being Sunday, in some places this would be considered rather irregular; at least, to do so with open doors would be considered setting a bad example to children and servants; and, in fact, considering myself on a pretty sociable footing, I could not help telling them that in my country they would all be read out of Church. The padre Congressman had met an Englishman in Mexico who told him the same thing, and also the manner of observing the Sunday in England, which they all thought must be very stupid.

Perhaps upon less ground than this the whole Spanish American priesthood has at times been denounced as a set of unprincipled gamblers, but I have too warm a recollection of their many kindnesses to hold them up in this light. They were all intelligent and good men, who would rather do benefits than an injury; in matters connected with religion they were most reverential, laboured diligently in their vocations, and were without reproach among their people. By custom and education they did not consider that they were doing wrong. From my agreeable intercourse with them, and my regard for their many good qualities, I would fain save them from denunciations of utter unworthiness which might be cast upon them. Nevertheless, it is true that dinner was delayed, and all the company kept waiting until they had finished their game of cards.

The table was set in an unoccupied house adjoining. Every white man in the village, except the prefect and alcalde, was present; the former being away at his hacienda, and the latter, from the sneering references he made to it, I suspected was not invited. In all there were fifteen or sixteen, and I was led to the seat of honour at the head of the table. I objected, but the padres seated me perforce. After the gentlemen were seated, it was found that, by sitting close, there was room for some ladies, and after the arrangements for the table were completed, they were invited to take seats. Unluckily, there was only room for three, who sat all together on my left. In a few minutes I felt very much as if the dinner was got up expressly for me. It was long since I had seen such a table, and I mourned in spirit that I had not sent notice for Mr. Catherwood to come to the village accidentally in time to get an invitation. But it was too late now; there was no time for reflection; every moment the dinner was going. In some places my position would have required me to devote myself to those on each side of me; but at Palenque they devoted themselves to me. If I stopped a moment my plate was whipped away, and another brought, loaded with something else. It may seem unmannerly, but I watched the fate of certain dishes, particularly some dolces or sweetmeats, hoping they would not be entirely consumed, as I purposed to secure all that should be left to take with me to the ruins. Wine was on the table, which was recommended to me as coming from New-York, but this was not enough to induce me to taste it. There was no water, and, by-the-way, water is never put on the table, and never drunk until after the dolces, which come on as the last course, when it is served in a large tumbler, which passes round for each one to sip from. It is entirely irregular and ill bred to ask for water during the meal. Each guest, as he rose from the table, bowed to Don Santiago, and said "muchas gratias," which I considered in bad taste, and not in keeping with the delicacy of Spanish courtesy, as the host ought rather to thank his guests for their society than they to thank him for his dinner. Nevertheless, as I had more reason to be thankful than any of them, I conformed to the example set me. After dinner my friends became drowsy and retired to siesta. I found my way back to Don Santiago's house, where, in a conversation with the ladies, I secured the remains of the dolces, and bought out his stock of vermicelli.

In the morning, my foot being sufficiently recovered,

I rode up to the house of the padres to escort them to the ruins. They had passed the evening sociably at cards, and again the padre of Palenque was wanting. We rode over to his house, and waited while he secured carefully on the back of a tall horse a little boy, who looked so wonderfully like him, that, out of respect to his obligation of celibacy, people felt delicate in asking whose son he was. This done, he tied an extra pair of shoes behind his own saddle, and we set off with the adios of all the village. The padres intended to pass the night at the ruins, and had a train of fifty or sixty Indians loaded with beds, bedding, provisions, sacate for mules, and multifarious articles, down to a white earthen washbowl; besides which, more favoured than we, they had four or five women.

Entering the forest, we found the branches of the trees, which had been trimmed on my return to the village, again weighed down by the rains; the streams were very bad; the padres were well mounted, but no horsemen, dismounted very often, and under my escort we got lost, but at eleven o'clock, very much to the satisfaction of all, our long, strange-looking, straggling party reached the ruins. The old palace was once more alive with inhabitants.

There was a marked change in it since I left; the walls were damp, the corridors wet; the continued rains were working through cracks and crevices, and opening leaks in the roof; saddles, bridles, boots, shoes, &c., were green and mildewed, and the guns and pistols covered with a coat of rust. Mr. Catherwood's appearance startled me. He was wan and gaunt; lame, like me, from the bites of insects; his face was swollen, and his left arm hung with rheumatism as if paralyzed.

We sent the Indians across the courtyard to the opposite corridor, where the sight of our loose traps might not tempt them to their undoing, and selecting a place for that purpose, the cartarets were set up immediately, and, with all the comforts of home, the padres lay down for an hour's rest. I had no ill-will toward these worthy men; on the contrary, the most friendly feeling; but, to do the honours of the palace, I invited them to dine with us. Catherwood and Pawling objected, and they would have done better if left to themselves; but they appreciated the spirit of the invitation, and returned me muchas gratias. After their siesta I escorted them over the palace, and left them in their apartment. Singularly enough, that night there was no rain; so that, with a hat before a candle, we crossed the courtyard and paid them a visit; we found the three reverend gentlemen sitting on a mat on the ground, winding up the day with a comfortable game at cards, and the Indians asleep around them.

The next morning, with the assistance of Pawling and the Indians to lift and haul them, I escorted them to the other buildings, heard some curious speculations, and at two o'clock, with many expressions of good-will, and pressing invitations to their different convents, they returned to the village.

Late in the afternoon the storm set in with terrific thunder, which at night rolled with fearful crashes against the walls, while the vivid lightning flashed along the corridors. The padres had laughed at us for their superior discrimination in selecting a sleeping-place, and this night their apartment was flooded. From this time my notebook contains memoranda only of the arrival of the Indians, with the time that the storm set in, its violence and duration, the deluges of rain, and the places to which we were obliged to move

our beds.   Every day our residence became more wet
and uncomfortable.   On Thursday, the thirtieth of May,
the storm opened with a whirlwind.   At night the crash
of falling trees rang through the forest, rain fell in deluges, the roaring of thunder was terrific, and as we lay
looking out, the aspect of the ruined palace, lighted
by the glare of lightning such as I never saw in this
country, was awfully grand; in fact, there was too much
of the sublime and terrible.   The storm threatened the
very existence of the building; and, knowing the tottering state of the walls, for some moments we had apprehensions lest the whole should fall and crush us.   In
the morning the courtyard and the ground below the
palace were flooded, and by this time the whole front
was so wet that we were obliged to desert it and move
to the other side of the corridor.   Even here we were
not much better off; but we remained until Mr. Catherwood had finished his last drawing; and on Saturday,
the first of June, like rats leaving a sinking ship, we
broke up and left the ruins.   Before leaving, however,
I will present a description of the remaining buildings.

GENERAL VIEW OF PALENQUE.

F. Catherwood.

North.

West

South.

East.

GENERAL PLAN

Of the Ruins of

PALENQUE.

This Plan is not to be regarded as perfectly correct. No means existed of cutting down the dense Forest which surrounds the Monuments, and consequently the bearings and distances must be considered only as close approximation to the truth.

Casa No. 5, is so much destroyed, that the Ground Plan cannot be made out.

The dotted lines show the paths to the different Monuments.

Casa No. 4.

Casa No. 1.

The Palace.

Acqueduct

Milpa, or Field of Maize.

Small Stream

Casa No. 2.

Casa No. 3.

Casa No. 5.

Scale of Feet.
100 40 0   1   2   3   4   5   6   7   8   9   1000 Feet

F. Catherwood.

CHAPTER XX.

THE plan opposite indicates the position of all the
buildings which have been discovered at Palenque.
There are remains of others in the same vicinity, but
so utterly dilapidated that we have not thought it worth
while to give any description of them, nor even to indicate their places on the plan.

From the palace no other building is visible.   Passing
out by what is called the subterraneous passage, you descend the southwest corner of the terrace, and at the foot
immediately commence ascending a ruined pyramidal
structure, which appears once to have had steps on all its
sides.   These steps have been thrown down by the trees,
and it is necessary to clamber over stones, aiding the feet
by clinging to the branches.   The ascent is so steep,
that if the first man displaces a stone it bounds down
the side of the pyramid, and wo to those behind.   About
half way up, through openings in the trees, is seen the

building represented in the engraving opposite. The height of the structure on which it stands is one hundred and ten feet on the slope. The engravings represent the actual condition of the building, surrounded and overgrown by trees, but no description and no drawing can give effect to the moral sublimity of the spectacle. From the multiplicity of engravings required to illustrate the architecture and arts of this unknown people, I have omitted a series of views, exhibiting the most picturesque and striking subjects that ever presented themselves to the pencil of an artist. The ruins and the forest made the deep and abiding impression upon our minds; but our object is to present the building as restored, as subjects for speculation and comparison with the architecture of other lands and times. The supposed restorations were made after a careful examination, and in each case the reader will see precisely what we had to guide us in making them. I must remark, however, that the buildings are the only parts which we attempted to restore; the specimens of sculpture and stuccoed ornaments were drawn as we found them.

Casa No. 1.

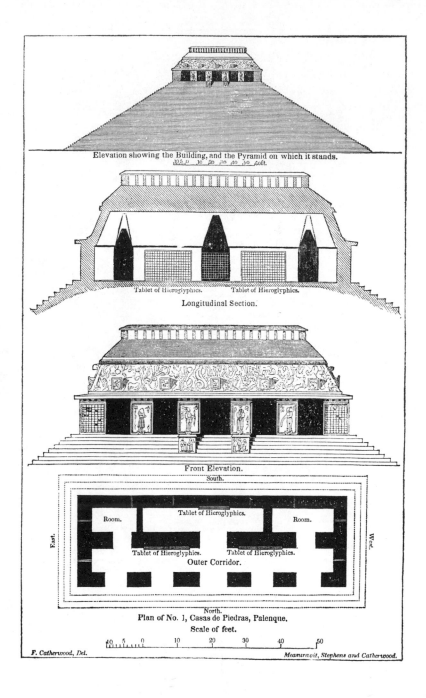

Elevation showing the Building, and the Pyramid on which it stands.

10.5 0 10 20 30 40 50 60ft.

Tablet of Hieroglyphics.   Tablet of Hieroglyphics.

Longitudinal Section.

Front Elevation.

South.

Room.   Tablet of Hieroglyphics.   Room.

East   West.

Tablet of Hieroglyphics.   Tablet of Hieroglyphics.

Outer Corridor.

North.

Plan of No. 1, Casas de Piedras, Palenque.

Scale of feet.

10.5 0   10   20   30   40   50

F. Catherwood, Del.   Measured by Stephens and Catherwood.

The engraving opposite represents the same building cleared from forest and restored, and, according to our division, marked on the plan No. 1. In the plate are given the ground-plan (beginning at the bottom), the front elevation, a section showing the position of tablets within, and the front elevation on a smaller scale, with the pyramidal structure on which it stands.

The building is seventy-six feet in front and twenty-five feet deep. It has five doors and six piers, all standing. The whole front was richly ornamented in stucco, and the corner piers are covered with hieroglyphics, each of which contains ninety-six squares.

The four piers are ornamented with human figures, two on each side, facing each other, which are represented in the following engravings in the order in which they stand upon the piers.

The first is that of a woman with a child in her arms; at least we suppose it to be intended for a woman from the dress. It is enclosed by an elaborate border, and stands on a rich ornament. The head is destroyed. Over the top are three hieroglyphics, and there are traces of hieroglyphics broken off in the corner. The other three are of the same general character; each probably had an infant in the arms, and over each are hieroglyphics.

At the foot of the two centre piers, resting on the steps, are two stone tablets with what seemed interesting figures, but so encumbered with ruins that it was impossible to draw them.

F. Catherwood del.

PIER Nº 1

BAS RELIEF IN STUCCO,
on one of the Piers of Nº 1 Casas de Piedra Palenque.

F. Catherwood del.

Pier Nº 2, North   **PALENQUE**   Nº 1, Casa de Piedra

On Stone by J. H. Colen.   F. Catherwood del.

Pier Nº 3.   **PALENQUE.** Nº1 Casas de Piedra.

Pier N.º 4.   PALENQUE.   N.º 1 Casas de Piedra.

The interior of the building is divided into two corridors, running lengthwise, with a ceiling rising nearly to
a point, as in the palace, and paved with large square
stones. The front corridor is seven feet wide. The
separating wall is very massive, and has three doors,
a large one in the centre, and a smaller one on each
side. In this corridor, on each side of the principal
door, is a large tablet of hieroglyphics, each thirteen
feet long and eight feet high, and each divided into two
hundred and forty squares of characters or symbols.
Both are set in the wall so as to project three or four
inches. In one place a hole had been made in the
wall close to the side of one of them, apparently for
the purpose of attempting its removal, by which we
discovered that the stone is about a foot thick. The

sculpture is in bas-relief. The tablets are represented in the engravings opposite.

The construction of the tablets was a large stone on each side, and smaller ones in the centre, as indicated by the dark lines in the engravings.

In the right-hand tablet one line is obliterated by water that has trickled down for an unknown length of time, and formed a sort of stalactite or hard substance, which has incorporated itself with the stone, and which we could not remove, though perhaps it might be detached by some chemical process. In the other tablet, nearly one half of the hieroglyphics are obliterated by the action of water and decomposition of the stone. When we first saw them both tablets were covered with a thick coat of green moss, and it was necessary to wash and scrape them, clear the lines with a stick, and scrub them thoroughly, for which last operation a pair of blacking-brushes that Juan had picked up in my house at Guatimala, and disobeyed my order to throw away upon the road, proved exactly what we wanted and could not have procured. Besides this process, on account of the darkness of the corridor, from the thick shade of the trees growing before it, it was necessary to burn candles or torches, and to throw a strong light upon the stones while Mr. Catherwood was drawing.

The corridor in the rear is dark and gloomy, and divided into three apartments. Each of the side apartments has two narrow openings about three inches wide and a foot high. They have no remains of sculpture, or painting, or stuccoed ornaments. In the centre apartment, set in the back wall, and fronting the principal door of entrance, is another tablet of hieroglyphics, four feet six inches wide and three feet six inches high. The roof above it is tight; consequently it has not suf-

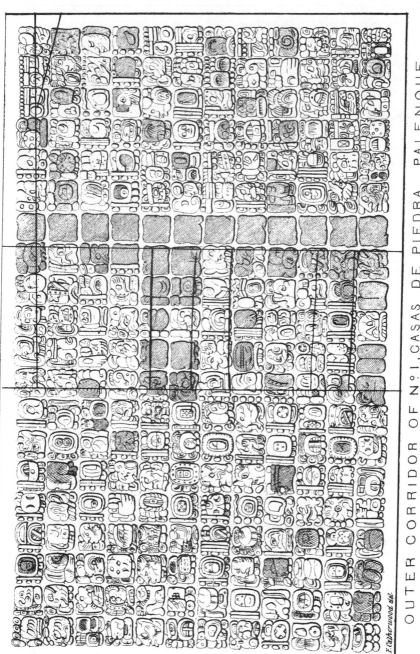

OUTER CORRIDOR OF N°I, CASAS DE PIEDRA PALENQUE

Right hand side Tablet.

F. Catherwood del.

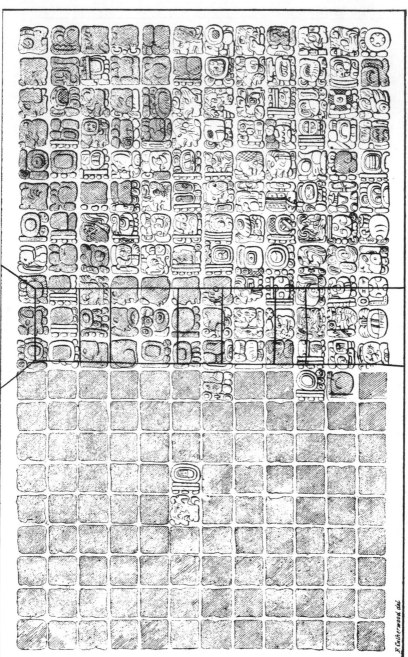

OUTER CORRIDOR OF Nº I, CASAS DE PIEDRA, PALENQUE.

Left hand side Tablet.

F. Catherwood del.

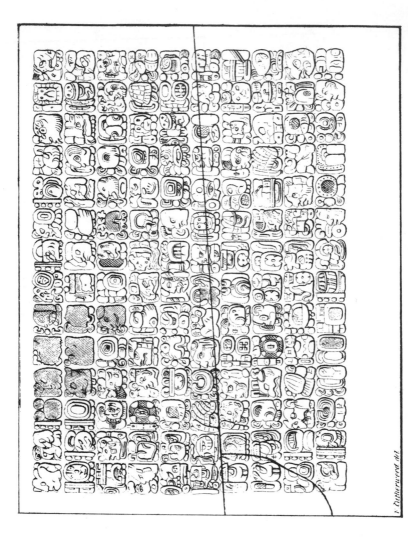

TABLET ON THE INNER WALL OF CASA Nº I.

J. Catherwood del.

fered from exposure, and the hieroglyphics are perfect, though the stone is cracked lengthwise through the middle, as indicated in the engraving.

The impression made upon our minds by these speaking but unintelligible tablets I shall not attempt to describe. From some unaccountable cause they have never before been presented to the public. Captains Del Rio and Dupaix both refer to them, but in very few words, and neither of them has given a single drawing. Acting under a royal commission, and selected, doubtless, as fit men for the duties intrusted to them, they cannot have been ignorant or insensible of their value. It is my belief they did not give them because in both cases the artists attached to their expedition were incapable of the labour, and the steady, determined perseverance required for drawing such complicated, unintelligible, and anomalous characters. As at Copan, Mr. Catherwood divided his paper into squares; the original drawings were reduced, and the engravings corrected by himself, and I believe they are as true copies as the pencil can make : the real written records of a lost people. The Indians call this building an escuela or school, but our friends the padres called it a tribunal of justice, and these stones, they said, contained the tables of the law.

There is one important fact to be noticed. The hieroglyphics are the same as were found at Copan and Quirigua. The intermediate country is now occupied by races of Indians speaking many different languages, and entirely unintelligible to each other ; but there is room for the belief that the whole of this country was once occupied by the same race, speaking the same language, or, at least, having the same written characters.

There is no staircase or other visible communication

between the lower and upper parts of this building, and the only way of reaching the latter was by climbing a tree which grows close against the wall, and the branches of which spread over the roof. The roof is inclined, and the sides are covered with stucco ornaments, which, from exposure to the elements, and the assaults of trees and bushes, are faded and ruined, so that it was impossible to draw them; but enough remained to give the impression that, when perfect and painted, they must have been rich and imposing. Along the top was a range of pillars eighteen inches high and twelve apart, made of small pieces of stone laid in mortar, and covered with stucco, crowning which is a layer of flat projecting stones, having somewhat the appearance of a low open balustrade.

In front of this building, at the foot of the pyramidal structure, is a small stream, part of which supplies the aqueduct before referred to. Crossing this, we come upon a broken stone terrace about sixty feet on the slope, with a level esplanade at the top, one hundred and ten feet in breadth, from which rises another pyramidal structure, now ruined and overgrown with trees; it is one hundred and thirty-four feet high on the slope, and on its summit is the building marked No. 2, like the first shrouded among trees, but presented in the engraving opposite as restored. The plate contains, as before, the ground-plan, front elevation, section, and front elevation on a smaller scale, with the pyramidal structure on which it stands.

This building is fifty feet front, thirty-one feet deep, and has three doorways. The whole front was covered with stuccoed ornaments. The two outer piers contain hieroglyphics; one of the inner piers is fallen, and

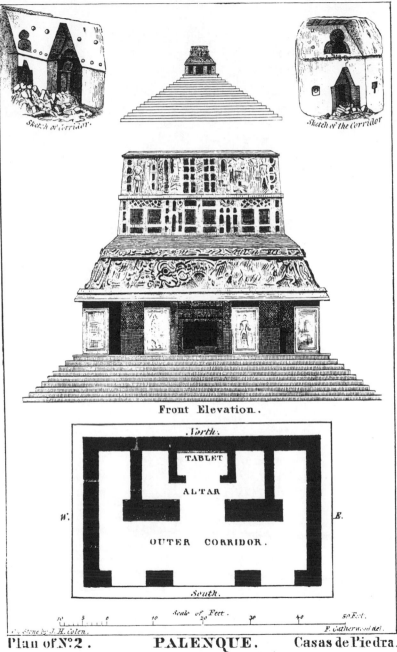

Sketch of Corridor.

Sketch of the Corridor.

Front Elevation.

North.

TABLET

ALTAR

W.   E.

OUTER   CORRIDOR.

South.

Scale of Feet.

10   5   0   10   20   30   40   50 Feet.

On Stone by J. H. Colen.   F. Catherwood del.

Plan of Nº 2 .   **PALENQUE.**   Casas de Piedra.

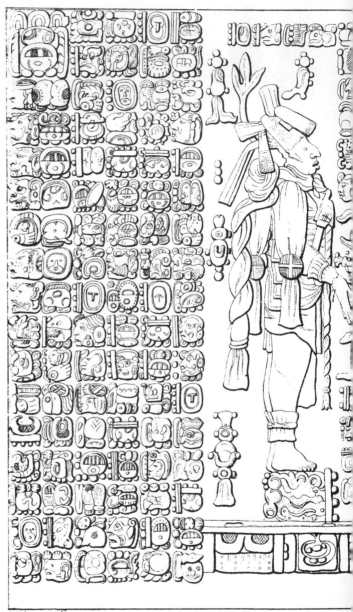

TABLET ON THE BAC

ALL OF ALTAR CASA Nº 2.

the other is ornamented with a figure in bas-relief, but faded and ruined.

The interior, again, is divided into two corridors running lengthwise, with ceilings as before, and pavements of large square stones, in which forcible breaches have been made, doubtless by Captain Del Rio, and excavations underneath. The back corridor is divided into three apartments, and opposite the principal door of entrance is an oblong enclosure, with a heavy cornice or moulding of stucco, and a doorway richly ornamented over the top, but now much defaced; on each side of the doorway was a tablet of sculptured stone, which, however, has been removed. Within, the chamber is thirteen feet wide and seven feet deep. There was no admission of light except from the door; the sides were without ornament of any kind, and in the back wall, covering the whole width, was the tablet given in the engraving opposite. It was ten feet eight inches wide, six feet four inches in height, and consisted of three separate stones. That on the left, facing the spectator, is still in its place. The middle one has been removed and carried down the side of the structure, and now lies near the bank of the stream. It was removed many years ago by one of the inhabitants of the village, with the intention of carrying it to his house; but, after great labour, with no other instruments than the arms and hands of Indians, and poles cut from trees, it had advanced so far, when its removal was arrested by an order from the government forbidding any farther abstraction from the ruins. We found it lying on its back near the banks of the stream, washed by many floods of the rainy season, and covered with a thick coat of dirt and moss. We had it scrubbed and propped up, and probably the next traveller will find it with the same props under it which we placed there. In the engraving it is given in its original position on the wall. The stone on the right is broken, and, unfortunately, altogether destroyed; most of the fragments have disappeared; but, from the few we found among the ruins in the front of the building, there is no doubt that it contained ranges of hieroglyphics corresponding in general appearance with those of the stone on the left.

The tablet, as given in the engraving, contains only two thirds of the original. In Del Rio's work it is not represented at all. In Dupaix it is given, not, however, as it exists, but as made up by the artist in Paris, so as to present a perfect picture. The subject is reversed, with the cross in the centre, and on each side a single row of hieroglyphics, only eight in number. Probably, when Dupaix saw it (thirty-four years before), it was entire, but the important features of six rows of hieroglyphics on each side of the principal figures, each row containing seventeen in a line, do not appear. This is the more inexcusable in his publishers, as in his report Dupaix expressly refers to these numerous hieroglyphics; but it is probable that his report was not accompanied by any drawings of them.

The principal subject of this tablet is the cross. It is surmounted by a strange bird, and loaded with indescribable ornaments. The two figures are evidently those of important personages. They are well drawn, and in symmetry of proportion are perhaps equal to many that are carved on the walls of the ruined temples in Egypt. Their costume is in a style different from any heretofore given, and the folds would seem to indicate that they were of a soft and pliable texture, like cotton. Both are looking toward the cross, and one seems in the act of making an offering, perhaps of a child; all speculations on the subject are of course entitled to little regard, but perhaps it would not be wrong to ascribe to these personages a sacerdotal character. The hieroglyphics doubtless explain all. Near them are other hieroglyphics, which reminded us of the Egyptian mode for recording the name, history, office, or character of the persons represented. This tablet of the cross has given rise to more learned speculations than perhaps any others found at Palenque. Dupaix and his commentators, assuming for the building a very remote antiquity, or, at least, a period long antecedent to the Christian era, account for the appearance of the cross by the argument that it was known and had a symbolical meaning among ancient nations long before it was established as the emblem of the Christian faith. Our friends the padres, at the sight of it, immediately decided that the old inhabitants of Palenque were Christians, and by conclusions which are sometimes called jumping, they fixed the age of the buildings in the third century.

There is reason to believe that this particular building was intended as a temple, and that the enclosed inner chamber was an adoratorio, or oratory, or altar. What the rites and ceremonies of worship may have been, no one can undertake to say.

The upper part of this building differs from the first. As before, there was no staircase or other communication inside or out, nor were there the remains of any. The only mode of access was, in like manner, by climbing a tree, the branches of which spread across the roof. The roof was inclined, and the sides were richly ornamented with stucco figures, plants, and flowers, but mostly ruined. Among them were the fragments of a beautiful head and of two bodies, in justness of proportion and symmetry approaching the Greek models. On the top of this roof is a narrow platform, supporting what, for the sake of description, I shall call two stories. The platform is but two feet ten inches wide, and the superstructure of the first story is seven feet five inches in height ; that of the second eight feet five inches, the width of the two being the same.   The ascent from one to the other is by square projecting stones, and the covering of the upper story is of flat stones laid across and projecting over.   The long sides of this narrow structure are of open stucco work, formed into curious and indescribable devices, human figures with legs and arms spreading and apertures between ; and the whole was once loaded with rich and elegant ornaments in stucco relief.   Its appearance at a distance must have been that of a high, fanciful lattice.   Altogether, like the rest of the architecture and ornaments, it was perfectly unique, different from the works of any other people with which we were familiar, and its uses and purposes entirely incomprehensible.   Perhaps it was intended as an observatory.   From the upper gallery, through openings in the trees growing around, we looked out over an immense forest, and saw the Lake of Terminos and the Gulf of Mexico.

Near this building was another interesting monument, which had been entirely overlooked by those who preceded us in a visit to Palenque, and I mention this fact in the hope that the next visiter may discover many things omitted by us.   It lies in front of the building, about forty or fifty feet down the side of the pyramidal structure.   When we first passed it with our guide it lay on its face, with its head downward, and half buried by an accumulation of earth and stones.   The outer side was rough and unhewn, and our attention was attract-

CATHERWOOD.

LOSSING.

Stone Statue in front of Casa No. 2.

12   6   0   1   2   3

Scale of feet.

12 6 0   1   2   3

Scale for the small Figure.

ed by its size; our guide said it was not sculptured; but, after he had shown us everything that he had knowledge of, and we had discharged him, in passing it again we stopped and dug around it, and discovered that the under surface was carved. The Indians cut down some saplings for levers, and rolled it over. The opposite engraving represents this monument. It is the only statue that has ever been found at Palenque. We were at once struck with its expression of serene repose and its strong resemblance to Egyptian statues, though in size it does not compare with the gigantic remains of Egypt. In height it is ten feet six inches, of which two feet six inches were under ground. The headdress is lofty and spreading; there are holes in the place of ears, which were perhaps adorned with earrings of gold and pearls. Round the neck is a necklace, and pressed against the breast by the right hand is an instrument apparently with teeth. The left hand rests on a hieroglyphic, from which descends some symbolical ornament. The lower part of the dress bears an unfortunate resemblance to the modern pantaloons, but the figure stands on what we have always considered a hieroglyphic, analogous again to the custom in Egypt of recording the name and office of the hero or other person represented. The sides are rounded, and the back is of rough stone. Probably it stood imbedded in a wall.

From the foot of the elevation on which the last-mentioned building stands, their bases almost touching, rises another pyramidal structure of about the same height, on the top of which is the building marked No. 3. Such is the density of the forest, even on the sides of the pyramidal structure, that, though in a right line but a short distance apart, one of these buildings cannot be seen from the other.

The engraving opposite represents this building as restored, not from any fancied idea of what it might have been, but from such remains and indications that it was impossible to make anything else of it. It is thirty-eight feet front and twenty-eight feet deep, and has three doors. The end piers are ornamented with hieroglyphics in stucco, two large medallions in handsome compartments, and the intermediate ones with bas-reliefs, also in stucco; in general character similar to those before given, and for that reason, not to multiply engravings, I omit them.

Front Elevation.

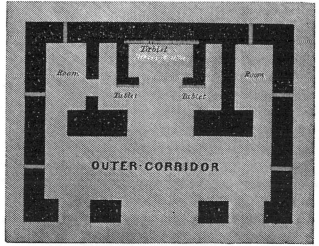

Plan of No. 3, Casas de Piedra, Palenque.

10   5   0   10   20   30

Scale of feet.

F. Catherwood.

Casa No. 4, Front Corridor.

The interior, again, is divided into two corridors, about nine feet wide each, and paved with stone. The engraving opposite represents the front corridor, with the ceiling rising nearly to a point, and covered at the top with a layer of flat stones. In several places on each side are holes, which are found also in all the other corridors; they were probably used to support poles for scaffolding while the building was in process of erection, and had never been filled up. At the extreme end, cut through the wall, is one of the windows before referred to, which have been the subject of speculation from analogy to the letter Tau.

The back corridor is divided into three apartments. In the centre, facing the principal door of entrance, is an enclosed chamber similar to that which in the last building we have called an oratory or altar. Its shadow is seen in the engraving. The top of the doorway was gorgeous with stuccoed ornaments, and on the piers at each side were stone tablets in bas-relief. Within, the chamber was four feet seven inches deep and nine feet wide. There were no stuccoed ornaments or paintings, but set in the back wall was a stone tablet covering the whole width of the chamber, nine feet wide and eight feet high.

The tablet is given in the frontispiece of this volume, and I beg to call to it the particular attention of the reader, as the most perfect and most interesting monument in Palenque. Neither Del Rio nor Dupaix has given any drawing of it, and it is now for the first time presented to the public. It is composed of three separate stones, the joints in which are shown by the blurred lines in the engraving. The sculpture is perfect, and the characters and figures stand clear and distinct on the stone. On each side are rows of hieroglyphics.

The principal personages will be recognised at once as the same who are represented in the tablet of the cross. They wear the same dress, but here both seem to be making offerings. Both personages stand on the backs of human beings, one of whom supports himself by his hands and knees, and the other seems crushed to the ground by the weight. Between them, at the foot of the tablet, are two figures, sitting cross-legged, one bracing himself with his right hand on the ground, and with the left supporting a square table ; the attitude and action of the other are the same, except that they are in reverse order. The table also rests upon their bended necks, and their distorted countenances may perhaps be considered expressions of pain and suffering. They are both clothed in leopard-skins. Upon this table rest two batons crossed, their upper extremities richly ornamented, and supporting what seems a hideous mask, the eyes widely expanded, and the tongue hanging out. This seems to be the object to which the principal personages are making offerings.

The pier on each side of the doorway contained a stone tablet, with figures carved in bas-relief, which are represented in the two following engravings. These tablets, however, have been removed from their place to the village, and set up in the wall of a house as ornaments. They were the first objects which we saw, and the last which Mr. Catherwood drew. The house belonged to two sisters, who have an exaggerated idea of the value of these tablets ; and, though always pleased with our coming to see them, made objections to having them copied. We obtained permission only by promising a copy for them also, which, however, Mr. Catherwood, worn out with constant labour, was entirely unable to make. I cut out of Del Rio's book the

F. Catherwood.

BAS RELIEF ON SIDE OF DOOR OF ALTAR.

BAS RELIEF ON SIDE OF DOOR OF ALTAR.

drawings of the same subjects, which I thought, being printed, would please them better; but they had examined Mr. Catherwood's drawing in its progress, and were not at all satisfied with the substitute. The moment I saw these tablets I formed the idea of purchasing them and carrying them home as a sample of Palenque, but it was some time before I ventured to broach the subject. They could not be purchased without the house; but that was no impediment, for I liked the house also. It was afterward included among the subjects of other negotiations which were undetermined when I left Palenque.

The two figures stand facing each other, the first on the right hand, fronting the spectator. The nose and eyes are strongly marked, but altogether the development is not so strange as to indicate a race entirely different from those which are known. The headdress is curious and complicated, consisting principally of leaves of plants, with a large flower hanging down; and among the ornaments are distinguished the beak and eyes of a bird, and a tortoise. The cloak is a leopard's skin, and the figure has ruffles around the wrists and ancles.

The second figure, standing on the left of the spectator, has the same profile which characterizes all the others at Palenque. Its headdress is composed of a plume of feathers, in which is a bird holding a fish in its mouth; and in different parts of the headdress there are three other fishes. The figure wears a richly-embroidered tippet, and a broad girdle, with the head of some animal in front, sandals, and leggins: the right hand is extended in a prayerful or deprecating position, with the palm outward. Over the heads of these mysterious personages are three cabalistic hieroglyphics.

We considered the oratorio or altar the most interesting portion of the ruins of Palenque ; and in order that the reader may understand it in all its details, the plate opposite is presented, which shows distinctly all the combinations of the doorway, with its broken ornaments, the tablets on each side ; and within the doorway is seen the large tablet on the back of the inner wall. The reader will form from it some idea of the whole, and of its effect upon the stranger, when, as he climbs up the ruined pyramidal structure, on the threshold of the door this scene presents itself. We could not but regard it as a holy place, dedicated to the gods, and consecrated by the religious observances of a lost and unknown people. Comparatively, the hand of ruin has spared it, and the great tablet, surviving the wreck of elements, stands perfect and entire. Lonely, deserted, and without any worshippers at its shrine, the figures and characters are distinct as when the people who reared it went up to pay their adorations before it. To us it'was all a mystery; silent, defying the most scrutinizing gaze and reach of intellect. Even our friends the padres could make nothing of it.

Near this, on the top of another pyramidal structure, was another building entirely in ruins, which apparently had been shattered and hurled down by an earthquake. The stones were strewed on the side of the pyramid, and it was impossible even to make out the groundplan.

Returning to No. 1 and proceeding south, at a distance of fifteen hundred feet, and on a pyramidal structure one hundred feet high from the bank of the river, is another building, marked on the plan No. 4, twenty feet front and eighteen feet deep, but in an unfortunately ruined condition. The whole of the front wall has fallen, leaving the outer corridor entirely exposed.

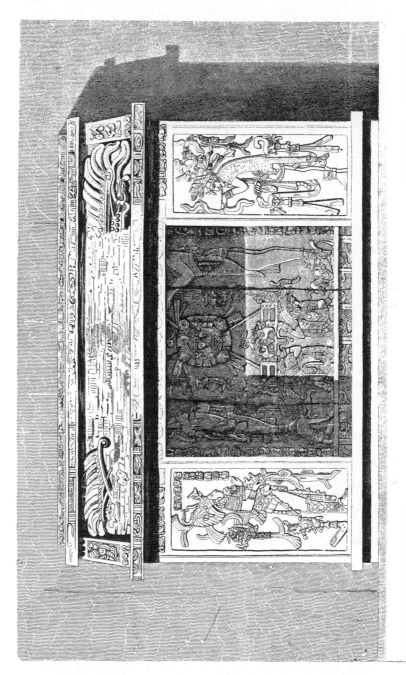

F. Catherwood.

A. L. Dick.

ADORATORIO OR ALTAR. CASA Nº 3.

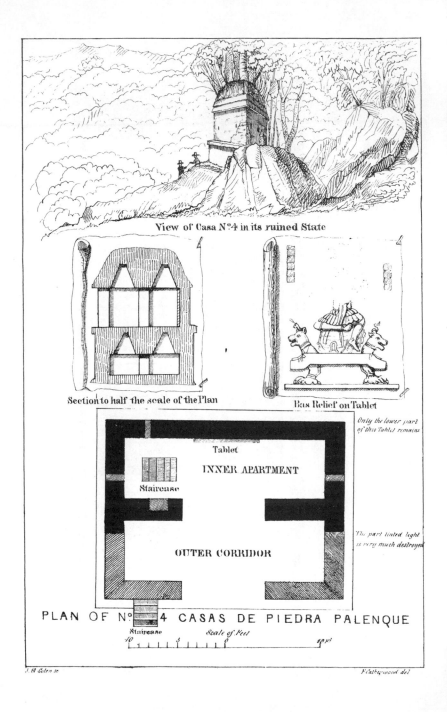

View of Casa Nº 4 in its ruined State

Section to half the scale of the Plan

Bas Relief on Tablet

Only the lower part
of this Tablet remains

Tablet

Staircase

INNER APARTMENT

The part tinted light
is very much destroyed

OUTER CORRIDOR

Staircase   Scale of Feet

PLAN OF Nº 4 CASAS DE PIEDRA PALENQUE

J. H. Coton sc   F. Catherwood del

Fronting the door, and against the back wall of the inner corridor, was a large stucco ornament representing a figure sitting on a couch; but a great part has fallen or been taken off and carried away. The body of the couch, with tiger's feet, is all that now remains. The outline of two tigers' heads and of the sitting personage is seen on the wall. The loss or destruction of this ornament is more to be regretted, as from what remains it appears to have been superior in execution to any other stucco relief in Palenque. The body of the couch is entire, and the leg and foot hanging down the side are elegant specimens of art and models for study. The plate opposite represents this relief, and also a plan, section, and general view of the building.

I have now given, without speculation or comment, a full description of the ruins of Palenque. I repeat what I stated in the beginning, there may be more buildings, but, after a close examination of the vague reports current in the village, we are satisfied that no more have ever been discovered; and from repeated inquries of Indians who had traversed the forest in every direction in the dry season, we are induced to believe that no more exist. The whole extent of ground covered by those as yet known, as appears by the plan, is not larger than our Park or Battery. In stating this fact I am very far from wishing to detract from the importance or interest of the subject. I give our opinion, with the grounds of it, and the reader will judge for himself how far these are entitled to consideration. It is proper to add, however, that, considering the space now occupied by the ruins as the site of palaces, temples, and public buildings, and supposing the houses of the inhabitants to have been, like those of the Egyptians and the present race of Indians, of frail and perishable

materials, and, as at Memphis and Thebes, to have disappeared altogether, the city may have covered an immense extent.

The reader is perhaps disappointed, but we were not.
There was no necessity for assigning to the ruined city
an immense extent, or an antiquity coeval with that of
the Egyptians or of any other ancient and known people. What we had before our eyes was grand, curious,
and remarkable enough. Here were the remains of a
cultivated, polished, and peculiar people, who had passed
through all the stages incident to the rise and fall of nations; reached their golden age, and perished, entirely
unknown. The links which connected them with the
human family were severed and lost, and these were
the only memorials of their footsteps upon earth. We
lived in the ruined palace of their kings; we went up
to their desolate temples and fallen altars; and wherever we moved we saw the evidences of their taste,
their skill in arts, their wealth and power. In the midst
of desolation and ruin we looked back to the past,
cleared away the gloomy forest, and fancied every
building perfect, with its terraces and pyramids, its
sculptured and painted ornaments, grand, lofty, and
imposing, and overlooking an immense inhabited plain;
we called back into life the strange people who gazed
at us in sadness from the walls; pictured them, in fanciful costumes and adorned with plumes of feathers, ascending the terraces of the palace and the steps leading to the temples; and often we imagined a scene of
unique and gorgeous beauty and magnificence, realizing the creations of Oriental poets, the very spot which
fancy would have selected for the "Happy Valley" of
Rasselas. In the romance of the world's history nothing ever impressed me more forcibly than the specta-

cle of this once great and lovely city, overturned, desolate, and lost; discovered by accident, overgrown with trees for miles around, and without even a name to distinguish it. Apart from everything else, it was a mourning witness to the world's mutations.

> " Nations melt
> From Power's high pinnacle, when they have felt
> The sunshine for a while, and downward go."

As at Copan, I shall not at present offer any conjecture in regard to the antiquity of these buildings, merely remarking that at ten leagues' distance is a village called Las Tres Cruces or the Three Crosses, from three crosses which, according to tradition, Cortez erected at that place when on his conquering march from Mexico to Honduras by the Lake of Peten. Cortez, then, must have passed within twenty or thirty miles of the place now called Palenque. If it had been a living city, its fame must have reached his ears, and he would probably have turned aside from his road to subdue and plunder it. It seems, therefore, but reasonable to suppose that it was at that time desolate and in ruins, and even the memory of it lost.

CHAPTER XXI.

Departure from the Ruins.—Bad Road.—An Accident.—Arrival at the Village.
—A Funeral Procession.—Negotiations for Purchasing Palenque.—Making
Casts.—Final Departure from Palenque.—Beautiful Plain.—Hanging Birds'-
nests.—A Sitio.—Adventure with a monstrous Ape.—Hospitality of Padres.—
Las Playas.—A Tempest.—Moschetoes.—A Youthful Merchant.—Alligators.
—Another Funeral.—Disgusting Ceremonials.

AMONG the Indians who came out to escort us to the
village was one whom we had not seen before, and
whose face bore a striking resemblance to those de-
lineated on the walls of the buildings.   In general the
faces of the Indians were of an entirely different character, but he might have been taken for a lineal de-
scendant of the perished race.   The resemblance was
perhaps purely accidental, but we were anxious to procure his portrait.   He was, however, very shy, and unwilling to be drawn.   Mr. Catherwood, too, was worn
out, and in the confusion of removing we postponed it
upon his promising to come to us at the village, but
we could not get hold of him again.

We left behind our kitchen furniture, consisting of
the three stones which Juan put together the first day
of our residence, vessels of pottery and calabashes, and
also our beds, for the benefit of the next comer.   Everything susceptible of injury from damp was rusty or
mouldy, and in a ruinous condition; we ourselves
were not much better; and with the clothes on our
backs far from dry, we bade farewell to the ruins.   We
were happy when we reached them, but our joy at
leaving them burst the bounds of discretion, and broke
out into extravagances poetical, which, however, fortu-

nately for the reader, did not advance much beyond the first line :

"Adios, Las Casas de Piedra."

The road was worse than at any time before; the streams were swollen into rivers, and along the banks were steep, narrow gullies, very difficult to pass. At one of these, after attempting to ascend with my macho, I dismounted. Mr. Catherwood was so weak that he remained on the back of his mule; and after he had crossed, just as he reached the top, the mule's strength gave way, and she fell backward, rolling over in the stream with Mr. Catherwood entirely under. Pawling was behind, and at that time in the stream. He sprang off and extricated Mr. Catherwood, unhurt, but very faint, and, as he was obliged to ride in his wet clothes, we had great apprehensions for him. At length we reached the village, when, exhausted by hard and unintermitted labour, he gave up completely, and took to bed and the medicine-chest. In the evening nearly all my friends of the dinner-party came to see us. That one day had established an intimacy. All regretted that we had had such an unfortunate time at the ruins, wondered how we had lived through it, and were most kind in offers of services. The padre remained after the rest, and went home with a lantern in the midst of one of those dreadful storms which had almost terrified us at the ruins.

The next day again was Sunday. It was my third Sunday in the village, and again it was emphatically a day of rest. In the afternoon a mournful interruption was given to the stillness of the place by the funeral of a young Indian girl, once the pride and beauty of the village, whose portrait Mr. Waldeck had taken to embellish his intended work on Palenque.   Her career, as often happens with beauty in higher life, was short, brilliant, and unhappy.   She had married a young Indian, who abandoned her and went to another village.   Ignorant, innocent, and unconscious of wrong, she was persuaded to marry another, drooped, and died.   The funeral procession passed our door.   The corpse was borne on a rude bier, without coffin, in a white cotton dress, with a shawl over the head, and followed by a slender procession of women and children only.   I walked beside it, and heard one of them say, " bueno Christiano, to attend the funeral of a poor woman." The bier was set down beside the grave, and in lifting the body from it the head turned on one side, and the hands dropped ; the grave was too short, and as the dead was laid within the legs were drawn up.   Her face was thin and wasted, but the mouth had a sweetness of expression which seemed to express that she had died with a smile of forgiveness for him who had injured her.   I could not turn my eyes from her placid but grief-worn countenance, and so touching was its expression that I could almost have shed tears.   Young, beautiful, simple, and innocent, abandoned and dead, with not a mourner at her grave.   All seemed to think that she was better dead ; she was poor, and could not maintain herself.   The men went away, and the women and children with their hands scraped the earth upon the body.   It was covered up gradually and slowly ; the feet stuck out, and then all was buried but the face. A small piece of muddy earth fell upon one of the eyes, and another on her sweetly smiling mouth, changing the whole expression in a moment ; death was now robed with terror.   The women stopped to comment upon the change ; the dirt fell so as to cover the whole face except the nose, and for two or three moments this alone was visible. Another brush covered this, and the girl was buried. The reader will excuse me. I am sorry to say that if she had been ugly, I should, perhaps, have regarded it as an every-day case of a wife neglected by her husband ; but her sweet face speaking from the grave created an impression which even yet is hardly effaced.

But to return to things more in my line. We had another long journey before us. Our next move was for Yucatan. From Mr. Catherwood's condition I had great fear that we would not be able to accomplish what we purposed ; but, at all events, it was necessary to go down to the seacoast. There were two routes, either by Tobasco or the Laguna, to Campeachy, and war again confronted us. Both Tobasco and Campeachy were besieged by the Liberals, or, as they were called, the Revolutionists. The former route required three days' journey by land, the latter one short day ; and as Mr. C. was not able to ride, this determined us. In the mean time, while waiting for his recovery, and so as not to rust and be utterly useless when I returned home, I started another operation, viz., the purchase of the city of Palenque. I am bound to say, however, that I was not bold enough to originate this, but fell into it accidentally, in a long conversation with the prefect about the richness of the soil, the cheapness of land, its vicinity to the seaboard and the United States, and easy communication with New-York. He told me that a merchant of Tobasco, who had visited the place, had proposed to purchase a tract of land and establish a colony of emigrants, but he had gone away and never returned. He added, that for two years a government order from the State of Chiapas, to which the region

belonged, had been lying in his hands for the sale of all
land in the vicinity lying within certain limits; but there
were no purchasers, and no sales were ever made.
Upon inquiry I learned that this order, in its terms,
embraced the ground occupied by the ruined city. No
exception whatever was made in favour of it. He
showed me the order, which was imperative; and he
said that if any exception was intended, it would have
been so expressed; wherefore he considered himself
bound to receive an offer for any portion of the land.
The sale was directed to be by appraisement, the appli-
cant to name one man, the prefect another, and, if necessary, they two to name a third; and the application,
with the price fixed and the boundaries, was to be sent
to Ciudad Real for the approval of the governor and a
deed.

The tract containing the ruins consisted of about six
thousand acres of good land, which, according to the
usual appraisement, would cost about fifteen hundred
dollars, and the prefect said that it would not be valued
a cent higher on account of the ruins. I resolved immediately to buy it. I would fit up the palace and re-
people the old city of Palenque. But there was one
difficulty: by the laws of Mexico no stranger can purchase lands unless married to a hica del pais, or daughter of the country. This, by-the-way, is a grand stroke
of policy, holding up the most powerful attraction of
the country to seduce men from their natural alle-
giance, and radicate them in the soil; and it is taking
them where weak and vulnerable; for, when wandering in strange countries, alone and friendless, buffeted
and battered, with no one to care for him, there are
moments when a lovely woman might root the stranger
to any spot on earth. On principle I always resisted

such tendencies, but I never before found it to my interest to give way. The ruined city of Palenque was a most desirable piece of property.

The case was embarrassing and complicated. Society in Palenque was small; the oldest young lady was not more than fourteen, and the prettiest woman, who already had contributed most to our happiness (she made our cigars), was already married. The house containing the two tablets belonged to a widow lady and a single sister, good-looking, amiable, and both about forty. The house was one of the neatest in the place. I always liked to visit it, and had before thought that, if passing a year at the ruins, it would be delightful to have this house in the village for recreation and occasional visits. With either of these ladies would come possession of the house and the two stone tablets; but the difficulty was that there were two of them, both equally interesting and equally interested. I am particular in mentioning these little circumstances, to show the difficulties that attended every step of our enterprise in that country. There was an alternative, and that was to purchase in the name of some other person; but I did not know any one I could trust. At length, however, I hit upon Mr. Russell, the American consul at Laguna, who was married to a Spanish lady, and already had large possessions in the country; and I arranged with the prefect to make the purchase in his name. Pawling was to accompany me to the Laguna, for the purpose of procuring and carrying back evidence of Mr. Russell's co-operation and the necessary funds, and was to act as my agent in completing the purchase. The prefect was personally anxious to complete it. The buildings, he said, were fast going to decay, and in a few years more would be mounds of ru-

ins. In that country they were not appreciated or understood, and he had the liberal wish that the tablets
of hieroglyphics particularly might find their way to
other countries, be inspected and studied by scientific
men, and their origin and history be ascertained. Besides, he had an idea that immense discoveries were still
to be made and treasures found, and he was anxious
for a thorough exploration, in which he should himself
co-operate. The two tablets which I had attempted to
purchase were highly prized by the owners, but he
thought they could be secured by purchasing the house,
and I authorized him to buy it at a fixed price.

In my many conversations with the prefect I had
broached the subject of making casts from the tablets.
Like every other official whom I met, he supposed that
I was acting under a commission from my government,
which idea was sustained by having in my employ a man
of such character and appearance as Pawling, though
every time I put my hand in my pocket I had a feeling
sense that the case was far otherwise. In the matter of
casts he offered every assistance, but there was no plaster of Paris nearer than the Laguna or Campeachy, and
perhaps not there. We had made an experiment at the
ruins by catching in the river a large quantity of snails
and burning the shells, but it did not answer. He referred us to some limestone in the neighbourhood, but
this would not do. Pawling knew nothing of casting.
The idea had never entered his mind before, but he
was willing to undertake this. Mr. Catherwood, who
had been shut up in Athens during the Greek Revolution, when it was besieged by the Turks, and in pursu-
ing his artistical studies had perforce made castings
with his own hands, gave him written instructions, and
it was agreed that when he returned with the creden-

tials from Mr. Russell he should bring back plaster of Paris, and, while the proceedings for completing the purchase were pending, should occupy himself in this new branch of business.

On the fourth of June we took our final departure from Palenque. Don Santiago sent me a farewell letter, enclosing, according to the custom of the country, a piece of silk, the meaning of which I did not understand, but learned that it was meant as a pledge of friendship, which I reciprocated with a penknife. The prefect was kind and courteous to the last; even the old alcalde, drawing a little daily revenue from us, was touched. Every male inhabitant came to the house to bid us farewell and wish us to return; and before starting we rode round and exchanged adios with all their wives: good, kind, and quiet people, free from all agitating cares, and aiming only at an undisturbed existence in a place which I had been induced to believe the abode of savages and full of danger.

In order to accompany us, the cura had postponed for two days a visit to his hacienda, which lay on our road. Pawling continued with us for the purpose before mentioned, and Juan according to contract. I had agreed to return him to Guatimala. Completely among strangers, he was absolutely in our power, and followed blindly, but with great misgivings asked the padre where we were taking him. His impression was that he was setting out for my country, and he had but little hope of ever seeing Guatimala again.

From the village we entered immediately upon a beautiful plain, picturesque, ornamented with trees, and extending five or six days' journey to the Gulf of Mexico. The road was very muddy, but, open to the sun in the morning, was not so bad as we feared. On the borders of a piece of woodland were singular trees, with a tall trunk, the bark very smooth, and the branches festooned with hanging birds'-nests. The bird was called the jagua, and built in this tree, as the padre told us, to prevent serpents from getting at the young. The cura, notwithstanding his strange figure, and a life of incident and danger, was almost a woman in voice, manner, tastes, and feelings. He had been educated at the capital, and sent as a penance to this retired curacy. The visit of the padres had for the first time broken the monotony of his life. In the political convulsions of the capital he had made himself obnoxious to the church government by his liberal opinions ; but unable, as he said, to find in him any tangible offence, his superiors had called him up on a charge of polluting the surplice, founded on the circumstance that, in the time of the cholera, when his fellow-creatures were lying all around him in the agonies of death, in leaning over their bodies to administer the sacrament, his surplice had been soiled by saliva from the mouth of a dying man. For this he was condemned to penance and prayers, from midnight till daybreak, for two years in the Cathedral, deprived of a good curacy, and sent to Palenque.

At half past two we reached his sitio or small hacienda. In the apprehension of the afternoon's rain, we would have continued to the end of our afternoon's journey ; but the padre watched carefully the appearance of the sky, and, after satisfying himself that the rain would not come on till late, positively forbade our passing on. His sitio was what would be called at home a " new" place, being a tract of wild land of I do not know what extent, but some large quantity, which had cost him twenty-five dollars, and about as much

more to make the improvements, which consisted of a
hut made of poles and thatched with corn-husks, and a
cucinera or kitchen at a little distance. The stables
and outhouses were a clearing bounded by a forest so
thick that cattle could not penetrate it, and on the roadside by a rude fence. Altogether, in that mild climate
the effect was good; and it was one of those occasions which make a man feel, away from the region
of fictitious wants, how little is necessary for the comforts of life. The furniture of the hut consisted of
two reed bedsteads, a table, and a bench, and in one
corner was a pile of corn. The cura sent out for half
a dozen fresh pineapples; and while we were refreshing ourselves with them we heard an extraordinary
noise in the woods, which an Indian boy told us was
made by "un animal." Pawling and I took our guns,
and entering a path in the woods, as we advanced
the noise sounded fearful, but all at once it stopped.
The boy opened a way through thickets of brush and
underwood, and through an opening in the branches I
saw on the limbs of a high tree a large black animal
with fiery eyes. The boy said it was not a mico or
monkey, and I supposed it to be a catamount. I had
barely an opening through which to take aim, fired, and
the animal dropped below the range of view; but, not
hearing him strike the ground, I looked again, and saw
him hanging by his tail, and dead, with the blood
streaming from his mouth. Pawling attempted to climb
the tree; but it was fifty feet to the first branch, and the
blood trickled down the trunk. Wishing to examine
the creature more closely, we sent the boy to the house,
whence he returned with a couple of Indians. They
cut down the tree, which fell with a terrible crash; and
still the animal hung by its tail. The ball had hit him

in the mouth and knocked out the fore teeth, passed out at the top of his back between his shoulders, and must have killed him instantly. The tenacity of his tail seemed marvellous, but was easily explained. It had no grip, and had lost all muscular power, but was wound round the branch with the end under, so that the weight of the body tightened the coil, and the harder the strain, the more secure was the hold. It was not a monkey, but so near a connexion that I would not have shot him if I had known it. In fact, he was even more nearly related to the human family, being called a monos or ape, and measured six feet including the tail; very muscular, and in a struggle would have been more than a match for a man; and the padre said they were known to have attacked women. The Indians carried him up to the house and skinned him; and when lying on his back, with his skin off and his eyes staring, the padre cried out, " es hombre," it is a man, and I almost felt liable to an indictment for homicide. The Indians cooked the body, and I contrived to preserve the skin as a curiosity, for its extraordinary size; but, unluckily, I left it on board a Spanish vessel at sea.

In the mean time the padre had a fowl boiled for dinner. Three guests at a time were not too much for his open hospitality, but they went beyond his dinner-service, which consisted of three bowls. There was no plate, knife, fork, or spoon, and for the cura himself not even a bowl. The fowl was served in an ocean of broth, which had to be disposed of first. Tortillas and a small cake of fresh cheese composed the rest of the meal. The reader will perhaps connect such an entertainment with vulgarity of manners; but the curate was a gentleman, and made no apologies, for he gave us the best he had. We had sent our carriers on be-

fore, the padre gave us a servant as a guide, and at
three o'clock we bade him farewell. He was the last
padre whom we met, and put a seal upon the kindness
we had received from all the padres of that country.

At five o'clock, by a muddy road, through a picturesque country, remarkable only for swarms of butterflies
with large yellow wings which filled the air, we reached
Las Playas. This village is the head of navigation of the
waters that empty in this direction into the Gulf of Mexico. The whole of the great plain to the sea is intersect-
ed by creeks and rivers, some of them in the summer dry,
and on the rising of the waters overflowing their banks.
At this season the plain on one side of the village was
inundated, and seemed a large lake. The village was
a small collection of huts upon what might be called its
banks. It consisted of one street or road, grass-grown
and still as at Palenque, at the extreme end of which
was the church, under the pastoral care of our friend
the padre. Our guide, according to the directions of
the padre, conducted us to the convent, and engaged the
sexton to provide us with supper. The convent was
built of upright sticks, with a thatched roof, mud floor,
and furnished with three reed bedsteads and a table.

At this place we were to embark in a canoe, and had
sent a courier a day beforehand, with a letter from the
prefect to the justitia, to have one ready for us. The
justitia was a portly mulatto, well dressed, and very civil,
had a canoe of his own, and promised to procure us
two bogadores or rowers in the morning. Very soon
the moschetoes made alarming demonstrations, and gave
us apprehensions of a fearful night. To make a show
of resistance, we built a large fire in the middle of the
convent. At night the storm came on with a high wind,
which made it necessary to close the doors. For two

hours we had a tempest of wind and rain, with terrific thunder and lightning. One blast burst open the door and scattered the fire, so that it came very near burning down the convent. Between the smoke and moschetoes, it was a matter of debate which of the two to choose, suffocation or torture. We preferred the former, and had the latter besides, and passed a miserable night.

The next morning the justitia came to say that the bogadores were not ready and could not go that day. The price which he named was about twice as much as the cura told us we ought to pay, besides possol (balls of mashed Indian corn), tortillas, honey, and meat. I remonstrated, and he went off to consult the mozos, but returned to say that they would not take less, and, after treating him with but little of the respect due to office, I was obliged to accede; but I ought to add, that throughout that country, in general, prices are fixed, and there is less advantage taken of the necessity of travellers than in most others. We were loth to remain, for, besides the loss of time and the moschetoes, the scarcity of provisions was greater than at Palenque.

The sexton bought us some corn, and his wife made us tortillas. The principal merchant in the place, or, at least, the one who traded most largely with us, was a little boy about twelve years old, who was dressed in a petate or straw hat. He had brought us some fruit, and we saw him coming again with a string over his naked shoulder, dragging on the ground what proved to be a large fish. The principal food of the place was young alligators. They were about a foot and a half long, and at that youthful time of life were considered very tender. At their first appearance on the table they had not an inviting aspect, but ce n'est que le premier pas qui coute, they tasted better than the fish, and they were the best food possible for our canoe voyage, being dried and capable of preservation.

Go where we will, to the uttermost parts of the earth, we are sure to meet one acquaintance. Death is always with us. In the afternoon was the funeral of a child. The procession consisted of eight or ten grown persons, and as many boys and girls. The sexton carried the child in his arms, dressed in white, with a wreath of flowers around its head. All were huddled around the sexton, walking together; the father and mother with him; and even more than in Costa Rica I remarked, not only an absence of solemnity, but cheerfulness and actual gayety, from the same happy conviction that the child had gone to a better world. I happened to be in the church as they approached, more like a wedding than a burial party. The floor of the church was earthen, and the grave was dug inside, because, as the sexton told me, the father was rich and could afford to pay for it, and the father seemed pleased and proud that he could give his child such a burial-place. The sexton laid the child in the grave, folded its little hands across its breast, placing there a small rude cross, covered it over with eight or ten inches of earth, and then got into the grave and stamped it down with his feet. He then got out and threw in more, and, going outside of the church, brought back a pounder, being a log of wood about four feet long and ten inches in diameter, like the rammer used among us by paviors, and again taking his place in the grave, threw up the pounder to the full swing of his arm, and brought it down with all his strength over the head of the child. My blood ran cold. As he threw it up a second time I caught his arm and remonstrated with

him, but he said that they always did so with those
buried inside the church ; that the earth must be all put
back, and the floor of the church made even.   My re-
monstrances seemed only to give him more strength and
spirit.   The sweat rolled down his body, and when
perfectly tired with pounding he stepped out of the
grave.   But this was nothing.   More earth was thrown
in, and the father laid down his hat, stepped into the
grave, and the pounder was handed to him.   I saw
him throw it up twice and bring it down with a dead,
heavy noise.   I never beheld a more brutal and disgusting scene.   The child's body must have been
crushed to atoms.

Toward evening the moschetoes began their operations.   Pawling and Juan planted sticks in the ground
outside the convent, and spread sheets over them for
nets; but the rain came on and drove them within, and
we passed another wretched night.   It may be asked
how the inhabitants live.   I cannot answer.   They
seemed to suffer as much as we, but at home they
could have conveniences which we could not carry in
travelling.   Pawling suffered so much, and heard such
dreadful accounts of what we would meet with below,
that, in a spirit of impetuosity and irritation, he resolved
not to continue any farther.   From the difficulty and
uncertainty of communications, however, I strongly apprehended that in such case all the schemes in which
he was concerned must fall through and be abandoned,
as I was not willing to incur the expense of sending
materials, subject to delays and uncertainties, unless in
special charge, and once more he changed his purpose.

I had but one leave-taking, and that was a trying
one.   I was to bid farewell to my noble macho.   He
had carried me more than two thousand miles, over the

worst roads that mule ever travelled. He stood tied
to the door of the convent; saw the luggage, and even
his own saddle, carried away by hand, and seemed
to have a presentiment that something unusual was
going on. I had often been solicited to sell him, but
no money could have tempted me. He was in poorer
condition than when we reached Palenque. Deprived
of corn and exposed to the dreadful rains, he was
worse than when worked hard and fed well every day,
and in his drooping state seemed to reproach me for
going away and leaving him forlorn. I threw my arms
around his neck; his eyes had a mournful expression,
and at that moment he forgot the angry prick of the
spur. I laid aside the memory of a toss from his back
and ineffectual attempts to repeat it, and we remembered only mutual kind offices and good-fellowship.
Tried and faithful companion, where are you now? I
left him, with two others, tied at the door of the convent,
to be taken by the sexton to the prefect at Palenque,
there to recover from the debilitating influence of the
early rains, and to roam on rich pasture-grounds, untouched by bridle or spur, until I should return to
mount him again.

CHAPTER XXII.

At seven o'clock we went down to the shore to embark. The boatmen whom the justice had consulted, and for whom he had been so tenacious, were his honour himself and another man, who, we thought, was hired as the cheapest help he could find in the village. The canoe was about forty feet long, with a toldo or awning of about twelve feet at the stern, and covered with matting. All the space before this was required by the boatmen to work the canoe, and, with all our luggage under the awning, we had but narrow quarters. The seeming lake on which we started was merely a large inundated plain, covered with water to the depth of three or four feet; and the justice in the stern, and his assistant before, walking in the bottom of the canoe, with poles against their shoulders, set her across. At eight o'clock we entered a narrow, muddy creek, not wider than a canal, but very deep, and with the current against us. The setting-pole could not touch bottom, but it was forked at one end, and, keeping close to the bank, the bogador or rower fixed it against the branches of overhanging trees and pushed, while the justice, whose pole had a rude hook, fastened it to other branches forward and pulled. In this way, with no view but that of the wooded banks, we worked slowly along the muddy stream. In turning a short bend, suddenly we saw on the banks eight or ten alligators, some of them twenty feet long, huge, hideous monsters, appropriate inhabitants of such a stream, and, considering the frailty of our little vessel, not very attractive neighbours. As we approached they plunged heavily into the water, sometimes rose in the middle of the stream, and swam across or disappeared. At half past twelve we entered the Rio Chico or Little River, varying from two to five hundred feet in width, deep, muddy, and very sluggish, with wooded banks of impenetrable thickness. At six o'clock we entered the great Usumasinta, five or six hundred yards across, one of the noblest rivers in Central America, rising among the mountains of Peten, and emptying into the Lake of Terminos.

At this point the three provinces of Chiapas, Tobasco, and Yucatan meet, and the junction of the waters of the Usumasinta and the Rio Chico presents a singular spectacle. Since leaving the sheet of water before the Playas we had been ascending the stream, but now, continuing in the same direction and crossing the line of junction, we came from the ascending current of the Rio Chico into the descending flow of the Usumasinta. Working out into the middle and looking back, we saw the Usumasinta and Rio Chico coming together, and forming an angle of not more than forty degrees, one running up and the other down. Amid the wildness and stillness of the majestic river, and floating in a little canoe, the effect was very extraordinary; but the cause was obvious. The Usumasinta, descending swiftly and with immense force, broke against a projecting headland on the left of its course ; and, while the main body forced its way past and hurried on to the ocean, part was turned back at this sharp angle with such power as to form the creeks which we had ascended, and flood the plain of the Playas.

At this time, away from the wooded banks, with the setting-poles at rest, and floating quietly on the bosom of the noble Usumasinta, our situation was pleasant and exciting. A strong wind sweeping down the river drove away the moschetoes, and there were no gathering clouds to indicate rain. We had expected to come to for the night, but the evening was so clear that we determined to continue. Unfortunately, we were obliged to leave the Usumasinta, and, about an hour after dark, turned to the north into the Rio Palisada. The whole great plain from Palenque to the Gulf of Mexico is broken by creeks and streams. The Usumasinta in its stately course receives many, and sends off others to find their way by other channels to the sea.

Leaving the broad expanse of the Usumasinta, with its comparative light, the Rio Palisada, narrow, and with a dark line of forest on each side, had an aspect fearfully ominous of moschetoes. Unfortunately, at the very beginning we brushed against the bank, and took on board enough to show us the bloodthirsty character of the natives. Of course that night afforded us little sleep.

At daylight we were still dropping down the river. This was the region of the great logwood country. We met a large bungo with two masts moving against the stream, set up by hauling and pushing on the branches of trees, on her way for a cargo. As we advanced, the banks of the river in some places were cleared and cultivated, and had whitewashed houses, and small sugar-mills turned by oxen, and canoes were lying on the water ; altogether the scene was pretty, but with the richness of the soil suggesting the idea how beautiful this country might be made.

At two o'clock we reached the Palisada, situated on the left bank of the river, on a luxuriant plain elevated some fifteen or twenty feet. Several bungoes lay along the bank, and in front was a long street, with large and well-built houses. This, our first point, was in the

State of Yucatan, then in revolution against the government of Mexico. Our descent of the river had been watched from the bank, and before we landed we were hailed, asked for our passports, and directed to present ourselves immediately to the alcalde. The intimation was peremptory, and we proceeded forthwith to the alcalde. Don Francisco Hebreu was superior to any man I had yet found at the head of a municipality ; in fact, he was chief of the Liberal party in that section of the state, and, like all the other officials in the Mexican provinces, received us with the respect due to an official passport of a friendly nation. We were again in the midst of a revolution, but had not the remotest idea what it was about. We were most intimately acquainted with Central American politics, but this was of no more use to us than a knowledge of Texan politics would be to a stranger in the United States. For several months the names of Morazan and Carrera had rung in our ears like those of our own candidates for the presidency at a contested election; but we had passed the limits of their world, and were obliged to begin anew.

For eight years the Central party had maintained the ascendancy in Mexico, during which time, as a mark of the *sympathy* between neighbouring people, the Liberal or Democratic party had been ascendant in Central America. Within the last six months the Centralists had overturned the Liberals in Central America, and during the same time the Liberalists had almost driven out the Centralists in Mexico. Along the whole coast of the Pacific the Liberals were in arms, waging a strong revolutionary war, and threatening the capital, which they afterward entered, but, after great massacre and bloodshed, were expelled. On the Atlantic side, the states of Tobasco and Yucatan had declared their independence of the general government, and in the interior of both states the officials of the Central government had been driven out. The seaports of Tobasco and Campeachy, garrisoned by Central troops, still held out, but they were at that time blockaded and besieged on land by the Federal forces. All communications by sea and land were cut off, their supplies were short, and Don Francisco thought they would soon be obliged by starvation to surrender.

The revolution seemed of a higher tone, for greater cause, and conducted with more moderation than in Central America. The grounds of revolt here were the despotism of the Central government, which, far removed by position, and ignorant of the condition and resources of the country, used its distant provinces as a quartering place for rapacious officers, and a source of revenue for money to be squandered in the capital. One little circumstance showed the impolicy and inefficiency of the laws. On account of high duties, smuggling was carried to such an extent on the coast that many articles were regularly sold at the Palisada for much less than the duties.

The revolution, like all others in that country, began with pronunciamentos, i. e., declarations of the municipality, or what we would call the corporation of a town, in favour of any particular party. The Palisada had made its pronunciamento but two weeks before, the Central officers had been turned out, and the present alcalde was hardly warm in his place. The change, however, had been effected with a spirit of moderation and forbearance, and without bloodshed. Don Francisco, with a liberality unusual, spoke of his immediate predecessor as an upright but misguided man, who was not persecuted, but then living in the place unmolested.

The Liberals, however, did not expect the same treatment at the hands of the Centralists. An invasion had been apprehended from Tobasco. Don Francisco had his silver and valuables packed up, and kept his bungo before the door to save his effects and family, and the place was alive with patriots brushing up arms and preparing for war.

Don Francisco was a rich man ; had a hacienda of thirty thousand head of cattle, logwood plantations and bungoes, and was rated at two hundred thousand dollars. The house in which he lived was on the bank of the river, newly built, one hundred and fifty feet front, and had cost him twenty thousand dollars. While we were with him dinner was about being served, in a liberal style of housekeeping unusual in that country, and, with the freedom of a man who felt sure that he could not be taken unaware, he asked us to join him at table. In all his domestic relations he was like the respectable head of a family at home. He had two sons, whom he intended to send, to the United States to be educated ; and minor things, too, called up home feelings. For the first time in a long while we had bread, made of flour from New-York, and the barrel-head had a Rochester brand. Don Francisco had never travelled farther than Tobasco and Campeachy, but he was well acquainted with Europe and the United States, geographically and politically ; indeed, he was one of the most agreeable companions and best-informed men we met in that country. We remained with him all the afternoon, and toward evening moved our chairs outside in front of the house, which at evening was the regular gathering-place of the family. The bank of the river was a promenade for the people of the town, who stopped to exchange greetings with Don Francisco and his wife ; a vacant chair was always at hand, and from time to time one took a seat with us. When the vesper bell struck conversation ceased, all rose from their seats, made a short prayer, and when it was over turned to each other with a buenos noces, reseated themselves, and renewed the conversation. There was always something imposing in the sound of the vesper bell, presenting the idea of an immense multitude of people at the same moment offering up a prayer.

During the evening a courier arrived with despatches for Don Francisco, advising him that a town which had " pronounced" in favour of the Liberals had pronounced back again, which seemed to give both him and his wife much uneasiness. At ten o'clock an armed patrol came for orders, and we retired to what we much needed, a good night's rest.

In the morning Don Francisco, half in jest and half in earnest, told us of the uneasiness we had given his wife. Pawling's Spanish, and constant use of idioms well known as belonging to the city of Mexico, had excited her suspicions ; she said he was not an American, but a Mexican from the capital, and she believed him to be a spy of the Centralists. Pawling did not like the imputation ; he was a little mortified at this visible mark of long absence from his country, and not at all flattered at being taken for a Mexican. Don Francisco laughed at it, but his wife was so pertinacious, that, if it had not been for the apparent propriety of my being attended by one perfectly familiar with the language of the country, I believe, in the state of apprehension and distrust, Pawling would have lost the benefit of his birthright, and been arrested as a spy.

We passed the next day in a quiet lounge and in

making arrangements for continuing our journey, and
the next day after, furnished with a luxurious supply of
provisions by the señora, and accompanied to the place
by Don Francisco, we embarked on board a bungo for
the Laguna. The bungo was about fifteen tons, flat-
bottomed, with two masts and sails, and loaded with
logwood. The deck was covered with mangoes, plantains, and other fruits and vegetables, and so encumbered that it was impossible to move. The stern had movable hatches. A few tiers of logwood had been taken
out, and the hatches put over so as to give us a shelter
against rain; a sail was rigged into an awning to protect us from the sun, and in a few minutes we pushed
off from the bank.

We had as passengers two young Central Americans
from Peten, both under twenty, and flying on account
of the dominion of the Carrera party. Coming, as we
did, direct from Central America, we called each other
countrymen. We soon saw that the bungo had a miserable crew. Above the men were called bogadores
or rowers; but here, as they were on board a bungo
with sails, and going down to the seacoast, they called
themselves marineros or sailors. The patron or master
was a mild, inoffensive, and inefficient man, who prefaced
all his orders to his breechless marineros with the conciliatory words, " Señores, haga me el favor ;" " Gentlemen, do me the favour."

Below the town commenced an island about four
leagues in length, at the end of which, on the main-
land, was a large clearing and farming establishment,
with canoes lying on the water. All travelling here is
along the river, and in canoes. From this place there
were no habitations; the river was very deep, the banks
densely wooded, with the branches spreading far over.

Very soon we came to a part of the river where the alligators seemed to enjoy undisturbed possession. Some lay basking in the sun on mudbanks, like logs of drift-wood, and in many places the river was dotted with their heads. The Spanish historian says that "They swim with their Head above the water, gaping at what-soever they see, and swallow it, whether Stick, Stone, or living Creature, which is the true reason of their swallowing Stones; and not to sink to the bottom, as some say, for they have no need to do so, nor do they like it, being extraordinary Swimmers; for the Tail serves instead of a Rudder, the Head is the Prow, and the Paws the Oars, being so swift as to catch any other fish as it swims. An hundred Weight and an half of fresh Fish has been found in the Maw of an Alligator, besides what was digested; in another was an Indian Woman whole, with her Cloaths, whom he had swallow-ed the Day before, and another with a pair of Gold Bracelets, with Pearls, the Enamel gone off, and Part of the Pearls dissolved, but the Gold entire."

Here they still maintained their dominion. Accidents frequently happen; and at the Palisada Don Francisco told us that a year before a man had had his leg bitten off and was drowned. Three were lying together at the mouth of a small stream which emptied into the river. The patron told us that at the end of the last dry season upward of two hundred had been counted in the bed of a pond emptied by this stream. The boatmen of several bungoes went in among them with clubs, sharp stakes, and machetes, and killed upward of sixty. The river itself, discoloured, with muddy banks, and a fiery sun beating upon it, was ugly enough; but these huge and ugly monsters, neither fish nor flesh, made it absolutely hideous. The boatmen called them

enemigos de los Christianos, by which they mean enemies of mankind. In a canoe it would have been unpleasant to disturb them, but in the bungo we brought
out our guns and made indiscriminate war. One monster, twenty-five or thirty feet long, lay on the arm of a
gigantic tree which projected forty or fifty feet, the
lower part covered with water, but the whole of the
alligator was visible. I hit him just under the white
line ; he fell off, and with a tremendous convulsion,
reddening the water with a circle of blood, turned over
on his back, dead. A boatman and one of the Peten
lads got into a canoe to bring him alongside. The canoe was small and tottering, and had not proceeded
fifty yards before it dipped, filled, upset, and threw
them both into the water. At that moment there were
perhaps twenty alligators in sight on the banks and
swimming in different parts of the river. We could do
nothing for the man and boy, and the old bungo, which
before hardly moved, seemed to start forward purpose-
ly to leave them to their fate. Every moment the distance between us and them increased, and on board all
was confusion ; the patron cried out in agony to the señores, and the señores, straining every nerve, turned the
old bungo in to the bank, and got the masts foul of the
branches of the trees, which held her fast. In the mean
time our friends in the water were not idle. The Peten lad struck out vigorously toward the shore, and we
saw him seize the branch of a tree which projected fifty
feet over the water, so low as to be within reach, haul
himself up like a monkey, and run along it to the shore.
The marinero, having the canoe to himself, turned her
bottom upward, got astride, and paddled down with his
hands. Both got safely on board, and, apprehension
over, the affair was considered a good joke.

In the mean time our masts had become so locked in the branches of the trees that we carried away some of our miserable tackling in extricating them; but at length were once more in the middle of the river, and renewed our war upon los enemigos de los Christianos.   The sun was so hot that we could not stand outside the awning, but the boatmen gave us notice when we could have a shot.   Our track down the river will be remembered as a desolation and scourge.   Old alligators, by dying injunction, will teach the rising generation to keep the head under water when the bungoes are coming.   We killed perhaps twenty, and others are probably at this moment sitting on the banks with our bullets in their bodies, wondering how they came there.   With rifles we could have killed at least a hundred.

At three o'clock the regular afternoon storm came on, beginning with a tremendous sweep of wind up the river, which turned the bungo round, drove her broadside up the stream, and before we could come to at the bank we had a deluge of rain.   At length we made fast, secured the hatch over the place prepared for us, and crawled under.   It was so low that we could not sit up, and, lying down, there was about a foot of room above us.   On our arrival at the Palisada we considered ourselves fortunate in finding a bungo ready, although she had already on board a full load of logwood from stem to stern.   Don Francisco said it would be too uncomfortable, and wished us to wait for a bungo of his own; but delay was to us a worse evil, and I made a bargain to have a portion of the logwood taken out behind the mainmast, so as to admit of a hatch on deck, and give room below.   But we had not given any personal superintendence; and when we came on board, though the logwood seemed of a rather hard species for sleeping on, we did not discover the extreme discomfort of the place until forced below by the rain. Even the small place engaged, and paid for accordingly, we had not to ourselves. The Peten lads crawled under with us, and the patron and señores followed. We could not drive them out into a merciless rain, and all lay like one mass of human flesh, animated by the same spirit of suffering, irritation, and helplessness. During this time the rain was descending in a deluge ; the thunder rolled fearfully over our heads; lightning flashed in through the crevices of our dark burrowing-place, dazzling and blinding our eyes; and we heard near us the terrific crash of a falling tree, snapped by the wind, or, as we then supposed, shivered by lightning.

Such was our position. Sometimes the knots in the logwood fitted well into the curves and hollows of the body, but in general they were just where they should not be. We thought we could not be worse off, but very soon we found our mistake, and looked back upon ourselves as ungrateful murmurers without cause. The moschetoes claimed us as waifs, and in murderous swarms found the way under the hatches, humming and buzzing

> "Fee, faw, fum,
> I smell the blood of an English-mun,
> Dead or alive I will have some."

I now look back upon our troubles at that place with perfect equanimity ; but at the moment, with the heat and confinement, we were in anything but an amiable humour, and at ten o'clock broke out furious, upbraided the patron and his lazy señores for not reaching the mouth of the river before night, as is usually done, and as he had been charged by the alcalde to do, and insisted upon his hauling out into the stream.

The rain had ceased, but the wind was still furious, and dead ahead. By the misty light we saw a large bungo, with one sail set, seemingly flying up the river like a phantom. We made the patron haul out from the bank, but we could not keep the river, and, after a few zigzag movements, were shot across to the opposite side, where we brought upon us new and more hungry swarms. Here we remained an hour longer, when the wind died away, and we pushed out into the stream. This was a great relief. The señores, though more used to the scourge of moschetoes than we, suffered quite as much. The clouds rolled away, the moon broke out, and, but for the abominable insects, our float down the wild and desolate river would have been an event to live in memory ; as it was, not one of us attempted to sleep ; and I verily believe a man could not have passed an entire night on the banks and lived.

At daylight we were still in the river. Very soon we reached a small lake, and, making a few tacks, entered a narrow passage called the Boca Chico, or Little Mouth. The water was almost even with the banks, and on each side were the most gigantic trees of the tropical forests, their roots naked three or four feet above the ground, gnarled, twisted, and interlacing each other, gray and dead-looking, and holding up, so as to afford an extended view under the first branches, a forest of vivid green. At ten o'clock we passed the Boca Chica and entered the Lake of Terminos. Once more in salt water and stretching out under full sail, on the right we saw only an expanse of water ; on the left was a border of trees with naked roots, which seemed growing out of the water ; and in front, but a little to the left, and barely visible, a long line of trees, marking the island of Carmen, on which stood the town of Laguna, our port of destination. The passage into the lake was shoal and narrow, with reefs and sandbars, and our boatmen did not let slip the chance of running her ashore. Their efforts to get her off capped the climax of stupidity and laziness ; one or two of them pushing on poles at a time, as if they were shoving off a rowboat, and then stopping to rest and giving up to others. Of what could be done by united force they seemed to have no idea ; and, after a few ineffectual efforts, the patron said we must remain till the tide rose. We had no idea of another night on board the bungo, and took entire command of the vessel. This we were entitled to do from the physical force we brought into action. Even Mr. Catherwood assisted; and, besides him, we were three able-bodied and desperate men. Juan's efforts were gigantic. From the great surface exposed, the moschetoes had tormented him dreadfully, and he was even more disgusted with the bungo than we. We put two of the men into the water to heave against the bottom with their shoulders, and ourselves bearing on poles all together, we shoved her off into deep water. With a gentle breeze we sailed smoothly along until we could distinguish the masts of vessels at the Laguna rising above the island, when the wind died away entirely, and left us under a broiling sun in a dead calm.

At two o'clock we saw clouds gathering, and immediately the sky became very black, the harbinger of one of those dreadful storms which even on dry land were terrible. The hatches were put down, and a tarpaulin spread over for us to take refuge under. The squall came on so suddenly that the men were taken unaware, and the confusion on board was alarming. The patron, with both hands extended, and a most beseech-

ing look, begged the señores to take in sail; and the señores, all shouting together, ran and tumbled over the
logwood, hauling upon every rope but the right one.
The mainsail stuck half way up, and would not come
down; and while the patron and all the men were
shouting and looking up at it, the marinero who had
been upset in the canoe, with tears of terror actually
streaming from his eyes, and a start of desperation, ran
up the mast by the rings, and, springing violently upon
the top one, holding fast by a rope, brought the sail
down with a run.   A hurricane blew through the naked
masts, a deluge of rain followed, and the lake was lash-
ed into fury; we lost sight of everything.   At the very
beginning, on account of the confusion on board, we
determined not to go under the hatch; if the bungo
swamped, the logwood cargo would carry her to the
bottom like lead.   We disencumbered ourselves of
boots and coats, and brought out life-preservers ready
for use.   The deck of the bungo was about three feet
from the water, and perfectly smooth, without anything
to hold on by, and, to keep from being blown or washed away, we lay down and took the whole brunt of the
storm.   The atmosphere was black; but by the flashes
we saw the bare poles of another bungo, tossed, like
ourselves, at the mercy of the storm.   This continued
more than an hour, when it cleared off as suddenly as it
came up, and we saw the Laguna crowded with more
shipping than we had seen since we left New-York.   In
our long inland journey we had almost forgotten the
use of ships, and the very sight of them seemed to bring
us into close relations with home.   The squall having
spent its fury, there was now a dead calm.   The men
took to their sweeps, but made very little headway;
and, with the port in full sight, we had great apprehen-

sions of another night on board, when another squall came on, not so violent, but blowing directly from the harbour. Tremendous rain accompanied it. We made two or three tacks under a close-reefed foresail; the old bungo seemed to fly through the water ; and, when under full way, the anchor, or, to speak more correctly, stone, was thrown out at some distance below the shipping, and brought us up all standing. There were breakers between us and the shore, and we hallooed to some men to come and take us off, but they answered that the breakers were too rough. The rain came on again, and for half an hour we stowed ourselves away under hatches.

As soon as it cleared off we were on deck, and in a little time we saw a fine jolly-boat, with a cockswain and four men, coasting along the shore against a rapid current, the men at times jumping into the water, and hauling by ropes fixed for the purpose. We hailed them in English, and the cockswain answered in the same language that it was too rough, but after a consultation with the sailors they pulled toward us, and took Mr. Catherwood and me on board. The cockswain was the mate of a French ship, and spoke English. His ship was to sail the next day, and he was going to take in some large turtles which lay on the beach waiting for him. As soon as we struck we mounted the shoulders of two square-built French sailors, and were set down on shore, and perhaps in our whole tour we were never so happy as at that moment in being rid of the bungo.

The town extended along the bank of the lake. We walked the whole length of it, saw numerous and well-filled stores, cafés, and even barbers' shops, and at the extreme end reached the American consul's. Two men were sitting on the portico, of a most homelike appearance. One was Don Carlos Russell, the consul. The face of the other was familiar to me ; and learning that we had come from Guatimala, he asked news of me, which I was most happy to give him in person. It was Captain Fensley, whose acquaintance I had made in New-York when seeking information about that country, and with whom I had spoken of sailing to Campeachy ; but at the moment I did not recognise him, and in my costume from the interior it was impossible for him to recognise me. He was direct from New-York, and gave the first information we had received in a long time from that place, with budgets of newspapers, burdened with suspension of specie payments and universal ruin. Some of my friends had been playing strange antics ; but in the important matters of marriages and deaths I did not find anything to give me either joy or sorrow.

Don Carlos Russell, or Mr. Charles Russell, was a native of Philadelphia, married to a Spanish lady of large fortune, and, though long absent, received us as one who had not forgotten his home. His house, his table, all that he had, even his purse, were at our service. Our first congratulations over, we sat down to a dinner which rivalled that of our friend of Totonicapan. We could hardly believe ourselves the same miserable beings who had been a few hours before tossing on the lake, in dread alike of the bottom and of another night on board the bungo. The reader must have gone through what we had to form any idea of our enjoyment. The negro who served us at table had been waiter at the house of an acquaintance in Broadway ; we seemed but a step from home, and at night we had clean sheets furnished us by our host.

CHAPTER XXIII.

THE town of Laguna stands on the island of Carmen, which is about seven leagues long, and which, with another island about four leagues in length, separates the Lake of Terminos from the Gulf of Mexico. It is the depôt of the great logwood country in the interior, and a dozen vessels were then in port awaiting cargoes for Europe and the United States. The town is well built and thriving; its trade has been trammelled by the oppressive regulations of the Central government, but it had made its pronunciamento, disarmed and driven out the garrison, and considered itself independent, subject only to the state government of Yucatan. The anchorage is shoal but safe, and easy of access for vessels not drawing over twelve or thirteen feet of water.

We could have passed some time with satisfaction in resting and strolling over the island, but our journey was not yet ended. Our next move was for Merida, the capital of Yucatan. The nearest port was Campeachy, a hundred and twenty miles distant, and the voyage was usually made by bungo, coasting along the shore of the open sea. With our experience of bungoes this was most disheartening. Nevertheless, this would have been our unhappy lot but for the kindness of Mr. Russell and Captain Fensley. The latter was bound directly to New-York, and his course lay along the coast of Yucatan. Personally he was disposed to do all in his power to serve us, but there might be some risk in putting into port to land us. Knowing his favourable disposition, we could not urge him; but Mr. Russell was his consignee, and by charter-party had a right to detain him ten days, and intended to do so; but he offered to load him in two days upon condition of his taking us on board, and, as Campeachy was blockaded, landing us at Sisal, sixty miles beyond, and the seaport of Merida. Captain Fensley assented, and we were relieved from what at the time we should have considered a great calamity.

In regard to the project for the purchase of the ruins of Palenque, which I have before referred to, Mr. Russell entered into it warmly; and with a generosity I cannot help mentioning, hardly to be expected from one so long from home, requested to be held liable for two thousand dollars as part of the cost of introducing them into the United States. In pursuance of my previous arrangement I wrote to the prefect, advising him of Mr. Russell's co-operation, and referring him to Pawling as my agent in settling the details of the purchase. This was enclosed in a letter from Mr. Russell to the same effect, which stated, besides, that the money should be paid the moment it was required, and both, with full instructions, were given to Pawling. The interest which Mr. Russell took in this matter gave me a flattering hope of success, and but for him, the scheme for making castings would have failed entirely. He was engaged in building an unusually fine house, and in order to finish it had sent to Campeachy for plaster of Paris, but not finding any there, had imported some from New-York. Fortunately, he had a few barrels left; and but for this accident—there was none nearer than Vera

Cruz or New-Orleans—Pawling's journey, so far as related to this object, would have been fruitless. We settled the details of sending the plaster with Pawling to Palenque, receiving and shipping the castings to me at New-York, and on Saturday morning at seven o'clock bade farewell to Mr. Russell, and embarked on board the Gabrielacho. Pawling accompanied us outside the bar, and we took leave of him as he got on board the pilot-boat to return. We had gone through such rough scenes together since he overtook us at the foot of the Sierra Madre, that it may be supposed we did not separate with indifference. Juan was still with us, for the first time at sea, and wondering where we would take him next.

The Gabrielacho was a beautiful brig of about one hundred and sixty tons, built under Captain Fensley's own direction, one half belonging to himself, and fitted up neatly and tastefully as a home. He had no house on shore; one daughter was at boarding-school in the United States, and the rest of his family, consisting of his wife and a little daughter about three years old, was with him on board. Since his marriage seven years before, his wife had remained but one year on shore, and she determined not to leave him again as long as he followed the seas, while he was resolved that every voyage should be the last, and looked forward to the consummation of every sailor's hopes, a good farm. His daughter Vicentia, or poor Centy, as she called herself, was the pet of all on board; and we had twelve passengers, interesting to the Common Council of New-York, being enormous turtles, one of which the captain hoped would gladden the hearts of the fathers of the city at their fourth of July dinner.

The reader cannot realize the satisfaction with which

we found ourselves in such comfortable quarters on board this brig. We had an afternoon squall, but we considered ourselves merely passengers, and, with a good vessel, master, and crew, laughed at a distant bungo crawling close along the shore, and for the first time feared that the voyage would end too soon. Perhaps no captain ever had passengers so perfectly contented under storm or calm. Oh you who cross the Atlantic in packet-ships, complaining of discomforts, and threaten to publish the captain because the porter does not hold out, may you one day be caught on board a bungo loaded with logwood!

The wear and tear of our wardrobe was manifest to the most indifferent observer ; and Mrs. Fensley, pitying our ragged condition, sewed on our buttons, darned, patched, and mended us, and put us in order for another expedition. On the third morning Captain Fensley told us we had passed Campeachy during the night, and, if the wind held, would reach Sisal that day. At eight o'clock we came in sight of the long low coast, and moving steadily toward it, at a little before dark anchored off the port, about two miles from the shore. One brig was lying there, a Spanish trader, bound to Havana, and the only vessel in port. The anchorage is an open roadstead outside of the breakers, which is considered perfectly safe except during a northeast storm, when Spanish vessels always slip their cables and stand out to sea.

In the uncertainty whether what we were going to see was worth the trouble, and the greater uncertainty of a conveyance when we wanted it, it was trying to leave a good vessel which in twenty days might carry us home. Nevertheless, we made the exertion. It was dusk when we left the vessel. We landed at the end of a long wooden dock, built out on the open shore of the sea, where we were challenged by a soldier. At the head of the pier was a guard and custom house, where an officer presented himself to escort us to the commandant. On the right, near the shore, was an old Spanish fortress with turrets. A soldier, barely distinguishable on the battlements, challenged us; and, passing the quartel, we were challenged again. The answer, as in Central America, was "Patria libre." The tone of the place was warlike, the Liberal party dominant. The revolution, as in all the other places, had been conducted in a spirit of moderation; but when the garrison was driven out, the commandant, who had been very tyrannical and oppressive, was taken, and the character of the revolution would have been stained by his murder, but he was put on board a bungo and escaped. We were well received by the commandant; and Captain Fensley took us to the house of an acquaintance, where we saw the captain of the brig in the offing, which was to sail in eight days for Havana, and no other vessel was expected for a long time. We made arrangements for setting out the next day for Merida, and early in the morning accompanied the captain to the pier, saw him embark in a bungo, waited till he got on board, and saw the brig, with a fine breeze and every sail set, stand out into the ocean for home. We turned our backs upon it with regret. There was nothing to detain us at Sisal. Though prettily situated on the seashore and a thriving place, it was merely the depôt of the exports and imports of Merida. At two o'clock we set out for the capital.

We were now in a country as different from Central America as if separated by the Atlantic, and we began our journey with an entirely new mode of conveyance.

It was in a vehicle called a calêche, built somewhat like the oldfashioned cab, but very large, cumbersome, made for rough roads, without springs, and painted red, green, and yellow.   One cowhide trunk for each was strapped on behind, and above them, reaching to the top of the calêche, was secured a pile of sacate for the horses.   The whole of this load, with Mr. Catherwood and me, was drawn by a single horse, having a rider on his back.   Two other horses followed for change, harnessed, and each with a boy riding him.   The road was perfectly level, and on a causeway a little elevated above the plain, which was stony and covered with scrub-trees.   At first it seemed a great luxury to roll along in a wheel carriage ; but, with the roughness of the road, and the calêche being without springs, in a little while this luxury began to be questionable.

After the magnificent scenery of Central America the country was barren and uninteresting, but we perceived the tokens of a rich interior in large cars drawn by mules five abreast, with high wheels ten or twelve feet apart, and loaded with hemp, bagging, wax, honey, and ox and deer skins.   The first incident of the 'road was changing horses, which consisted in taking out the horse in the shafts and putting in one of the others, already in a sweat.   This occurred twice ; and at one o'clock we entered the village of Hunucama, pleasantly situated, imbowered among trees, with a large plaza, at that time decorated with an arbour of evergreens all around, preparatory to the great fête of Corpus Christi, which was to be celebrated the next day.   Here we took three fresh horses ; and changing them as before, and passing two villages, through a vista two miles long saw the steeples of Merida, and at six o'clock rode into the city.   The houses were well built, with balconied

windows, and many had two stories. The streets were
clean, and many people in them well dressed, animated,
and cheerful in appearance; calêches fancifully painted and curtained, having ladies in them handsomely
dressed, without hats, and their hair ornamented with
flowers, gave it an air of gayety and beauty that, after
the sombre towns through which we had passed, was
fascinating and almost poetic. No place had yet made
so agreeable a first impression; and there was a hotel
in a large building kept by Donna Michaele, driving up
to which we felt as if by some accident we had fallen
upon a European city.

The reader will perhaps be surprised, but I had a
friend in Merida who expected me. Before embarking from New-York, I had been in the habit of dining
at a Spanish hotel in Fulton-street, frequented principally by Spanish Americans, at which place I had
met a gentleman of Merida, and learned that he was
the proprietor of the ruins of Uxmal. As yet I knew
nothing of the position or character of my friend, but I
soon found that everybody in Merida knew Don Simon
Peon. In the evening we called at his house. It was
a large, aristocratic-looking mansion of dark gray stone,
with balconied windows, occupying nearly the half of
one side of the plaza. Unfortunately, he was then at
Uxmal; but we saw his wife, father, mother, and sisters,
the house being a family residence, and the different
members of it having separate haciendas. They had
heard from him of my intended visit, and received me
as an acquaintance. Don Simon was expected back in
a few days, but, in the hope of finding him at Uxmal,
we determined to go on immediately. Donna Joaquina, his mother, promised to make all necessary arrangements for the journey, and to send a servant with

us. It was long since we passed so pleasant an evening ; we saw many persons who in appearance and manner would do credit to any society, and left with a strong disposition to make some stay in Merida.

The plaza presented a gay scene. It was the eve of the fête of El Corpus. Two sides of the plaza were occupied by corridors, and the others were adorned with arbours of evergreens, among which lights were interspersed. Gay parties were promenading under them, and along the corridors and in front of the houses were placed chairs and benches for the use of the promenaders, and all who chose to take them.

The city of Merida contains about twenty thousand inhabitants. It is founded on the site of an old Indian village, and dates from a few years after the conquest. In different parts of the city are the remains of Indian buildings. As the capital of the powerful State of Yucatan, it had always enjoyed a high degree of consideration in the Mexican Confederacy, and throughout the republic is famed for its sabios or learned men. The State of Yucatan had declared its independence of Mexico ; indeed, its independence was considered achieved. News had been received of the capitulation of Campeachy and the surrender of the Central garrison. The last remnant of despotism was rooted out, and the capital was in the first flush of successful revolution, the pride of independence. Removed by position, it was manifest that it would be no easy matter for Mexico to reconquer it ; and probably, like Texas, it is a limb forever lopped from that great, but feeble and distracted republic. It was pleasant to find that political animosities were not cherished with the same ferocity ; and Centralists and Liberals met like men of opposite parties at home.

The next day was the fête of Corpus Domini through-out all Spanish America, the greatest in the Catholic Church. Early in the morning, at the tolling of the bell, we went to the Cathedral, which, with the palace of the bishop, occupied one entire side of the plaza. The interior was grand and imposing, having a vaulted roof of stone, and two rows of lofty stone pillars; the choir was in the centre, the altar richly adorned with silver; but the great attraction was in the ladies kneel-ing before the altars, with white or black veils laid over the top of the head, some of them of saintlike purity and beauty, in dress, manners, and appearance realizing the pictures of Spanish romance. Indeed, the Spanish la-dies appear nowhere so lovely as in church.

The associations of one of my acquaintances having turned out so well, I determined to present a letter of introduction from friends in New-York to Don Joaquim Gutierrez, whose family-name stood high in Merida, and who, to my surprise, spoke English quite as well as we did. He had gone the rounds of society in Europe and the United States, and, like a good citizen, had returned to marry one of the belles and beauties of his own coun-try. His family was from Merida, but he himself was resident at Campeachy; and, being a prominent Cen-tralist, had left that city on account of its blockade by the Federalists, and in apprehensions of excesses that might be committed against obnoxious individuals should the place fall into their hands. From his house we went to the plaza to see the procession. After those we had seen in Guatimala this was inferior, and there were no devils; but the gathering of people under the arbour and in the corridors presented a beautiful spectacle. There was a large collection of Indians, both men and women, the best-looking race we had seen, and all were neatly dressed. In the whole crowd there was not a single garment that was not clean that day, and we were told that any Indian too poor to appear in a fitting dress that morning would be too proud to appear at all. The Indian women were really handsome ; all were dressed in white, with a red border around the neck, sleeves, and hem of their garments, and their faces had a mild, contented, and amiable expression ; the higher class were seated under the arbours before the doors of the houses and along the corridors, elegantly attired, without hats, and with veils or flowers in their hair, combining an elegance of appearance with simplicity of manners that made almost a scene of poetic beauty; and they had an air of gayety and freedom from disquietude, so different from the careworn faces of Guatimala, that they seemed as if what God intended them to be, happy. In fact, at this place it would have been no hardship to comply with the condition of purchasing Palenque ; and yet perhaps some of the effect of this strong impression was only the result of comparison.

After the procession Don Joaquim proposed to call either upon the bishop or a lady who had a beautiful daughter. The bishop was the greatest man in Merida, and lived in the greatest style ; but, determined to make the best of our day in Merida, we chose the other branch of the alternative. In the evening, however, we called upon him. His palace was adjoining the Cathedral, and before the door was a large cross ; the entrance was through a courtyard with two rows of corridors. We ascended to a second flight, and entered an anteroom, where we were received by a well-dressed official, who notified the bishop of our coming, and shortly afterward conducted us through three stately saloons with high ceilings and lighted with lamps, in one of which was a chair of state covered with red damask, which was carried up on the wall behind and ceiling over it. From the last a door opened into a large room elegantly fitted up as a sleeping apartment, in one corner of which was a large silver wash-hand basin with a silver pitcher; and in the centre, not a moveable or not very easily moved, sat the bishop, a man several feet round, handsomely dressed, and in a chair made to fit, stuffed and covered with red morocco, neither pinching him nor permitting him to roll, with a large, firmly-secured projecting ear-piece on each side to catch his head during the siesta. It had arms broad enough to support books and papers, and seemed the work of a man of genius. The lines of the bishop's face, however, indicated a man of high tone and character, and his conversation sustained the impression. He was a Centralist, and a great politician; and spoke of letters from generals, sieges, blockades, and battles, in tones which brought up a vivid picture of some priestly warrior or grand master of the Temple. In conclusion, he said that his influence, his house, and his *table* were at our service, asked us to name a day for dining with him, and said he would invite some friends to meet us. We had many trials in our journey, and it was not the least to decline this invitation; but we had some hope that we might be able to share his hospitality on our return from Uxmal.

From the bishop's palace we went to the theatre, a large building built expressly for the purpose, with two rows of boxes and a pit. The upper tier of boxes was private. The prima donna was a lady who sat next me at dinner at the hotel; but I had better employment than attending to the performance, in conversation with ladies who would have graced any circle.   One of them told me that there was to be a tertulia and a baglio at a country-house near the town in a few days, and to forego this was a harder trial than the loss of the bishop's dinner.   Altogether, the evening at the theatre consummated the satisfaction of the only day we passed in Merida, so that it remains impressed on my mind in bright relief to months of dulness.

The next morning at half past six we set out for Uxmal on horseback, escorted by a servant of Señor Peon, with Indians before us, one of whom carried a load not provided by us, in which a box of claret was conspicuous.   Leaving the city, we entered upon a level stony road, which seemed one bed of limestone, cut through a forest of scrub trees.   At the distance of a league we saw through a vista in the trees a large hacienda belonging to the Peon family, the entrance to which was by a large gate into a cattle-yard.   The house was built of stone, and had a front of about one hundred and fifty feet, with an arcade running the whole length.   It was raised about twenty feet, and at the foot was a large water-trough extending the whole length, about ten feet wide and of the same depth, filled with water for cattle.   On the left was a flight of stone steps, leading to a stone platform on which the hacienda stood.   At the end of this structure was an artificial reservoir or tank, also built of stone and cemented, about one hundred and fifty feet square, and perhaps twenty feet deep.   At the foot of the wall of the tank was a plantation of henniken, a species of aloe, from the fibres of which hemp is made. The style of the house, the strong and substantial character of the reservoir, and its apparent costliness, gave an imposing character to the hacienda.

At this place our Indian carriers left us, and we took others from the hacienda, with whom we continued three leagues farther to another hacienda of the family, of much the same character, where we stopped to breakfast. This over, we set out again, and by this time it had become desperately hot.

The road was very rough, over a bed of stone thinly covered, with barely soil enough for the growth of scrubtrees ; our saddles were of a new fashion, and most painfully trying to those unused to them ; the heat was very oppressive, and the leagues very long, till we reached another hacienda, a vast, irregular pile of buildings of dark gray stone, that might have been the castle of a German baron in feudal times. Each of these haciendas had an Indian name ; this was called the hacienda of Vayalquex, and it was the only one of which Donna Joaquina, in speaking of our route, had made any particular mention. The entrance was by a large stone gateway, with a pyramidal top, into a long lane, on the right of which was a shed, built by Don Simon since his return from the United States as a ropewalk for manufacturing hemp raised on the hacienda ; and there was one arrangement which added very much to the effect, and which I did not observe anywhere else : the cattleyard and water-tanks were on one side and out of sight. We dismounted under the shade of noble trees in front of the house, and ascended by a flight of broad stone steps to a corridor thirty feet wide, with large mattings, which could be rolled up, or dropped as an awning for protection against the sun and rain. On one side the corridor was continued around the building, and on the other it conducted to the door of a church having a large cross over it, and within ornamented with figures like the churches in towns, for the tenants of the hacienda. The whole establishment was lordly in its appearance. It had fifteen hundred Indian tenants, bound to the master by a sort of feudal tenure, and, as the friends of the master, escorted by a household servant, the whole was ours.

We had fallen unexpectedly upon a state of things new and peculiar. The peninsula of Yucatan, lying between the bays of Campeachy and Honduras, is a vast plain. Cape Catoche, the northeastern point of the peninsula, is but fifty-one leagues from San Antonio, the western extremity of the Island of Cuba, which is supposed at a remote period to have formed part of the American Continent. The soil and atmosphere are extremely dry ; along the whole coast, from Campeachy to Cape Catoche, there is not a single stream or spring of fresh water. The interior is equally destitute ; and water is the most valuable possession in the country. During the season of rains, from April to the end of October, there is a superabundant supply ; but the scorching sun of the next six months dries up the earth, and unless water were preserved man and beast would perish, and the country be depopulated. All the enterprise and wealth of the landed proprietors, therefore, are exerted in procuring supplies of water, as without it the lands are worth nothing. For this purpose each hacienda has large tanks and reservoirs, constructed and kept up at great expense, to supply water for six months to all dependant upon it, and this creates a relation with the Indian population which places the proprietor somewhat in the position of a lord under the old feudal system.

By the act of independence, the Indians of Mexico, as well as the white population, became free. No man can buy and sell another, whatever may be the colour of his skin; but as the Indians are poor, thriftless, and improvident, and never look beyond the immediate hour, they are obliged to attach themselves to some hacienda which can supply their wants; and, in return for the privilege of using the water, they come under certain obligations of service to the master, which place him in a lordly position; and this state of things, growing out of the natural condition of the country, exists, I believe, nowhere in Spanish America except in Yucatan. Each hacienda has its major-domo, who attends to all the details of the management of the estate, and in the absence of the master is his viceroy, and has the same powers over the tenants. At this hacienda the major-domo was a young Mestitzo, and had fallen into his place in an easy and natural way by marrying his predecessor's daughter, who had just enough white blood to elevate the dulness of the Indian face into one of softness and sweetness; and yet it struck me that he thought quite as much of the place he got with her as of herself.

It would have been a great satisfaction to pass several days at this lordly hacienda; but, not expecting anything to interest us on the road, we had requested Donna Joaquina to hurry us through, and the servant told us that the señora's orders were to conduct us to another hacienda of the family, about two leagues beyond, to sleep. At the moment we were particularly loth to leave, on account of the fatigue of the previous ride. The servant suggested to the major-domo llamar un coché; in English, to "call a coach," which the latter proposed to do if we wished it. We made a few inquiries, and said, unhesitatingly and peremptorily, in effect, "Go call a coach, and let a coach be called." The major-domo ascended by a flight of stone steps

outside to the belfry of the church, whither we followed
him; and, turning around with a movement and tone
of voice that reminded us of a Mussulman in a minaret
calling the faithful to prayers, he called for a coach.
The roof of the church, and of the whole pile of buildings connected, was of stone cemented, firm and strong
as a pavement. The sun beat intensely upon it, and for
several minutes all was still. At length we saw a single Indian trotting through the woods toward the hacienda, then two together, and in a quarter of an hour
there were twenty or thirty. These were the horses;
the coaches were yet growing on the trees. Six Indians were selected for each coach, who, with a few
minutes' use of the machete, cut a bundle of poles,
which they brought up to the corridor to manufacture
into coaches. This was done, first, by laying on the
ground two poles about as thick as a man's wrist, ten
feet long and three feet apart. These were fastened
by cross-sticks tied with strings of unspun hemp, about
two feet from each end; grass hammocks were secured between the poles, bows bent over them and covered with light matting, and the coaches were made.
We placed our ponchas at the head for pillows, crawled inside, and lay down. The Indians took off little
cotton shirts covering the breast, and tied them around
their petates as hatbands. Four of them raised up
each coach, and placed the end of the poles on little
cushions on their shoulders. We bade farewell to the
major-domo and his wife, and, feet first, descended the
steps and set off on a trot, while an Indian followed
leading the horses. In the great relief we experienced
we forgot our former scruples against making beasts of
burden of men. They were not troubled with any sense
of indignity or abasement, and the weight was not much.

There were no mountains; only some little inequalities which brought the head lower than the heels, and they seldom stumbled.   In this way they carried us about three miles, and then laid us down gently on the ground. Like the Indians in Merida, they were a fine-looking race, with a good expression of countenance, cheerful, and even merry in their toil.   They were amused at us because we could not talk with them.   There is no diversity of Indian languages in Yucatan ; the Maya is universal, and all the Spaniards speak it.

Having wiped off the perspiration and rested, they took us up again; and, lulled by the quiet movement and the regular fall of the Indians' feet upon the ear, I fell into a doze, from which I was roused by stopping at a gate, on entering which I found we were advancing to a range of white stone buildings, standing on an elevation about twenty feet high, which by measurement afterward I found to be three hundred and sixty feet long, with an imposing corridor running the whole length; and on the extreme right of the building the platform was continued one or two hundred feet, forming the top of a reservoir, on which there was a windlass with long arms; and Indian women, dressed in white, were moving round in a circle, drawing water and filling their water-jars.   This was called the hacienda of Mucuyche.   We entered, as usual, through a large cattle-yard.   At the foot of the structure on which the building stood, running nearly the whole length, was a gigantic stone tank, about eight or ten feet wide, and of the same depth, filled with water.   We were carried up an inclined stone platform about the centre of the range of buildings, which consisted of three distinct sets, each one hundred and twenty feet front.   In that on the left was the church, the door of which was

open, and an old Indian was then lighting candles at
the altar for vesper prayers. In front, setting a little
back, were the apartments of the major-domo, and at
the other end of the range the mansion of the master,
in the corridor of which we were set down, and crawled out of our coaches. There was something mon-
strously aristocratic in being borne on the shoulders of
tenants from such a hacienda as that we had left to this
stately pile. The whole appearance of things gave an
idea of country residence upon a scale of grand hospitality, and yet we learned, to our astonishment, that
most of the family had never seen it. The only one by
whom it was ever visited was the son who had it in
charge, and he came only for a few days at a time, to
see how things were conducted, and examine the accounts of the major-domo. The range consisted of a
single suite of rooms, one in the centre about eighty
feet long, and one on each side, communicating, about
forty feet long each, and a noble corridor extended
along the whole front and rear.

We had an hour of daylight, which I could have employed very satisfactorily on the spot, but the servant
urged us to go immediately and see a cenote. What a
cenote was we had no idea, and Mr. C., being much
fatigued, turned into a hammock ; but, unwilling to lose
anything where all was strange and unexpected, I followed the servant, crossed the roof of the reservoir, cemented as hard as stone, passed on to an open tank
built of stone, covered with cement inside and out,
about one hundred and fifty feet square and twenty feet
deep, filled with water, in which twenty or thirty Indians were swimming ; and, descending to the foot of
the tank, at the distance of about a hundred yards
came to a large opening in the ground, with a broad

flight of more than fifty steps; descending which, I saw unexpectedly a spectacle of such extraordinary beauty, that I sent the servant back to tell Mr. Catherwood to come to me forthwith, if he had to be carried in his hammock. It was a large cavern or grotto, with a roof of broken, overhanging rock, high enough to give an air of wildness and grandeur, impenetrable at midday to the sun's rays, and at the bottom water pure as crystal, still and deep, resting upon a bed of white limestone rock. It was the very creation of romance; a bathing-place for Diana and her nymphs. Grecian poet never imagined so beautiful a scene. It was almost a profanation, but in a few minutes we were swimming around the rocky basin with feelings of boyish exultation, only regretting that such a freak of nature was played where so few could enjoy its beauties. On a nobleman's estate in England it would be above all price. The bath reinvigorated our frames. It was after dark when we returned; hammocks were waiting for us, and very soon we were in a profound sleep.

CHAPTER XXIV.

Journey resumed.—Arrival at Uxmal.—Hacienda of Uxmal. — Major-domos.—
    Adventures of a young Spaniard.—Visit to the Ruins of Uxmal.—First Sight
    of the Ruins.—Character of the Indians.—Details of Hacienda Life.—A delicate
    Case.—Illness of Mr. Catherwood.—Breaking up.

At daybreak the next morning, with new Indians
and a guide on horseback from the hacienda, we resumed our journey.   The surface of the country was the
same, limestone with scrub trees.   There was not soil
enough to absorb the water, which rested in puddles in
the hollows of the stones.   At nine o'clock we reached
another hacienda, smaller than the last, but still having
a lordly appearance, where, as before, the women were
drawing water by a wheel.   The major-domo expressed
his sense of the honour conferred upon him by our visit,
and his anxiety to serve us, gave us a breakfast of milk,
tortillas, and wild honey, and furnished us with other
Indians and a guide.   We mounted again ; very soon
the sun became intensely hot ; there were no trees to
shade us, and we suffered excessively.   At half past
twelve we passed some mounds of ruins a little off the
road, but the sun was so scorching that we could not
stop to examine them, and at two o'clock we reached
Uxmal.   Little did I think, when I made the acquaintance of my unpretending friend at the Spanish hotel in
Fulton-street, that I should ride upward of fifty miles
on his family estates, carried by his Indians, and breakfasting, dining, and sleeping at his lordly haciendas,
while the route marked out for our return would bring
us to others, one of which was larger than any we had

seen. The family of Peon, under the Spanish dominion, had given governors to the province of Yucatan.
On the establishment of independence, its present head,
a stanch Royalist, retired in disgust from all kinds of
employment, and the whole of the large family estates
were managed by the Señora Donna Joaquina. Unfortunately, Don Simon had left for Merida, and we had
missed him on the way. Moreover, owing to the heat
of the sun and our awkward saddles, we arrived at the
end of this triumphal march in a dreadfully jaded and
forlorn condition, and perhaps we never dismounted
more utterly worn out and uncomfortable.

The hacienda of Uxmal was built of dark gray stone,
ruder in appearance and finish than any of the others,
with a greater appearance of antiquity, and at a distance
looked like an old baronial castle. A year before it
had been given to Don Simon by his father, and he
was making large repairs and additions to the building,
though, as his family never visited it, and he only for a
few days at a time, for what purpose I could not conceive. It had its cattle-yard in front, with tanks of
water around, some with green vegetation on the top,
and there was an unwholesome sensation of dampness.
It had, too, its church, which contained a figure of nu-
estra Señor, " Our Lord," revered by the Indians of all
the haciendas around, the fame of which had reached
the household servants at Merida, and which was the
first object that attracted the attention of our guide.
The whole hacienda was immediately at our disposal;
but, worn down with heat and fatigue, we took at once
to our hammocks.

The hacienda had two major-domos, one a Mestitzo,
who understood the language and business, and in the
other we found an acquaintance, or, at least, what seem-

ed so, for about the time that we left New-York he was
a waiter at Delmonico's.   It was a strange encounter
at this out-of-the-way place, to be brought into close
connexion with this well-known restaurant, which in
that country seemed the seat of art and fountain of happiness.   He was a young Spaniard from Catalonia,
who, with a friend, having taken part in some defeated
insurrection, fled to Cuba, whence, on the point of being
discovered, they escaped to New-York, penniless.   Ignorant of the language, with no means of getting a live-
lihood, both were received by Delmonico as waiters at
his restaurant, where the friend rose to be head choco-
late-maker; but he was languishing as simple waiter,
when Don Simon proposed to him to go to Uxmal.
Without knowing where he was going, except that it
was to some part of Spanish America, or what was to
be his business, he found himself in a retired place, surrounded by Indians whose language he could not understand, and having no one near him with whom he
could exchange a word except the major-domo.   These
major-domos form a class in Yucatan who need sharp
looking after.   Like the Scotch servant applying for a
place, they are not particular about wages, and are satisfied with what little they can pick up about the house.
This is the character of most of the major-domos ; and
the position of the young man, being white, intelligent,
and honest, had advantages in that country, as Don Simon intended to give him, as soon as he understood the
business, a superintendence over the major-domos of
three or four haciendas ; but, unfortunately, he wanted
energy, felt the want of society and the loneliness of
his situation, remembered scenes of enjoyment with his
friend and other waiters, and at Uxmal talked of the
opera ; and when at dinner-time he drew a feeling pic-

ture of Delmonico's saloon, we sympathized with him
cordially.

In the afternoon, rested and refreshed, we set out for
a walk to the ruins.   The path led through a noble
piece of woods, in which there were many tracks, and
our Indian guide lost his way.   Mr. C., being unwell,
returned to the hacienda.   We took another road, and,
emerging suddenly from the woods, to my astonishment came at once upon a large open field strewed
with mounds of ruins, and vast buildings on terraces,
and pyramidal structures, grand and in good preservation, richly ornamented, without a bush to obstruct the
view, and in picturesque effect almost equal to the ruins
of Thebes ; for these, standing on the flat valley of the
Nile, and extending on both sides of the river, nowhere
burst in one view upon the sight.   Such was the report
I made to Mr. Catherwood on my return, who, lying in
his hammock unwell and out of spirits, told me I was
romancing ; but early the next morning we were on the
ground, and his comment was that the reality exceeded
my description.

The place of which I am now speaking was beyond
all doubt once a large, populous, and highly civilized
city, and the reader can nowhere find one word of it
on any page of history.   Who built it, why it was lo-
cated on that spot, away from water or any of those
natural advantages which have determined the sites of
cities whose histories are known, what led to its aban-
donment and destruction, no man can tell.   The only
name by which it is known is that of the hacienda on
which it stands.   In the oldest deed belonging to the
Peon family, which goes back a hundred and forty
years, the buildings are referred to, in the boundaries
of the estate, as Las Casas de Piedra.   This is the only

ancient document or record in existence in which the place is mentioned at all, and there are no traditions except the wild superstitions of Indians in regard to particular buildings. The ruins were all exhumed; within the last year the trees had been cut down and burned, and the whole field of ruins was in view, enclosed by the woods and planted with corn.

We passed a most interesting and laborious day, and at evening returned to the hacienda to mature our plans for a thorough exploration; but, unfortunately, during the night Mr. Catherwood, I believe affected by the immensity of the work, had a violent attack of fever, which continued upon him in the morning, with a prospect of serious illness.

It was Monday, and very early all the Indians of the hacienda, according to their obligation to the master, presented themselves to receive directions from the major-domo for the day's work. In remaining about the house I had an opportunity of learning somewhat of hacienda discipline and the character of the Indians.

The hacienda of Uxmal is ten leagues or thirty miles square, but only a small portion is cultivated, and the rest is a mere roaming-ground for cattle. The Indians are of two classes: vaceros, or tenders of cattle and horses, who receive twelve dollars per year, with five almudas of maize per week; and labradores or labourers, who are also called Luneros, from their obligation, in consideration of their drinking the water of the hacienda, to work for the master without pay on Lunes or Monday. These last constitute the great body of the Indians; and, besides their obligation to work on Monday, when they marry and have families, and, of course, need more water, they are obliged to clear, sow, and gather twenty micates of maize for the master, each

micate being twenty-four square yards. When the bell
of the church is struck five times, every Indian is obliged to go forthwith to the hacienda, and, for a real a
day and a ration of three cents' worth of maize, do
whatever work the master or his delegate, the major-
domo, may direct. The authority of the master or his
delegate over these is absolute. He settles all disputes
between the Indians themselves, and punishes for offences, acting both as judge and executioner. If the
major-domo punish an Indian unreasonably, the latter
may complain to his master; and if the master refuse to
give him redress, or himself punishes an Indian unreasonably, the latter may apply for his discharge. There
is no obligation upon him to remain on the hacienda
unless he is in debt to the master, but, practically, this
binds him hand and foot. The Indians are all improvident, anticipate their earnings, never have two days'
provisions in store, and never keep any accounts. A
dishonest master may always bring them in debt, and
generally they are really so. If able to pay off the debt,
the Indian is entitled to his immediate discharge; but if
not, the master is obliged to give him a writing to the
effect following: " Whatever señor wishes to receive
the Indian named ———, can take him, provided he
pays me the debt he owes me." If the master refuses
him this paper, the Indian may complain to the justitia.
When he has obtained it, he goes round to the different
haciendas until he finds a proprietor who is willing to
purchase the debt, with a mortgage upon him until it is
paid. The account is settled, and the master gives the
Indian a writing of this purport: " The account of my
former servant ——— being adjusted, which is twenty
dollars, and having paid me the said debt, I, his present master, give him this receipt;" and with this he

enters into the service of a new master. There is but little chance of his ever paying off the smallest debt. He will never work merely to clear off the encumbrance, considers all he can get on his body clear gain, and virtually, from the time he receives his first dollar, goes through life in bondage, varied only by an occasional change of masters. In general they are mild, amiable, and very docile; bear no malice; and when one of them is whipped and smarting under stripes, with tears in his eyes he makes a bow to the major-domo, and says "buenos tarde, señor;" "good evening, sir." But they require to be dealt with sternly, and kept at a distance; are uncertain, and completely the creatures of impulse; and one bad Indian or a bad Mestitzo may ruin a whole hacienda. They inherit all the indolence of their ancestors, are wedded to old usages, and unwilling to be taught anything new. Don Simon has attempted to introduce improvements in agriculture, but in vain; they cannot work except in their own old way. Don Simon brought out the common churn from the United States, and attempted to introduce the making of butter and cheese; but the Indians could not be taught the use of them, the churns were thrown aside, and hundreds of cows wander in the woods unmilked. The master is not obliged to maintain the Indian when sick; though, as he derives a profit from his labour, it is his interest to do so; and, on broad grounds, as it is an object always to increase his labradores, it is his interest to treat them in such a manner as to acquire among the Indians a reputation as a good master.

In the course of the morning I visited many of the huts of the Indians. They were built in an oblong form, of round poles set upright in the ground and thatched, and some appeared clean and comfortable.

The men were all away at work, and all day there was a procession of women in white cotton dresses moving from the gate to the well and drawing water. It was pleasant to find that marriage was considered proper and expedient, conducing to good order and thrift certainly, and probably to individual happiness. Don Simon encouraged it; he did not like to have any single men on the estate, and made every young Indian of the right age take unto himself a wife. When, as often happened, the Indian, in a deprecating tone, said, "No tengo muger," "I have no woman," Don Simon looked through the hacienda and found one for him. On his last visit he made four matches, and the day before our arrival the Delmonico major-domo had been to the nearest village to escort the couples and pay the padre for marrying them, the price being thirteen shillings each. He was afraid to trust them with the money, for fear they would spend it and not get married.

The old major-domo was energetic in carrying out the views of his master on this important subject, and that day a delicate case was brought before him. A young Indian girl brought a complaint against a married woman for slander. She said that she was engaged to be married to a young man whom she loved and who loved her, and the married woman had injured her fair fame by reporting that she was already in "an interesting situation;" she had told the young man of it, said that all the women in the hacienda saw it, and taunted him with marrying such a girl; and now, she said, the young man would not have her. The married woman was supported by a crowd of witnesses, and it must be admitted that appearances were very much against the plaintiff; but the old major-domo, without going into the merits at all, decided in her fa-

vour on broad grounds. Indignant at a marriage being
prevented, he turned to the married woman and asked,
What was it to her ? what right had she to meddle ?
what if it was true ?—it was none of her business. Perhaps the young man knew it and was party to it, and
still intended to marry the girl, and they might have
lived happily but for her busy tongue ; and, without
more ado, he brought out a leather whip cut into long
lashes, and with great vigour began applying it to the
back of the indiscreet communicator of unwelcome tidings. He wound up with an angry homily upon busy-
bodies, and then upon women generally, who, he said,
made all the difficulties on the hacienda, and but for
them the men would be quiet enough. The matrons
of the hacienda stood aghast at this unexpected turn of
things ; and, when the case was dismissed, all crowded
around the victim and went away with her, giving such
comfort as they could. The young girl went away
alone ; the hearts of her sex were steeled against her ;
in savage as in civilized life,

> " Every wo a tear may claim,
> Except an erring sister's shame."

In the afternoon Mr. Catherwood's fever left him,
but in a very low state. The hacienda was unhealthy
at this season ; the great troughs and tanks of water
around the house were green, and, with the regular afternoon rains, induced fatal fevers. Mr. Catherwood's
constitution was already severely shattered. Indeed, I
became alarmed, and considered it indispensable for
him to leave the hacienda, and, if possible, the country
altogether. To carry out my other plans, we intended
at all events to return. We made a calculation that,
by setting out the next morning, we could reach the

Spanish brig in time to embark for Havana, and in ten minutes' consultation we determined to break up and go home. Immediately we communicated our purpose to the major-domo, who ascended to the belfry of the church and called a coach, to be ready at two o'clock the next morning.

F. Catherwood

CENOTE.

CHAPTER XXV.

In the mean time I returned for one more view of the ruins.   Mr. Waldeck's work on these ruins had appeared before we left this country.   It was brought out in Paris in a large folio edition, with illustrations fancifully and beautifully coloured, and contains the result of a year's residence at Merida and eight days at Uxmal. At the time of his visit the ruins were overgrown with trees, which within the last year had been cleared away, and the whole was laid bare and exposed to view.   In attempting a description of these ruins, so vast a work rises up before me that I am at a loss where to begin. Arrested on the very threshold of our labours, I am unable to give any general plan; but, fortunately, the whole field was level, clear of trees, and in full sight at once.   The first view stamped it indelibly upon my mind, and Mr. Catherwood's single day was well employed.

The first object that arrests the eye on emerging from the forest is the building represented on the right hand of the engraving opposite.   Drawn off by mounds of ruins and piles of gigantic buildings, the eye returns and again fastens upon this lofty structure.   It was the first building I entered.   From its front doorway I counted sixteen elevations, with broken walls and

F. Catherwood.

H. Jordan.

U X M A L,

HOUSE OF THE DWARF AND HOUSE OF THE NUNS.

mounds of stones, and vast, magnificent edifices, which at that distance seemed untouched by time and defying ruin. I stood in the doorway when the sun went down, throwing from the buildings a prodigious breadth of shadow, darkening the terraces on which they stood, and presenting a scene strange enough for a work of enchantment.

This building is sixty-eight feet long. The elevation on which it stands is built up solid from the plain, entirely artificial. Its form is not pyramidal, but oblong and rounding, being two hundred and forty feet long at the base, and one hundred and twenty broad, and it is protected all around, to the very top, by a wall of square stones. Perhaps the high ruined structures at Palenque, which we have called pyramidal, and which were so ruined that we could not make them out exactly, were originally of the same shape. On the east side of the structure is a broad range of stone steps between eight and nine inches high, and so steep that great care is necessary in ascending and descending ; of these we counted a hundred and one in their places. Nine were wanting at the top, and perhaps twenty were covered with rubbish at the bottom. At the summit of the steps is a stone platform four feet and a half wide, running along the rear of the building. There is no door in the centre, but at each end a door opens into an apartment eighteen feet long and nine wide, and between the two is a third apartment of the same width, and thirty-four feet long. The whole building is of stone ; inside, the walls are of polished smoothness ; outside, up to the height of the door, the stones are plain and square ; above this line there is a rich cornice or moulding, and from this to the top of the building all the sides are covered with rich and elaborate sculptured ornaments,

forming a sort of arabesque.   The style and character
of these ornaments were entirely different from those of
any we had ever seen before, either in that country or
any other ; they bore no resemblance whatever to those
of Copan or Palenque, and were quite as unique and
peculiar.   The designs were strange and incomprehensible, very elaborate, sometimes grotesque, but often
simple, tasteful, and beautiful.   Among the intelligible
subjects are squares and diamonds, with busts of human
beings, heads of leopards, and compositions of leaves
and flowers, and the ornaments known everywhere as
grecques.   The ornaments, which succeed each other,
are all different ; the whole form an extraordinary
mass of richness and complexity, and the effect is both
grand and curious.   And the construction of these ornaments is not less peculiar and striking than the general effect.   There were no tablets or single stones,
each representing separately and by itself an entire
subject ; but every ornament or combination is made
up of separate stones, on each of which part of the subject was carved, and which was then set in its place in
the wall.   Each stone, by itself, was an unmeaning
fractional part ; but, placed by the side of others, helped
to make a whole, which without it would be incomplete.
Perhaps it may, with propriety, be called a species of
sculptured mosaic.

From the front door of this extraordinary building a
pavement of hard cement, twenty-two feet long by fifteen broad, leads to the roof of another building, seated
lower down on the artificial structure, as shown in the
engraving.   There is no staircase or other visible communication between the two ; but, descending by a pile
of rubbish along the side of the lower one, and groping
around the corner, we entered a doorway in front four

feet wide, and found inside a chamber twelve feet high, with corridors running the whole breadth, of which the front one was seven feet three inches deep, and the other three feet nine inches. The inner walls were of smooth and polished square stones, and there was no inner door or means of communication with any other place. Outside the doorway was loaded with ornaments, and the whole exterior was the same as that of the building described above. The steps leading from the doorway to the foot of the structure were entirely destroyed.

The Indians regard these ruins with superstitious reverence. They will not go near them at night, and they have the old story that immense treasure is hidden among them. Each of the buildings has its name given to it by the Indians. This is called the Casa del Anano, or House of the Dwarf, and it is consecrated by a wild legend, which, as I sat in the doorway, I received from the lips of an Indian, as follows :

There was an old woman who lived in a hut on the very spot now occupied by the structure on which this building is perched, and opposite the Casa del Gobernador (which will be mentioned hereafter), who went mourning that she had no children. In her distress she one day took an egg, covered it with a cloth, and laid it away carefully in one corner of the hut. Every day she went to look at it, until one morning she found the egg hatched, and a criatura, or creature, or baby, born. The old woman was delighted, and called it her son, provided it with a nurse, took good care of it, so that in one year it walked and talked like a man ; and then it stopped growing. The old woman was more delighted than ever, and said he would be a great lord or king. One day she told him to go to the house of the gober-

nador and challenge him to a trial of strength. The
dwarf tried to beg off, but the old woman insisted, and
he went. The guard admitted him, and he flung his
challenge at the gobernador. The latter smiled, and
told him to lift a stone of three arrobas, or seventy-five
pounds, at which the little fellow cried and returned to
his mother, who sent him back to say that if the gobernador lifted it first, he would afterward. The gobernador lifted it, and the dwarf immediately did the same.
The gobernador then tried him with other feats of
strength, and the dwarf regularly did whatever was
done by the gobernador. At length, indignant at being
matched by a dwarf, the gobernador told him that, unless he made a house in one night higher than any in
the place, he would kill him. The poor dwarf again
returned crying to his mother, who bade him not to be
disheartened, and the next morning he awoke and found
himself in this lofty building. The gobernador, seeing
it from the door of his palace, was astonished, and sent
for the dwarf, and told him to collect two bundles of
cogoiol, a wood of a very hard species, with one of
which he, the gobernador, would beat the dwarf over
the head, and *afterward* the dwarf should beat him with
the other. The dwarf again returned crying to his
mother; but the latter told him not to be afraid, and
put on the crown of his head a tortillita de trigo, a small
thin cake of wheat flour. The trial was made in the
presence of all the great men in the city. The gobernador broke the whole of his bundle over the dwarf's
head without hurting the little fellow in the least. He
then tried to avoid the trial on his own head, but he
had given his word in the presence of his officers, and
was obliged to submit. The second blow of the dwarf
broke his scull in pieces, and all the spectators hailed

the victor as their new gobernador. The old woman then died; but at the Indian village of Mani, seventeen leagues distant, there is a deep well, from which opens a cave that leads under ground an immense distance to Merida. In this cave, on the bank of a stream, under the shade of a large tree, sits an old woman with a serpent by her side, who sells water in small quantities, not for money, but only for a criatura or baby to give the serpent to eat; and this old woman is the mother of the dwarf. Such is the fanciful legend connected with this edifice; but it hardly seemed more strange than the structure to which it referred.

The other building indicated in the plate is called by a name which may originally have had some reference to the vestals who in Mexico were employed to keep burning the sacred fire; but I believe in the mouths of the Indians of Uxmal it has no reference whatever to history, tradition, or legend, but is derived entirely from Spanish associations. It is called Casa de las Monjas, or House of the Nuns, or the Convent. It is situated on an artificial elevation about fifteen feet high. Its form is quadrangular, and one side, according to my measurement, is ninety-five paces in length. It was not possible to pace all around it, from the masses of fallen stones which encumber it in some places, but it may be safely stated at two hundred and fifty feet square. Like the house of the dwarf, it is built entirely of cut stone, and the whole exterior is filled with the same rich, elaborate, and incomprehensible sculptured ornaments.

The principal entrance is by a large doorway into a beautiful patio or courtyard, grass-grown, but clear of trees, and the whole of the inner façade is ornamented more richly and elaborately than the outside, and in a

more perfect state of preservation. On one side the
combination was in the form of diamonds, simple, chaste,
and tasteful; and at the head of the courtyard two gigantic serpents, with their heads broken and fallen,
were winding from opposite directions along the whole
façade.

In front, and on a line with the door of the convent,
is another building, on a lower foundation, of the same
general character, called Casa de Tortugas, from sculptured turtles over the doorway. This building had in
several places huge cracks, as if it had been shaken by
an earthquake. It stands nearly in the centre of the
ruins, and the top commands a view all round of singular but wrecked magnificence.

Beyond this, a little to the right, approached by passing over mounds of ruins, was another building, which
at a great distance attracted our attention by its conspicuous ornaments. We reached it by ascending two high
terraces. The main building was similar to the others,
and along the top ran a high ornamented wall in this

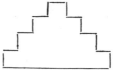

form, from which it was called Casa de Palomos, or
House of Pigeons, and at a distance it looked more like
a row of pigeon-houses than anything else.

In front was a broad avenue, with a line of ruins on
each side, leading beyond the wall of the convent to a
great mound of ruins, which probably had once been a
building with which it was connected; and beyond this
is a lofty building in the rear, to which this seemed but
a vestibule or porter's lodge. Between the two was a
large patio or courtyard, with corridors on each side,

and the ground of the courtyard sounded hollow. In one place the surface was broken, and I descended into a large excavation, cemented, which had probably been intended as a granary. At the back of the courtyard, on a high, broken terrace, which it was difficult to climb, was another edifice more ruined than the others, but which, from the style of its remains and its commanding position, overlooking every other building except the house of the dwarf, and apparently having been connected with the distant mass of ruins in front, must have been one of the most important in the city, perhaps the principal temple. The Indians called it the quartel or guard-house. It commanded a view of other ruins not contained in the enumeration of those seen from the house of the dwarf; and the whole presented a scene of barbaric magnificence, utterly confounding all previous notions in regard to the aboriginal inhabitants of this country, and calling up emotions which had not been wakened to the same extent by anything we had yet seen.

There was one strange circumstance connected with these ruins. No water had ever been discovered; and there was not a single stream, fountain, or well, known to the Indians, nearer than the hacienda, a mile and a half distant. The sources which supplied this element of life had disappeared; the cisterns were broken, or the streams dried up. This, as we afterward learned from Don Simon, was an object of great interest to him, and made him particularly anxious for a thorough exploration of the ruins. He supposed that the face of the country had not changed, and that somewhere under ground must exist great wells, cisterns, or reservoirs, which supplied the former inhabitants of the city with water. The discovery of these wells or reservoirs would, in that region, be like finding a fountain in the desert, or, more poetically, like finding money. The supply of water would be boundless. Luneros without number might draw from it, and the old city be repeopled without any new expense for wells or tanks.

While I was making the circuit of these ruins, Mr. Catherwood proceeded to the Casa del Gobernador, which title, according to the naming of the Indians, indicates the principal building of the old city, the residence of the governor, or royal house. It is the grandest in position, the most stately in architecture and proportions, and the most perfect in preservation of all the structures remaining at Uxmal.

The plate opposite represents the ground-plan, with the three ranges of terraces on which it stands. The first terrace is six hundred feet long and five feet high. It is walled with cut stone, and on the top is a platform twenty feet broad, from which rises another terrace fifteen feet high. At the corners this terrace is supported by cut stones, having the faces rounded so as to give a better finish than with sharp angles. The great platform above is flat and clear of trees, but abounding in green stumps of the forest but lately cleared away, and now planted, or, rather, from its irregularity, sown with corn, which as yet rose barely a foot from the ground. At the southeast corner of this platform is a row of round pillars eighteen inches in diameter and three or four feet high, extending about one hundred feet along the platform; and these were the nearest approach to pillars or columns that we saw in all our exploration of the ruins of that country. In the middle of the terrace, along an avenue leading to a range of steps, was a broken, round pillar, inclined and falling, with trees growing around it. It was part of our purpose to make an

ESPLANADE.

Grand Esplanade or Terrace, three hundred and fifty feet long.

Remains of what are supposed once to have been a Flight of Steps.

Flight of Steps.

Stone Ornament on Façade of Building.

terrace raised about twenty feet

Terrace raised about six feet

300 Feet

200

Scale of Feet

Remains of what are supposed once to have been a Flight of Steps

PLAN

Of a large Stone Building at UXMAL IN YUCATAN.

The front extends 315 feet, and the whole of the upper part, the sides, and the back, are covered with a rich and intricate design, skilfully worked in stone, and originally coloured, of which some remains are still seen.

Remains of Columns

Terrace raised about six feet

Whole extent of Ground occupied by the Edifice

100   50   0

Remains of what are supposed once to have been a Flight of Steps

F. Catherwood.

79.

excavation in this platform, from the impression that
underneath would be found a vault, forming part of the
immense reservoirs for supplying the city with water.

In the centre of the platform, at a distance of two
hundred and five feet from the border in front, is a range
of stone steps more than a hundred feet broad, and thirty-five in number, ascending to a third terrace, fifteen
feet above the last, and thirty-five feet from the ground,
about equal to the height of the City Hall, which, being
elevated on a naked plain, formed a most commanding
position.   The erection of these terraces alone was an
immense work.   On this third terrace, with its principal
doorway facing the range of steps, stands the noble
structure of the Casa del Gobernador.   The façade
measures three hundred and twenty feet.   Away from
the region of dreadful rains, and the rank growth of
forest which smothers the ruins of Palenque, it stands
with all its walls erect, and almost as perfect as when
deserted by its inhabitants.   The whole building is of
stone, plain up to the moulding that runs along the tops
of the doorway, and above filled with the same rich,
strange, and elaborate sculpture, among which is particularly conspicuous the ornament before referred to as
la grecque.   There is no rudeness or barbarity in the design or proportions ; on the contrary, the whole wears
an air of architectural symmetry and grandeur ; and as
the stranger ascends the steps and casts a bewildered eye
along its open and desolate doors, it is hard to believe
that he sees before him the work of a race in whose
epitaph, as written by historians, they are called ignorant of art, and said to have perished in the rudeness
of savage life.   If it stood at this day on its grand artificial terrace in Hyde Park or the Garden of the Tuil-
eries, it would form a new order, I do not say equal-

ling, but not unworthy to stand side by side with the remains of Egyptian, Grecian, and Roman art.

But there was one thing which seemed in strange want of conformity with all the rest. It was the first object that had arrested my attention in the house of the dwarf, and which I had marked in every other building. I have mentioned that at Ocosingo we saw a wooden beam, and at Palenque the fragment of a wooden pole; at this place *all the lintels had been of wood, and throughout the ruins most of them were still in their places over the doors.* These lintels were heavy beams, eight or nine feet long, eighteen or twenty inches wide, and twelve or fourteen thick. The wood, like that at Ocosingo, was very hard, and rang under the blow of the machete. As our guide told us, it was of a species not found in the neighbourhood, but came from the distant forests near the Lake of Peten. Why wood was used in the construction of buildings otherwise of solid stone seemed unaccountable; but if our guide was correct in regard to the place of its growth, each beam must have been carried on the shoulders of eight Indians, with the necessary relief carriers, a distance of three hundred miles; consequently, it was rare, costly, and curious, and for that reason may have been considered ornamental. The position of these lintels was most trying, as they were obliged to support a solid mass of stone wall fourteen or sixteen feet high, and three or four in thickness. Once, perhaps, they were strong as stone, but they showed that they were not as durable, and contained within them the seeds of destruction. Most, it is true, were in their places, sound, and harder than lignum vitæ; but others were perforated by wormholes; some were cracked in the middle, and the walls, settling upon them, were fast overcoming their remaining strength;

and others had fallen down altogether. In fact, except in the house of the nuns the greatest destruction was from the decay and breaking of these wooden beams. If the lintels had been of stone, the principal buildings of this desolate city would at this day be almost entire; or, if the edifices had been still occupied under a master's eye, a decaying beam would have been replaced, and the buildings saved from ruin. In the moment of greatness and power, the builders never contemplated that the time would come when their city would be a desolation.

The Casa del Gobernador stands with its front to the east. In the centre, and opposite the range of steps leading up the terrace, are three principal doorways. The middle one is eight feet six inches wide, and eight feet ten inches high; the others are of the same height, but two feet less in width. The centre door opens into an apartment sixty feet long and twenty-seven feet deep, which is divided into two corridors by a wall three and a half feet thick, with a door of communication between of the same size with the door of entrance. The plan is the same as that of the corridor in front of the palace at Palenque, except that here the corridor does not run the whole length of the building, and the back corridor has no door of egress. The floors are of smooth square stone, the walls of square blocks nicely laid and smoothly polished. The ceiling forms a triangular arch without the keystone, as at Palenque $\triangle$; but, instead of the rough stones overlapping or being covered with stucco, the layers of stone are bevilled as they rise, and present an even and polished surface. Throughout, the laying and polishing of the stones are as perfect as under the rules of the best modern masonry.

In this apartment we determined to take up our abode, once more in the palace of an unknown king, and under a roof tight as when sheltering the heads of its former occupants. Different from ruins in the Old World, where every fragment is exaggerated by some prating cicerone, in general, in this country, the reality exceeded our expectations. When we left Captain Fensley's brig we did not expect to find occupation for more than two or three days. But a vast field of interesting labour was before us, and we entered upon it with advantages of experience, the protection and kind assistance of the proprietor, and within the reach of comforts not procurable at any other place. We were not buried in the forest as at Palenque. In front of our door rose the lofty house of the dwarf, seeming almost to realize the Indian legend, and from every part of the terrace we looked over a field of ruins.

From the centre apartment the divisions on each wing corresponded exactly in size and finish, the details of which appear in the plan, and the same uniformity was preserved in the ornaments. Throughout the roof was tight, the apartments were dry, and, to speak understandingly, a *few thousand dollars expended in repairs* would have restored it, and made it fit for the reoccupation of its royal owners. In the apartment marked A the walls were coated with a very fine plaster of Paris, equal to the best seen on walls in this country. The rest were all of smooth polished stone. There were no paintings, stucco ornaments, sculptured tablets, or other decorations whatever.

In the apartment marked B we found what we regarded as a most interesting object. It was a *beam of wood*, about ten feet long and very heavy, which had fallen from its place over the doorway, and for some purpose or other been hauled inside the chamber into a dark corner. On the face was a line of characters

carved or stamped, almost obliterated, but which we
made out to be hieroglyphics, and, so far as we could
understand them, similar to those at Copan and Palenque. Several Indians were around us, with an idle
curiosity watching all our movements ; and, not wishing to call their attention to it, we left it with an Indian
at the moment sitting upon it. Before we were out of
the doorway we heard the ring of his machete from a
blow which, on rising, he had struck at random, and
which chipped off a long shaving within a few inches
of the characters. It almost gave us a shivering fit,
and we did not dare tell him to spare it, lest from ignorance, jealousy, or suspicion, it should be the means of
ensuring its destruction. I immediately determined to
secure this mystical beam. Compelled to leave in haste,
on my arrival at Merida Don Simon kindly promised
to send it to me, together with a sculptured stone which
formed one of the principal ornaments in all the buildings. The latter is now in my possession, but the former has never arrived. In the multitude of regrets
connected with our abrupt departure from these ruins,
I cannot help deploring the misfortune of not being assured of the safety of this beam. By what feeble light
the pages of American history are written ! There are
at Uxmal no " idols," as at Copan ; not a single stuccoed figure or carved tablet, as at Palenque. Except
this beam of hieroglyphics, though searching earnestly,
we did not discover any one absolute point of resemblance ; and the wanton machete of an Indian may destroy the only link that can connect them together.

The ornament above referred to is introduced in one
of the compartments of the " plan." It is the face of a
death's head, with wings expanded, and rows of teeth
projecting, in effect somewhat like the figure of a death's

head on tombstones with us. It is two feet wide across the wings, and has a stone staple behind, about two feet long, by which it was fastened in the wall. It had been removed by Don Simon entire, with the intention of setting it up as an ornament on the front of his hacienda.

It was our purpose to present full drawings of the exterior of this building, and, in fact, of all the others. The plate opposite represents one division, with its sculptured ornaments, or what I have called mosaic.* As at Copan, Mr. Catherwood was obliged to make several attempts before he could comprehend the subject so as to copy the characters. The drawing was begun late in the afternoon, was unfinished when we left to return to the hacienda, and, unfortunately, Mr. C. was never able to resume it. It is presented in the state given by the last touches of the pencil on the spot, wanting many of the minute characters with which the subject was charged, and without any attempt to fill them in. The reader will see how utterly insufficient any verbal description must be, and he will be able to form from it some idea of the imposing exterior of the building. The exterior of every building in Uxmal was ornamented in the same elaborate manner. The part represented in the engraving embraces about twenty feet of the Casa del Gobernador. The whole exterior of this building presents a surface of seven hundred feet; the Casa de las Monjas is two thousand feet, and the extent of sculptured surface exhibited by the other buildings I am not able to give. Complete drawings of the whole would form one of the most magnificent series ever offered to the public, and such it is yet our hope one day to be able to present. The reader will be able to form some idea of the time, skill, and labour required

* Since the above was in type it has been determined not to give the engraving.

PART OF FRONT CASA DEL GOBERNADOR

F. Catherwood.

SCULPTURED FRONT OF THE CASA DEL GOBERNADOR.

for making them; and, more than this, to conceive the immense time, skill, and labour required for carving such a surface of stone, and the wealth, power, and cultivation of the people who could command such skill and labour for the mere decoration of their edifices. Probably all these ornaments have a symbolical meaning; each stone is part of an allegory or fable, hidden from us, inscrutable under the light of the feeble torch we may burn before it, but which, if ever revealed, will show that the history of the world yet remains to be written.

CHAPTER XXVI.

Exploration finished.—Who built these ruined Cities?—Opinion of Dupaix.—
These Ruins bear no Resemblance to the Architecture of Greece and Rome.—
Nothing like them in Europe.—Do not Resemble the known Works of Japan
and China.—Neither those of Hindu.—No Excavations found.—The Pyramids
of Egypt, in their original State, do not resemble what are called the Pyramids
of America.—The Temples of Egypt not like those of America.—Sculpture not
the same as that of Egypt.—Probable Antiquity of these Ruins.—Accounts of
the Spanish Historians.—These Cities probably built by the Races inhabiting
the Country at the time of the Spanish Conquest.—These Races not yet extinct.

I HAVE now finished the exploration of ruins. The
reader is perhaps pleased that our labours were brought
to an abrupt close (my publishers certainly are) ; but I
assure him that I could have found it in my heart to be
prolix beyond all bounds, and that in mercy I have been
very brief ; in fact, I have let slip the best chance that
author ever had to make his reader remember him.   I
will make no mention of other ruins of which we heard
at more remote places.   I have no doubt a year may
be passed with great interest in Yucatan.   The field of
American antiquities is barely opened ; but for the present I have done.

And here I would be willing to part, and leave the
reader to wander alone and at will through the laby-
rinth of mystery which hangs over these ruined cities ;
but it would be craven to do so, without turning for a
moment to the important question, Who were the people that built these cities ?

Since their discovery, a dark cloud has been thrown
over them in two particulars.   The first is in regard to
the immense difficulty and danger, labour and expense,
of visiting and exploring them.   It has been my object
to clear away this cloud.   It will appear from these

pages that the accounts have been exaggerated; and, as regards Palenque and Uxmal at least, the only places which have been brought before the public at all, there is neither difficulty in reaching nor danger in exploring them.

The second is in regard to the age of the buildings; but here the cloud is darker, and not so easily dispelled.

I will not recapitulate the many speculations that have already been presented. The most irrational, perhaps, is that of Captain Dupaix, who gives to the ruins of Palenque an antediluvian origin; and, unfortunately for him, he gives his reason, which is the accumulation of earth over the figures in the courtyard of the palace. His visit was thirty years before ours; and, though he cleared away the earth, the accumulation was again probably quite as great when we were there. At all events, by his own showing, the figures were not entirely buried. I have a distinct recollection of the condition of those monuments, and have no scruple in saying that, if entirely buried, one Irishman, with the national weapon that has done such service on our canals, would in three hours remove the whole of this antediluvian deposite. I shall not follow the learned commentaries upon this suggestion of Captain Dupaix, except to remark that much learning and research have been expended upon insufficient or incorrect data, or when a bias has been given by a statement of facts; and, putting ourselves in the same category with those who have furnished these data, for the benefit of explorers and writers who may succeed us I shall narrow down this question to a ground even yet sufficiently broad, viz., a comparison of these remains with those of the architecture and sculpture of other ages and people.

I set out with the proposition that they are not Cyclopean, and do not resemble the works of Greek or Roman ; there is nothing in Europe like them. We must look, then, to Asia and Africa.

It has been supposed that at different periods of time vessels from Japan and China have been thrown upon the western coast of America. The civilization, cultivation, and science of those countries are known to date back from a very early antiquity. Of Japan I believe some accounts and drawings have been published, but they are not within my reach ; of China, during the whole of her long history, the interior has been so completely shut against strangers that we know nothing of her ancient architecture. Perhaps, however, that time is close at hand. At present we know only that they have been a people not given to change ; and if their ancient architecture is the same with their modern, it bears no resemblance whatever to these unknown ruins.

The monuments of India have been made familiar to us. The remains of Hindu architecture exhibit immense excavations in the rock, either entirely artificial or made by enlarging natural caverns, supported in front by large columns cut out of the rock, with a dark and gloomy interior.

Among all these American ruins there is not a single excavation. The surface of country, abounding in mountain sides, seems to invite it ; but, instead of being under ground, the striking feature of these ruins is, that the buildings stand on lofty artificial elevations ; and it can hardly be supposed that a people emigrating to a new country, with that strong natural impulse to perpetuate and retain under their eyes memorials of home, would have gone so directly counter to national and religious associations.

In sculpture, too, the Hindus differ entirely. Their

subjects are far more hideous, being in general representations of human beings distorted, deformed, and unnatural, very often many-headed, or with three or four arms or legs thrown out from the same body.

Lastly we come to the Egyptians. The point of resemblance upon which the great stress has been laid is the pyramid. The pyramidal form is one which suggests itself to human intelligence in every country as the simplest and surest mode of erecting a high structure upon a solid foundation. It cannot be regarded, as a ground for assigning a common origin to all people among whom structures of that character are found, unless the similarity is preserved in its most striking features. The pyramids of Egypt are peculiar and uniform, and were invariably erected for the same uses and purposes, so far as those uses and purposes are known. They are all square at the base, with steps rising and diminishing until they come to a point. The nearest approach to this is at Copan; but even at that place there is no entire pyramid standing alone and disconnected, nor one with four sides complete, but only two, or, at most, three sides, and intended to form part of other structures. All the rest, without a single exception, were high elevations, with sides so broken that we could not make out their form, which, perhaps, were merely walled around, and had ranges of steps in front and rear, as at Uxmal, or terraces or raised platforms of earth, at most of three or four ranges, not of any precise form, but never square, and with small ranges of steps in the centre. Besides, the pyramids of Egypt are known to have interior chambers, and, whatever their other uses, to have been intended and used as sepulchres. These, on the contrary, are of solid earth and stone. No interior chambers have ever been discovered, and probably none exist. And the most radical difference of all is, the pyramids of Egypt are complete in themselves; the structures of this country were erected only to serve as the foundations of buildings. There is no pyramid in Egypt with a palace or temple upon it; there is no pyramidal structure in this country without; at least none from whose condition any judgment can be formed.

But there is one farther consideration, which must be conclusive. The pyramids of Egypt, as I have considered them, and as they stand now, differ most materially from the original structures. Herodotus says that in his time the great pyramid was coated with stone, so as to present a smooth surface on all its sides from the base to the top. The second pyramid of Ghizeh, called the Pyramid of Cephrenes, in its present condition, presents on the lower part ranges of steps, with an accumulation of angular stones at the base, which originally filled up the interstices between the steps, but have fallen down. In the upper part the intermediate layers are still in their places, and the sides present a smooth surface to the top. There is no doubt that originally every pyramid in Egypt was built with its sides perfectly smooth. The steps formed no part of the plan. It is in this state only that they ought to be considered, and in this state any possible resemblance between them and what are called the pyramids of America, ceases.

Next to the pyramids, the oldest remains of Egyptian architecture, such as the temple of Absamboul in Nubia, like those of the Hindus, are excavations in the rock, from which it has been supposed that the Egyptians derived their style from that people. In later times they commenced erecting temples above ground, retaining the same features of gloomy grandeur, and

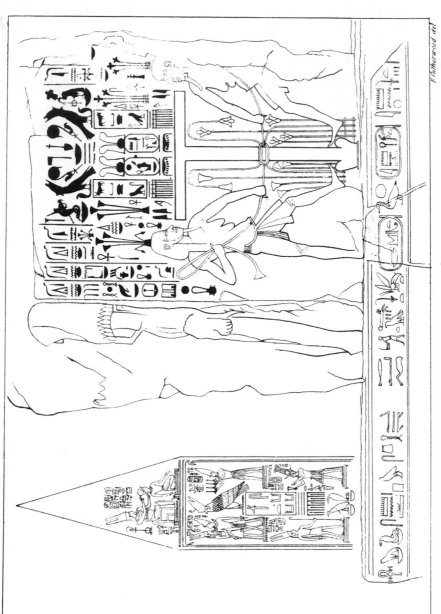

EGYPTIAN HIEROGLYPHICS.

F. Catherwood del

remarkable for their vastness and the massiveness of the stone used in their construction. This does not seem to have been aimed at by the American builders. Among all these ruins we did not see a stone worthy of being laid on the walls of an Egyptian temple. The largest single blocks were the "idols" or "obelisks," as they have been called, of Copan and Quirigua ; but in Egypt stones large as these are raised to a height of twenty or thirty feet and laid in the walls, while the obelisks which stand as ornaments at the doors, towering, a single stone, to the height of ninety feet, so overpower them by their grandeur, that, if imitations, they are the feeblest ever attempted by aspiring men.

Again: columns are a distinguishing feature of Egyptian architecture, grand and massive, and at this day towering above the sands, startling the wondering traveller in that mysterious country. There is not a temple on the Nile without them ; and the reader will bear in mind, that among the whole of these ruins not one column has been found. If this architecture had been derived from the Egyptian, so striking and important a feature would never have been thrown aside. The dromos, pronaos, and adytum, all equally characteristic of Egyptian temples, are also here entirely wanting.

Next, as to sculpture. The idea of resemblance in this particular has been so often and so confidently expressed, and the drawings in these pages have so often given the same impression, that I almost hesitate to declare the total want of similarity. What the differences are I will not attempt to point out ; but, that the reader may have the whole subject before him at once, I have introduced a plate of Egyptian sculpture taken from Mr. Catherwood's portfolio. The subject on the right is from the side of the great monument at Thebes known as the vocal Memnon, and has never before been engraved. The other is the top of the fallen obelisk of Carnac; and I think, by comparison with the engravings before presented, it will be found that there is no resemblance whatever. If there be any at all striking, it is only that the figures are in profile, and this is equally true of all good sculpture in bas-relief.

There is, then, no resemblance in these remains to those of the Egyptians; and, failing here, we look elsewhere in vain. They are different from the works of any other known people, of a new order, and entirely and absolutely anomalous: they stand alone.

I invite to this subject the special attention of those familiar with the arts of other countries; for, unless I am wrong, we have a conclusion far more interesting and wonderful than that of connecting the builders of these cities with the Egyptians or any other people. It is the spectacle of a people skilled in architecture, sculpture, and drawing, and, beyond doubt, other more perishable arts, and possessing the cultivation and refinement attendant upon these, not derived from the Old World, but originating and growing up here, without models or masters, having a distinct, separate, independent existence; like the plants and fruits of the soil, indigenous.

I shall not attempt to inquire into the origin of this people, from what country they came, or when, or how; I shall confine myself to their works and to the ruins.

I am inclined to think that there are not sufficient grounds for the belief in the great antiquity that has been ascribed to these ruins; that they are not the works of people who have passed away, and whose history has become unknown; but, opposed as is my idea to all previous speculations, that they were constructed by the races who occupied the country at the time of the invasion by the Spaniards, or of some not very distant progenitors.

And this opinion is founded, first, upon the appearance and condition of the remains themselves. The climate and rank luxuriance of soil are most destructive to all perishable materials. For six months every year exposed to the deluge of tropical rains, and with trees growing through the doorways of buildings and on the tops, it seems impossible that, after a lapse of two or three thousand years, a single edifice could now be standing.

The existence of wooden beams, and at Uxmal in a perfect state of preservation, confirms this opinion. The durability of wood will depend upon its quality and exposure. In Egypt, it is true, wood has been discovered sound and perfect, and certainly three thousand years old; but even in that dry climate none has ever been found in a situation at all exposed. It occurs only in coffins in the tombs and mummy-pits of Thebes, and in wooden cramps connecting two stones together, completely shut in and excluded from the air.

Secondly, my opinion is founded upon historical accounts. Herrera, perhaps the most reliable of the Spanish historians, says of Yucatan : " The whole country is divided into eighteen districts, and in all of them were so many and such stately Stone Buildings that it was amazing, and the greatest Wonder is, that having no Use of any Metal, they were able to raise such Structures, which seem to have been Temples, for their Houses were always of Timber and thatched. In those Edifices were carved the Figures of naked Men, with Earrings after the Indian manner, Idols of all Sorts, Lions, Pots or Jarrs," &c.; and again, " after the parting of these lords, for the space of twenty years there was such plenty through the Country, and the People multiplied so much, that old Men said the whole Province looked like one Town, and then they applied themselves to build more Temples, which produced so great a number of them."

Of the natives he says, " They *flattened their Heads and Foreheads, their Ears bor'd with Rings in them.* Their Faces were generally good, and not very brown, *but without Beards,* for they scorched them when young, that they might not grow. Their Hair was *long like Women,* and in Tresses, with which they made a Garland about the Head, and a *little Tail hung behind.*" " The prime Men wore a *Rowler eight Fingers broad round about them* instead of Breeches, and *going several times round the Waste, so that one end of it hung before and the other behind,* with fine Feather-work, and had large *square Mantles knotted on their Shoulders,* and *Sandals* or *Buskins* made of Deer's Skins." The reader almost sees here, in the flatted heads and costumes of the natives, a picture of the sculptured and stuccoed figures at Palenque, which, though a little beyond the present territorial borders of Yucatan, was perhaps once a part of that province.

Besides the glowing and familiar descriptions given by Cortez of the splendour exhibited in the buildings of Mexico, I have within my reach the authority of but one eyewitness. It is that of Bernal Diaz de Castillo, a follower and sharer in all the expeditions attending the conquest of Mexico.

Beginning with the first expedition, he says, " On approaching Yucatan, we perceived a large town at the distance of two leagues from the coast, which, from its size, it exceeding any town in Cuba, we named Grand Cairo." Upon the invitation of a chief, who came off in a canoe, they went ashore, and set out to march to the town, but on their way were surprised by the natives, whom, however, they repulsed, killing fifteen. " Near the place of this ambuscade," he says, " were three buildings *of lime and stone*, wherein were idols of clay with *diabolical countenances*," &c. " The buildings of *lime and stone*, and the gold, gave us a high idea of the country we had discovered."

In fifteen days' farther sailing, they discovered from the ships a large town, with an inlet, and went ashore for water. While filling their casks they were accosted by fifty Indians, " dressed in cotton mantles," who " by signs invited us to their town." Proceeding thither, they " arrived at some large and very well-constructed buildings of *lime and stone*, with figures of *serpents* and of *idols* painted upon the walls."

In the second expedition, sailing along the coast, they passed a low island, about three leagues from the main, where, on going ashore, they found " two buildings of lime and stone, well constructed, each with steps, and an altar placed before certain hideous figures, the representations of the gods of these Indians."

His third expedition was under Cortez, and in this his regard for truth and the reliance that may be placed upon him are happily shown in the struggle between deep religious feeling and belief in the evidence of his senses, which appears in his comment upon Gomara's account of their first battle. " In his account of this action, Gomara says that, previous to the arrival of the main body under Cortez, Francisco de Morla appeared in the field upon a gray dappled horse, and that it was one of the holy apostles, St. Peter or St. Jago, disguised under his person. I say that all our works and victories are guided by the hand of our Lord Jesus Christ, and that in this battle there were so many enemies to every one of us, that they could have buried us under the dust they could have held in their hands, but that the great mercy of God aided us throughout. What Gomara asserts may be the case, and I, sinner as I am, was not permitted to see it. What I did see was Francisco de Morla riding in company with Cortez and the rest upon a chestnut horse. But although I, unworthy sinner that I am, was unfit to behold either of these apostles, upward of four hundred of us were present. Let their testimony be taken. Let inquiry also be made how it happened that, when the town was founded on that spot, it was not named after one or other of these holy apostles, and called St. Jago de la Vittoria or St. Pedro de la Vittoria, as it was Santa Maria, and a church erected and dedicated to one of these holy saints. Very bad Christians were we, indeed, according to the account of Gomara, who, when God sent us his apostles to fight at our head, did not every day after acknowledge and return thanks for so great a mercy!"

Setting out on their march to Mexico, they arrived at Cempoal, entering which, he says, " We were surprised with the beauty of the buildings." " Our advanced guard having gone to the great square, the buildings of which had been lately whitewashed and *plastered, in which art these people are very expert*, one of our horsemen was so struck with the splendour of their appearance in the sun, that he came back in full speed to Cortez to tell him that the walls of the houses were of silver."

Offended by the abominable custom of human sacrifices, Cortez determined to suppress by force their idolatrous worship, and destroy their false gods. The chiefs ordered the people to arm in defence of their temple ; " but when they saw that we were preparing to ascend *the great flight of steps*," they said " they could not help themselves ; and they had hardly said this, when fifty of us, *going up* for the purpose, threw down and broke in pieces the enormous idols which we found within the temple." Cortez then caused a number of " *Indian masons* to be collected, *with lime, which abounded* in that place, and had the walls cleared of blood and *new plastered.*"

As they approached the territory of Mexico, he continues, " Appearances demonstrated that we had entered a new country, for the *temples were very lofty*, and, together with the *terraced dwellings* and the houses of the cacique, being *plastered* and whitewashed, appeared very well, and resembled some of our towns in Spain."

Farther on he says, " We arrived at a kind of fortification, built of *lime and stone*, of so strong a nature that nothing but tools of iron could have any effect upon it. The people informed us that it was built by the Tlascalans, on whose territory it stood, as a defence against the incursions of the Mexicans."

At Tehuacingo, after a sanguinary battle, in which the Indians " drew off and left the field to them, who were too much fatigued to follow," he adds, " As soon as we found ourselves clear of them, we returned thanks to God for his mercy, and, entering a *strong and spacious temple*, we dressed our wounds with the fat of Indians."

Arrived at Cholula, Cortez immediately " sent some soldiers to a *great temple* hard by our quarters, with orders to bring, as quietly as they could, two priests." In this they succeeded. One of them was a person of rank and authority over *all the temples* of the city. Again · " *within the high walls of the courts* where we were quartered." And again : the city of Cholula, he says, " much resembled Valladolid." It " had at that time above a hundred *lofty white towers,* which were the temples of their idols. The principal temple was higher than that of Mexico, and each of these buildings was placed *in a spacious court.*"

Approaching the city of Mexico, he gives way to a burst of enthusiasm. " We could compare it to nothing but the enchanted scenes we had read of in Amadis de Gaul, from the *great towers,* and *temples,* and other *edifices of lime and stone* which seemed to rise up out of the water."

" We were received by great lords of that country, relations of Montezuma, who conducted us to our lodgings there in *palaces* magnificently built *of stone,* the timber of which was cedar, with *spacious courts* and apartments furnished with canopies of the *finest cotton.* The whole was ornamented with *works of art painted,* and *admirably plastered* and whitened, and it was rendered more delightful by numbers of beautiful birds."

" The palace in which we were lodged was very light, airy, clean, and pleasant, the entry being through a great court."

Montezuma, in his first interview with Cortez, says, " The Tlascalans have, I know, told you that I am like a god, and that all about me is gold, and silver, and precious stones ; but you now see that I am mere flesh and blood, and that my *houses are built like other houses, of lime, and stone, and timber.*"

" At the great square we were astonished at the crowds of people and the regularity which prevailed, and the vast quantities of merchandise."

" The entire square was enclosed in piazzas."

" From the square we proceeded to the great temple,

but before we entered it we made a circuit through a number of *large courts,* the smallest of which appeared to me to contain more ground than the great square of Salamanca, with double enclosures, *built of lime and stone,* and the *courts* paved with large white *cut* stones, or, where not paved, they were *plastered and polished.*"

",The ascent to the great temple was by *a hundred and fourteen steps.*"

" From the platform on the summit of the temple, Montezuma, taking Cortez by the hand, pointed out to him the different parts of the city and its vicinity, all of which were commanded from that place." " We observed also the temples and adoratories of the adjacent cities, built in the form of *towers* and *fortresses,* and others on the causeway, all whitewashed and wonderfully brilliant."

" The noise and bustle of the market-place could be heard almost a league off, and *those who had been at Rome and Constantinople* said that for convenience, regularity, and population they had never seen the like."

During the siege he speaks of being " quartered in a *lofty temple;*" " marching *up the steps of the temple;*" " *some lofty temples* which we now battered with our artillery;" " the *lofty temples* where Diego Velasquez and Salvatierra were posted;" "the *breaches* which they had made in the *walls;*" " *cut stone* taken from the buildings from the terraces."

Arrived at the great temple, instantly above four thousand Mexicans rushed up into it, who for some time prevented them from ascending. " Although the cavalry several times attempted to charge, the stone pavements of the courts of the temple were so smooth that the horses could not keep their feet, and fell."

" Their numbers were such that we could not make
any effectual impression or *ascend the steps*.   At length
we *forced our way up*.   Here Cortez showed himself
the man that he really was.   What a desperate engagement we then had !   Every man of us was covered with
blood."

" They drove us *down six, and even ten of the steps;*
while others who were in the corridors, or within side
of the railings and concavities of the great temple, shot
such clouds of arrows at us that we could not maintain our ground," " began our retreat, every man of us
being wounded, and forty-six of us left dead on the
spot.   I have often seen this engagement represented
in the *paintings* of the natives both of Mexico and Tlas-
cala, and *our ascent into the great temple.*"

Again, he speaks of arriving at a village and taking
up their " quarters *in a strong temple;*" " assaulting
them at their *posts in the temples* and *large walled enclosures.*"

At Tezcuco " we took up our quarters in some buildings which consisted of *large halls and enclosed courts.*"
" Alvarado, De Oli, and some soldiers, whereof I was
one, then ascended to the top of *the great temple*, which
was *very lofty*, in order to notice what was going on in
the neighbourhood."

" We proceeded to another town called Terrayuco,
but which we named the town of the *serpents*, on account of the *enormous figures of those animals* which we
found in their temples, and which they worshipped as
gods."

Again : " In this garden our whole force lodged for
the night.   I certainly never had seen one of such magnificence ; and Cortez and the treasurer Alderete, after
they had walked through and examined it, declared that

it was admirable, and equal to any they had ever seen in Castille."

" I and ten more soldiers were posted as a guard upon a *wall of lime and stone.*"

" When we arrived at our quarters at Jacuba it rained heavily, and we remained under it for two hours in some *large enclosed courts.* The general, with his captains, the treasurer, our reverend father, and many others of us, mounted to the *top of the temple,* which commanded all the lake."

" We crossed the water up to our necks at the pass they had left open, and followed them until we came to a place where were *large temples* and *towers of idols.*"

" As Cortez now lodged at Cuejoacan, in large buildings with white walls, very well adapted for scribbling on, there appeared every morning libels against him in prose and verse. I recollect the words of one only:

' Que trista esta el alma mea
Hasta que la parte vea.'

How anxious I am for a share of the plunder."

" When our party (for I went with Sandoval) arrived at Tustepeque, I took up my lodgings in the summit of a *tower in a very high temple,* partly for the fresh air and to avoid the moschetoes, which were very troublesome below, and partly to be near Sandoval's quarters."

" We pursued our route to the city of Chiapas, in the same province with Palenque, and a city it might be called, from the regularity of its streets and houses. It contained not less than four thousand families, not reckoning the population of the many dependant towns in its neighbourhood." " We found the whole force of Chiapas drawn up to receive us. Their troops were adorned with plumage."

" On our arrival we found it too closely built to be

safely occupied by us, and we therefore pitched our camp in the open field.   In their *temples* we found idols of a horrid figure."

Now it will be recollected that Bernal Diaz wrote to do justice to himself and others of the "true conquerors," his companions in arms, whose fame had been obscured by other historians not actors and eyewitnesses; all his references to buildings are incidental; he never expected to be cited as authority upon the antiquities of the country.   The pettiest skirmish with the natives was nearer his heart than all the edifices of lime and stone which he saw, and it is precisely on that account that his testimony is the more valuable.   It was written at a time when there were many living who could contradict him if incorrect or false.   His "true history" never was impeached; on the contrary, while its style was considered rude and inelegant, its fidelity and truth have been acknowledged by all contemporaneous and subsequent historians.   In my opinion, it is as true and reliable as any work of *travels* on the countries through which he fought his way.   It gives the hurried and imperfect observations of an unlettered soldier, whose sword was seldom in its scabbard, surrounded by dangers, attacking, retreating, wounded, and flying, with his mind constantly occupied by matters of more pressing moment.

The reader cannot fail to be struck with the general resemblance between the objects described by him and the scenes referred to in these pages.   His account presents to my mind a vivid picture of the ruined cities which we visited, as they once stood, with *buildings of lime and stone, painted* and *sculptured ornaments*, and *plastered; idols, courts, strong walls*, and *lofty temples with high ranges of steps.*

But if this is not sufficient, I have farther and strong-

er support.   After the siege of Mexico, on the re-entry
of the Spaniards, a ruthless and indiscriminate destruction fell upon every building and monument in the city.
No memorials of the arts of the Mexicans were left;
but in the year 1790, two statues and a flat stone, with
sculptured characters relative to the Mexican calendar,
were discovered and dug up from among the remains
of the great Teocalli in the plaza of the city of Mexico.
The statues excited great interest among the Mexican
Indians, and the priests, afraid of their relapsing into
idolatry, and to destroy all memorials of their ancient
rites, buried them in the court of the Franciscan Convent.   The calendar was fixed in a conspicuous place
in the wall of the Cathedral, where it now stands.   In
the centre, and forming the principal subject of this
calendar, is a face, published in Humboldt's work,
which in one particular bears so strong a resemblance
to that called the mask, in the frontispiece of this volume,
as to suggest the idea that they were intended for the
same.   There are palpable differences, but perhaps the
expression of the eyes is changed and improved in the
engraving published, and, at all events, in both the peculiar and striking feature is that of the tongue hanging
out of the mouth.   The calendar is in bas-relief, and,
as I understand from a gentleman who has seen it, the
sculpture is good.*

And, lastly, among the hieroglyphical paintings which
escaped destruction from monkish fanaticism are certain Mexican manuscripts now in the libraries of Dres-
den and Vienna.   These have been published in Humboldt's work and in that of Lord Kingsborough, and, on
a careful examination, we are strongly of the opinion
that the characters are the same with those found on

* Vues de las Cordilleras, vol. xiii., p. 276.

the monuments and tablets at Copan and Palenque. For the sake of comparison I have introduced again the engraving of the top of the altar at Copan, and another from a hieroglyphical manuscript published in Humboldt's work. Differences, it is true, are manifest;

CATHERWOOD D.   ANDERSON S.

but it must be borne in mind that in the former the characters are carved on stone, and in the latter written on paper (made of the Agave Mexicana). Probably, for this reason, they want the same regularity and finish; but, altogether, the reader cannot fail to mark the strong similarity, and this similarity cannot be accidental. The inference is, that the Aztecs or Mexicans, at the time of the conquest, had the same written language with the people of Copan and Palenque.

I have thus very briefly, and without attempting to controvert the opinions and speculations of others, presented our own views upon the subject of these ruins. As yet we perhaps stand alone in these views, but I repeat my opinion that we are not warranted in going back to any ancient nation of the Old World for the builders of these cities; that they are not the work of people who have passed away and whose history is lost, but that there are strong reasons to believe them the creations of the same races who inhabited the country at the time of the Spanish conquest, or some not very distant progenitors. And I would remark that we began our exploration without any theory to support. Our feelings were in favour of going back to a high and venerable antiquity. During the greater part of our journey we were groping in the dark, in doubt and uncertainty, and it was not until our arrival at the ruins of Uxmal that we formed our opinion of their comparatively modern date. Some are beyond doubt older than others; some are known to have been inhabited at the time of the Spanish conquest, and others, perhaps, were really in ruins before; and there are points of difference which as yet cannot very readily be explained; but in regard to Uxmal, at least, we believe that it was an existing and inhabited city at the time of the arrival of the

Spaniards.   Its desolation and ruin since are easily accounted for.   With the arrival of the Spaniards the sceptre of the Indians departed.   In the city of Mexico every house was razed to the ground, and, beyond doubt, throughout the country every gathering-place or stronghold was broken up, the communities scattered, their lofty temples thrown down, and their idols burned, the palaces of the caciques ruined, the caciques themselves made bondmen, and, by the same ruthless policy which from time immemorial has been pursued in a conquered country, all the mementoes of their ancestors and lost independence were destroyed or made odious in their eyes.   And, without this, we have authentic accounts of great scourges which swept over, and for a time depopulated and desolated, the whole of Yucatan.

It perhaps destroys much of the interest that hangs over these ruins to assign to them a modern date; but we live in an age whose spirit is to discard phantasms and arrive at truth, and the interest lost in one particular is supplied in another scarcely inferior; for, the nearer we can bring the builders of these cities to our own times, the greater is our chance of knowing all. Throughout the country the convents are rich in manuscripts and documents written by the early fathers, caciques, and Indians, who very soon acquired the knowledge of Spanish and the art of writing. These have never been examined with the slightest reference to this subject; and I cannot help thinking that some precious memorial is now mouldering in the library of a neighbouring convent, which would determine the history of some one of these ruined cities; moreover, I cannot help believing that the tablets of hieroglyphics will yet be read.   No strong curiosity has hitherto been directed to them; vigour and acuteness of intellect, knowledge and learning, have never been expended upon them. For centuries the hieroglyphics of Egypt were inscrutable, and, though not perhaps in our day, I feel persuaded that a key surer than that of the Rosetta stone will be discovered. And if only three centuries have elapsed since any one of these unknown cities was inhabited, the race of the inhabitants is not extinct. Their descendants are still in the land, scattered, perhaps, and retired, like our own Indians, into wildernesses which have never yet been penetrated by a white man, but not lost; living as their fathers did, erecting the same buildings of "lime and stone," "with ornaments of sculpture and plastered," "large courts," and "lofty towers with high ranges of steps," and still carving on tablets of stone the same mysterious hieroglyphics; and if, in consideration that I have not often indulged in speculative conjecture, the reader will allow one flight, I turn to that vast and unknown region, untraversed by a single road, wherein fancy pictures that mysterious city seen from the topmost range of the Cordilleras, of unconquered, unvisited, and unsought aboriginal inhabitants.

In conclusion, I am at a loss to determine which would be the greatest enterprise, an attempt to reach this mysterious city, to decipher the tablets of hieroglyphics, or to wade through the accumulated manuscripts of three centuries in the libraries of the convents.

CHAPTER XXVII.

Journey to Merida.—Village of Moona.—A Pond of Water, a Curiosity.—Aboula.
—Indian Runners.—Merida.—Departure.—Hunucama.—Siege of Campeachy.
—Embarcation for Havana.—Incidents of the Passage.—Fourth of July at Sea.
—Shark-fishing.—Getting lost at Sea.—Relieved by the Helen Maria.—Pas-
sage to New-York.—Arrival.—Conclusion.

BUT to return to ourselves. At three, by the light of
the moon, we left Uxmal by the most direct road for Merida, Mr. Catherwood in a coach and I on horseback,
charged with a letter from the junior major-domo to his
compatriot and friend, Delmonico's head chocolate-ma-
ker. As I followed Mr. C. through the woods, borne on
the shoulders of Indians, the stillness broken only by the
shuffle of their feet, and under my great apprehensions for
his health, it almost seemed as if I were following his bier.
At the distance of three leagues we entered the village of
Moona, where, though a fine village, having white people and Mestitzoes among its inhabitants, travellers were
more rare than in the interior of Central America. We
were detained two hours at the casa real, waiting for a
relief coach. At a short distance beyond, my guide
led me out of the road to show me a pond of water,
which in that country was a curiosity. It was surrounded by woods; wild cattle were drinking on the
borders, and started like deer at our approach. At the
distance of four leagues we reached the village of
Aboula, with a plaza enclosed by a rough picket-fence,
a good casa real and fine old alcalde, who knew our
servant as belonging to the Peon family.

There was no intermediate village, and he undertook

to provide us with relief Indians to carry the coach through to Merida, twenty-seven miles. It was growing late, and I went on before with a horse for change, to reach Merida in time to make arrangements for a calêche the next day.

Toward evening it rained hard. At dark I began to have apprehension of leaving Mr. Catherwood behind, sent the servant on to secure the calêche, and dismounted to wait. I was too dreadfully fatigued to ride back, and sat down in the road; by degrees I stretched myself on a smooth stone, with the bridle around my wrist, and, after a dreamy debate whether my horse would tread on me or not, fell asleep. I was roused by a jerk which nearly tore my arm off, and saw coming through the woods Indian runners with blazing pine torches, lighting the way for the coach, which had an aspect so funereal that it almost made me shudder. Mr. C. had had his difficulties. After carrying him about a league, the Indians stopped, laid him down, and, after an animated conversation, took him up, went on, but in a little while laid him down again, and, thrusting their heads under the cover of the coach, made him an eager and clamorous address, of which he did not understand one word. At length he picked up dos pesos, or two dollars, and gathered that they wanted two dollars more. As the alcalde had adjusted the account, he refused to pay, and, after a noisy wrangle, they quietly took him up on their shoulders, and began trotting back with him to the village. This made him tractable, and he paid the money, threatening them as well as he could with vengeance; but the amusing part was that they were right. The alcalde had made a mistake in the calculation; and, on a division and distribution on the road, by hard pounding and calculating, each one

knowing what he ought to receive himself, they discovered that they had been paid two dollars short. The
price was twenty-five cents per man for the first, and
eighteen cents for every subsequent league, besides fifty
cents for making the coach ; so that, with four men for
relief, it was two dollars for the first league, and a dollar and a half for every subsequent one ; and a calculation of the whole amount for nine leagues was rather
complicated.

It was half past one when we reached Merida, and
we had been up and on the road since two in the morning.   Fortunately, with the easy movement of the coach,
Mr. C. had suffered but little.   I was tired beyond all
measure ; but I had, what enabled me to endure any
degree of fatigue, a good cot, and was soon asleep.

The next morning we saw my friend Don Simon,
who was preparing to go back and join us.   I cannot
sufficiently express my sense of the kindness we received from himself and his family, and only hope that I
may have an opportunity at some future time of returning it in my own country.   He promised, when we returned, to go down with us and assist in a thorough
exploration of the ruins.   The Spanish vessel was to
sail the next day.   Toward evening, after a heavy rain,
as the dark clouds were rolling away, and the setting
sun was tinging them with a rich golden border, we left
Merida.   At eleven o'clock we reached Hunucama,
and stopped in the plaza two hours to feed the horses.
While here, a party of soldiers arrived from the port,
waving pine torches, having just returned victorious
from the siege of Campeachy.   They were all young,
ardent, well dressed, and in fine spirits, and full of
praises of their general, who, they said, had remained
at Sisal to attend a ball, and was coming on as soon as

it was over.   Resuming our journey, in an hour more
we met a train of calêches, with officers in uniform.
We stopped, congratulated the general upon his victory
at Campeachy, inquired for a United States' sloop-of-
war which we had heard was there during the blockade, and, with many interchanges of courtesy, but without seeing a feature of each other's faces, resumed our
separate roads.   An hour before daylight we reached
Sisal, at six o'clock we embarked on board the Spanish
brig Alexandre for Havana, and at eight we were under way.

It was the twenty-fourth of June; and now, as we
thought, all our troubles were ended.   The morning
was fine.   We had eight passengers, all Spanish; one
of whom, from the interior, when he came down to the
shore and saw the brig in the offing, asked what animal it was.   From my great regard to the captain, I
will not speak of the brig or of its condition, particularly the cabin, except to say that it was Spanish.   The
wind was light; we breakfasted on deck, making the
top of the companion-way serve as a table under an
awning.   The captain told us we would be in Havana
in a week.

Our course lay along the coast of Yucatan toward
Cape Catoche.   On Sunday, the 28th, we had made,
according to the brig's reckoning, about one hundred
and fifty miles, and were then becalmed.   The sun was
intensely hot, the sea of glassy stillness, and all day a
school of sharks were swimming around the brig.   From
this time we had continued calms, and the sea was like
a mirror, heated and reflecting its heat.   On the Fourth
of July there was the same glassy stillness, with light
clouds, but fixed and stationary.   The captain said we
were incantado or enchanted, and really it almost seem-

ed so. We had expected to celebrate this day by dining
with the American consul in Havana; but our vessel lay
like a log, and we were scorching, and already pinched
for water; the bare thought of a Fourth of July dinner
meanwhile making Spanish ship-cookery intolerable.
We had read through all the books in the mate's library, consisting of some French novels translated into
Spanish, and a history of awful shipwrecks. To break
the monotony of the calm, we had hooks and lines out
constantly for sharks; the sailors called them, like the
alligators, ennemigos de los Christianos, hoisted them
on deck, cut out their hearts and entrails, and then
threw them overboard. We were already out ten days,
and growing short of provisions; we had two young
sharks for dinner. Apart from the associations, they
were not bad—quite equal to young alligators; and the
captain told us that in Campeachy they were regularly
in the markets, and eaten by all classes. In the afternoon they gathered around us fearfully. Everything that
fell overboard was immediately snapped up; and the
hat of a passenger which fell from his head had hardly
touched the water before a huge fellow turned over on
his side, opened his ugly mouth above the water, and
swallowed it: luckily, the man was not under it. Toward evening we caught a leviathan, raised him four or
five feet out of the water with the hook, and the sailors, leaning over, beat his brains with the capstan bars
till he was motionless; then fastening a rope with
a slipnoose under his fins, with the ship's tackle they
hoisted him on deck. He seemed to fill half the side
of the vessel. The sailors opened his mouth, and fastened the jaws apart with a marlinspike, turned him
over on his back, ripped him open, and tore out his
heart and entrails. They then chopped off about a foot

of his tail and threw him overboard; what he did I will not mention, lest it should bring discredit upon other parts of these pages which the reader is disposed to think may be true; but the last we saw of him he seemed to be feeling for his tail.

In the afternoon of the next day we crossed a strong current setting to northwest, which roared like breakers; soundings before one hundred and twenty fathoms; during the evening there was no bottom, and we supposed we must have passed Cape Catoche.

On the sixth, seventh, eighth, ninth, tenth, eleventh, and twelfth there was the same dead calm, with a sea like glass and intense heat. We were scant of provisions, and alarmed for entire failure of water. The captain was a noble Spaniard, who comforted the passengers by repeating every morning that we were enchanted, but for several days he had been uneasy and alarmed. He had no chronometer on board. He had been thirty years trading from Havana to different ports in the Gulf of Mexico, and had never used one; but out of soundings, among currents, with nothing but the log, he could not determine his longitude, and was afraid of getting into the Gulf Stream and being carried past Havana. Our chronometer had been nine months in hard use, jolted over severe mountain roads, and, as we supposed, could not be relied upon. Mr. Catherwood made a calculation with an old French table of logarithms which happened to be on board, but with results so different from the captain's reckoning that we supposed it could not be correct. At this time our best prospect was that of reaching Havana in the midst of the yellow fever season, sailing from there in the worst hurricane month, and a quarantine at Staten Island.

On the thirteenth of July everything on board was

getting scarce, and with crew and passengers twenty
in number, we broached our last cask of water. The
heat was scorching, and the calm and stillness of the
sea were fearful. All said we were enchanted ; and the
sailors added, half in earnest, that it was on account of
the heretics; sharks more numerous than ever ; we
could not look over the side of the vessel without seeing three or four, as if waiting for prey.

On the fourteenth the captain was alarmed. The log
was thrown regularly, but could not give his position.
Toward evening we saw an enormous monster, with. a
straight black head ten feet out of water, moving directly toward us. The captain, looking at it from the
rigging with a glass, said it was not a whale. Another
of the same kind appeared at the stern, and we were
really nervous ; but we were relieved by hearing them
spout, and seeing a column of water thrown into the air.
At dark they were lying huge and motionless on the
surface of the water.

On the fifteenth, to our great joy, a slight breeze
sprang up in the morning, and the log gave three miles
an hour. At twelve o'clock we took the latitude, which
was in 25° 10', and found that in steering *southward* at
the rate of three miles an hour by the log, we were fifty-
five miles to the northward of the reckoning of the day
before. The captain now believed that we were in the
midst of the Gulf Stream, had been so perhaps two or
three days, and were then two or three hundred miles
past Havana. Mr. Catherwood's chronometer gave 88°
longitude ; but this was so far out of the way by our
dead reckoning, that, with our distrust of the chronometer, we all disregarded it, and the captain especially.
We were then in a very bad position, short of provisions and water, and drifted past our port. The captain

called aft passengers, sailors, cook, and cabin-boy, spread
the chart on the companion-way, and pointed out our
supposed position, saying that he wished to take the
advice of all on board as to what was best to be done.
The mate sat by with the log-book to take notes. All
remained silent until the cook spoke, and said that the
captain knew best; the sailors and passengers assented;
for, although we considered it all uncertain, and that we
were completely lost, we believed that he knew better
than anybody else. The captain pointed out the course
of the Gulf Stream, said it would be impossible to turn
back against it, and, having a light, favourable breeze,
recommended that we should follow the stream, and
bear up for New Providence for a supply of provisions
and water. All assented, and so we put about from
the south and squared the yards for the northeast. At
that moment we considered ourselves farther from Havana than when we started.

With most uncomfortable feelings we sat down to a
scanty meal. Supposing that we were in the Gulf
Stream and in the track of vessels, the captain sent a
man aloft to look out for a sail, who very soon, to our
great joy, reported a brig to leeward. We hoisted our
flag and bore down upon her. As we approached she
answered our signal, and with a glass we recognised
the American ensign. In an hour we were nearly within hailing distance; the captain could not speak English, and gave me the speaking-trumpet; but fancying,
from his movements, that our countryman did not like
he Spanish colours, and afraid of some technical irregularity in my hail, which would make us an object of
suspicion, we begged him to lower the jolly-boat. This
was lying on the deck, with her bottom upward and her
seams opened by the sun. The water poured into her,

and before we were fifty yards from the brig she was
half full.   We sat up on the gunwale, and two of the
men had as much as they could do to keep her afloat,
while we urged the others to pull.   Sharks were playing around us, and for a few moments we wished to be
back on board the old brig.   A breeze seemed to strike
the vessel, which for two or three minutes kept steadily
on ; but, to our great relief, she hove to and took us on
board.   Our Spanish colours, and our irregular movement in attempting to board without hailing, had excited suspicion, and the sailors said we were pirates ; but
the captain, a long, cool-headed down-easter, standing
on the quarter with both his hands in his pockets, and
seeing the sinking condition of our boat, said, " Them's
no pirates."   The brig was the Helen Maria, of North
Yarmouth, Sweetzer, master, from Tobasco, and bound
to New-York !   The reader cannot imagine the satisfaction with which I greeted on the high seas a countryman bound for New-York.   My first question was
whether he could take us on board, next for provisions
and water for our friends, and then where we were.
He showed us his observation for the day.   We were
about four hundred miles from the spot we supposed.
The current which sets up between Cape Catoche and
Cape Antonio the captain had taken for the Gulf Stream.
If we had attended to Mr. C.'s chronometer we should
not have been far out of the way.   As it was, we were
perfectly lost ; and if we had not met this vessel, I do not
know what would have become of us.   The captain
was but seven days from Tobasco, with a wind that had
carried away one of his sails, and had lost one of his men.
He had no surplus of provisions, particularly with two
additional passengers ; but he sent on board what he
could, and a supply of water.   We returned, told the

captain, much to his surprise and astonishment, of his position, not more than two hundred miles from Sisal, and bade all hands farewell. They were not sorry to get rid of us, for the absence of two mouths was an object; and though, perhaps, in their hearts they thought their bad luck was on account of the heretics, it was pleasant, that with all our vexations, parting thus on the wide ocean, we shook hands with captain, passengers, sailors, cook, and cabin-boy, having no unkind feeling with any one on board. How long they were out I do not know, but I heard that they arrived at Havana in wretched condition, having eaten up the last morsel on board.

Our new vessel had a full cargo of logwood, the deck being loaded even with the quarter, and stowed so close that the cabin-door was taken off, and the descent was over a water-cask; but the change from the Spanish to the American vessel was a strange transition. The former had a captain, two mates, and eight sailors; the latter one mate and three sailors, with plank over the deck-load for sailors to run on, an enormous boom mainsail, and a tiller instead of a wheel, sweeping the whole quarter-deck, and at times requiring two men to hold it. In the evening we had two or three hours of calm; we were used to it, but the captain was annoyed; he detested a calm; he had not had one since he left Tobasco; he could bear anything but a calm. In the evening the charm was broken by a squall. The captain hated to take in sail, held on till the last moment, and then, springing from the tiller, hauled on the ropes himself, and was back again at the rudder, all in a flash. Mr. C. and I were so well pleased with the change that we were in no hurry; and, noticing the shortness of hands, and stumbling over logwood, we suggested to the cap-

tain that if he lost another man he would have difficulty
in carrying his vessel into port; but he put this down
at once by swearing that, if he lost every hand on board,
the mate and he could carry her in themselves, deck-
load and all.

On the thirty-first of July we arrived at New-York,
being ten months less three days since we sailed, and
nine without having received any intelligence whatever
from our friends at home; deducting the time passed
at sea, but seven months and twenty-four days in the
prosecution of our work.   This, I am sure, must recommend us to every true American; and here, on the same
spot from which we set out together, and with but little
hope of ever journeying with him again, I bid the reader
farewell.

APPENDIX.

Having mentioned in the preceding pages efforts to introduce into this country some of the antiquities therein described, the author considers it proper to say that, immediately on his return home, a few friends, whose names he would have great pleasure in making known if he were at liberty to do so, undertook to provide the sum of $20,000 for the purpose of carrying that object into effect. Under their direction, the author wrote to his agent at Guatimala, to purchase the ruins of Quirigua, or such monuments as it might be considered advisable to remove, at a price beyond what would have been accepted for them when he left Guatimala; but, unfortunately, in the mean time, a notice taken from Mr. Catherwood's memoranda, and inserted by the proprietors in a Guatimala paper, had reached this country, been translated and copied into some of our own journals, and one eulogistic paragraph, probably forgotten as soon as written, was sent back to Guatimala, which gave the proprietor such an exaggerated notion of their value that he refused the offer. From vague conversations with foreigners who had never seen and knew nothing of them, he conceived the idea that all the governments of Europe would vie with each other for their possession; and still entertaining the foolish belief that the author was acting on behalf of his government, said that, if the President of the United States wanted them, he must pay $20,000 for them; in the mean time, he resolved to wait for offers from England and France. By the last advices he was still under the same hallucination.

In regard to Palenque, the author has just received a letter from Mr. Russell, enclosing four documents brought to him by Mr. Pawling, which, translated so far as the manuscripts can be made out, are as follows:

" The governor has been informed that the vice-governor of
Balize" (meaning, no doubt, Mr. Secretary Walker and Captain
Caddy) " came to explore the ruins a few days since, with fourteen
armed men, and you have neither prevented him nor given any
information to this government.

" Now he is again informed that some citizens of the United
States of the North are doing the same ; in virtue of which, his
excellency orders me to tell you to inform him immediately upon
the truth of these facts, that he may take the necessary measures.

" God and liberty.

" ENRIQUE RUIZ.

"San Cristobal,* October 1, 1840."

" The subscribers, inhabitants of this town, as true patriots,
and lovers of the prosperity and advancement of their country,
before you, with due respect, and with the legal right that we
may have, appear, saying that it is something like more than
three months since a citizen of North America, named Henry
Paulin, has fixed his residence on the ruins in this district, with
the view of making moulds of every monument and precious
thing that there is on them ; as, in fact, he is making them,
since, up to this date ; he has already made something like
thirty moulds of plaster of Paris, including two which he took to
the town of Carmen, without giving notice to anybody, and with
the object of shipping them for the North" (these two have been
received by the author).   " The said moulds are so much like
the originals, that at the first sight it may be observed that they
may be taken, surely, for second originals, and no doubt they
may serve to mould after them as many copies as might be
wished, and in this manner they may supply the world with
these precious things without a six cents' piece expense.   *Mr.
William Brown*, married to Donna Trinidad Garrido, offered
from eight to ten thousand dollars only for the leave to extract
four or six principal stones from these ruins, in quality of a loan
* * * * or to * * * *" (the precise nature of MR. WILLIAM
BROWN's offer cannot be made out, from the illegible character

* Or Ciudad Real, the capital of the State of Chiapas.

of the handwriting), " promising all these things with the most satisfactory guarantees. Saving you, sir, from any responsibility, we take it upon ourselves, since we arc aware of your bad state of health, and we suppose that you do not know of this fact" (manuscript illegible), " on account of this master operation, or whosoever is concerned in it, make this gentleman pay four or five thousand dollars, to apply them to benevolent works, and to the embellishment of this town, or else let him in no manner take away with him any of the mouids of plaster of Paris he has made and continues making. Indeed, if this treasure is ours, and by right belongs to our town, why should it not be benefited by it?

" It is an honour to us, sir, to make a demand of this nature, since we have not heard that any offer whatever has been made at all about this undertaking up to this date. Let the visiters of these ruins make moulds, drawings, &c., but let them also contribute with sums proportionate to their operations. This is, sir, if we are not mistaken, a business of a great speculation. The persons concerned in this affair are men of importance. Therefore we beg of you most earnestly, and in virtue of our legal right, not to permit the removal of any of the said moulds of plaster of Paris from this town without the said sums being paid, grounded on the great utility that the extractors may derive from it, as well as on the aforesaid offer made by *Mr. Brown.*

" SANTIAGO FRONCOSO,
" BARTOLO BRAVO,
" MIGUEL CASTILLO.

" Palenque, October 15, 1840."

" Don Santiago Froncoso having informed the governor that he and two other inhabitants of that town have presented a memorial before you in regard to the removal of the antiquities of the ruins at Palenque, his excellency consulted the departmental junta on the subject, which junta answered by approving the petition, which copy I send you enclosed, with the decree of his excellency written under it, that you may cause it to be fulfilled. I send you, likewise, two copies of the regulations for passports for the archives of that subprefecture, with the object that the

subprefect should act according to it, in the introduction of foreigners in your district, and also a copy of the order of the 17th
of June, 1835, and his excellency orders me to tell you to inform
him immediately with regard to the issue of the fulfilment of his
said decree.

"It is a copy.   God and liberty.

"DOMINGO GONZALEZ.

"San Cristobal, December 1, 1840."

"His excellency the governor, having read your information
of the 15th inst., orders me to tell you to keep a watchful eye
upon the strangers who visit the ruins ; and when any of them
arrive, to give notice of it to this government without delay, ex-
pressing their numbers, whence they come, and what is their object, without allowing them to make any operation or excavation, and much less to remove anything whatever, however in-
significant it may appear.

"Consequently, if they arrive with the only object of visiting,
let them do it in company with one, two, or more officers of that
subprefecture, that the above dispositions may be fulfilled.

"It is a copy from the original.

"God and liberty.

"DOMINGO GONZALEZ.

"San Cristobal, November 30, 1840."

Under these orders Mr. Pawling has been compelled to leave
the ruins, and the casts belonging to the author, for the making of
which he had subjected himself to considerable expense, have
been seized and detained by the prefect. Perhaps, instead of
unavailing regrets, he ought rather to congratulate himself that
he had left the ruins, and that Mr. Catherwood's drawings were
safe, before the news of their visit reached the capital. He can
imagine the excitement in the village, and the annoyance and
vexation to which future travellers will be subjected ; but he cannot understand exactly the cause. His purpose of leaving Pawling to make casts was known in the village, and no objections
whatever were made. Don Santiago Froncoso, the first of the
"true patriots" whose names are signed to the complaint, was

his particular friend, from whom, late in the evening before he
left Palenque, he received the following note (translation) :

"Mr. —— (I do not know your surname), at his house, June 3, 1840.

"My most respected Sir,

"I have just arrived, because my wife sent me notice yesterday
that *you* (permit me to address you on the footing of a friend*)
and your estimable companion depart to-morrow without fail.
If it is really true, continue your journey with all the felicity
which my great affection desires.   I send you, together with my
gratitude and affection, this raw silk from the ruins to keep for
my sake.

"Farewell, my friend and dearest sir.   Command whatever
you wish, and from whatever distance.

"Your most affectionate friend,

"Santiago Froncoso.

"Senor ex-plenipotentiary envoy near the government of Central America from the government of North America."

The author feels assured that, if he had been on the spot himself, Don Santiago would have been the last man in the place to
embarrass his operations.   He is now violent against foreigners.
The author has received no letter from Mr. Pawling, and fears
that he has in some way got into difficulty with the people of the
village, or else the author's plans have been defeated, and his casts
are detained and kept from being introduced into the United
States, by the agency and offers of *Mr. William Brown.*   In
the absence of any farther information than what appears in these
documents, the author makes no comments ; but he mentions,
that this *Mr. William Brown* is an *American,* known in this
city as *Captain William Brown,* having been for several years
master of a vessel trading between this port and Tobasco.

It was the hope of the gentlemen before referred to, with
the monuments of Quirigua, casts from Copan and Palenque,
or the tablets themselves, and other objects from other places
within their reach, to lay the foundation of a Museum of American Antiquities which might deserve the countenance of the Gen-

* Don Santiago apologizes for not using the title *your excellency.*

eral Government, and draw to it Catlin's Indian Gallery, and every
other memorial of the aboriginal races, whose history within our
own borders has already become almost a romance and fable.
The author does not despair of this yet. The difficulty will perhaps be increased (the author trusts he will not be considered
presumptuous) by the attention that will be directed to the remains of Palenque and the other ruined cities by the publication
of these pages, and the consequently exaggerated notions that
the inhabitants will form of their value ; but then he is persuaded that the Government of Mexico will, on proper representations, order a restitution of the casts now detained at Palenque,
and that the republic, without impoverishing herself, will enrich
her neighbours of the North with the knowledge of the many
other curious remains scattered through her country. And he
entertains the belief also that England and France, whose formidable competition has already been set up, as it were in ter-
rorem, by one proprietor, having their capitals enriched by the
remains of art collected throughout the Old World, will respect
the rights of nations and discovery, and leave the field of American
antiquities to us ; that they will not deprive a destitute country
of its only chance of contributing to the cause of science, but rather encourage it in the work of bringing together, from remote
and almost inaccessible places, and retaining on its own soil, the
architectural remains of its aboriginal inhabitants.

THE END.

A CATALOGUE OF SELECTED DOVER BOOKS
IN ALL FIELDS OF INTEREST

AMERICA'S OLD MASTERS, James T. Flexner. Four men emerged unexpectedly from provincial 18th century America to leadership in European art: Benjamin West, J. S. Copley, C. R. Peale, Gilbert Stuart. Brilliant coverage of lives and contributions. Revised, 1967 edition. 69 plates. 365pp. of text.
21806-6 Paperbound $2.75

FIRST FLOWERS OF OUR WILDERNESS: AMERICAN PAINTING, THE COLONIAL PERIOD, James T. Flexner. Painters, and regional painting traditions from earliest Colonial times up to the emergence of Copley, West and Peale Sr., Foster, Gustavus Hesselius, Feke, John Smibert and many anonymous painters in the primitive manner. Engaging presentation, with 162 illustrations. xxii + 368pp.
22180-6 Paperbound $3.50

THE LIGHT OF DISTANT SKIES: AMERICAN PAINTING, 1760-1835, James T. Flexner. The great generation of early American painters goes to Europe to learn and to teach: West, Copley, Gilbert Stuart and others. Allston, Trumbull, Morse; also contemporary American painters—primitives, derivatives, academics—who remained in America. 102 illustrations. xiii + 306pp.
22179-2 Paperbound $3.00

A HISTORY OF THE RISE AND PROGRESS OF THE ARTS OF DESIGN IN THE UNITED STATES, William Dunlap. Much the richest mine of information on early American painters, sculptors, architects, engravers, miniaturists, etc. The only source of information for scores of artists, the major primary source for many others. Unabridged reprint of rare original 1834 edition, with new introduction by James T. Flexner, and 394 new illustrations. Edited by Rita Weiss. 6⅝ x 9⅝.
21695-0, 21696-9, 21697-7 Three volumes, Paperbound $13.50

EPOCHS OF CHINESE AND JAPANESE ART, Ernest F. Fenollosa. From primitive Chinese art to the 20th century, thorough history, explanation of every important art period and form, including Japanese woodcuts; main stress on China and Japan, but Tibet, Korea also included. Still unexcelled for its detailed, rich coverage of cultural background, aesthetic elements, diffusion studies, particularly of the historical period. 2nd, 1913 edition. 242 illustrations. lii + 439pp. of text.
20364-6, 20365-4 Two volumes, Paperbound $5.00

THE GENTLE ART OF MAKING ENEMIES, James A. M. Whistler. Greatest wit of his day deflates Oscar Wilde, Ruskin, Swinburne; strikes back at inane critics, exhibitions, art journalism; aesthetics of impressionist revolution in most striking form. Highly readable classic by great painter. Reproduction of edition designed by Whistler. Introduction by Alfred Werner. xxxvi + 334pp.
21875-9 Paperbound $2.25

A CATALOGUE OF SELECTED DOVER BOOKS
IN ALL FIELDS OF INTEREST

VISUAL ILLUSIONS: THEIR CAUSES, CHARACTERISTICS, AND APPLICATIONS, Matthew Luckiesh. Thorough description and discussion of optical illusion, geometric and perspective, particularly; size and shape distortions, illusions of color, of motion; natural illusions; use of illusion in art and magic, industry, etc. Most useful today with op art, also for classical art. Scores of effects illustrated. Introduction by William H. Ittleson. 100 illustrations. xxi + 252pp.
21530-X Paperbound $1.50

A HANDBOOK OF ANATOMY FOR ART STUDENTS, Arthur Thomson. Thorough, virtually exhaustive coverage of skeletal structure, musculature, etc. Full text, supplemented by anatomical diagrams and drawings and by photographs of undraped figures. Unique in its comparison of male and female forms, pointing out differences of contour, texture, form. 211 figures, 40 drawings, 86 photographs. xx + 459pp. 5⅜ x 8⅜.
21163-0 Paperbound $3.00

150 MASTERPIECES OF DRAWING, Selected by Anthony Toney. Full page reproductions of drawings from the early 16th to the end of the 18th century, all beautifully reproduced: Rembrandt, Michelangelo, Dürer, Fragonard, Urs, Graf, Wouwerman, many others. First-rate browsing book, model book for artists. xviii + 150pp. 8⅜ x 11¼.
21032-4 Paperbound $2.00

THE LATER WORK OF AUBREY BEARDSLEY, Aubrey Beardsley. Exotic, erotic, ironic masterpieces in full maturity: Comedy Ballet, Venus and Tannhauser, Pierrot, Lysistrata, Rape of the Lock, Savoy material, Ali Baba, Volpone, etc. This material revolutionized the art world, and is still powerful, fresh, brilliant. With *The Early Work*, all Beardsley's finest work. 174 plates, 2 in color. xiv + 176pp. 8⅛ x 11.
21817-1 Paperbound $3.00

DRAWINGS OF REMBRANDT, Rembrandt van Rijn. Complete reproduction of fabulously rare edition by Lippmann and Hofstede de Groot, completely reedited, updated, improved by Prof. Seymour Slive, Fogg Museum. Portraits, Biblical sketches, landscapes, Oriental types, nudes, episodes from classical mythology—All Rembrandt's fertile genius. Also selection of drawings by his pupils and followers. "Stunning volumes," *Saturday Review*. 550 illustrations. lxxviii + 552pp. 9⅛ x 12¼.
21485-0, 21486-9 Two volumes, Paperbound $6.50

THE DISASTERS OF WAR, Francisco Goya. One of the masterpieces of Western civilization—83 etchings that record Goya's shattering, bitter reaction to the Napoleonic war that swept through Spain after the insurrection of 1808 and to war in general. Reprint of the first edition, with three additional plates from Boston's Museum of Fine Arts. All plates facsimile size. Introduction by Philip Hofer, Fogg Museum. v + 97pp. 9⅜ x 8¼.
21872-4 Paperbound $1.75

GRAPHIC WORKS OF ODILON REDON. Largest collection of Redon's graphic works ever assembled: 172 lithographs, 28 etchings and engravings, 9 drawings. These include some of his most famous works. All the plates from *Odilon Redon: oeuvre graphique complet,* plus additional plates. New introduction and caption translations by Alfred Werner. 209 illustrations. xxvii + 209pp. 9⅛ x 12¼.
21966-8 Paperbound $4.00

DESIGN BY ACCIDENT; A BOOK OF "ACCIDENTAL EFFECTS" FOR ARTISTS AND DESIGNERS, James F. O'Brien. Create your own unique, striking, imaginative effects by "controlled accident" interaction of materials: paints and lacquers, oil and water based paints, splatter, crackling materials, shatter, similar items. Everything you do will be different; first book on this limitless art, so useful to both fine artist and commercial artist. Full instructions. 192 plates showing "accidents," 8 in color. viii + 215pp. 8⅜ x 11¼.   21942-9 Paperbound $3.50

THE BOOK OF SIGNS, Rudolf Koch. Famed German type designer draws 493 beautiful symbols: religious, mystical, alchemical, imperial, property marks, runes, etc. Remarkable fusion of traditional and modern. Good for suggestions of timelessness, smartness, modernity. Text. vi + 104pp. 6⅛ x 9¼.
                    20162-7 Paperbound $1.25

HISTORY OF INDIAN AND INDONESIAN ART, Ananda K. Coomaraswamy. An unabridged republication of one of the finest books by a great scholar in Eastern art. Rich in descriptive material, history, social backgrounds; Sunga reliefs, Rajput paintings, Gupta temples, Burmese frescoes, textiles, jewelry, sculpture, etc. 400 photos. viii + 423pp. 6⅜ x 9¾.   21436-2 Paperbound $3.50

PRIMITIVE ART, Franz Boas. America's foremost anthropologist surveys textiles, ceramics, woodcarving, basketry, metalwork, etc.; patterns, technology, creation of symbols, style origins. All areas of world, but very full on Northwest Coast Indians. More than 350 illustrations of baskets, boxes, totem poles, weapons, etc. 378 pp.
                    20025-6 Paperbound $2.50

THE GENTLEMAN AND CABINET MAKER'S DIRECTOR, Thomas Chippendale. Full reprint (third edition, 1762) of most influential furniture book of all time, by master cabinetmaker. 200 plates, illustrating chairs, sofas, mirrors, tables, cabinets, plus 24 photographs of surviving pieces. Biographical introduction by N. Bienenstock. vi + 249pp. 9⅞ x 12¾.   21601-2 Paperbound $3.50

AMERICAN ANTIQUE FURNITURE, Edgar G. Miller, Jr. The basic coverage of all American furniture before 1840. Individual chapters cover type of furniture—clocks, tables, sideboards, etc.—chronologically, with inexhaustible wealth of data. More than 2100 photographs, all identified, commented on. Essential to all early American collectors. Introduction by H. E. Keyes. vi + 1106pp. 7⅞ x 10¾.
                    21599-7, 21600-4 Two volumes, Paperbound $7.50

PENNSYLVANIA DUTCH AMERICAN FOLK ART, Henry J. Kauffman. 279 photos, 28 drawings of tulipware, Fraktur script, painted tinware, toys, flowered furniture, quilts, samplers, hex signs, house interiors, etc. Full descriptive text. Excellent for tourist, rewarding for designer, collector. Map. 146pp. 7⅞ x 10¾.
                    21205-X Paperbound $2.00

EARLY NEW ENGLAND GRAVESTONE RUBBINGS, Edmund V. Gillon, Jr. 43 photographs, 226 carefully reproduced rubbings show heavily symbolic, sometimes macabre early gravestones, up to early 19th century. Remarkable early American primitive art, occasionally strikingly beautiful; always powerful. Text. xxvi + 207pp. 8⅜ x 11¼.   21380-3 Paperbound $3.00

ALPHABETS AND ORNAMENTS, Ernst Lehner. Well-known pictorial source for decorative alphabets, script examples, cartouches, frames, decorative title pages, calligraphic initials, borders, similar material. 14th to 19th century, mostly European. Useful in almost any graphic arts designing, varied styles. 750 illustrations. 256pp. 7 x 10.   21905-4 Paperbound $3.50

PAINTING: A CREATIVE APPROACH, Norman Colquhoun. For the beginner simple guide provides an instructive approach to painting: major stumbling blocks for beginner; overcoming them, technical points; paints and pigments; oil painting; watercolor and other media and color. New section on "plastic" paints. Glossary. Formerly *Paint Your Own Pictures.* 221pp.   22000-1 Paperbound $1.75

THE ENJOYMENT AND USE OF COLOR, Walter Sargent. Explanation of the relations between colors themselves and between colors in nature and art, including hundreds of little-known facts about color values, intensities, effects of high and low illumination, complementary colors. Many practical hints for painters, references to great masters. 7 color plates, 29 illustrations. x + 274pp.
20944-X Paperbound $2.50

THE NOTEBOOKS OF LEONARDO DA VINCI, compiled and edited by Jean Paul Richter. 1566 extracts from original manuscripts reveal the full range of Leonardo's versatile genius: all his writings on painting, sculpture, architecture, anatomy, astronomy, geography, topography, physiology, mining, music, etc., in both Italian and English, with 186 plates of manuscript pages and more than 500 additional drawings. Includes studies for the Last Supper, the lost Sforza monument, and other works. Total of xlvii + 866pp. 7⅞ x 10¾.
22572-0, 22573-9 Two volumes, Paperbound $10.00

MONTGOMERY WARD CATALOGUE OF 1895. Tea gowns, yards of flannel and pillow-case lace, stereoscopes, books of gospel hymns, the New Improved Singer Sewing Machine, side saddles, milk skimmers, straight-edged razors, high-button shoes, spittoons, and on and on . . . listing some 25,000 items, practically all illustrated. Essential to the shoppers of the 1890's, it is our truest record of the spirit of the period. Unaltered reprint of Issue No. 57, Spring and Summer 1895. Introduction by Boris Emmet. Innumerable illustrations. xiii + 624pp. 8½ x 11⅝.
22377-9 Paperbound $6.95

THE CRYSTAL PALACE EXHIBITION ILLUSTRATED CATALOGUE (LONDON, 1851). One of the wonders of the modern world—the Crystal Palace Exhibition in which all the nations of the civilized world exhibited their achievements in the arts and sciences—presented in an equally important illustrated catalogue. More than 1700 items pictured with accompanying text—ceramics, textiles, cast-iron work, carpets, pianos, sleds, razors, wall-papers, billiard tables, beehives, silverware and hundreds of other artifacts—represent the focal point of Victorian culture in the Western World. Probably the largest collection of Victorian decorative art ever assembled—indispensable for antiquarians and designers. Unabridged republication of the Art-Journal Catalogue of the Great Exhibition of 1851, with all terminal essays. New introduction by John Gloag, F.S.A. xxxiv + 426pp. 9 x 12.
22503-8 Paperbound $4.50

A History of Costume, Carl Köhler. Definitive history, based on surviving pieces of clothing primarily, and paintings, statues, etc. secondarily. Highly readable text, supplemented by 594 illustrations of costumes of the ancient Mediterranean peoples, Greece and Rome, the Teutonic prehistoric period; costumes of the Middle Ages, Renaissance, Baroque, 18th and 19th centuries. Clear, measured patterns are provided for many clothing articles. Approach is practical throughout. Enlarged by Emma von Sichart. 464pp. 21030-8 Paperbound $3.00

Oriental Rugs, Antique and Modern, Walter A. Hawley. A complete and authoritative treatise on the Oriental rug—where they are made, by whom and how, designs and symbols, characteristics in detail of the six major groups, how to distinguish them and how to buy them. Detailed technical data is provided on periods, weaves, warps, wefts, textures, sides, ends and knots, although no technical background is required for an understanding. 11 color plates, 80 halftones, 4 maps. vi + 320pp. 6⅛ x 9⅛. 22366-3 Paperbound $5.00

Ten Books on Architecture, Vitruvius. By any standards the most important book on architecture ever written. Early Roman discussion of aesthetics of building, construction methods, orders, sites, and every other aspect of architecture has inspired, instructed architecture for about 2,000 years. Stands behind Palladio, Michelangelo, Bramante, Wren, countless others. Definitive Morris H. Morgan translation. 68 illustrations. xii + 331pp. 20645-9 Paperbound $2.50

The Four Books of Architecture, Andrea Palladio. Translated into every major Western European language in the two centuries following its publication in 1570, this has been one of the most influential books in the history of architecture. Complete reprint of the 1738 Isaac Ware edition. New introduction by Adolf Placzek, Columbia Univ. 216 plates. xxii + 110pp. of text. 9½ x 12¾. 21308-0 Clothbound $10.00

Sticks and Stones: A Study of American Architecture and Civilization, Lewis Mumford.One of the great classics of American cultural history. American architecture from the medieval-inspired earliest forms to the early 20th century; evolution of structure and style, and reciprocal influences on environment. 21 photographic illustrations. 238pp. 20202-X Paperbound $2.00

The American Builder's Companion, Asher Benjamin. The most widely used early 19th century architectural style and source book, for colonial up into Greek Revival periods. Extensive development of geometry of carpentering, construction of sashes, frames, doors, stairs; plans and elevations of domestic and other buildings. Hundreds of thousands of houses were built according to this book, now invaluable to historians, architects, restorers, etc. 1827 edition. 59 plates. 114pp. 7⅞ x 10¾. 22236-5 Paperbound $3.00

Dutch Houses in the Hudson Valley Before 1776, Helen Wilkinson Reynolds. The standard survey of the Dutch colonial house and outbuildings, with constructional features, decoration, and local history associated with individual homesteads. Introduction by Franklin D. Roosevelt. Map. 150 illustrations. 469pp. 6⅝ x 9¼. 21469-9 Paperbound $3.50

CATALOGUE OF DOVER BOOKS

THE ARCHITECTURE OF COUNTRY HOUSES, Andrew J. Downing. Together with Vaux's *Villas and Cottages* this is the basic book for Hudson River Gothic architecture of the middle Victorian period. Full, sound discussions of general aspects of housing, architecture, style, decoration, furnishing, together with scores of detailed house plans, illustrations of specific buildings, accompanied by full text. Perhaps the most influential single American architectural book. 1850 edition. Introduction by J. Stewart Johnson. 321 figures, 34 architectural designs. xvi + 560pp.
22003-6 Paperbound $3.50

LOST EXAMPLES OF COLONIAL ARCHITECTURE, John Mead Howells. Full-page photographs of buildings that have disappeared or been so altered as to be denatured, including many designed by major early American architects. 245 plates. xvii + 248pp. 7⅞ x 10¾.
21143-6 Paperbound $3.00

DOMESTIC ARCHITECTURE OF THE AMERICAN COLONIES AND OF THE EARLY REPUBLIC, Fiske Kimball. Foremost architect and restorer of Williamsburg and Monticello covers nearly 200 homes between 1620-1825. Architectural details, construction, style features, special fixtures, floor plans, etc. Generally considered finest work in its area. 219 illustrations of houses, doorways, windows, capital mantels. xx + 314pp. 7⅞ x 10¾.
21743-4 Paperbound $3.50

EARLY AMERICAN ROOMS: 1650-1858, edited by Russell Hawes Kettell. Tour of 12 rooms, each representative of a different era in American history and each furnished, decorated, designed and occupied in the style of the era. 72 plans and elevations, 8-page color section, etc., show fabrics, wall papers, arrangements, etc. Full descriptive text. xvii + 200pp. of text. 8⅜ x 11¼.
21633-0 Paperbound $4.00

THE FITZWILLIAM VIRGINAL BOOK, edited by J. Fuller Maitland and W. B. Squire. Full modern printing of famous early 17th-century ms. volume of 300 works by Morley, Byrd, Bull, Gibbons, etc. For piano or other modern keyboard instrument; easy to read format. xxxvi + 938pp. 8⅜ x 11.
21068-5, 21069-3 Two volumes, Paperbound $8.00

HARPSICHORD MUSIC, Johann Sebastian Bach. Bach Gesellschaft edition. A rich selection of Bach's masterpieces for the harpsichord: the six English Suites, six French Suites, the six Partitas (Clavierübung part I), the Goldberg Variations (Clavierübung part IV), the fifteen Two-Part Inventions and the fifteen Three-Part Sinfonias. Clearly reproduced on large sheets with ample margins; eminently playable. vi + 312pp. 8⅛ x 11.
22360-4 Paperbound $5.00

THE MUSIC OF BACH: AN INTRODUCTION, Charles Sanford Terry. A fine, nontechnical introduction to Bach's music, both instrumental and vocal. Covers organ music, chamber music, passion music, other types. Analyzes themes, developments, innovations. x + 114pp.
21075-8 Paperbound $1.25

BEETHOVEN AND HIS NINE SYMPHONIES, Sir George Grove. Noted British musicologist provides best history, analysis, commentary on symphonies. Very thorough, rigorously accurate; necessary to both advanced student and amateur music lover. 436 musical passages. vii + 407 pp.
20334-4 Paperbound $2.25

JOHANN SEBASTIAN BACH, Philipp Spitta. One of the great classics of musicology, this definitive analysis of Bach's music (and life) has never been surpassed. Lucid, nontechnical analyses of hundreds of pieces (30 pages devoted to St. Matthew Passion, 26 to B Minor Mass). Also includes major analysis of 18th-century music. 450 musical examples. 40-page musical supplement. Total of xx + 1799pp.
(EUK) 22278-0, 22279-9 Two volumes, Clothbound $15.00

MOZART AND HIS PIANO CONCERTOS, Cuthbert Girdlestone. The only full-length study of an important area of Mozart's creativity. Provides detailed analyses of all 23 concertos, traces inspirational sources. 417 musical examples. Second edition. 509pp. (USO) 21271-8 Paperbound $3.50

THE PERFECT WAGNERITE: A COMMENTARY ON THE NIBLUNG'S RING, George Bernard Shaw. Brilliant and still relevant criticism in remarkable essays on Wagner's Ring cycle, Shaw's ideas on political and social ideology behind the plots, role of Leitmotifs, vocal requisites, etc. Prefaces. xxi + 136pp.
21707-8 Paperbound $1.50

DON GIOVANNI, W. A. Mozart. Complete libretto, modern English translation; biographies of composer and librettist; accounts of early performances and critical reaction. Lavishly illustrated. All the material you need to understand and appreciate this great work. Dover Opera Guide and Libretto Series; translated and introduced by Ellen Bleiler. 92 illustrations. 209pp.
21134-7 Paperbound $1.50

HIGH FIDELITY SYSTEMS: A LAYMAN'S GUIDE, Roy F. Allison. All the basic information you need for setting up your own audio system: high fidelity and stereo record players, tape records, F.M. Connections, adjusting tone arm, cartridge, checking needle alignment, positioning speakers, phasing speakers, adjusting hums, trouble-shooting, maintenance, and similar topics. Enlarged 1965 edition. More than 50 charts, diagrams, photos. iv + 91pp. 21514-8 Paperbound $1.25

REPRODUCTION OF SOUND, Edgar Villchur. Thorough coverage for laymen of high fidelity systems, reproducing systems in general, needles, amplifiers, preamps, loudspeakers, feedback, explaining physical background. "A rare talent for making technicalities vividly comprehensible," R. Darrell, *High Fidelity.* 69 figures. iv + 92pp. 21515-6 Paperbound $1.00

HEAR ME TALKIN' TO YA: THE STORY OF JAZZ AS TOLD BY THE MEN WHO MADE IT, Nat Shapiro and Nat Hentoff. Louis Armstrong, Fats Waller, Jo Jones, Clarence Williams, Billy Holiday, Duke Ellington, Jelly Roll Morton and dozens of other jazz greats tell how it was in Chicago's South Side, New Orleans, depression Harlem and the modern West Coast as jazz was born and grew. xvi + 429pp.
21726-4 Paperbound $2.00

FABLES OF AESOP, translated by Sir Roger L'Estrange. A reproduction of the very rare 1931 Paris edition; a selection of the most interesting fables, together with 50 imaginative drawings by Alexander Calder. v + 128pp. 6½x9¼.
21780-9 Paperbound $1.25

AGAINST THE GRAIN (A REBOURS), Joris K. Huysmans. Filled with weird images, evidences of a bizarre imagination, exotic experiments with hallucinatory drugs, rich tastes and smells and the diversions of its sybarite hero Duc Jean des Esseintes, this classic novel pushed 19th-century literary decadence to its limits. Full unabridged edition. Do not confuse this with abridged editions generally sold. Introduction by Havelock Ellis. xlix + 206pp. 22190-3 Paperbound $2.00

VARIORUM SHAKESPEARE: HAMLET. Edited by Horace H. Furness; a landmark of American scholarship. Exhaustive footnotes and appendices treat all doubtful words and phrases, as well as suggested critical emendations throughout the play's history. First volume contains editor's own text, collated with all Quartos and Folios. Second volume contains full first Quarto, translations of Shakespeare's sources (Belleforest, and Saxo Grammaticus), Der Bestrafte Brudermord, and many essays on critical and historical points of interest by major authorities of past and present. Includes details of staging and costuming over the years. By far the best edition available for serious students of Shakespeare. Total of xx + 905pp. 21004-9, 21005-7, 2 volumes, Paperbound $5.25

A LIFE OF WILLIAM SHAKESPEARE, Sir Sidney Lee. This is the standard life of Shakespeare, summarizing everything known about Shakespeare and his plays. Incredibly rich in material, broad in coverage, clear and judicious, it has served thousands as the best introduction to Shakespeare. 1931 edition. 9 plates. xxix + 792pp. (USO) 21967-4 Paperbound $3.75

MASTERS OF THE DRAMA, John Gassner. Most comprehensive history of the drama in print, covering every tradition from Greeks to modern Europe and America, including India, Far East, etc. Covers more than 800 dramatists, 2000 plays, with biographical material, plot summaries, theatre history, criticism, etc. "Best of its kind in English," *New Republic*. 77 illustrations. xxii + 890pp. 20100-7 Clothbound $7.50

THE EVOLUTION OF THE ENGLISH LANGUAGE, George McKnight. The growth of English, from the 14th century to the present. Unusual, non-technical account presents basic information in very interesting form: sound shifts, change in grammar and syntax, vocabulary growth, similar topics. Abundantly illustrated with quotations. Formerly *Modern English in the Making*. xii + 590pp. 21932-1 Paperbound $3.50

AN ETYMOLOGICAL DICTIONARY OF MODERN ENGLISH, Ernest Weekley. Fullest, richest work of its sort, by foremost British lexicographer. Detailed word histories, including many colloquial and archaic words; extensive quotations. Do not confuse this with the Concise Etymological Dictionary, which is much abridged. Total of xxvii + 830pp. 6½ x 9¼. 21873-2, 21874-0 Two volumes, Paperbound $5.50

FLATLAND: A ROMANCE OF MANY DIMENSIONS, E. A. Abbott. Classic of science-fiction explores ramifications of life in a two-dimensional world, and what happens when a three-dimensional being intrudes. Amusing reading, but also useful as introduction to thought about hyperspace. Introduction by Banesh Hoffmann. 16 illustrations. xx + 103pp. 20001-9 Paperbound $1.00

POEMS OF ANNE BRADSTREET, edited with an introduction by Robert Hutchinson. A new selection of poems by America's first poet and perhaps the first significant woman poet in the English language. 48 poems display her development in works of considerable variety—love poems, domestic poems, religious meditations, formal elegies, "quaternions," etc. Notes, bibliography. viii + 222pp.
22160-1 Paperbound $2.00

THREE GOTHIC NOVELS: THE CASTLE OF OTRANTO BY HORACE WALPOLE; VATHEK BY WILLIAM BECKFORD; THE VAMPYRE BY JOHN POLIDORI, WITH FRAGMENT OF A NOVEL BY LORD BYRON, edited by E. F. Bleiler. The first Gothic novel, by Walpole; the finest Oriental tale in English, by Beckford; powerful Romantic supernatural story in versions by Polidori and Byron. All extremely important in history of literature; all still exciting, packed with supernatural thrills, ghosts, haunted castles, magic, etc. xl + 291pp.
21232-7 Paperbound $2.00

THE BEST TALES OF HOFFMANN, E. T. A. Hoffmann. 10 of Hoffmann's most important stories, in modern re-editings of standard translations: Nutcracker and the King of Mice, Signor Formica, Automata, The Sandman, Rath Krespel, The Golden Flowerpot, Master Martin the Cooper, The Mines of Falun, The King's Betrothed, A New Year's Eve Adventure. 7 illustrations by Hoffmann. Edited by E. F. Bleiler. xxxix + 419pp.
21793-0 Paperbound $2.25

GHOST AND HORROR STORIES OF AMBROSE BIERCE, Ambrose Bierce. 23 strikingly modern stories of the horrors latent in the human mind: The Eyes of the Panther, The Damned Thing, An Occurrence at Owl Creek Bridge, An Inhabitant of Carcosa, etc., plus the dream-essay, Visions of the Night. Edited by E. F. Bleiler. xxii + 199pp.
20767-6 Paperbound $1.50

BEST GHOST STORIES OF J. S. LEFANU, J. Sheridan LeFanu. Finest stories by Victorian master often considered greatest supernatural writer of all. Carmilla, Green Tea, The Haunted Baronet, The Familiar, and 12 others. Most never before available in the U. S. A. Edited by E. F. Bleiler. 8 illustrations from Victorian publications. xvii + 467pp.
20415-4 Paperbound $2.50

THE TIME STREAM, THE GREATEST ADVENTURE, AND THE PURPLE SAPPHIRE—THREE SCIENCE FICTION NOVELS, John Taine (Eric Temple Bell). Great American mathematician was also foremost science fiction novelist of the 1920's. *The Time Stream,* one of all-time classics, uses concepts of circular time; *The Greatest Adventure,* incredibly ancient biological experiments from Antarctica threaten to escape; The *Purple Sapphire,* superscience, lost races in Central Tibet, survivors of the Great Race. 4 illustrations by Frank R. Paul. v + 532pp.
21180-0 Paperbound $2.50

SEVEN SCIENCE FICTION NOVELS, H. G. Wells. The standard collection of the great novels. Complete, unabridged. *First Men in the Moon, Island of Dr. Moreau, War of the Worlds, Food of the Gods, Invisible Man, Time Machine, In the Days of the Comet.* Not only science fiction fans, but every educated person owes it to himself to read these novels. 1015pp.
20264-X Clothbound $5.00

LAST AND FIRST MEN AND STAR MAKER, TWO SCIENCE FICTION NOVELS, Olaf Stapledon. Greatest future histories in science fiction. In the first, human intelligence is the "hero," through strange paths of evolution, interplanetary invasions, incredible technologies, near extinctions and reemergences. Star Maker describes the quest of a band of star rovers for intelligence itself, through time and space: weird inhuman civilizations, crustacean minds, symbiotic worlds, etc. Complete, unabridged. v + 438pp. 21962-3 Paperbound $2.00

THREE PROPHETIC NOVELS, H. G. WELLS. Stages of a consistently planned future for mankind. *When the Sleeper Wakes,* and *A Story of the Days to Come,* anticipate *Brave New World* and *1984,* in the 21st Century; *The Time Machine,* only complete version in print, shows farther future and the end of mankind. All show Wells's greatest gifts as storyteller and novelist. Edited by E. F. Bleiler. x + 335pp. (USO) 20605-X Paperbound $2.00

THE DEVIL'S DICTIONARY, Ambrose Bierce. America's own Oscar Wilde— Ambrose Bierce—offers his barbed iconoclastic wisdom in over 1,000 definitions hailed by H. L. Mencken as "some of the most gorgeous witticisms in the English language." 145pp. 20487-1 Paperbound $1.25

MAX AND MORITZ, Wilhelm Busch. Great children's classic, father of comic strip, of two bad boys, Max and Moritz. Also Ker and Plunk (Plisch und Plumm), Cat and Mouse, Deceitful Henry, Ice-Peter, The Boy and the Pipe, and five other pieces. Original German, with English translation. Edited by H. Arthur Klein; translations by various hands and H. Arthur Klein. vi + 216pp. 20181-3 Paperbound $1.50

PIGS IS PIGS AND OTHER FAVORITES, Ellis Parker Butler. The title story is one of the best humor short stories, as Mike Flannery obfuscates biology and English. Also included, That Pup of Murchison's, The Great American Pie Company, and Perkins of Portland. 14 illustrations. v + 109pp. 21532-6 Paperbound $1.00

THE PETERKIN PAPERS, Lucretia P. Hale. It takes genius to be as stupidly mad as the Peterkins, as they decide to become wise, celebrate the "Fourth," keep a cow, and otherwise strain the resources of the Lady from Philadelphia. Basic book of American humor. 153 illustrations. 219pp. 20794-3 Paperbound $1.25

PERRAULT'S FAIRY TALES, translated by A. E. Johnson and S. R. Littlewood, with 34 full-page illustrations by Gustave Doré. All the original Perrault stories— Cinderella, Sleeping Beauty, Bluebeard, Little Red Riding Hood, Puss in Boots, Tom Thumb, etc.—with their witty verse morals and the magnificent illustrations of Doré. One of the five or six great books of European fairy tales. viii + 117pp. 8⅛ x 11. 22311-6 Paperbound $2.00

OLD HUNGARIAN FAIRY TALES, Baroness Orczy. Favorites translated and adapted by author of the *Scarlet Pimpernel.* Eight fairy tales include "The Suitors of Princess Fire-Fly," "The Twin Hunchbacks," "Mr. Cuttlefish's Love Story," and "The Enchanted Cat." This little volume of magic and adventure will captivate children as it has for generations. 90 drawings by Montagu Barstow. 96pp. (USO) 22293-4 Paperbound $1.95

THE RED FAIRY BOOK, Andrew Lang. Lang's color fairy books have long been children's favorites. This volume includes Rapunzel, Jack and the Bean-stalk and 35 other stories, familiar and unfamiliar. 4 plates, 93 illustrations x + 367pp.
21673-X Paperbound $1.95

THE BLUE FAIRY BOOK, Andrew Lang. Lang's tales come from all countries and all times. Here are 37 tales from Grimm, the Arabian Nights, Greek Mythology, and other fascinating sources. 8 plates, 130 illustrations. xi + 390pp.
21437-0 Paperbound $1.95

HOUSEHOLD STORIES BY THE BROTHERS GRIMM. Classic English-language edition of the well-known tales — Rumpelstiltskin, Snow White, Hansel and Gretel, The Twelve Brothers, Faithful John, Rapunzel, Tom Thumb (52 stories in all). Translated into simple, straightforward English by Lucy Crane. Ornamented with head-pieces, vignettes, elaborate decorative initials and a dozen full-page illustrations by Walter Crane. x + 269pp.
21080-4 Paperbound $2.00

THE MERRY ADVENTURES OF ROBIN HOOD, Howard Pyle. The finest modern versions of the traditional ballads and tales about the great English outlaw. Howard Pyle's complete prose version, with every word, every illustration of the first edition. Do not confuse this facsimile of the original (1883) with modern editions that change text or illustrations. 23 plates plus many page decorations. xxii + 296pp.
22043-5 Paperbound $2.00

THE STORY OF KING ARTHUR AND HIS KNIGHTS, Howard Pyle. The finest children's version of the life of King Arthur; brilliantly retold by Pyle, with 48 of his most imaginative illustrations. xviii + 313pp. 6⅛ x 9¼.
21445-1 Paperbound $2.00

THE WONDERFUL WIZARD OF OZ, L. Frank Baum. America's finest children's book in facsimile of first edition with all Denslow illustrations in full color. The edition a child should have. Introduction by Martin Gardner. 23 color plates, scores of drawings. iv + 267pp.
20691-2 Paperbound $1.95

THE MARVELOUS LAND OF OZ, L. Frank Baum. The second Oz book, every bit as imaginative as the Wizard. The hero is a boy named Tip, but the Scarecrow and the Tin Woodman are back, as is the Oz magic. 16 color plates, 120 drawings by John R. Neill. 287pp.
20692-0 Paperbound $1.75

THE MAGICAL MONARCH OF MO, L. Frank Baum. Remarkable adventures in a land even stranger than Oz. The best of Baum's books not in the Oz series. 15 color plates and dozens of drawings by Frank Verbeck. xviii + 237pp.
21892-9 Paperbound $2.00

THE BAD CHILD'S BOOK OF BEASTS, MORE BEASTS FOR WORSE CHILDREN, A MORAL ALPHABET, Hilaire Belloc. Three complete humor classics in one volume. Be kind to the frog, and do not call him names . . . and 28 other whimsical animals. Familiar favorites and some not so well known. Illustrated by Basil Blackwell. 156pp.
(USO) 20749-8 Paperbound $1.25

EAST O' THE SUN AND WEST O' THE MOON, George W. Dasent. Considered the best of all translations of these Norwegian folk tales, this collection has been enjoyed by generations of children (and folklorists too). Includes True and Untrue, Why the Sea is Salt, East O' the Sun and West O' the Moon, Why the Bear is Stumpy-Tailed, Boots and the Troll, The Cock and the Hen, Rich Peter the Pedlar, and 52 more. The only edition with all 59 tales. 77 illustrations by Erik Werenskiold and Theodor Kittelsen. xv + 418pp. 22521-6 Paperbound $3.00

GOOPS AND HOW TO BE THEM, Gelett Burgess. Classic of tongue-in-cheek humor, masquerading as etiquette book. 87 verses, twice as many cartoons, show mischievous Goops as they demonstrate to children virtues of table manners, neatness, courtesy, etc. Favorite for generations. viii + 88pp. 6½ x 9¼.
22233-0 Paperbound $1.25

ALICE'S ADVENTURES UNDER GROUND, Lewis Carroll. The first version, quite different from the final Alice in Wonderland, printed out by Carroll himself with his own illustrations. Complete facsimile of the "million dollar" manuscript Carroll gave to Alice Liddell in 1864. Introduction by Martin Gardner. viii + 96pp. Title and dedication pages in color. 21482-6 Paperbound $1.25

THE BROWNIES, THEIR BOOK, Palmer Cox. Small as mice, cunning as foxes, exuberant and full of mischief, the Brownies go to the zoo, toy shop, seashore, circus, etc., in 24 verse adventures and 266 illustrations. Long a favorite, since their first appearance in St. Nicholas Magazine. xi + 144pp. 6⅝ x 9¼.
21265-3 Paperbound $1.75

SONGS OF CHILDHOOD, Walter De La Mare. Published (under the pseudonym Walter Ramal) when De La Mare was only 29, this charming collection has long been a favorite children's book. A facsimile of the first edition in paper, the 47 poems capture the simplicity of the nursery rhyme and the ballad, including such lyrics as I Met Eve, Tartary, The Silver Penny. vii + 106pp. 21972-0 Paperbound $1.25

THE COMPLETE NONSENSE OF EDWARD LEAR, Edward Lear. The finest 19th-century humorist-cartoonist in full: all nonsense limericks, zany alphabets, Owl and Pussycat, songs, nonsense botany, and more than 500 illustrations by Lear himself. Edited by Holbrook Jackson. xxix + 287pp. (USO) 20167-8 Paperbound $1.75

BILLY WHISKERS: THE AUTOBIOGRAPHY OF A GOAT, Frances Trego Montgomery. A favorite of children since the early 20th century, here are the escapades of that rambunctious, irresistible and mischievous goat—Billy Whiskers. Much in the spirit of Peck's Bad Boy, this is a book that children never tire of reading or hearing. All the original familiar illustrations by W. H. Fry are included: 6 color plates, 18 black and white drawings. 159pp. 22345-0 Paperbound $2.00

MOTHER GOOSE MELODIES. Faithful republication of the fabulously rare Munroe and Francis "copyright 1833" Boston edition—the most important Mother Goose collection, usually referred to as the "original." Familiar rhymes plus many rare ones, with wonderful old woodcut illustrations. Edited by E. F. Bleiler. 128pp. 4½ x 6⅜. 22577-1 Paperbound $1.25

TWO LITTLE SAVAGES; BEING THE ADVENTURES OF TWO BOYS WHO LIVED AS INDIANS AND WHAT THEY LEARNED, Ernest Thompson Seton. Great classic of nature and boyhood provides a vast range of woodlore in most palatable form, a genuinely entertaining story. Two farm boys build a teepee in woods and live in it for a month, working out Indian solutions to living problems, star lore, birds and animals, plants, etc. 293 illustrations. vii + 286pp.

20985-7 Paperbound $2.50

PETER PIPER'S PRACTICAL PRINCIPLES OF PLAIN & PERFECT PRONUNCIATION. Alliterative jingles and tongue-twisters of surprising charm, that made their first appearance in America about 1830. Republished in full with the spirited woodcut illustrations from this earliest American edition. 32pp. 4½ x 6⅜.

22560-7 Paperbound $1.00

SCIENCE EXPERIMENTS AND AMUSEMENTS FOR CHILDREN, Charles Vivian. 73 easy experiments, requiring only materials found at home or easily available, such as candles, coins, steel wool, etc.; illustrate basic phenomena like vacuum, simple chemical reaction, etc. All safe. Modern, well-planned. Formerly *Science Games for Children*. 102 photos, numerous drawings. 96pp. 6⅛ x 9¼.

21856-2 Paperbound $1.25

AN INTRODUCTION TO CHESS MOVES AND TACTICS SIMPLY EXPLAINED, Leonard Barden. Informal intermediate introduction, quite strong in explaining reasons for moves. Covers basic material, tactics, important openings, traps, positional play in middle game, end game. Attempts to isolate patterns and recurrent configurations. Formerly *Chess*. 58 figures. 102pp. (USO) 21210-6 Paperbound $1.25

LASKER'S MANUAL OF CHESS, Dr. Emanuel Lasker. Lasker was not only one of the five great World Champions, he was also one of the ablest expositors, theorists, and analysts. In many ways, his Manual, permeated with his philosophy of battle, filled with keen insights, is one of the greatest works ever written on chess. Filled with analyzed games by the great players. A single-volume library that will profit almost any chess player, beginner or master. 308 diagrams. xli x 349pp.

20640-8 Paperbound $2.50

THE MASTER BOOK OF MATHEMATICAL RECREATIONS, Fred Schuh. In opinion of many the finest work ever prepared on mathematical puzzles, stunts, recreations; exhaustively thorough explanations of mathematics involved, analysis of effects, citation of puzzles and games. Mathematics involved is elementary. Translated by F. Göbel. 194 figures. xxiv + 430pp. 22134-2 Paperbound $3.00

MATHEMATICS, MAGIC AND MYSTERY, Martin Gardner. Puzzle editor for Scientific American explains mathematics behind various mystifying tricks: card tricks, stage "mind reading," coin and match tricks, counting out games, geometric dissections, etc. Probability sets, theory of numbers clearly explained. Also provides more than 400 tricks, guaranteed to work, that you can do. 135 illustrations. xii + 176pp.

20338-2 Paperbound $1.50

MATHEMATICAL PUZZLES FOR BEGINNERS AND ENTHUSIASTS, Geoffrey Mott-Smith. 189 puzzles from easy to difficult—involving arithmetic, logic, algebra, properties of digits, probability, etc.—for enjoyment and mental stimulus. Explanation of mathematical principles behind the puzzles. 135 illustrations. viii + 248pp.
20198-8 Paperbound $1.25

PAPER FOLDING FOR BEGINNERS, William D. Murray and Francis J. Rigney. Easiest book on the market, clearest instructions on making interesting, beautiful origami. Sail boats, cups, roosters, frogs that move legs, bonbon boxes, standing birds, etc. 40 projects; more than 275 diagrams and photographs. 94pp.
20713-7 Paperbound $1.00

TRICKS AND GAMES ON THE POOL TABLE, Fred Herrmann. 79 tricks and games— some solitaires, some for two or more players, some competitive games—to entertain you between formal games. Mystifying shots and throws, unusual caroms, tricks involving such props as cork, coins, a hat, etc. Formerly *Fun on the Pool Table*. 77 figures. 95pp.
21814-7 Paperbound $1.00

HAND SHADOWS TO BE THROWN UPON THE WALL: A SERIES OF NOVEL AND AMUSING FIGURES FORMED BY THE HAND, Henry Bursill. Delightful picturebook from great-grandfather's day shows how to make 18 different hand shadows: a bird that flies, duck that quacks, dog that wags his tail, camel, goose, deer, boy, turtle, etc. Only book of its sort. vi + 33pp. 6½ x 9¼. 21779-5 Paperbound $1.00

WHITTLING AND WOODCARVING, E. J. Tangerman. 18th printing of best book on market. "If you can cut a potato you can carve" toys and puzzles, chains, chessmen, caricatures, masks, frames, woodcut blocks, surface patterns, much more. Information on tools, woods, techniques. Also goes into serious wood sculpture from Middle Ages to present, East and West. 464 photos, figures. x + 293pp.
20965-2 Paperbound $2.00

HISTORY OF PHILOSOPHY, Julián Marias. Possibly the clearest, most easily followed, best planned, most useful one-volume history of philosophy on the market; neither skimpy nor overfull. Full details on system of every major philosopher and dozens of less important thinkers from pre-Socratics up to Existentialism and later. Strong on many European figures usually omitted. Has gone through dozens of editions in Europe. 1966 edition, translated by Stanley Appelbaum and Clarence Strowbridge. xviii + 505pp.
21739-6 Paperbound $2.75

YOGA: A SCIENTIFIC EVALUATION, Kovoor T. Behanan. Scientific but non-technical study of physiological results of yoga exercises; done under auspices of Yale U. Relations to Indian thought, to psychoanalysis, etc. 16 photos. xxiii + 270pp.
20505-3 Paperbound $2.50

Prices subject to change without notice.
Available at your book dealer or write for free catalogue to Dept. GI, Dover Publications, Inc., 180 Varick St., N. Y., N. Y. 10014. Dover publishes more than 150 books each year on science, elementary and advanced mathematics, biology, music, art, literary history, social sciences and other areas.